*Also in the Variorum Collected Studies Series:*

**JOHN W. O'MALLEY**
Religious Culture in the 16th Century: Preaching,
Rhetoric, Spirituality, and Reform

**ANDRÉ-E. SAYOUS**
Structure et évolution du capitalisme européen,
XVIe–XVIIe siècles

**I.A.A. THOMPSON**
Crown and Cortes: Government, Institutions and
Representation in Early Modern Castile

**I.A.A. THOMPSON**
War and Society in Habsburg Spain

**J.S. CUMMINS**
Jesuit and Friar in the Spanish Expansion to the East

**GUY BEAUJOUAN**
Science médiéval d'Espagne et d'alentour

**CHARLES JULIAN BISHKO**
Studies in Medieval Spanish Frontier History

**NELSON H. MINNICH**
The Catholic Reformation: Council, Churchmen,
Controversies

**PAUL FREEDMAN**
Church, Law and Society in Catalonia, 900–1500

**TEOFILO F. RUIZ**
The City and the Realm: Burgos and Castile, 1080–1492

**ANGUS MacKAY**
Society, Economy and Religion in Late Medieval Castile

**HENRY KAMEN**
Crisis and Change in Early Modern Spain

**E. WILLIAM MONTER**
Enforcing Morality in Early Modern Europe

**J.B. TRAPP**
Essays in the Renaissance and Classical Tradition

BX 1584 ORE

DATE DUE FOR RETURN

COLLECTED STUDIES SERIES

# From Ignatius Loyola to John of the Cross

(Eoin Stephenson)

Professor Terence O'Reilly

Terence O'Reilly

# From Ignatius Loyola to John of the Cross

## Spirituality and literature in sixteenth-century Spain

VARIORUM
1995

This edition copyright © 1995 by Terence O'Reilly.

Published by VARIORUM
Ashgate Publishing Limited
Gower House, Croft Road,
Aldershot, Hampshire GU11 3HR
Great Britain

Ashgate Publishing Company
Old Post Road,
Brookfield, Vermont 05036
USA

ISBN 0-86078-459-2

**British Library CIP Data**
O'Reilly, Terence
From Ignatius to John of the Cross.
(Variorum Collected Studies Series; CS 484)
I. Title  II. Series
274.06

**US Library of Congress CIP Data**
O'Reilly, Terence
From Ignatius to John of the Cross / Terence O'Reilly.
p. cm. — (Collected Studies Series: CS484)
Includes index.            ISBN 0-86078-459-2
1. Spirituality—Spain—history—16th century.  2. Monasticism and
religious orders—Spain—history—16th century.  3. Spirituality—
Catholic Church—history—16th century.  4. Mysticism—Spain—
history 16th century.  5. Ignatius, of Loyola, Saint, 1491–1556,
6. John of the Cross, Saint, 1542–1591.  7. Catholic Church—
Spain—history—16th century.  8. Spain—Church history—16th
century. I. Title. II. Series: Collected Studies: CS484.
BX1584.074  1994                              94–37037
248'.0946'09031—dc20                                CIP

Printed by Galliard (Printers) Ltd
Great Yarmouth, Norfolk, Great Britain

COLLECTED STUDIES SERIES CS484

# CONTENTS

Preface                                      viii–ix

*ST IGNATIUS LOYOLA*

I     Ignatius of Loyola and the Counter-Reformation:
the hagiographic tradition                439–470
*Heythrop Journal 31.*
*London: Heythrop College, 1990*

II    St Ignatius Loyola and Spanish Erasmianism    301–321
*Archivum Historicum Societatis Iesu 43.*
*Rome: Institutum Historicum Societatis Iesu, 1974*

III   Erasmus, Ignatius Loyola, and Orthodoxy     115–127
*Journal of Theological Studies 30.*
*Oxford: Clarendon Press, 1979*

IV   Melchor Cano and the Spirituality of
St Ignatius Loyola                    369–380
*Ignacio de Loyola y su tiempo, ed. Juan*
*Plazaola. Bilbao: Ediciones Mensajero, 1992*

V     Melchor Cano's *Censura y parecer contra el*
*Instituto de los Padres Jesuitas:* a transcription
of the British Library manuscript        1–22
*First publication*

*THE SPIRITUAL EXERCISES*

VI   The Spiritual Exercises and the Crisis of
Medieval Piety                    101–113
*The Way Supplement 70.*
*London: Institute of Spirituality, 1991*

VII    The Structual Unity of the *Exercitatorio*
*de la Vida Spiritual*    287–324
*Studia Monastica 15.*
*Barcelona: Abadia de Montserrat, 1973*

VIII    The Exercises of Saint Ignatius Loyola and the
*Exercitatorio de la Vida Spiritual*    301–323
*Studia Monastica 16.*
*Barcelona: Abadia de Montserrat, 1974*

IX    Saint Ignatius Loyola and Castles in Palestine    421–425
*Modern Language Notes 96. Baltimore:*
*The Johns Hopkins University Press, 1981*

*SPIRITUALITY AND LITERATURE*

X    The Erasmianism of *Lazarillo de Tormes*    91–100
*Essays in Honour of Robert Brian Tate*
*from his Colleagues and Pupils, ed.*
*Richard A. Cardwell. University of*
*Nottingham, 1984*

XI    The Ode to Francisco Salinas    107–113
*What's Past is Prologue, A Collection of*
*Essays in Honour of L.J. Woodward, ed.*
*Salvador Bacarisse et al. Edinburgh:*
*Scottish Academic Press, 1984*

XII    Courtly Love and Mysticism in Spanish Poetry
of the Golden Age    53–76
*Journal of Hispanic Research 1.*
*London: Impart Publishing, 1992*

*ST JOHN OF THE CROSS*

XIII    St John of the Cross and the Traditions of
Monastic Exegesis    105–126
*Leeds Papers on Saint John of the Cross,*
*ed. Margaret A. Rees. Leeds: Trinity and*
*All Saints College, 1991*

XIV   The Literary and Devotional Context of the
      *Pastorcico*                                              363–370
      *Forum for Modern Language Studies 18.*
      *Edinburgh: Scottish Academic Press and*
      *The University of St Andrews, 1982*


XV    The *Cántico Espiritual* of Saint John of the Cross
      and the Mystical Interpretation of the *Song of Songs*      5–16
      *Hallel, A Review of Monastic Spirituality and*
      *Liturgy 19. Roscrea, Co. Tipperary:*
      *Mount Saint Joseph Abbey, 1994*

Index                                                            1–5

This volume contains x + 271 pages

***Publisher's Note:*** *The articles in this volume, as in all others in the Collected Studies Series, have not been given a new, continuous pagination. In order to avoid confusion, and to facilitate their use where these same studies have been referred to elsewhere, the original pagination has been maintained wherever possible.*

*Each article has been given a Roman number in order of appearance, as listed in the Contents. This number is repeated on each page and quoted in the index entries.*

# PREFACE

The essays collected in this volume have been written on divers occasions over many years, but despite their various origins they may be said to have in common a concern with two strands in the life of sixteenth-century Spain. The first consists of the movements of religious reform that made the history of the period such a ferment. Among them some stand out: the dissemination of *devotio moderna* piety from Montserrat; the illuminism of the *alumbrados* of Toledo; the Christian humanism of Erasmus; the apostolic spirituality of the first Jesuits; the discalced Carmelite reform. At the heart of each of these lay a drive to interiorise and deepen the spiritual life by renewing the disciplines of Christian living through the practice of meditation, and to encourage in varying degrees an openness to mystical prayer.

The second strand is composed of the literary conventions that flourished during the period. Many were inherited from medieval Castile: the commentary on scripture; the *florilegium;* the popular lyric; the courtly poetry of the *cancioneros*; the chivalric romance. Gradually these were crossed with new conventions drawn from Northern Europe and Italy, among them the meditation manual, the humanist satire, and a range of fresh poetic metres and forms, including the Horatian epistle and ode. In the hundred years that passed between the birth of Ignatius Loyola (1491) and the death of John of the Cross (1591) these two strands became intertwined, and the result was a literature that has held the fascinated gaze of many scholars.

The essays have been grouped in four sections, the first two of which focus on the life and writings of Ignatius Loyola. Until the present century he was associated with the period of the militant Counter-Reform, but now he can be seen more accurately as belonging to an earlier world. The essays in the first section (I-V) seek to locate him in this world by examining the connections between his spirituality and the teachings of the Spanish Erasmians and illuminists. One of the essays (V), published here for the first time, presents a treatise long thought lost in which the Dominican theologian Melchor Cano argued that Ignatius was an *alumbrado*.

Ignatius was not a "writer" in the modern sense of the word, but few writers have chosen their words with more care or wielded such influence through their works. His *Spiritual Exercises* are still used extensively today, and the variety of ways in which they are practised has raised new questions about their interpretation in the time of Ignatius himself. The essays in the second section (VI-IX) centre on the *Exercises*, and seek to answer some of these questions by examining the origins of the text in his experience of conversion, and in the books he read at Loyola, Manresa and Montserrat.

In the remaining two sections the focus of attention shifts towards the later sixteenth century and the writings of John of the Cross. The connections between spirituality and literature are often hard to trace, and the essays in the third section (X-XII) consider a number of cases in which they have proved problematic: the Erasmianism of the *Lazarillo*, the mysticism of the great ode to Salinas, and (most thorny of all) the relationship between courtly love and mysticism in the poetry of the age. The latter essay, naturally enough, devotes attention to the lyrics of St. John, and the fourth section (essays XIII-XV) is concerned entirely with his work, particularly with how his poetry was shaped by liturgical texts, devotional writings and the exegesis of Scripture.

I should like to thank Dr. John Smedley and Variorum Reprints, the editors and publishers of the works in which the essays first appeared, and my colleagues Professor Terence Folley and Mr. Stephen Boyd who with the Dean and the Faculty of Arts in University College Cork have supported my research over the years. I am grateful to Professor Alan Deyermond who was helpful when, at an earlier stage, I thought of gathering some of these essays in another form. And I thank the friends whose encouragement and learning, generously shared, have made this volume possible, particularly Dr. Barry Taylor, Professor R.B. Tate, Professor L.J. Woodward, Professor J.S. Cummins, Mr. George Every, Fr. Simon Tugwell O.P., Professor Bernard Hamilton, Mrs. Janet Hamilton, Mr. Aidan MacDonald, and Dr. Elisabeth Stopp. I am indebted too to the secretaries in my department, Mrs. Kay Doyle and Ms. Aisling O'Leary, who worked with unfailing patience and good humour to prepare the text for publication.

**Terence O'Reilly**

*Cork*
*August 1994*

Sponsae et amicae meae

# I

# IGNATIUS OF LOYOLA AND THE COUNTER-REFORMATION: THE HAGIOGRAPHIC TRADITION

Many of our popular images of Ignatius Loyola go back to the first official biographies which were written towards the end of the sixteenth century by Pedro de Ribadeneira and Gian Pietro Maffei.[1] The first and more important of these, by Ribadeneira, is in many ways an invaluable source of information about the saint. He knew Ignatius well, and the other companions with whom Ignatius had founded the Society of Jesus in 1539-1540; he based his biography on earlier, unpublished lives, and on some of Ignatius's own writings; and he strove, in accordance with his humanist ideals, for accuracy, balance and completeness.[2]

None the less, like all historians, Ribadeneira had a view of the past that was shaped by the preoccupations of his own time and place. His biography appeared in the aftermath of the Council of Trent, when the Catholic Church in Europe was struggling to turn the tide of the Protestant Reformation. The decrees of the Council were being implemented gradually, and a determined counterattack on Protestantism — political, scholarly, apologetic — was growing in urgency and force. These events directly involved the numerous members of the Society of Jesus, among them many younger Jesuits who had never had an opportunity to know Ignatius themselves.[3]

The Counter-Reformation world in which and for which Ribadeneira wrote left its mark on his biography. He presented Ignatius as a soldier of the Church, leading its victorious armies against the Antichrist, Martin Luther; as a person hostile to earlier movements in the Catholic Reform, such as Illuminism and Erasmianism; and as a staunch defender of Catholic tradition. In this portrait of Ignatius there is, undoubtedly, an element of truth, especially in the case of his later years when he was General of the Society, the period during which Ribadeneira knew him. In recent decades, however, a number of developments in scholarship have indicated that it needs to be qualified.[4]

One of these developments has been the general improvement in our understanding of the nature and the course of the Catholic Reform of the early sixteenth century, including its origins in the late medieval Church, and the various reform movements in Spain and Italy among which Ignatius and his companions first appeared: the *alumbrados,* the Erasmian humanists, and the disciples of Juan de Avila in Spain, and the *spirituali* in Italy.[5] Another has been the publication in critical editions of Ignatius's writings, and of the earliest documents relating to his life, including the ones to which Ribadeneira himself had access.

Three of the earliest biographical accounts, all of them written before the death of Ignatius in 1556, have proved to be of particular importance. The first is in the form of a letter, dated 16 June 1547, by Ignatius's close friend and companion, Diego Laínez. It is addressed to Juan Polanco, who had been appointed secretary to Ignatius a few months earlier, and was anxious to gather information about the origins of the Society. The second is by Polanco himself: a chronicle, in Spanish, on the origins of the order, which he completed in 1547 or 1548. It is based on the information he had gathered, including Laínez's letter, and on what he had learned from the other founders, among them Ignatius. The third is Ignatius's own account of his life which he dictated between 1553 and 1556 to a Portuguese Jesuit, Luis Gonçalves da Cámara. The text, which has come to be known as the *Autobiography,* is in Spanish and Italian.[6]

These early documents were known and read within the Society during the lifetime of Ignatius, and in the decade following his death, and they were consulted by both Ribadeneira and Maffei. In 1567, however, they were withdrawn from general circulation, apparently at Ribadeneira's prompting, and they did not become widely known again until the present century. The letter of Laínez was first published in 1904; Polanco's Spanish chronicle in 1943. The *Autobiography* fared better: an early Latin translation was published by the Bollandists in the eighteenth century; but the original text was not edited until 1904, and only in 1943 did a satisfactory critical edition appear in print.[7]

These developments in scholarship have drawn attention to the fact that Ignatius's formative years were far removed from the late Counter-Reformation world in which Ribadeneira wrote. His spirituality and his ideals were shaped during the 1520s and 1530s, in a period before the opening of the first session of the Council of Trent when the boundaries between orthodoxy and heresy were not always clear. They have also revealed that in the course of his life Ignatius's views and priorities developed and changed, sometimes radically. Now it is no longer possible to see him, with Ribadeneira, as a man whose concerns were shaped fundamentally by the occurrence of the Lutheran Reform.

## I. PROTESTANTISM

In the writings of the early Jesuits one often encounters a dramatic contrast between Ignatius, the faithful servant of the Church, and Martin Luther, its ardent foe. Some of the earliest mentions of the two occur in the papers of Ignatius's helper and companion, Jerónimo Nadal. In his *Apologia pro Exercitiis,* written between 1554 and 1556, he affirmed that all Ignatius's life and efforts were directed against the Lutherans. [8] Later, in January 1557, six months after Ignatius's death, he noted that when Luther began his schism Ignatius was still a soldier in the world, striving for wordly honours.[9] Sometime between 1559 and 1566 Ribadeneira, who was busy preparing his biography, made the parallel into a contrast: the very year in which Luther broke with Rome (he wrote) Ignatius was converted to Christ.[10] At about the same time, in 1564, Juan Polanco made the point with dramatic effect:

> . . . al tiempo que permitió Dios por nuestros peccados que començase Martín Lutero en Alemagna a levantar vandera contra la santa Sede Apostólica y cathólica religión . . . al mismo tiempo, poco más o menos, su divina Providentia comenzó a preparar como un antídoto contra este veneno, con una conversión notable del Padre Ignatio de Loyola . . .[11]

In his Latin biography published in 1572, and later in the elaborated Spanish version of 1583, Ribadeneira developed the contrast further. He emphasized the military aspects of Ignatius and of the Church he served, portraying Catholicism as a kingdom at war that God provides with reinforcements. Ignatius, he affirmed, was the great reinforcement sent by God to do battle with Luther, whose contrary he was in everything:

> . . . quando salió del abismo Martín Lutero como un monstruo infernal . . . al mismo tiempo embió Dios nuestro Señor de socorro otro varón y capitán a su Yglesia, en todo contrario a Lutero, para que con su espíritu invencible y armas poderosas y divinas valerosamente le resistiesse y peleasse las batallas del Señor . . .[12]

Ribadeneira also noted precisely the Catholic traditions that Ignatius had been sent to defend. One of these was belief in the primacy of the pope, which Luther had repudiated. Ignatius, by contrast, had exemplified it, and had defended it energetically, calling on his 'soldiers' to make it the subject of a special vow.[13] Another was the religious life, based on vows of poverty, chastity and obedience whose value and justification the Protestants had challenged. The purpose of the Society founded by Ignatius was to support other orders in the heat of battle, and to fight their cause single-handed when this was necessary.[14] A third was the sacraments and devotions that the Protestants had spurned: auricular confession, the Mass, invocation of the saints, indulgences and the veneration of relics. Ignatius's constant and all-consuming purpose, according to Ribadeneira, was to preserve the Catholic faith that Luther and his followers had tried to destroy:

> Finalmente, todos los consejos, pensamientos y cuydados de nuestro padre Ignacio tiravan a este blanco de conservar en la parte sana, o restaurar en la caída, por sí y por los suyos, la sinceridad y limpieza de la fe católica, assí como sus enemigos la procura destruir.[15]

The image of Ignatius as the captain of the troops of Rome was destined to enjoy a long life. It informed the second official biography by Maffei which appeared in 1585, and which became, with Ribadeneira's, the main source for subsequent biographies until the eighteenth century.[16] When Ignatius was canonized in 1622 his feast was commemorated in the Roman Breviary by a prayer that recalled how through him God had reinforced the Church Militant with a fresh supply of soldiers, and by readings in which it was stated that he and the Society had been raised up to overthrow Luther and his fellow heretics.[17] One book that popularized the image throughout Catholic Europe was the *Exercicio de perfección* by the Spanish Jesuit Alonso Rodríguez, first published in Seville in 1609. In this work of devotion, whose popularity in the course of the next three centuries rivalled that of the *Imitation of Christ,* Rodríguez portrayed Ignatius as a valiant soldier whose leg was broken at Pamplona so that God might 'heal him . . . and make him his captain, his general, and the defender of his Church against Luther', and he carried the military images further in his description of the Jesuits as 'the squadron and company of soldiers' always ready 'like light infantry . . . to meet the enemy in battle'.[18] In the late eighteenth and early nineteenth centuries the image was taken up by the great German Protestant historians among whom the term 'Counter-Reformation' was first used.[19] Von Ranke devoted several pages to Ignatius in his history of the popes, and contrasted his life and personality with those of Luther.[20] Detailed contrasts between Luther and Loyola became a set piece in the work of subsequent historians, and survived into the present century in innumerable biographies and Church histories.

### The Early Years
A different picture of Ignatius emerges from the earliest accounts of his formative years. These provide most of the information we possess about the period between his conversion in 1521 and the founding of the Society of Jesus in 1540. From them it is clear that in this period, when the Protestant Reform was erupting in Germany and overflowing into France and Italy, it was not Ignatius's main concern to stem the tide of schism.

The years Ignatius spent in Spain between his conversion, in 1521, and 1527, coincided with the infiltration of Lutheran ideas into the peninsula. In April

1521 the Royal Council prohibited the writings of Luther and discussion of his ideas, and the Inquisition began to hunt and destroy the Lutheran books that were being smuggled into the country by the *marrano* community in Antwerp.[21] A few years later, in September 1525, the Inquisition in Toledo issued an edict against the *dexados,* a group of illuminists whom it suspected of Lutheran leanings.[22] In his own account of these years, however, Ignatius never mentions Luther, and later he was able to claim that he had never come across any Lutherans or illuminists.[23] The prompt action of the authorities ensured that the number of people who read Lutheran works was small, and confined on the whole to clerics and academic theologians; among the general population there was a certain curiosity about Luther's views, but little informed understanding of their nature.[24]

Instead of a desire to combat heresy, we note in Ignatius at this time a constant need and concern to prove that he was not a heretic himself. After his return from the Holy Land in 1524 he gave himself to a life of study and evangelical poverty, and began to gather like-minded companions.[25] In Alcalá his apostolic life style attracted the attention of the Inquisition of Toledo, and he was suspected of being a *dexado.*[26] Later, in Salamanca, he was suspected of being sympathetic to the Erasmians, a movement associated by some conservatives with a certain crypto-Lutheranism.[27] In 1526 and 1527 his activities were investigated four times. Although he was cleared of the charge of heresy, the authorities placed restrictions on his activities that made him feel unable to follow his apostolic call, and that eventually drove him to leave Spain for Paris.[28]

The situation in France, where Ignatius spent eight years between 1527 and 1535, was very different. In Paris he was surrounded on all sides by signs of religious dissent. When he began to study in the Collège de Montaigu in 1528, one of his fellow students, who had just completed a course of studies, was John Calvin. A few years later the two men lived opposite each other, Loyola at the Collège de Sainte Barbe and Calvin at the Collège de Furet, separated by a street. While Ignatius was a student in Sainte Barbe, the acting Principal, Andrés de Gouveia, was accused of heresy, and broke with his conservative and influential uncle, Diego. Ignatius must have heard about, and may even have attended, the pro-Lutheran sermon delivered on 1 November 1533 by Nicholas Cop, Rector of the University, which was followed by his flight from Paris with Calvin.[29] He was certainly present in Paris on 18 October 1534 when the city was filled with placards denouncing the Mass, and during the widespread repression that followed he helped a number of people who feared they would be persecuted as heretics.[30]

However, these upheavals are not mentioned in Ignatius's account of his Paris years. His chief concerns continued to be study and the gathering of friends who wished to share his apostolic way of life. His activities once again incurred suspicion, and on two occasions he was obliged to defend himself before the Paris Inquisition against accusations and rumours that he was a covert heretic.[31] The suspicions of heresy may have been fuelled by accounts of the earlier inquiries by the Inquisition in Spain. One of his fellow students in Paris, Jerónimo Nadal, had witnessed his activities in Alcalá in 1526 and 1527, and had serious qualms about his orthodoxy. He refused to join his circle of friends, and did not change his mind until 1546, by which time the Society had been approved by the pope.[32]

Similar accusations troubled Ignatius later in Italy. For about eighteen months, between early 1536 and July 1537, he lived in Venice, one of the centres of Protestant influence in the peninsula. In his *Autobiography* there is no mention of any concern at this time to combat heresy. Instead he was himself suspected of Protestant sympathies. The extent and depth of the suspicion is apparent in the account of his meeting with Diego Hoces from Málaga, to whom he gave the *Spiritual Exercises* in 1536. Hoces knew of Ignatius's reputation, and was so fearful of being led into unorthdox views that he brought along theological works to consult during the retreat.[33] Eventually rumours that he was a heretic, on the run from Spain and France, obliged Ignatius to seek ratification of his orthodoxy from the Vicar of the Papal Legate to the city.[34] Later in Rome his companions became involved in a dispute with a preacher, Mainardi, whose sympathies were Lutheran, and who eventually became a Protestant. Soon, however, the centre of attention became Ignatius himself, who was accused by some Spanish supporters of Mainardi of holding heretical views, and once again he was obliged to seek an official inquiry in order to clear his name.[35]

*Jerusalem*

Ignatius's apparent detachment from the religious revolution occurring around hin in the 1520s and 1530s is remarkable, and at first sight hard to understand. It is made easier to explain by the fact that for long periods during the 1520s and 1530s he was convinced that his true vocation lay outside Europe altogether. His recurrent ambition at this time was to travel to the Holy Land and spend the rest of his life in Jerusalem.

The origins of the ambition lie in the works of devotion that he read at Loyola while he was recovering from the wounds he had sustained earlier in the battle at Pamplona. The *Vita Christi* of Ludolph the Carthusian and the *Legenda aurea* of Jacopo di Voragine kindled in him an intense devotion to the person of Jesus, a longing to practise penance and the desire to travel to the Holy Places. Ludolph urges the reader of his work to imagine himself in Palestine, or even better to go there; Voragine describes many saints who went to Jerusalem on pilgrimage.[36] As Ignatius read these books and day-dreamed, he thought of making the pilgrimage himself: 'pensaba . . . en ir a Jerusalem descalço, y en no comer sino yerbas, y en hacer todos los demás rigores que veía haber hecho los santos'.[37] Once he was resolved to follow Christ, the idea of the pilgrimage became a firm purpose: 'todo lo que deseaba de hacer, luego como sanase, era la ida de Hierusalem, como arriba es dicho, con tantas disciplinas y tantas abstinencias, quantas un ánimo generoso, encendido de Dios, suele desear hacer'.[38]

With this ambition Ignatius set out from Loyola at the end of February 1522, heading for the port of Barcelona. After reaching the shrine of the Virgin at Montserrat he changed his plans, for reasons that are obscure, and went to Manresa where he stayed almost a year.[39] When he resumed his pilgrimage in February 1523, the original ambition was modified in two ways: his desire was now to stay in Jerusalem permanently; and his original longing to lead a life of devotion and penance in the Holy Places was complemented by the hope that he might be able to 'help others'.[40] In Jerusalem, however, it was made clear to him that he would not be permitted to stay, and for a while he was confused and unsure what to do; eventually he decided to study, and he put his decision into effect on his return to Barcelona in 1525.[41]

During the twelve years of study that followed, and that took him to Alcalá, Paris and Venice, a deep inner call to Jerusalem continued to inform his life. This is apparent from the fact that several of his followers to whom he gave the *Spiritual Exercises* in these years, and who wished to embrace his way of life, also conceived the desire to go on pilgrimage there. When he began his initial attempt to gather companions, in Barcelona, the first person to join him was a young man of Portuguese origin, Calisto de Sá. On Ignatius's advice, and following his example, Calisto visited the Holy Land as a pilgrim, before returning to Spain.[42] Later in Alcalá Ignatius became friendly with Diego and Esteban de Eguía, brothers of the printer Miguel, the enthusiastic publisher of Erasmus. They too made the pilgrimage to Jerusalem, and met up with Ignatius afterwards in Italy, where eventually they entered the Society.[43] In Paris, in 1529, Ignatius made a second attempt to gather companions, giving the *Exercises* to three young Spaniards, Juan Castro, Pedro de Peralta and Amador de Elduayen, who caused a furore by deciding to adopt his life of evangelical poverty. Later Peralta made the pilgrimage on foot to Jerusalem.[44]

When Ignatius made his third, and successful, attempt to gather companions, Jerusalem once again played a central role. His six friends — Francisco Javier, Pierre Favre, Alfonso Salmerón, Diego Laínez, Nicolás Alonso Bobadilla and Simon Rodrigues — decided to travel to the Holy Land. Each took the decision independently, though under his guidance. Later they formally expressed their resolve together, in the vow at Montmartre on 15 August, 1534. Although the exact nature of the vow is hard to determine, partly because its text has not survived, and partly because the various accounts of it vary, it is clear that all agreed to travel to Jerusalem in poverty, though they differed about what they should do once they had arrived. Some were inclined to stay there for a limited period of time; others wished to spend the rest of their lives there in devotion and service.[45] The latter included Ignatius, for whom this was an opportunity to realize the ambition conceived in Spain years before. As Polanco later put it: 'que no le habiendo salido la primera vez, pretendía el padre Ignacio probarlo la segunda'.[46]

It was in order to await a boat to Jerusalem that the companions met up in Italy in 1537, and there they sought the pope's blessing on their pilgrimage. When it became apparent that they would not be able to make the journey, because of conflict in the Mediterranean between Venice and the Turks, Ignatius's longing to go to Jerusalem did not subside. With his other companions he was ordained in Venice on 24 June 1537, but unlike them he did not say his first Mass shortly afterwards, apparently hoping that he would be able to say it in the Holy Land. Eventually he said it in Rome, on 25 December 1538, in a chapel in Santa Maria Maggiore reputed to hold a true relic of the manger in which Christ had been laid in Bethlehem.[47]

*The Society of Jesus*

Ignatius's sense of a personal involvement in the fight against heresy appears to have developed after the decision was taken in 1539 to found the Society of Jesus. In the original foundation document that Cardinal Contarini presented to Paul III in September 1539, the purpose of the Society was said to be 'the advancement of souls in Christian life and doctrine and . . . the propagation of the faith'. It was considered a missionary enterprise with world-wide concerns. Work in Protestant countries was mentioned as one task in which the Society might become involved, but it was not given prominence: it was listed third, after missions to the Turks and to the New World.[48] One year later this definition of purpose was incorporated into the bull *Regimini militantis ecclesiae* by which the Society was officially established.[49] In 1550, however, it was revised by Ignatius, and appeared in a different form in the bull *Exposcit debitum*. The purpose of the Society was now defined as 'the defence and propagation of the faith and . . . the advancement of souls'.[50] Nadal later explained what this meant: 'la defensa de la fe, frente a los herejes; su propagación respecto a los no creyentes; la salvación y perfección de nuestro prójimo para todos'.[51]

The sequence of aims in the bull of 1550 reversed the order in which they had developed in Ignatius's own life. A concern for interior renewal came first, during his conversion; the desire to help others grow spiritually developed alongside the ambition to 'spread the faith' in the Holy Land; the commitment to 'defend' the faith emerged last of all, during the 1540s, when the Society became involved in the battle against heresy in Italy and Northern Europe. Ignatius worked for the establishment of the Roman Inquisition in 1542; throughout the decade he directed Jesuit missions in Protestant lands; and he laboured tirelessly to found a college in Rome for the training of ordinands from the various German provinces.[52] In a letter of 1554 to Peter Canisius in Germany he expressed his growing awareness of the importance of this aspect of the Society's calling:

> Vedendo il progresso che hanno fatto gli eretici in così breve tempo, dilatando il veleno della loro mala dottrina per tanti popoli e regioni . . . pare che la Compagnia nostra, essendo accettata dalla providenza divina fra li mezzi efficaci per riparare a tanto male, non solamente debba essere sollecita a preparare remedi buoni, ma pronti e che possano molto estendersi, adoperandosi, quanto più presto potrà, a preservare quello che resta sano, e a curare quello che già è ammorbato dalla peste eretica . . .[53]

In another letter to Canisius, written on the same day, he expressed his agreement in principle with the use of political means to suppress religious dissent, including the censorship of books, the establishment of the Inquisition and the imposition, under certain circumstances, of the death penalty. In such remarks one notes a Counter-Reformation spirit that became increasingly important after his death.[54]

Ignatius himself, however, was not inclined towards polemic. He had some knowledge of Protestant views, having studied theology for eighteen months in Paris and for one year in Venice, and he urged Jesuits in Germany to keep up to date with theological controversies. None the less he never debated Protestant beliefs in his own writings, and hardly ever alluded to Luther in his letters. His gifts were not those of an academic theologian or a publicist, but of a pastor, and he preferred the simple affirmation of his beliefs to defending them in disputation.[55] This is apparent in his advice to Jesuits to counter heresy not primarily by persecution or polemic but by private conversation, preaching on Catholic doctrines, administration of the sacraments and, above all, the example of Christian lives. To members of the Society who were sent to Cologne and Ingolstadt he wrote:

> Será manera más pacífica ésta de predicar, y leer, y enseñar la doctrina católica, y probarla, y confirmarla, más bien que armar ruido persiguiendo a los herejes, los cuales se obstinarían más si se predicaba contra ellos abiertamente.[56]

On two occasions recorded by Gonçalves da Cámara he remarked that the reform of the Church would be accomplished if the pope simply reformed himself, his household and the city of Rome. This conviction, expressed by many reformers in the late fifteenth and early sixteenth centuries, stemmed from his belief that the basis of orthodoxy was, or should be, orthopraxis.[57] Although it is true that he approved, in principle, of using political means to combat heresy, he was not an extremist: he did not believe that the Inquisition or the death penalty should be used in Germany;[58] and he held that the Society's role should be mainly a defensive one, in Southern Europe.[59]

The missions to Protestant lands, moreover, were only a part of the Society's many activities, and never the part to which Ignatius himself was most attracted.[60] When planning them, and missions outside Europe to places such as Japan and Brazil, he was efficient but detached: 'his mind directed the operations with serenity and thoroughness, but his emotions seemed asleep'.[61] His enthusiasm was evident, however, in matters to do with the Muslim world and the Middle East. In 1546 he was prepared to resign his position as General of the Society in order to participate in a mission to Ethiopia.[62] In 1550 he was prompt to offer spiritual assistance to the viceroy of Sicily, Juan de Vega, who was engaged in a military expedition to the North African coast.[63] From 1552 onwards he worked with great energy for the foundation of Jesuit colleges in Cyprus, Constantinople and Jerusalem.[64] In 1554 he longed to join a mission to North Africa to convert the Moors, despite advanced years and poor health.[65] Such moments reveal the continuing force, even in old age, of his deep-rooted attraction to the Holy Land.

## II. THE PAPACY

Ribadeneira's biography depicts Ignatius not only as Luther's foe, but also as a staunch defender of the pope. In one vivid passage it contrasts Luther's refusal to submit to Rome with Loyola's determination to obey it, and to promote obedience to the Holy See by instituting the fourth vow of the Society of Jesus:[66]

> Y quando Lutero quitava la obediencia a la Yglesia Romana y hazía gente para combatilla con todas sus fuerças entonces levantó Dios a este santo capitán, para que allegasse soldados por todo el mundo, los quales con nuevo voto se obligassen de obedecer al sumo pontífice, y resistiessen con obras y con palabras a la perversa y herética dotrina de los sequazes de Lutero.[67]

This interpretation of Ignatius's attitude to the papacy, which rapidly became the standard one, contains a core of truth, but, like the notion of his hostility to Protestantism, it omits important details. It does not mention, for instance, that his view of the papal office and of his relation to it passed through several phases between his conversion and his death; nor does it indicate that throughout his life he experienced serious difficulties in the matter of obedience to Church authority.

## The Early Years

In the period before his conversion, and immediately after it, the papacy formed part of Ignatius's received understanding of the Church, but it does not appear to have had for him any special or urgent importance. When he was a
young man he had a devotion to St Peter, who was venerated in the locality
of Azpeitia where he was raised, and later he was struck by the fact that it
was on St Peter's feast day in 1521 that he began to recover from the serious
illness that afflicted him after the battle at Pamplona.[68] There is no evidence,
however, that at this stage in his life he connected devotion to St Peter with
devotion to his successor in Rome. In the *Spiritual Exercises,* which he began
to write at Manresa in 1522, the papacy is not mentioned, and apart from
the *Rules of Orthodoxy,* which were composed later, there are few allusions
to the Church.[69] Two of the exercises that probably date from Manresa por-
tray in vivid images the kingdom of God in the world. In the first, the meditation on the Kingdom, Jesus is pictured as a monarch summoning his troops
to a war of conquest; and in the second, the meditation on Two Standards,
his followers in Jerusalem are contrasted with the enemy forces in Babylon.
In these exercises the kingdom of God is interior and spiritual, the realm of
men's souls: it is not identified with the Church; and the foe is not said to
be heresy, but the devil who rules through sin.[70]

The first indication of a special role of the papacy in Ignatius's life appeared
during the years he spent in Paris gathering companions. Just before taking
the vow of Monmartre in 1534, his friends, with one exception, received the
*Exercises* individually, under his direction, and their decision to go to the Holy
Land was probably influenced by the image in the meditation on Two Standards of Jesus in Palestine calling his followers to join him.[71] They agreed,
in addition, that if they could not go to Jerusalem, or if they decided not to
stay there, they would turn to the pope and ask him to send them wherever
he chose. This mention of the pope has been interpreted as the earliest sign
of what later became the 'romanità' of the Society of Jesus.[72] It is important to note, however, that in 1534 it was of secondary significance, not
primary. Their ideal was, and continued to be, a life of prayer and service
in Jerusalem, and recourse to the pope was envisaged only as a last resort,
as a method of discerning God's will if events should frustrate their plans
unexpectedly and throw them into confusion. This ranking of priorities is clearly implied in the remarks of Pierre Favre, who afterwards reflected that he
would always feel bound to give thanks to Christ for disclosing their vocation 'by the voice of his Vicar',[73] and in the account of the fourth vow that
Ignatius later included in the *Constitutions* of the Society:

La intención del 4° voto del Papa no era pará lugar particular, sino pará ser esparcidos en varias partes del mundo. Porque como fuesen los que primero se jun-taron de la Compañía de diversas provincias y reinos, no sabiendo entre qué regiones andar, entre fieles o infieles, por no errar in via Domini hicieron la tal promesa o voto, para que su Santidad hiciesse la división dellos a mayor gloria divina.[74]

## The Society of Jesus

A further phase began in 1539 when Ignatius and his companions decided, after lengthy deliberations, to found a religious order. Gradually they came to realize that an important development had occurred in the ideal that had inspired them since the Montmartre vow. Jerusalem had ceased to be the place to which they felt called; Rome had become instead their centre and their base; and their longing to serve Christ had found a new expression in their resolve to serve his vicar on earth, the pope.

Their acknowledgement of this crucial development was reflected in the im-ages they drew from the *Exercises* in order to articulate the revised concep-tion of their goal. In later years Jerónimo Nadal repeatedly affirmed that the original inspiration of the Society lay in the meditations on the Kingdom and Two Standards.[75] His perception is confirmed by close study of the founda-tion document submitted to Paul III in September 1539. Here the Society pro-claimed that its members were enlisted under the pope to fight his cause:

> Sciant omnes socii . . . Societatem hanc universam et singulos sub sanctissimi Domini nostri Pauli III et successorum ejus fideli obedientia Deo militare . . .[76]

These words recall the section of the meditation on the Kingdom in which the retreatant is asked to imagine Christ calling on men to enlist in his service and fight on his behalf.[77] The foundation document went on to state that although all clerics had a duty to obey the pope, members of the Society would go further and take a special vow to obey him in all matters concerned with mission:

> . . . atque ita sub Vicarii Christi imperio divinaque ejus potestate subesse, ut non solum ei iuxta commune clericorum omnium debitum parere, sed etiam voti vinculo ita alligari ut quicquid Sanctitas ejus iusserit ad profectum animarum et fidei propagationem pertinens . . . illico, quantum in nobis fuerit, exequi teneamur.[78]

In much the same way it is noted in the *Exercises* that although all men of sound judgement will respond to the call of Christ, some will wish to go fur-ther and make a special promise to serve him with zeal.[79]

As these parallels suggest, the vow to serve the pope sprang originally from devotional concerns, not apologetic ones. It expressed a fervent longing, shaped by the *Exercises,* to serve Christ throughout the world, rather than a particular desire to defend the papal office in schism-torn Europe. When

Ribadeneira looked back to the origins of the vow, he saw in them a providential anticipation of the needs of the Church in the 1570s and 1580s, but it is likely that in 1539 Ignatius and his companions were looking not so much to the future as to the past. A number of medieval orders, such as the Franciscans, had established a direct relationship with the pope, and in Italy, only fifteen years earlier, the Theatines had resolved to live 'under immediate subjection to, and the special protection of, the Supreme Pontiff and the Apostolic See'.[80] Ignatius was aware of such precedents: he had come into contact with the Theatines, for instance, in 1536, when he first arrived in Venice, and during his stay in the city he had made a thorough study of their way of life and constitutions.[81]

## General of the Society

In the years between 1541 and 1556, which he spent as General of the new order, Ignatius's understanding of the Society's relation to the pope developed in important ways that may be traced by comparing his various redactions of the fourth vow. The earliest formulation, in the foundation document of 1539, was soon found to be inadequate. When Cardinal Ghinucci was asked to examine it he could not see why the vow was necessary since, as the document itself affirmed, all clerics were obliged to obey the pope.[82] Ignatius responded to this objection in a redrafted version which eventually formed part of the bull *Regimini militantis ecclesiae:*

> Et quamvis Evangelio doceamur, et fide orthodoxa cognoscamus, ac firmiter profiteamur omnes Christi fideles Romano Pontifici, tamquam capiti ac Iesu Christi vicario, subesse, ad maiorem tamen nostrae Societatis humilitatem, ac perfectam unius cuiusque mortificationem et voluntatum nostrarum abnegationem, summopere conducere iudicavimus, singulos nos, ultra illud commune vinculum speciali voto adstringi, ita ut quidquid modernus et alii Romani Pontifices pro tempore exsistentes iusserint, ad profectum animarum et fidei propagationem pertinens . . . sine ulla tergiversatione aut excusatione, illico, quantum in nobis fuerit, exsequi teneamur.[83]

The emphasis in this passage on the devotional reasons for taking the vow calls to mind, once more, the *Exercises,* where it is said, in the meditation on the Kingdom, that the promise made by the king's close followers to serve him with zeal is undertaken in a spirit of mortification and self-denial.[84]

The second redaction remained untouched for ten years. In 1550, however, it was replaced by another version which Ignatius prepared for inclusion in the bull *Exposcit debitum.* In this he set out three separate reasons for taking the vow, the first of which was devotion to the papacy: 'we have judged . . . that the . . . procedure will be supremely profitable to each of us . . . for the sake of our greater devotion in obedience to the Apostolic See, of greater abnegation of our own wills, and of surer direction from the Holy Spirit'.[85] It is interesting to note that the sequence of reasons in the bull reversed the order in which they had evolved in Ignatius's own life.[86] The fourth vow began in the 1530s as a means of discerning God's will in perplexity; gradually, in the years that followed, it came to embody and express the ideal of serving Jesus with zeal that informs the meditation on the Kingdom; only in the 1540s did its role in the fight against heresy become clear, and only in 1550 was this aspect given pride of place in a papal bull.

The primacy accorded in *Exposcit debitum* to 'devotion in obedience to the Apostolic See' is in keeping with the emphasis elsewhere in the bull on 'defending' the Catholic faith; and it is matched by other evidence that after the foundation of the Society Ignatius became increasingly aware of the need to uphold the authority of the Church, and particularly the authority of the pope. The *Rules of Orthodoxy,* for instance, which were probably composed between 1539 and 1541, encourage praise of ecclesiastical decrees, customs and traditions, and affirm the importance of obeying the Church, which is termed (in words that focus attention on the magisterium) 'la nuestra sancta madre iglesia hierárchica'.[87] In the original Spanish text of the rules there is no allusion to the papal office, but later, when the first Latin translation (the *versio prima*) was being finalized, Ignatius remedied this by adding to the phrase 'hierarchical Church' the three words 'quae romana est'.[88]

The rule in which Church authority is exalted most conspicuously is the thirteenth, which urges that private judgement should be submitted unreservedly to pronouncements by the hierarchy: 'We must always hold, in order to be correct in everything, that what I see as white, I shall believe to be black, if the hierarchical Church so determines'.[89] It has been suggested that these words contain an allusion to an earlier statement by Erasmus in the *Supputationes errorum in censuris Beddae* of 1527: 'black would not be white, even if the Roman Pontiff pronounced it so, which I know he would never do'.[90] The parallels are not exact: Erasmus writes of black being called white, Ignatius of one's perception of white being called black; Erasmus imagines a pronouncement of the pope, Ignatius a pronouncement of the hierarchical Church. There is, none the less, a striking contrast: Erasmus expresses confidence that the pope would not call black white, but he is clear that if the pope did so, he would be mistaken; Ignatius affirms that if the Church did make such a judgement it would be correct, and entitled to one's obedient faith.[91]

A similar concern to uphold Church authority is evident in some of the letters Ignatius wrote as General, such as the instructions he drew up for Jesuits on missions to Protestant lands, in which he urged them to rally Catholics by stressing loyalty to the local bishops and the Holy See.[92] There is also the famous letter to the ruler of Ethiopia that he wrote towards the end of his life, in which he emphasized repeatedly the authority of the pope, set out in detail its basis in Scripture, and affirmed that its acceptance was the touchstone of authentic Christian faith.[93] By the standards of the time, however, Ignatius's papalism was not extreme. His letter to Ethiopia, for instance, cannot be taken as a statement of his ideas about the precise nature and extent of papal authority, for it had a specific pastoral purpose. The king of Ethiopia appeared to be following his predecessor's policy of protecting his country from Muslim attack by drawing close to Portugal, thus weakening the traditional allegiance of the Ethiopian Church to the Patriarchate of Alexandria. It was natural, therefore, that Ignatius should rehearse the traditional arguments for the primacy of Rome. The context of the letter is not the divided state of the Western Church, but the older schism between East and West.[94]

One of the most controversial theological issues in Ignatius's time was the precise relation between the authority of a pope and that of a council. It had been debated with particular urgency since the Conciliar controversies of the fifteenth century, and in the 1520s and 1530s it was still sufficiently controversial to deter Rome from summoning a Council of Reform. Ignatius did not allude to the problem in his writings, no doubt out of a wish, evident in other matters, to avoid an issue that was contentious and unresolved.[95] The *Rules of Orthodoxy,* in fact, seem carefully framed to avoid all allusion to it: they praise, in general terms, the authority of the hierarchical Church, and they mention specifically the decrees of councils, but they nowhere refer to the prerogatives of the papacy, nor to the relationship between council and pope.[96]

In general, Ignatius's concern to defend papal authority differed in tone and substance from polemical celebrations of it in the later sixteenth century. He was certainly opposed to papalism of an exaggerated kind. In his instructions to Jesuits destined for Germany in 1549 he wrote: 'Let them defend the Apostolic See and its authority and draw men to authentic obedience to it in such a way that they do not make themselves, like "papists", unworthy of credence by exaggerated defences'.[97]

### Conflict

Ribadeneira's portrait of Ignatius as the faithful servant of the Church does not allude to the difficulties that Ignatius himself frequently encountered in the matter of obedience. From the time of his conversion in the 1520s to his death in 1556 he often experienced conflict, sometimes painful, between the decisions of Church authority and his own discernment of the divine will.[98]

At Manresa, in 1522 and 1523, he found no guide with whom he could share all his concerns, even though he had a confessor and some like-minded friends, and later he reflected that he had been led throughout this period by God himself:

> En este tiempo le trataba Dios de la misma manera que trata un maestro de escuela a un niño, enseñándole; y ora esto fuese por su rudeza y grueso ingenio, o porque no tenía quien le enseñase, o por la firme voluntad que el mismo Dios le había dado para servirle, claramente él juzgaba y siempre ha juzgado que Dios le trataba desta manera.[99]

It was his own inner promptings that led him to Jerusalem, and when he was denied permission to stay there he experienced a clash between authority and his own discernment of God's plans. When the Franciscan superior threatened to excommunicate him if he did not comply, he concluded that he was not meant to stay, but the inner conviction that he was meant to dwell in Jerusalem subsequently returned.[100]

Similar agonizing situations arose later during his visits to Alcalá and Salamanca. Restrictions were placed on his teaching in these places because his source of inspiration was not formal theology but personal and interior. This is clear from his interview in 1527 with the subprior of the Dominican house of San Esteban in Salamanca, who reproached him for teaching matters of moral theology without having received a proper education:

> Vosotros no sois letrados, dice el fraile, y habláis de virtudes y de vicios; y desto ninguno puede hablar sino en una de dos maneras: o por letras, o por el Espíritu Santo. No por letras; ergo por Espíritu Santo.[101]

In both towns he complied, at first, with the restrictions, but because they clashed with his inner sense of divine vocation he protested against them, and strove to have them countermanded.[102] When his efforts failed, he left Spain for Paris in order to continue teaching as well as studying.[103]

In Spain in the 1520s Ignatius, without disobeying the 'letter' of ecclesiastical decisions, was prepared to follow his inner light as far as he could. In the 1530s the same 'discernment of spirits' took him from Paris to Rome, and eventually, after much perplexity, prompted him to found the Society. It was an inner certainty that led him to insist that the Society should take the name, not of its founder, but of Jesus. Polanco recorded the tenacity with which he clung to this certainty, which he believed he had received from God:

> Y en esto del nombre tuvo tantas visitaciones . . . de aquel cuyo nombre tomaron, y tantas señales de su aprobación y confirmación deste apellido, que le oí decir al mismo que pensaría ir contra Dios y ofenderle, si dudase que este nombre convenía; y siéndole dicho y escrito de mudarle . . . él me acuerdo me dijo que si todos juntos los de la Compañía juzgasen y todos los otros, a quienes no es obligado a creer so pena de pecado, que se debía mudar este nombre, que él solo nunca vendría en ello.

Such tenacity, added Polanco, was typical of Ignatius in matters in which he felt 'directly' guided: 'Y esta seguridad tan inmovible suele tener . . . en las cosas que tiene por vía superior a la humana, y así en las tales no se rinde a razones ningunas'.[104]

Once the Society had been founded Ignatius continued to experience a conflict between obedience and inner discernment. As General he was resolutely opposed to members of the Society accepting ecclesiastical dignities. Paul III, however, wished to appoint Claude Le Jay bishop of Trieste, and Peter Canisius bishop of Vienna; Julius III planned to make Francis Borgia a cardinal; and Paul IV cherished the same ambition for Diego Laínez. In each of these cases Ignatius refused to acquiesce, and made use of every means to frustrate the decision, visiting prelates and cardinals, and even applying indirect diplomatic pressure, on one occasion, through the daughter of Charles V.[105]

Ignatius's behaviour in such matters was consistent with the understanding of divine inspiration that he set out in the *Rules of Orthodoxy:* '. . . entre Christo nuestro Señor, esposo, y la Iglesia su esposa, es el mismo espíritu que nos gobierna y rige . . .'[106] Since the Spirit who ruled the individual was the same Spirit that ruled the Church, the conflict between personal discernment and Church authority could be, and would be, reconciled. He expressed the principle in one of his letters in order to justify his opposition to Borgia's promotion: '. . . there was no contradiction seeing that the same divine Spirit could move me to this for some reasons, and others (in a contrary direction) for other reasons'.[107]

The confusion, even anguish, to which this could give rise is evident in his reactions to the pontificate of Paul IV. As a cardinal, Carafa had differed from Ignatius in his conception of the religious life, and had desired to merge the Jesuits with his own Theatines, a move that Ignatius had implacably opposed. He also disapproved profoundly of the way in which Ignatius ran the Society, and of its rule of life.[108] After the Society had been founded, Ignatius always feared that Carafa would be elected pope. He confided in Gonçalves da Cámara, 'Yo he pensado en qué cosa me podría dar melancolía y no hallé cosa ninguna sino si el Papa deshiciera la Compañía del todo'. In 1555, after the sudden death of Marcellus II, he asked for prayers that the conclave would not elect a pope hostile to the Society, 'por haber algunos papables de quien se temía la mutarían'. And when he heard that Carafa had been elected, he shook in every bone of his body. The perfectly justified fear that Carafa would alter the Society's constitutions remained with him to the end of his life.[109]

It has been said, with reason, that Ignatius was 'the best servant the papacy ever had'.[110] It is not always recognized, however, that service of the pope became a priority rather late in his life, eighteen years after his conversion,

I

and that it was neither uncritical nor extreme. In many ways his notion of the papal office was medieval rather than Counter-Reformation. He never questioned its authority, but he did not see the defence of that authority as his vocation until the 1540s; and when he did so it was as an expression of his devotion to Christ, a devotion first kindled in his reading at Loyola. Only late in his life does one note the impact of the growing centralization around the papal office by which the medieval Church adjusted to the pressures of a new age.

### III. THE MEDIEVAL ORDERS

One of the priorities of the Council of Trent was to reaffirm the value of traditional forms of the religious life, and of the monastic vows on which they were based, and in the late sixteenth century the Society of Jesus, true to its calling as 'defender' of the faith, became increasingly involved in the defence as well as the renewal of the medieval orders. These concerns were reflected in Ribadeneira's biography:

> Y porque una de las cosas que más avía de perseguir este dragón (Luther) . . . son las sagradas religiones . . . con grandíssima sabiduría ordenó la divina providencia que se instituyesse una nueva orden para defender principalmente nuestra santíssima fe, cuyo instituto es socorrer y ayudar a los soldados valerosos de las otras santas religiones, que de día y de noche, con tanto esfuerço y fruto pelean donde los ay, y donde no, salir ella con las armas en las manos al encuentro del común enemigo.[111]

Ribadeneira's words convey Ignatius's commitment to the renewal of the religious life, but they do not indicate that it developed gradually and passed through various stages, nor that his attitude to the medieval orders was complex, even ambiguous.

From his conversion onwards, Ignatius had some close connections with the religious orders, and valued many of their traditions. When, during his convalescence at Loyola, he read the *Legenda aurea,* the medieval saints whose lives impressed him most deeply were Francis and Dominic, the founders of the Franciscans and Dominicans.[112] At Loyola, too, he considered becoming a Carthusian, and only hesitated when it occurred to him that he might not be permitted the rigorous, monastic penances that he was resolved to undertake.[113] At the Benedictine abbey of Montserrat he made a general confession to a monk in the community, Jean Chanones, who probably taught him the methodical meditation practised in the monastery. Later this type of meditation formed the basis of the *Spiritual Exercises.*[114] When Ignatius left Montserrat and went to Manresa, he stayed for a while in the Dominican house there, and developed the custom of visiting an elderly Cistercian whose wisdom he respected.[115] At this time he was regular in his attendance at the choral office and sung Mass, and he said the 'layman's breviary' in a book of hours.[116] A love of music, specifically Church music, remained with him to the end of his life.[117] On his return from the Holy Land, in 1523, he felt drawn, for a while, to enter an established order, preferably an unreformed house where he might suffer.[118] When he left Spain and went to Paris, a number of his friends there, who wished to emulate his apostolic zeal, entered religious orders. They included Juan Castro, a student from Burgos, who became a Carthusian in the Charterhouse of Vall de Cristo where Ignatius visited him in 1535.[119]

Despite this intimate contact with the religious life, Ignatius himself never entered a traditional order, and was extremely reluctant to found one. For fifteen years after his conversion he remained a layman, becoming a priest only in 1537.[120] During these years most of his close companions were laymen too: in Paris the one exception was Pierre Favre, who presided at Mass in Montmartre on the occasion of the famous vow.[121] The young men who took the vow, and who later travelled to Italy, followed no rule: they were united simply by the vow, and by the desire, underlying it, to share Ignatius's evangelical mode of life. At this stage they were not an order, but a group of pilgrims.[122] Ignatius's apparent lack of interest in founding an order led some of his followers in Paris to leave him, and to enter one or other of the traditional congregations.[123] Looking back on this period in the 1540s Polanco marvelled that Ignatius and his friends had not become friars or monks. To him this seemed a sign of the working of Providence, preserving them for another enterprise.[124]

## The Founding of the Society

Some of the reasons for Ignatius's reluctance to become a religious may be inferred from the deliberations about forming the Society which took place in 1539. After their submission to the pope the companions were split up on a variety of missions, and they were therefore led to ask if they should in some way maintain the bond of unity that had brought them together. They decided, without disagreement, that they should; but a further question followed: should they preserve their unity by promising to obey a common superior? The deliberations about this second issue were intense and prolonged. A number had grave reservations, among them, it would seem, Ignatius. Two arguments against a promise of obedience were articulated. First, the vow of obedience to a superior had fallen into disrepute in the existing orders, and this might dissuade others from joining the companions. Second, if they tried to found an order, the Church authorities might impose on them one of the traditional rules.[125]

Eventually it was decided to go ahead, but when the foundation document was drawn up it omitted many features of traditional religious life. Instead of taking the name of Ignatius, its founder, the Society would be called after Jesus, in accord with Ignatius's own adamant wishes; members were to wear no distinctive habit; instead of the fixed penances prescribed in traditional orders, there would be freedom for the individual to choose his own; unlike monks, canons and friars, the Society would not chant the office in common: instead each member would say it in private; they would dispense with organ and choir; and before taking their final vows, novices would be submitted to a longer period of probation than the established orders required.[126]

These breaks with monastic tradition suggest that if Ignatius and his friends did not join one of the existing orders it was because they knew that the way of life they wished to follow required new structures. They also imply that, like most reformers of the day, they were critical of certain features of conventional religious life. Erasmus, for instance, had criticized undue attachment to the externals of an order, including the memory and name of the founder, the habit, and prescribed penances; and he had been critical too of the insufficient testing of novices. Ignatius, though personally more sympathetic to monastic tradition than the Dutch reformer, appears to have had similar views on the need for renewal in the religious life, and the form it might take.[127]

The fact that the new Society implied a radical critique of monastic tradition explains the controversy that it provoked in the Roman curia in 1539 and 1540, and the long delay of twelve months before it was approved. When the document drawn up by the companions was presented to Paul III in September 1539, he gave it his verbal approval, but passed it for detailed examination to the curia, where Cardinal Ghinucci was alarmed by a number of passages that might, if approved by the Church, provide the Protestants with ammunition. The deadlock that resulted was prolonged, and for a while the ideals of Ignatius and the companions seemed, to their great consternation, to be in jeopardy. Eventually, in order to resolve the disagreement between Ghinucci and Contarini, the document was passed to a third cardinal, Guidiccioni, and after further delays a revised and modified version was prepared.[128]

Two passages in the revised version, which appeared in the papal bull of 1540, reveal the reasons for Ghinucci's concern. First, the decision to abandon the choral office was expressed in the original document in the following terms:

> All the members who are in holy orders . . . shall be bound to say the divine

office according to the ritual of the Church, but not in choir, lest they be drawn away from charitable works, to which we have dedicated ourselves completely. For the same reason they may not use an organ, nor choral liturgical chant, at Mass or any other function; since we have learnt from experience that all the things by which other clerics or religious laudably ornament the liturgy, and that have been invented to excite or move souls by hymns and mysteries, are for us no mean impediment. For, in accordance with our vocation, it is right that we, in addition to other necessary duties, should often spend a large part of the day and even of the night comforting the sick in body as well as soul.[129]

Although this forthright statement was worded carefully to indicate that the companions had no wish to impugn the traditions of the established orders, it was pared down to one succinct sentence when it appeared, reformulated, in the bull: 'All the members who are in holy orders . . . shall be bound to say the divine office according to the ritual of the Church, each one privately and individually and not in common'. [130] The suggestion that the choral office could be an impediment to works of charity was dropped; and the decision to abandon choir and organ was suppressed altogether.

Second, the original document mentioned, among dangers to be avoided, the external observances of the traditional religious life: 'Let no one, under pain of moral sin, impose on us fasts, disciplines, the obligation to keep head or feet uncovered, to wear clothing of a particular colour or to observe a particular diet, nor penances, hair shirts and other mortifications of the flesh'.[131] It went on to affirm that the companions did not question the value of such things in themselves: 'Each individual may (unless his superior refuses) choose devoutly the penances he finds useful and necessary'; and it explained that their concern was to accomplish the work to which they felt called: 'we do not wish to bind our members with so many chains all together, nor to provide them with an excuse for suspending, at times, the activities we propose to engage in'.[132] Despite the caveats, this entire section, with its Erasmian overtones, was dropped from the final version.

*General of the Society*

The circumstances in which the Society was founded ensured that from the very beginning its relation to traditional forms of the religious life was double-edged: on the one hand it affirmed the value of these forms and sought to defend them against Protestant attack; on the other its own rule of life broke sharply with them, and implied a criticism of how they were being observed by contemporaries. This complex inheritance explains some of the difficulties that Ignatius faced as General between 1541 and 1556, when he was obliged to defend the new order's way of life against two challenges: uncertainty and incomprehension amongst its own members and growing hostility from without.[133]

Ignatius's assurance that the Society's distinctive features were valuable and should be preserved was not shared by all his followers. While it was being established, his co-founder, Simon Rodrigues, wrote to him from Portugal asking that the word 'compañía' should not be used in the title, for it was causing confusion among canon lawyers who held that, strictly speaking, the term denoted not an 'order' but an association.[134] Uncertainty about the Society's legal status appears to have been widespread and prolonged,[135] and to have coexisted with some misunderstanding of its particular life style and goals. In August 1553, for instance, Ignatius received a letter from a Spanish Jesuit, Miguel de Torres, to whom he had entrusted a number of important missions, asking him to explain 'the Society's way of life, because, to be honest, . . . I do not understand it, nor how it accords with the Society's aim'.[136] Other Jesuits were inclined to question the wisdom of breaking with the traditions of the religious life, among them Francis Borgia and the friends with whom he had entered the Society, who felt drawn to a more contemplative vocation. Borgia believed that the time allowed for meditation was inadequate, and he was inclined to practise rigorous penances of a monastic kind. On both points Ignatius differed, and was obliged to take restraining action; but after his death similar tendencies resurfaced in Seville, where one of Borgia's followers, Bustamante, briefly ran the Jesuit house on monastic lines. Later, when Borgia became General, he introduced into the Society the duty of spending one hour a day in meditation, a measure that the Fourth General Congregation in 1581 voted to retain, even though it ran counter to Ignatius's own preferences; and in 1566, when the Muslim threat to Europe was particularly intense, he ordered the Jesuit communities to recite litanies, a practice Ignatius himself had rejected, but which was retained after the Muslim threat had decreased. The result of such developments was confusion within the order about its authentic spirit, some holding that a central place should be given to mental prayer and penance, others that these practices should be subordinated to the demands of apostolic activity. Divided views continued until the end of the century, when the whole matter came to a head during the generalate of Claudio Aquaviva.[137]

Such uncertainties are understandable, for throughout the 1540s Ignatius's ideas on many aspects of the Society's life, even the role within it of obedience, were still evolving.[138] Moreover, apart from the foundation documents incorporated into the papal bulls of 1540 and 1550, the Society in this period had no official constitutions. Ignatius laboured to produce the constitutions, and in 1549 and 1550 he managed to complete an initial draft which, based on a careful study of other orders, placed the new features of the Society in the context of tradition. He continued, however, to introduce revisions and corrections, and the text had not been promulgated when he died in 1556. The constitutions were approved officially two years later, in 1558, but further changes were subsequently introduced, and the final version was ratified only in 1594.[139]

Hostility from without to the Society's innovations was connected with the changing situation inside the Church during the 1540s and 1550s. The arrival in Italy of Ignatius and his companions had coincided with the ascendancy in the Roman curia of humanist cardinals committed to seeking reconciliation with the Protestants on the basis of common theological ground.[140] The leading member of the group, Gasparo Contarini, received the cardinal's hat in 1535 at a consistory that was originally to have included Erasmus himself, and in 1536 he was joined by Sadolet and Pole. It was in these quarters that Ignatius sought and received patronage and support. Contarini, who had earlier been guided through the *Exercises* by Ignatius himself, presented the foundation document to Paul III in 1539, and acted as its advocate in the troubled year that followed, aided in this by Lattanzio Tolomei, a Sienese humanist to whom Ignatius had also given the *Exercises* after his arrival in Rome.[141] Ignatius enjoyed close relations too with Morone, Cervini and Pole.[142]

The politics advocated by Contarini and the *spirituali* did not receive the support of all members of the curia, many of whom had grave reservations about the wisdom and viability of a rapprochement with the heretics. These reservations were held vigorously by Cardinal Carafa, and they underlay the reluctance of Cardinal Ghinucci to approve the new Society. While the future of the proposed order lay in the balance, or in the months immediately following the papal bull of 1540, Ignatius composed the *Rules of Orthodoxy,* several of which concern the vows and practices of the medieval congregations. The third, for instance, calls for praise of 'chants, psalms and long prayers in churches and outside them'; the fourth encourages warm praise for 'religious orders, virginity, continence'; the fifth praises 'the vows of religion, obedience, poverty, chastity and all other supererogatory works'; the seventh praises 'regulations to do with fasts and abstinence . . . and penances, not only interior but external'.[143] These rules call to mind the phrases in the foundation document of 1539 in which monastic traditions are said to be of value in their own right. They express convictions that Ignatius no doubt held sincerely. In 1539-1541, however, they also served the practical purpose of distinguishing his position from that of extreme reformers inside and outside the Roman Church: they were his response to the fears of conservatives who were opposed to making any concessions, even apparent ones, to the Protestant Reform.[144]

Soon after 1540, the fortunes of the group around Contarini began to wane. The collapse in May 1541 of the conference of Regensburg confirmed that doctrinal agreement with the Protestants was no longer possible. It was follow- ed in 1542 by Contarini's death. The result was the gradual, but decisive, rise of the more conservative party, which reached a height in July 1555 when Carafa was elected pope in succession to Cervini. The new pontiff threw Morone into prison, refused to reconvene the Council of Trent, tried to recall Pole from England and issued an Index of prohibited books that included all the works of Erasmus. A recent historian has written: 'Sometime around the year 1542, the group led by Carafa and other like-minded individuals seized the direction of "Catholic Reform". In the vast complexity of Catholicism, their policies were not consistently implemented, sometimes received setbacks, and could not altogether prevail. None the less, they were among the factors that set the Church in a direction that lasted for centuries'.[145]

Ignatius appears to have looked on the growing influence of the conser- vatives with alarm, recognizing in them a threat to the innovatory features of the Society. His anxiety is clear in his household remarks recorded by Gon- çalves da Cámara between January and October 1555, the period preceding and following Carafa's election. A number concern the wearing of a habit: a distinctive dress is not, he insists, important, and men who have become accustomed to wearing a habit in another order, even briefly as novices, may not be accepted into the Society. Other remarks concern the choral office, which Ignatius insists is not part of the Society's calling: repudiation of the choral office is a public sign of their dedication to apostolic work. He also expresses firm disapproval of monastic modes of address: members of the Society should use their ordinary names, and not call one another 'Father' or 'Brother'.[146] Events subsequently showed that his anxiety was well found- ed. After his death Carafa made important changes in the Society's way of life, cutting the General's tenure of office from life to three years, and im- posing the obligation to chant the office in choir. When the pope died in 1559 these changes lapsed, but the pressures that had produced them did not cease. The obligation to chant the choral office was reimposed by Pius V, and re- mained in force for five years. Later still, controversy about the lifetime tenure of the General was renewed when Clement VIII expressed grave reservations about its wisdom. In the end it proved possible to safeguard Ignatius's provi- sions on both matters, but only at the cost of damaging conflict within and outside the order.[147]

\* \* \*

The earliest accounts of Ignatius's life indicate that in the formative period between his conversion and the founding of the Society of Jesus his ideals and his spirituality were not shaped, or even profoundly influenced, by the concerns of the Counter-Reformation Church. In the 1520s and 1530s he drew together small groups of reform-minded individuals who wished to renew the Christian life in themselves and in those with whom they came into contact. Many such groups flourished in Europe in the late fifteenth and early sixteenth centuries, and, like Ignatius and his companions, most of them were dedicated not to 'self-concious and ambitious programmes for the reform of the Church as a whole', but to 'the taking up, refertilising and modernising . . . of the disciplines of prayer, self-control, and charitable activity . . . in the personal search for the kingdom of God and for the good of their neighbours'.[148] Ignatius's own conception of the 'kingdom of God' was shaped by the medieval works of piety that he read at the time of his conversion, which inspired him with an ardent desire to spend the rest of his life in the Holy Places. Until the late 1530s this desire was more important than any wish to combat the spread of Protestantism in Europe.

In this period, moreover, Ignatius pursued his various apostolic activities outside the established clerical structures of the Church. For fifteen years after his conversion he remained a layman, strongly disinclined to join a religious order or to found one, despite his respect for monasticism and his longing for its reform. For most of the time he lacked any formal training in theology, and he taught and guided others by drawing on his own interior and mystical experience. Not surprisingly he had uneasy, sometimes troubled, relations with the Church authorities, who were fearful of movements that might further the spread of Protestant ideas; and, as the fear of schism deepened in Spain, France and Italy, he came under increasing pressure to distinguish his views from those of the heretics by affirming the legitimacy and value of the Catholic traditions they rejected. This pressure became intense in the late 1530s when he was involved in the delicate process of founding a religious congregation whose rule was an implicit critique of the established orders.

Towards the end of the 1530s Ignatius's position in the Catholic reform underwent a decisive change. His studies over eleven years culminated in a theological education that enabled him to combine inner inspiration with formal learning; in 1537 he chose to become a priest; two years later, after some hesitation, he agreed to found the Society of Jesus. At the same time he was led by unforeseen events to relinquish his ambition to travel to the Holy Land, and he became involved in the papal programme of reform that had been initiated by Paul III. Rome replaced Jerusalem in his plans, and obedience to the pope became an expression of his devotion to Jesus. During the 1540s and early 1550s the ends of the papal reform became increasingly his own, particularly the defence of the Church against heresy, which he defined in

1550 as the principal concern of the Society, and which implied the defence of papal authority and of the medieval orders.

Such developments, however, did not take place without serious tensions in his own life and in the Society. The fight against heresy was for him a duty, not an inner ideal — the concrete application of one point of his programme, not the guiding purpose of his life. The defence and celebration of papal authority coexisted with repeated, sometimes anguished, inner conflict in his own practice of obedience, particularly during the reign of Paul IV; and it was never extreme. To the end of his days he was obliged to defend the innovatory features of the Society against incomprehension among its own members and active hostility from conservatives in Rome. This pattern of steady, sometimes radical, change was not recorded fully in the first official biographies, which appeared between 1572 and 1585. They were formed by, and directed to, a different, later world, in which the battle-lines between Catholic and Protestant were firmly drawn, and in which the Society of Jesus was playing a vital role in the restoration of Catholic tradition. They portrayed Ignatius, naturally enough, as a prophetic figure, sent by God to realize, and eventually symbolize, the defence of the Church in a Counter-Reformation world.

## Notes

1  Ribadeneira's biography appeared in Latin (Naples, 1572) and, revised, in Spanish (Madrid, 1583): *Vita Ignatii Loyolae. Textus latinus et hispanus cum censuris,* edited by Cándido de Dalmases, Rome, 1965; Ioannes Petrus Maffeius, *De vita et moribus Ignatii Loiolae qui Societatem Iesu fundavit,* Rome, 1585.

2  Manuel Ruiz Jurado, 'Ribadeneira (Pierre de)', *Dictionnaire de Spiritualité* 13 (part 2), cols.526-532; I. Iparraguirre, 'La figura de San Ignacio a través de los siglos', in San Ignacio de Loyola, *Obras completas,* edited by I. Iparraguirre and C. de Dalmases, fourth edition (Madrid, 1982), pp.3-38.

3  For a general survey see Irwin Iserloh, Joseph Glazik and Hubert Jedin, *Reformation and Counter-Reformation,* London, 1980.

4  I. Iparraguirre, 'Desmitificación de San Ignacio. La imagen de San Ignacio en el momento actual', *AHSI* 41 (1972), pp.357-373.

5  A general survey of scholarship is provided by John W. O'Malley, 'Catholic Reform' in *Reformation Europe: a Guide to Research,* edited by Steven Ozment (St Louis, 1982), pp.297-319; and 'The Jesuits, St Ignatius and the Counter-Reformation. Some Recent Studies and their Implications for Today', *Studies in the Spirituality of Jesuits* 14 (1982), part 1, pp.1-28.

6  All these texts are published in *Fontes Narrativi de S. Ignatio de Loyola et de Societatis Iesu initiis,* volume 1, edited by D. Fernández Zapico and C. de Dalmases, Rome, 1943 (the series is referred to henceforth as *FN*).

7  In *FN* 1 the history of the text is provided before each document. Other writings of Ignatius have been published for the first time this century: the Journal in 1934 in *MI Constitutiones,* volume 1, and the complete letters between 1903 and 1911 in *MI Epistolae et Instructiones.*

8  *FN* 1, p.317.

9  *FN* 2, p.5.

10  Ibid., p.331.

11  Ibid, pp.306-307: '. . . at the time when God, because of our sins, permitted Martin Luther in Germany to declare war on the apostolic Holy See and the Catholic religion . . . at the very same time, more or less, his divine Providence began to prepare an antidote, as it were, to counter this poison, in the striking conversion of Fr Ignatius Loyola . . .'

12  *FN* 4, p.339: 'When Martin Luther came out of hell like an infernal monster . . . at the same time God our Lord sent to the aid of his Church another man and captain, contrary to 'Luther in everything, so that with his invincible spirit and powerful divine arms he might valiantly resist him and fight the battles of the Lord . . .'

13  Ibid., p.715.

14  Ibid., p.341.

15  Ibid., p.715: 'Finally, all the counsels, thoughts and cares of our father Ignatius were directed to the goal of conserving (in so far as it was healthy) and restoring (in so far as it had declined) the sincerity and purity of the Catholic faith, by his efforts and those of his followers, in the same way as its enemies try to destroy it . . .'

16  Iparraguirre, 'La figura de San Ignacio', p.6.

17  The prayer and readings are those for 31 July, feast of Ignatius.

18  Alonso Rodríguez, *Exercicio de perfección y virtudes religiosas,* 3 volumes (Seville, 1609), volume 3, pp.2, 5. See Manuel Ruiz Jurado, 'Rodriguez (Alphonse)', *Dictionnaire de Spiritualité* 13, part 2, cols.853-860.

19  On the history of ther term see H. Outram Evennett, *The Spirit of the Counter-Reformation* (Cambridge, 1968), pp.4ff.; Ricardo García Villoslada, 'La contrarreforma, su nombre y su concepto histórico', *Miscellanea Historiae Pontificiae* 21 (1959), pp.189-242.

20  Leopold von Ranke, *The History of the Popes during the Last Four Centuries,* volume 1 (London, 1908), pp.145-153.

21  Augustin Redondo, 'Luther et l'Espagne de 1520 à 1536', *Mélanges de la Casa de Velázquez* 1 (1965), pp.109-165 (here pp.120-127).

22  Angela Selke de Sánchez, 'Algunos datos nuevos sobre los primeros Alumbrados. El edicto de 1525 y su relación con el proceso de Alcaraz', *Bulletin Hispanique* 54 (1952), pp.125-152.

23  *FN* 1, p.53.

24  J. Ignacio Tellechea Idígoras, 'La reacción española ante el luteranismo (1520-1559)', *Diálogo Ecuménico* 6 (1971), pp.325-341 (here p.329), reprinted in his *Tiempos recios. Inquisición y heterodoxias* (Salamanca, 1977), pp.23-32; Carlos Gilly, 'Juan de Valdés: Übersetzer und Bearbeiter von Luthers Schriften in seinem *Diálogo de Doctrina'*, *Archiv für Reformationsgeschichte* 74 (1983), pp.257-305.

25  *FN* 1, pp.170, 430, 438.

26  Ibid., p.442.

27  Ibid., p.454.

28  Ibid., p.462.

29  Cándido de Dalmases, 'San Ignacio de Loyola y la Contrarreforma', *Studia missionalia* 34 (1985), pp.321-350 (here pp.325-326).

30  *FN* 1, p.180.

31  Ibid., pp.180, 480.

32  Manuel Ruiz Jurado, 'Polanco (Jean Alphonse de)', *Dictionnaire de Spiritualité* 12 (part 2), cols.1838-1843.

33  *FN* 1, pp.490-492.

34  Ibid., p.493.

35  Ibid., pp.500-502. See M. Del Pazzo and C. de Dalmases, 'Il processo sull' ortodossia di S. Ignazio e dei suoi compagni svoltosi a Roma nel 1538', *AHSI* 38 (1969), pp.431-453. The sentences in favour of Ignatius in Venice and Rome have been published in *Fontes Documentales de S. Ignatio de Loyola,* edited by C. de Dalmases, Rome, 1977.

36 Pedro de Leturia, 'Jerusalén y Roma en los designios de San Ignacio de Loyola', in *Estudios ignacianos,* edited by I. Iparraguirre, 2 volumes (Rome, 1957), volume 1, pp.181-200 (here p.183); James W. Reites, 'Ignacio y los musulmanes de Tierra Santa', *Manresa* 52 (1980), pp.291-318.

37 *FN* 1, 372: 'he thought . . . of going to Jerusalem barefoot, and of eating nothing except grass, and of carrying out all the other mortifications that he saw that the saints had done . . .'

38 Ibid., p.374: 'all he desired to do, once he recovered, was the journey to Jerusalem, as is said above, with as many scourgings and as many fasts as a noble soul, enflamed with God, usually desires to carry out . . .'

39 *Obras completas,* p.102, note 11.

40 *FN* 1, p.422.

41 Ibid., p.430.

42 Ibid., p.171.

43 Ibid., pp.108-110.

44 Ibid., p.468.

45 Manuel Ruiz Jurado, 'The Montmartre Vows: History and Spirituality', *Centrum Ignatianum Spiritualitatis* 16 (1985), part 2, pp.15-89.

46 *MHSI Polanci Complementa,* 1, p.509: quoted in Leturia, *Estudios ignacianos,* volume 1, p.312: 'for since it had not worked out for him the first time, father Ignatius intended to try it a second time'.

47 Pedro de Leturia, 'La primera misa de San Ignacio de Loyola y sus relaciones con la fundación de la Companía', op.cit., pp.223-235.

48 The document is published in *MHSI Constitutiones* 1, pp.14-21.

49 Ibid., pp.24-32.

50 Ibid., pp.375-382.

51 *Monumenta Nadal* IV, p.173: 'the defence of the faith in the face of heretics; its propagation with respect to non-believers; the salvation and perfection of our neighbour with regard to everyone'. Nadal's words date from 1592.

52 See Cándido de Dalmases, 'San Ignacio de Loyola y la Contrarreforma', pp.328ff.; and 'Les Idées de saint Ignace sur la réforme catholique', *Christus* 18 (1958), pp.239-256.

53 *MI Epp.* 12, pp.259-260 (13 August 1554): 'Seeing the progress that the heretics have made in such a short time, spreading the poison of their evil teaching among so many peoples and regions . . . it seems that our Society, having been accepted by divine Providence among the effective means of repairing so much evil, should not only be concerned to prepare good remedies, but remedies that are swift and capable of wide expansion, adapting itself, as quickly as it can, to preserving that which is still healthy, and to healing that which has already succumbed to the plague of heresy'.

54 *MI Epp.* 7, pp.398-404. On the context and interpretation of this letter see Dominique Bertrand, 'De la décision en politique. Lettre de saint Ignace de Loyola sur la question allemande', *Revue d'Ascétique et de Mystique* 45 (1969), pp.47-64; and Cándido de Dalmases, *El padre maestro Ignacio. Breve biografía ignaciana* (Madrid, 1986), pp.169-171.

55 Piet Penning de Vries, 'Protestants and Other Spirituals. Ignatius' Vision and Why he Took this Position', *AHSI* 40 (1971), pp.463-483; John W. O'Malley, 'The Fourth Vow in its Ignatian Context. A Historical Study', *Studies in the Spirituality of Jesuits* 15 (1983) part 1, pp.1-59.

56 Quoted in Dalmases, *El padre maestro Ignacio,* p.167: 'This means, namely, preaching, and expounding and teaching Catholic doctrine, proving its truth and confirming it, will be a more peaceful method than noisily persecuting heretics, who would become more obstinate if one preached against them openly'.

57 *FN* 1, pp.582-583, 719.

58 This is clear from the letter to Canisius mentioned in note 54.

59 *MI Epp.* 12, p.260: '. . . massimamente nelle nazioni settentrionali . . .'

60 Dalmases, 'San Ignacio y la Contrarreforma', pp.323-324, 341.

61  Leturia, *Estudios ignacianos,* volume 1, p.312: 'su mente dirige serena y comprensiva el movimiento pero su afectividad parece dormida'.

62  Ibid., pp.199, 312: Dalmases, *El padre maestro Ignacio,* p.196.

63  James W. Reites, 'Ignacio y los musulmanes del norte de Africa', *Manresa* 56 (1984), pp.5-31 (here p.10).

64  Leturia, op.cit., pp.192, 312; Dalmases, op.cit., pp.193-194.

65  *MI Epp.* 6, pp.188-189; see Reites, art.cit., pp.24-25.

66  On the fourth vow, by which professed members of the Society promised 'a special obedience to the sovereign pontiff concerning the missions', see O'Malley, 'The Fourth Vow in its Ignatian Context', and, for an opposing view, John R. Sheets, 'The Fourth Vow of the Jesuits', *Review for Religious* 42 (1983), pp.518-529.

67  *FN* 4, p.715: 'And when Luther was withdrawing obedience from the Roman Church and gathering people to combat it with all their strength, then God raised up this holy captain to gather soldiers throughout the world, that they might commit themselves by a new vow to obey the supreme pontiff, and resist by words and deeds the perverse and heretical doctrine of Luther's followers'.

68  *FN 1, p.368; Pedro de Leturia, El gentilhombre Iñigo López de Loyola,* second edition (Barcelona, 1949), pp.139-140.

69  Apart from the *Rules of Orthodoxy,* the Church is referred to in five sections of the *Exercises*: 18, 42, 170, 177, 229.

70  See Cándido de Dalmases, 'The Church in the Personal Experience of St Ignatius', *Centrum Ignatianum Spiritualitatis* 14 (1983), pp.51-66, (here pp.53, 54).

71  Manuel Ruiz Jurado in 'The Montmartre Vows', pp.18-23, 25.

72  Pedro de Leturia, 'A las fuentes de la romanidad de la Compañía de Jesús', in *Estudios ignacianos,* volume 1, pp.239-256; published in a revised form as 'Aux sources de la "romanité" de la Compagnie de Jésus', *Christus* 2 (1955), pp.81-100.

73  *FN* 1, p.42.

74  *Constitutiones* 2; section 605: 'The intention of the fourth vow concerning the Pope was not to (designate) a particular place, but (for members) to be distributed in various parts of the world. For, since those members of the Society who (first) came together were from different provinces and realms, and unsure which regions they should go into, whether among the faithful or unbelievers, they made the aforesaid promise or vow to avoid erring in the path of the Lord, so that his Holiness might distribute them to the greater glory of God'

75  *MHSI Nadal* IV, p.649; V, pp.40, 288-302. On the origins of the Society see Antonio Jiménez Oñate, *El origen de la Compañía de Jesús: carisma fundacional y génesis histórica,* Rome, 1966; Javier Osuna, *Friends in the Lord,* London, 1974.

76  *MI Constitutiones* 1, p.17: 'Let all members know . . . that this entire Society and all its members are engaged in a battle for God under faithful obedience to our most holy Lord Paul III and his successors . . .'

77  *Sp. Exx.,* 95.

78  'And that it is subject to the command of the Vicar of Christ and to his divine power in such a way that not only should it obey him in accordance with the common duty of all clerics but it is bound by the bond of a vow so that whatsoever his Holiness demands for the advancement of souls and the propagation of the faith we shall be obliged to obey instantly as far as lies within us, without evasion or excuse'.

79  *Sp. Exx.,* 96, 97.

80  O'Malley, 'The Fourth Vow', p.3.

81  Georges Bottereau, 'La "lettre" d'Ignace de Loyola à Gian Pietro Carafa', *AHSI* 44 (1975), pp.139-152.

82  Cardinal Ghinucci's reflections on the proposed vow were communicated to Contarini by Lattanzio Tolomei on 28 September 1539; the letter is published in Franz Dittrich, *Regesten und Briefe des Cardinals G. Contarini* (Braunsberg, 1881), p.379.

83  *MI Constitutiones* 1, pp.27-28: 'And though we are taught by the Gospel, and know from the orthodox faith, and firmly profess, that all Christ's faithful are subject to the Roman

Pontiff, as their head and as Vicar of Christ, nevertheless we have judged that it will be supremely conducive to the greater humility of our Society, to the perfect mortification of each of its members, and to the abnegation of our wills, if, in addition to that common bond, each of us is obliged by a special vow to carry out, without hesitation or excuse, as far as we are able, whatever the present Roman Pontiff and his successors may command that pertains to the progress of souls and the propagation of the faith'.

84   *Sp. Exx.*, 97: '. . . haciendo contra su propia sensualidad y contra su amor carnal y mundano . . .'

85   *MI Constitutiones* 1, pp.377-378.

86   See O'Malley, 'The Fourth Vow', p.27.

87   *Sp. Exx.*, 353-370 (the phrase 'la nuestra sancta madre Iglesia hierárchica' occurs in 353). On the dating of the Rules see Cándido de Dalmases in *Obras completas,* pp.191-192.

88   The early texts of the *Exercises,* including the Spanish 'autograph' and the *versio prima,* have been edited in *Exercitia spiritualia: Textuum antiquissimorum nova editio,* edited by J. Calveras and C. de Dalmases, Rome, 1969.

89   *Sp. Exx.,* 365.

90   *Opera omnia* (Leyden, 1706), volume 9, col.517: 'Neque enim ideo nigrum esset album, si ita pronuntiaret Romanus Pontifex, quod illum scio nequaquam facturum'.

91   On the backgrounds to the two passages and their interpretation, see O'Malley, 'The Fourth Vow', p.15.

92   Dalmases, 'San Ignacio y la Contrarreforma', pp.328-329.

93   *MI Epp.* 8, pp.460-467.

94   Dalmases, *El padre maestro Ignacio,* pp.194-198.

95   O'Malley, 'The Fourth Vow', pp.27-30; 14-21.

96   *Sp. Exx.,* 353, 363.

97   *MI Epp.* 12, 244: 'Sic sedem apostolicam et eius auctoritatem defendant, et homines ad eius veram obedientiam trahant, ut ne per incautas defensiones, tanquam papiste, minus credantur' (quoted in O'Malley, 'The Fourth Vow', p.37).

98   On Ignatius's own practice of obedience see Carlos Palmés de Genover, 'Algunos casos de la obediencia personal de san Ignacio', *Manresa* 34 (1962), pp.263-280; Raymund Schwager, *Das dramatische Kirchenverständnis bei Ignatius von Loyola,* Zurich, 1970: Hugo Rahner, 'Geist und Kirche. Ein Kapital aus der Theologie des hl. Ignatius von Loyola', *Geist und Leben* 31 (1958), pp.117-131.

99   *FN* 1, p.400: 'At this time God treated him just as a schoolmaster treats a boy, to teach him: and whether this was because of his uncouthness and unformed understanding, or because he had no one to teach him, or because of the firm will God had given him to serve him, he clearly judged and always has judged that God treated him in this way'.

100   *FN* 1, pp.424-430; 90.

101   Ibid., p.454: ' "You are not educated men", says the friar, "and you speak about virtues and vices: and this no one can speak about except in one of two ways: either through learning, or through the Holy Spirit. Not through learning, therefore through the Holy Spirit" '.

102   *FN* 1, pp.444; 450; 460-462.

103   Ibid., pp.462; 177.

104   Ibid., p.204: 'And in this matter of the name he had so many visitations . . . from him whose name they took, and so many signs of his approval and confirmation of their (proposed) name, that I heard him (Ignatius) say that he would think he was going against God and offending him if he doubted that this name was right; and when he was urged by word and in writing to change it . . . I remember he told me that if all those in the Society, and everyone else that he was not obliged under pain of sin to believe, considered that this name should be changed, he alone would never consent to it'; 'and this certainty, so unassailable, is usual in him . . . in matters that he has by a supernatural means, and therefore in such matters he gives in to no arguments'.

105   Dalmases, 'The Church in the Personal Experience of St Ignatius', pp.63-64.

106   *Sp. Exx.,* 365.

107   *MI Epp.,* 4, p.284.

108   *FN* 1, p.582 n.14: 2, p.575; Victor Codina Mir, 'San Ignacio y Paulo IV. Notas para una teología del carisma', *Manresa* 40 (1968), pp.337-362; Peter A. Quinn, 'Ignatius Loyola and Gian Petro Carafa: Catholic Reformers At Odds', *Catholic Historical Review* 67 (1981), pp.386-400.

109   *FN* 1, pp.182; 712; 581-582; 720; J. Ignacio Tellechea Idígoras, *Ignacio de Loyola solo y a pie,* second edition (Madrid, 1987), pp.370-374.

110   Tellechea Idigoras, *Ignacio de Loyola,* p.374.

111   *FN* 4, p.341: 'And since one of the things that this dragon was to persecute the most . . . were the sacred religious orders . . . divine Providence with the utmost wisdom commanded the foundation of a new order with the purpose of defending first and foremost our most holy faith, (an order) whose calling is to succour and aid the valiant soldiers of the other holy orders who day and night, and with so much strength and fruit, fight in places where they are present; and where they are not present (its calling is) to go forth itself, bearing its weapons, to encounter the common foe'. See too the discussion of the same subject by Nadal, writing in the early 1560s, in *FN* 2, pp.266-267.

112   *FN* 1, p.372.

113   Ibid., pp.376; 378.

114   Terence O'Reilly, 'The *Exercises* of Saint Ignatius Loyola and the *Exercitatorio de la vida spiritual',* *Studia monastica* 16 (1974), pp.301-323; Manuel Ruiz Jurado, '¿ Influyó en S. Ignacio el *Ejercitatorio* de Cisneros?', *Manresa* 51 (1979), pp.65-75; O. Steggink, 'De moderne devotie in het Montserrat van Ignatius van Loyola', *Ons Geestelijk Erf* 59 (1985), pp.383-392.

115   *FN* 1, pp.394 n.10; 436 n.3; 437; 404 n.22.

116   Pedro de Leturia, 'Libros de horas, *Anima Christi* y *Ejercicios espirituales* de San Ignacio', *AHSI* 17 (1948), pp.3-50; reprinted in *Estudios ignacianos,* volume 2, pp.99-148.

117   *FN* 1, pp.712; 636.

118   Ibid., p.462.

119   Ibid., pp.183, 468, 486.

120   Ibid., p.118.

121   Marcel Bataillon, 'D'Erasme à la Compagnie de Jésus. Protestation et intégration dans la Réforme Catholique au xviᵉ siècle', *Archives de Sociologie des Religions,* 24 (1967) pp.57-81 (here p.68).

122   After their ordination in Venice in 1536 they were known as 'preti pellegrini': Bataillon, loc.cit.

123   *FN* 1, p.183.

124   Ibid., pp.184-185.

125   *MI Constitutiones* 1, pp.6-7; Bataillon, pp.68-70. A detailed account of the deliberations is given in Javier Osuna, *Friends in the Lord.*

126   The *Fórmula* of 1539 is published in *MI Constitutiones* 1, pp.14-21; and in Pietro Tacchi Venturi, *Storia della Compagnia di Gesù in Italia,* 2 volumes (Rome, 1950-1951), volume 1, part 1, pp.556-567.

127   Bataillon, pp.62-63, 67.

128   For an account of the delays and of the roles played by Ghinucci and Guidiccioni, see Tacchi Venturi; the consternation of Ignatius and his companions is noted by Polanco, *FN* 1, pp.206-207.

129   Tacchi Venturi, p.563.

130   Ibid.

131   Ibid., p.564.

132   Ibid.

133   Bataillon, p.81.

134   *MHSI Epistolae Broëti,* p.622; quoted in T. Baumann, 'Compagnie de Jésus. Origine et sens primitif de ce nom', *Revue d'Ascétique et de Mystique* 37 (1961), pp.47-60 (here p.50).

I

135  Estanislao Olivares, 'Aportación de la Compañía de Jesús a la vida religiosa en su época', *Manresa* 56 (1984), pp.229-259, 345-364; Philip Endean, 'Who Do you Say Ignatius Is? Jesuit Fundamentalism and Beyond', *Studies in the Spirituality of Jesuits* 19 (1987) part 5, pp.1-53 (here pp.16-18).

136  *MHSI Epp. Nadal* 1, p.774; quoted by Bataillon, pp.80-81.

137  Bataillon, p.81; William V. Bangert, *A History of the Society of Jesus* (St Louis, 1972), pp.48-52.

138  Endean, pp.18-22 (on obedience, pp.19-21).

139  Antonio María de Aldama, 'La composición de las Constituciones de la Compañía de Jesús, *AHSI* 42 (1973), pp.201-245.

140  Bataillon, pp.70-71; Dermot Fenlon, *Heresy and Obedience in Tridentine Italy. Cardinal Pole and the Counter-Reformation,* Cambridge, 1972; Elizabeth Gleason, 'On the Nature of Sixteenth-Century Italian Evangelism: Scholarship 1953-1978', *The Sixteenth-Century Journal* 9 (1978), number 3, pp.3-25; Paolo Simoncelli, *Evangelismo italiano del Cinquecento,* Rome, 1979; Silvana Seidel Menchi, *Erasmo in Italia 1520-1580,* Turin, 1987.

141  *FN* 1, p.196.

142  O'Malley, 'The Jesuits, St Ignatius and the Counter-Reformation', pp.19-21; Joseph H. Crehan, 'Saint Ignatius and Cardinal Pole', *AHSI* 25 (1956), pp.72-98.

143  *Sp. Exx.,* 355-357, 359.

144  Bataillon, pp.72-73. The bibliography on the rules is vast; a useful collection of studies is *'Sentire cum ecclesia:* History, Pedagogy, Challenge Today', *Centrum Ignatianum Spiritualitatis* 14 (1983).

145  O'Malley, 'The Jesuits, St Ignatius, and the Counter-Reformation', p.25.

146  *FN* 1, pp.609, 612, 623 (habit); 609, 729-730 (choir); 612-613 (modes of address): discussed in Bataillon, pp.77-78.

147  Bangert, pp.97-105.

148  H. Outram Evennett, *The Spirit of the Counter-Reformation,* p.28.

# II

## SAINT IGNATIUS LOYOLA AND SPANISH ERASMIANISM

The years between the birth of St. Ignatius and his departure from Spain in 1527 saw a growth in the country of popular interest in methods of mental prayer, a growth attested by the large number of devotional works translated into Castilian, and by the development of indigenous forms of spirituality. This development passed through three important stages before 1530.

First, devotion to the Passion, which flourished at the turn of the century and which was related to anxiety about personal salvation, prevalent at the time [1]. It was expressed in a wide variety of pious practices [2], all of which involved or could involve imaginative evocation of, and meditation on, Christ's death. About 1520 a second, distinct form of spirituality appeared. It has received the generic title of illuminism, but it included at least two different teachings on prayer, « dejamiento » and « recogimiento » [3]. One point on which adherents of both appear to have agreed is condemnation of contemporary devotion to the Passion. Neither group favoured making the humanity of Christ a central part of meditation : the « dejados » tended to prefer reflection on the gifts of God, the « recogidos » contemplation of Christ's divinity [4]. Both favoured prayer which did not involve much use of the imagination or of discursive thought, and in each case the form of prayer practised involved openness to the work of grace in the soul [5].

A third development occurred in the mid-1520's when the writings of Erasmus became a matter of controversy. The centre of the debate was initially Alcalá de Henares, where in 1526 the Spanish translation of the *Enchiridion militis christiani* enjoyed immediate popularity. Marcel

---

[1] See J. DELUMEAU, *Naissance et affirmation de la Réforme* (Paris 1965) 53. — On the Passion poetry written in Spain at this time see J. RODRÍGUEZ-PUÉRTOLAS, *Fray Iñigo de Mendoza y sus Coplas de vita Christi* (Madrid 1968) ; M. BATAILLON, *Chanson pieuse et poésie de dévotion : Fray Ambrosio Montesino*, in *Bulletin hispanique*, 27 (1925) 228-238 ; K. WHINNOM, *The supposed sources of inspiration of Spanish 15th. century narrative religious verse*, in *Symposium*, 17 (1963) 268-291.

[2] See L. GOUGAUD, *Devotional and Ascetic practices in the Middle Ages* (tr. London 1927).

[3] M. BATAILLON, *Erasmo y Espana*[2] (México 1966) 166-176.

[4] BATAILLON, notes to Juan DE VALDÉS, *Diálogo de doctrina cristiana* (Coimbra 1925) 274-276. — See the edict of 1525 against the « dejados » issued by the Inquisition of Toledo, edited by V. BELTRÁN DE HEREDIA O. P. in *Revista española de teología*, 10 (1950) 105-130 ; and, for views of « recogidos », the prologue of Francisco DE OSUNA to his *Tercer Abecedario espiritual* (Madrid 1911 = Nueva biblioteca de autores españoles, 16). Cf. A. MÁRQUEZ, *Los alumbrados*, Madrid 1972 (edict, p. 273-283); and M. ANDRÉS, *Recogidos y alumbrados. Nueva visión conjunta del alumbradismo español*, en *Salmanticensis*, 21 (1974) 151-162.

[5] BATAILLON, *Diálogo*, 35 ; but see R. GARCÍA-VILLOSLADA, *Loyola y Erasmo* (Madrid 1965) 81 sqq.

302

Bataillon has argued that it was read enthusiastically by many illuminists and that the spiritual teaching of Erasmus was grafted on to the already established illuminist tradition [6].

Ignatius grew up in the years of popular devotion to the Passion, and he witnessed the reaction against it. His conversion in 1521 and his stay in Manresa occurred about the time that the *alumbrados* first flourished. In 1526 he was a student at Alcalá, where his friends included Miguel Eguía, printer of the *Enchiridion* [7]. Both there and later in Salamanca he was suspected of illuminism and his apostolic work was investigated by the authorities [8]. When he eventually left Spain for France it was partly because of restrictions which had been placed on his activities [9]. He was in fact fully involved in the life of the Church in Spain ; and in view of this it is legitimate to ask if the developments he witnessed left their mark on his own spirituality and on his attitude towards reform of the Church.

This question has been answered in a variety of ways [10]. One point on which scholars have disagreed is the extent of his knowledge of the *Enchiridion*. Study of the *Exercises* suggests that he was aware of its purport [11], and there are textual parallels between one passage in it and part of the « Principio y Fundamento » [12]. The external evidence that he read it, however, is fraught with problems. According to Ribadeneira [13] he was advised to read it for its spiritual content and to improve his Latin while a student in Barcelona : that is, between 1524 and 1526. He did so, but noticed after a while that it cooled his devotion and ardour ; and when this happened

---

[6] BATAILLON, *Erasmo*, 166-225.

[7] MI, *Fontes narrativi*, I 442 n. 14.

[8] Ibid., 442 sqq., 452-462. Documents of the enquiries in Alcalá may be seen in MI, *Scripta de sancto Ignatio*, I 598 sqq. See J. E. LONGHURST, *Saint Ignatius at Alcalá*, AHSI 26 (1957) 252-256 ; also V. BELTRÁN DE HEREDIA, *Estancia de san Ignacio de Loyola en San Estéban de Salamanca*, in *Ciencia tomista*, 83 (1956) 507-528 ; now in *Miscelánea Beltrán de Heredia*, II (Salamanca 1972) 343-362.

[9] MI, *Fontes narrativi* I, 462.

[10] BATAILLON, *Erasmo*, 212-214 ; GARCÍA-VILLOSLADA, op. cit. and his earlier article, *San Ignacio de Loyola y Erasmo de Rotterdam*, in *Estudios eclesiásticos*, 16 (1942) 235-263, 399-426 ; 17 (1943) 77-103 ; J. DE GUIBERT, *La spiritualité de la Compagnie de Jésus* (Rome 1953) 153-155 ; M. OLPHE GAILLARD, *Erasme et Ignace de Loyola*, in *Revue d'ascétique et de mystique*, 35 (1959) 337-352 ; J. GRANERO, *Loyola y Erasmo*, in *Manresa*, 38 (1966) 155-164 ; R. M. HORNEDO, *Loyola y Erasmo*, in *Razón y Fe*, 173 (1966) 403-416 ; M. ROTSAERT, *Les premiers contacts de saint Ignace avec l'érasmisme espagnol*, in *Revue de l'histoire de la spiritualité*, 49 (1973) 443-464.

[11] P. LETURIA, *Estudios ignacianos* (Rome 1957) II, 160 ; M. BATLLORI, *Sobre l'humanisme a Barcelona durant els estudis de Sant Ignasi (1524-1526)* : *Nebrija i Erasme*, in *Quaderni ibero-americani*, nos. 19-20 (1956) 219-232.

[12] H. WATRIGANT, *La « Méditation fondamentale » avant S. Ignace* (Enghien 1907 = Bibliothèque des Exercices, 9) 71 ; L. DE GRANDMAISON, *Les Exercices de Saint Ignace dans l'édition des « Monumenta »*, in *Recherches de science religieuse*, 11 (1920) 396 ; A. CODINA, *Los orígenes de los Ejercicios espirituales de San Ignacio* (Barcelona 1926), 184-187 ; VILLOSLADA, op. cit., 39 sqq. ; LETURIA, op. cit., 22 n. 76 ; BATLLORI, art. cit., 229.

[13] *Vida del Bienaventurado Padre Ignacio de Loyola*, lib. I, c. XIII : MI, *Fontes narrativi*, IV, 173.

several times he abandoned it. After this he looked on it and the other writings of Erasmus with suspicion and dislike [14]. The event, as Ribadeneira described it, is not mentioned in any earlier records of the Saint's life ; and one of them, the notes taken down during his lifetime by Fr. Luis Gonçalves da Cámara, contains a different version of it [15]. According to this, it took place in Alcalá, (i.e. at a later date 1526-1527). Ignatius was advised to take it as his manual of devotion by several people including his confessor [16], but he refused to do so having heard its author criticised by preachers and others in authority and preferring the uncontroversial *Imitation of Christ* [17].

Several explanations have been advanced to account for this apparent conflict in evidence.

Some scholars suppose that Ribadeneira had access to a source of information of which we know nothing, and accept both versions of the incident. In their view Ignatius tried to read the work in Barcelona, but when offered it again in Alcalá declined it [18].

Bataillon, on the other hand, is of the opinion that Ribadeneira based his account on Gonçalves but altered the details of time and place, and mentioned the academic reason for reading the text, in order to dampen the religious significance of the event and to highlight the saint's instinct of orthodoxy [19].

A middle, balanced position has been taken by Fr. Batllori who points out that there are no *a priori* grounds for doubting Ribadeneira (there was a nucleus of Erasmians in Barcelona at the time) but that his version is open to question nonetheless. In the first place, his dependence on Gonçalves is close enough to doubt that he had another source [20]. And secondly, Barcelona was never a lively Erasmian centre like Alcalá and there is no mention of the *Enchiridion* in any surviving library, bookshop or printer's records of the first half of the century [21].

It is a matter which, for want of information, cannot be fully resolved ; one of those moments in Ignatius' life which must be interpreted by hypothesis and where, as Fr. Batllori puts it, « history easily becomes dialectic » [22]. This, however, is why it is interesting : although of minor importance in itself, it raises issues which affect the whole interpretation of Ignatius' life. Bataillon, for example, believes that in the

---

[14] Ibid., 174 : « a la fin echó el libro de sí, y cobró con él y con las demás obras deste autor tan grande ojeriza y aborrecimiento, que después jamás quiso leerlas él, ni consintió que en nuestra Compañía se leyessen sino con mucho delecto y mucha cautela».

[15] *Fontes narrativi*, I, 585, 669.

[16] This seems the likely interpretation of the phrase ' lhe aconselhavão ... que lesse pollo « Enchiridion»' : see BATAILLON, review of *Font. narr.* I in *Bulletin Hispanique*, 49 (1947) 100 n. 2 ; *Erasmo*, 213 n. 15. — On his confessor, Miona, see *Font. narr.* I, 585 n. 49 ; BATAILLON, intro. to *El Enquiridion o Manual del caballero cristiano* ed. D. Alonso (Madrid, 1932) 75 n. 3, 76 n. 2 ; VILLOSLADA, op. cit., 100-103.

[17] See *Memoriale* of Câmara n. 97 : *Font. narr.*, I, 584. See below, n. 102.

[18] LETURIA, op. cit., I, 331 n. 33 ; II, 160 ; VILLOSLADA, op. cit., 23-31 ; C. DE DALMASES, in *Fontes narrativi*, II, 417 n. 15 ; IV, 172-173 n. 12.

[19] BATAILLON, *Erasmo*, 213 n. 15.

[20] BATLLORI, art. cit., loc. cit.

[21] Ibid., 230.

[22] Ibid., 228 : « Són els punts on fàcilment la història devé dialèctica».

1520's Ignatius was part of, and by no means opposed to, the movement of renewal in Spain of which Erasmus was the figurehead and the *Enchiridion* the « libro de moda » [23]. For this reason his evangelical, lay apostolate was investigated [24]. Only subsequently, perhaps in the late 1530's [25], did he begin to distinguish his position from that of the Erasmians, and then under pressure, as the Society became suspect for its break with monastic tradition [26] and as the Church in general moved to the right [27]. Ribadeneira, writing towards the end of the century, attributed to the Ignatius of Barcelona an attitude to evangelical humanism which he came to hold only later [28]. This interpretation was challenged by Fr. García-Villoslada [29]. He argued that Ignatius was quite consistent in his attitude to Erasmus [30] : « El Iñigo de Alcalá es, en los rasgos esenciales de su espiritualidad, el Ignacio de Roma. En él se encuentra en germen la Contrarreforma, la pura y primitiva Contrarreforma » [31].

The weak point in Bataillon's case, and one of which Fr. Villoslada did not take full advantage, is undoubtedly his view of the *Spiritual Exercises*. For he considers that they prolonged and repopularised devotion to the Passion [32], a devotion which radicals of all shades of opinion — « dejados », « recogidos » and Erasmians — were united in deploring [33]. In this respect they differed from the kind of exercise favoured by Erasmus and his Spanish followers [34]. Now it seems certain that Ignatius had completed the substance of the *Exercises* before he began his studies in Spain [35]. If even in the 1520's he differed from Erasmians about a matter of central importance in his own life of prayer and in his teaching, can it really be said that he came only later to distinguish his position from theirs ?

\* \* \*

In the pages that follow I wish to re-examine the problem by comparing the *Exercises* with the *Enchiridion*. Their similarities and differences do, I think, clarify the nature of the Spanish renewal movement and of Ignatius' part in it, by explaining how he could have reacted adversely to the *Enchiridion* without being unsympathetic to many of the ideals it voiced.

---

[23] BATAILLON, *Enquiridion*, 72-79 ; *Erasmo*, 212-214 ; *Les commencements de la Compagnie de Jésus en Espagne*, in *Annuaire du Collège de France* (1946) 164-168.

[24] Ibid.

[25] BATAILLON, *Les commencements...*, 165-166.

[26] Ibid. ; *Erasmo*, 213-214. This view disputed by VILLOSLADA, op. cit., 74.

[27] See most recent study : *D'Erasme à la Compagnie de Jésus. Protestation et intégration dans la Réforme catholique au XVI^e siècle*, in *Archives de sociologie des religions*, 12 (1967) 57-81, and *Erasmo*, 726, 752.

[28] Ibid., 213 n. 15 ; review of *Font. narr.* I, in *Bulletin Hispanique*, 49 (1947) 97-101.

[29] See above, nn. 5 and 10.

[30] Art. cit., 259-260 ; op. cit., 77-79, 271-273.

[31] Op. cit., 78 ; an opinion accepted by LETURIA, op. cit., II, 183.

[32] BATAILLON, *Erasmo*, 589.

[33] BATAILLON, *Diálogo*, 274-276.

[34] BATAILLON, *Erasmo*, loc. cit., where he writes of Erasmian meditation : « Se opone de modo muy especial a la meditación imaginativa de la Pasión... a la cual los *Ejercicios* de San Ignacio están dando en ese momento un vigor absolutamente nuevo ».

[35] J. CALVERAS - C. DE DALMASES, *Sancti Ignatii de Loyola Exercitia spiritualia*[2] (Rome 1969 = MHSI, 100) 27-33.

There is one similarity between the two works which spring to mind immediately and it concerns, surprisingly, the reform of popular piety. The rules on orthodoxy at the end of the *Exercises* might seem to indicate the contrary, for they are clearly directed, at least in part, against Erasmian criticism of attachment to externals [36]. But, as Fr. Leturia pointed out, they are intended for the retreatant and cannot be separated from the rest of the work which in general reveals a concern to interiorise and christianise the devotional life [37]. This concern with interiority, with the spirit rather than the letter, was common to all reforming movements of the time and is not exclusively Erasmian, but it found particularly forceful and popular expression in the *Enchiridion* [38]. It has been suggested that Ignatius would not have approved of the satirical spirit in which Erasmus criticised popular piety [39]; but although this may be so, it is unlikely to have been his main reason for disliking the work since Erasmus makes it quite evident that he approves of popular devotions if they are practised for truly devout motives [40]. Apart from this, the actual methods of interior renewal recommended by both men are, in some respects, similar.

In the *Enchiridion* Erasmus writes that the attainment of perfection involves a two-fold process. One must detach one's affections from the world of sense and at the same time raise one's mind to the things of Heaven [41]. He drew this notion from Plato and introduces it to the reader as Socrates' teaching on how best to prepare for death. True to his conception of the *philosophia Christi* he equates it with St. Paul's exhortation to die with Christ in order to live with God [42]. This is the solution he recommends to the crisis in popular religion. He identifies excessive concern for externals with Paul's definition of the flesh that kills the spirit and which must be crucified by self-denial [43]. The ideal is to be moved by selfless love of Christ, for He is the only true end of piety [44].

---

[36] LETURIA, op. cit., I, 160 ; VILLOSLADA, art. cit., 424-426, 85-87 ; op. cit., 174-182.

[37] LETURIA, op. cit., 162 ; BATLLORI, art. cit., 227.

[38] BATAILLON, *Erasmo*, 190-205.

[39] LETURIA, op. cit., loc. cit.

[40] *Enquiridion*, 258 : « Assí que yo apruebo lo que hazes, con tanto que el fin y la intención ... no sea viciosa ; y demás desto con tanto que no hagas hincapié ni te detengas en el escalón que está puesto para subir más arriba a cosas más apropriadas a tu salud». All quotations from this work are from the Spanish translation of 1526 by Alonso Fernández de Madrid, Arcediano del Alcor ; variations from the original are in italics (see above, n. 16). Fr. Leturia's suggestion that it was this translation, printed by Eguía, that Ignatius was recommended in Alcalá (op. cit., 331 n. 33) is quite plausible. It should be noted, however, that Gonçalves gives no details of the version in question (see BATLLORI, art. cit.).

[41] *Enquiridion*, 231.

[42] Ibid., 236 : « Y esta manera de enajenamiento con que desasimos nuestra afición destas cosas baxas, para arraygarla mejor con Dios, es aquella cruz a que Christo nos combida y con que él mesmo nos requiere...».

[43] Ibid., 267.

[44] Ibid., 217 : « De manera que a sólo Christo como a único y summo bien endereces tu intención ; y assí ninguna cosa ames, ninguna tengas en mucho y ninguna tampoco dessees, sino a Jesu Christo, o por amor de Jesu Christo».

Ignatius, likewise, confronts his retreatant with the highest motives for serving God, in the « Principio y Fundamento» and before each exercise [45]. And one effect of the retreat is to alter radically one's motives for leading a Christian life. This interior renewal is achieved by dying to self-love with Christ on the Cross. In the contemplations on the Passion in the third « week» the retreatant, aware that Christ died because of his sins and to redeem him, and consequently moved by gratitude and shame, prays to share His suffering [46]. In the fourth « week» his joy on contemplating the Resurrection is disinterested [47].

In the case of particular devotions, such as imaginative meditation on the Passion, it is true that, at first sight, the two men appear to have disagreed. There are, however, reasons for supposing that they did not differ in this matter as radically as Bataillon has suggested. Objections to devotion to the Passion that one encounters in the writings of illuminists and Erasmians fall, broadly speaking, into five categories. Underlying them all is the conviction that those who practised it paid more attention to externals than to its inner spiritual meaning. It is one of those practices of the flesh that kill the spirit.

First, they objected to an inordinate importance given to the humanity of Christ, and wanted more attention to be fixed on the article of faith that He was God as well as man. In the *Enchiridion* Erasmus deplores that pity aroused by the Passion is of the kind one might feel for any good man in pain, and that it does not involve recognising it as the means by which God and man were reconciled [48]. He states his case forcefully by pointing out that if the superficial attention to Christ as man suffices to make one religious, what is one to say of the Jews who saw, heard and touched Him, or of Judas who actually kissed Him ? The apostles failed to grasp His purposes while He was with them : He had to ascend to Heaven for them to know Him truly [49]. This notion, that the Ascension was necessary for the disciples to believe in Christ's divinity, was invoked by Osuna, a « recogido» who does not seem to have been an Erasmian, to make the same point : one should not concentrate on the humanity of Jesus in prayer [50]. It is alluded to in the *Diálogo de doctrina cristiana* of Juan de Valdés [51], which includes a translation of the Erasmian colloquy *Inquisitio de fide* about the Creed. In the passage on the Ascension, Valdés omits some severe criticism of devotion to relics and inserts in its place a few lines of his own in which attachment to the externals of piety is equated with the state of the apostles before Christ left them [52].

---

[45] *Ejercicios espirituales*, 23, 46. All references are to the numbered subsections in the edition by I. IPARRAGUIRRE, in *Obras completas de San Ignacio de Loyola²*, Madrid 1963.

[46] Ibid., 203.

[47] Ibid., 221 : « ... pedir gracia para me alegrar y gozar intensamente de tanta gloria y gozo de Christo nuestro Señor».

[48] *Enquiridion*, 254, 369.

[49] Ibid., 255-256.

[50] *Tercer Abecedario*, prologue.

[51] See above, n. 4.

[52] *Diálogo*, fol. 13v.

Their second objection, related to the first, was that the devotion did not inspire compunction. It was made with force by the Arcediano del Alcor in some phrases that he inserted into his translation of the *Enchiridion*. Erasmus writes that many venerate the Passion of Our Lord, «no para más de averle lástima como a un buen ombre que padeció todo aquello sin culpa ninguna *por la embidia y maldad de aquellos malvados ingratos que fueron en la traición y le crucificaron*» [53]. By his interpolation the translator makes explicit one consequence of not regarding Christ as divine that Erasmus only implies : lack of faith that by His death He saved one from one's sins. The insertion is intentionally ironical : «aquellos malvados ingratos» are really the devotees and not just those historically responsible for crucifying Him. Out of hypocrisy or lack of faith they do not acknowledge that all men caused the Passion, just as they all profited by it. The Arcediano reiterates the point in a subsequent passage : «¿ Es muy gran cosa por ventura que un pecador como tú perdone a otro aviendo Christo *inocentíssimo* rogado al Padre por los mesmos *pecadores* que le crucificaron ?» [54]. By interpolating *pecadores* he explicitly associates the reader with those who crucified Christ. What they have in common is sinfulness, and the hope of pardon.

Their third objection was that the devotion did not result in resolutions to avoid vice and practise virtue, and so had no influence on morals. This objection was voiced by Osuna in the *Tercer Abecedario* [55]. Erasmus connected it with the absence of self-denial which he identified as the cause of all aberrations in devotion [56]. He argues in the *Enchiridion* that those devoted to the Passion do not climb high enough into the Tree of Life, the Cross, to pick its true fruit, which is conformity with Christ by mortification of one's sinful inclinations [57]. The alternative form of the devotion which he proposes involves calling to mind the Passion whenever one is tempted to sin, and practising the contrary virtue exemplified by Jesus. His counsel is firmly underwritten by the Arcediano who, to the statement that self-denial can express gratitude, adds the lines : «las quales gracias tanto más aceptas serán assí por la obra, que no de boca, quanto va dezir a hazer o a padecer» [58].

Their fourth objection was that the devotion did not inspire hope, thanksgiving and joy, but was wearisome and sad. This criticism was expressed by the early illuminists [59], particularly by Osuna, who compared the devotion unfavourably with the more joyful « recogimiento » [60]. Erasmus makes clear that the kinds of mortification involved by the devotions of which he approves should not be harsh and unpleasant, if inspired by the Spirit and by love [61]. Similarly, in the *Diálogo*, Valdés explains

---

[53] *Enquiridion*, 369.
[54] Ibid., 405.
[55] *Tercer Abecedario*, 525.
[56] *Enquiridion*, 255: « Si crees que es muy gran cosa tener en tu casa un pedacito de la cruz, cree que es mucho mayor tener dentro de tu coraçón escondido todo el misterio de la cruz».
[57] Ibid., 369.
[58] Ibid., 372.
[59] See Edict of 1525 (above, n. 4), proposition 22 : « tenía por defecto pensar en la passión y consolarse en ella, y … le pesava porque una dueña llorava cierto passo de la passión … y el juebes de la Cena avía tenido mucho regocixo y placer, como si fuesse día de Pascua».
[60] *Tercer Abecedario*, 478.
[61] *Enquiridion*, 369 ; see also VILLOSLADA, art. cit., 405, who mentions a phrase in the *Paraphrases in Novum Testamentum* condemned by the Sorbonne : « Mortem Christi non deplorari, sed adorari» ; op. cit., 95 n. 29.

that God asks men to love Him with all their hearts because if they do so they will obey the Law happily and learn the truth of Christ's assurance, « My yoke is easy and my burden light » [62]. The method of mental prayer that he favours has for subject the Law, understood in the light of the New Testament. Unlike imaginative meditation on the Passion which, he says, leaves the soul « muy fria y seca », it results in an appreciation of the good news of God's love for man [63]. In another passage he expands a reference to Christ's death in the *Inquisitio de fide* to stress that He was no passive victim but willingly chose to suffer out of love [64].

A fifth objection to the devotion appears to have concerned excessive rigidity of method. In the *Alfabeto cristiano* Valdés advises his friend, Giulia Gonzaga, to set aside each day four short periods for meditation. She is inclined to be over-scrupulous, and so he warns her not to feel restricted to fixed hours or particular places [65]. He deplores fixed rules about prayer partly because they inhibit one's freedom to respond to special graces ; he tells Giulia never to undertake to recite a specified number of vocal prayers, so that she may remain able to pass on to mental prayer if she wishes [66]. In his earlier work, the *Diálogo*, he does not explain precisely why he disapproves of imaginative meditations, but it may well be because they involved an elaborate reconstruction of the Passion down to tiny details, as Bataillon suggests, which would, of course, have impeded mental prayer [67].

These five objections constitute an indictment of devotion to the Passion as it was practised when Ignatius began to compose his *Exercises*. Among the works with which he was familiar at the time is the book to which Bataillon attributes in part the devotion's popularity, the *Vita Christi* of Ludolph the Carthusian [68]. In the *Exercitatorio* too, which he probably read [69], there are lengthy meditations on Christ's life, most of them on the Passion [70]. The devotion is recommended also in the *Imitation of Christ* [71]. In the *Exercises* themselves the retreatant contemplates the Passion events during the third « week», and in the other « weeks » is often reminded of them. The first meditation of the first « week» ends with a colloquy to the crucified Christ [72]. In the second « week» he considers at one moment all the suffering Christ bore for him, including Cal-

---

[62] *Diálogo*, fol. 38v.

[63] Ibid., fol. 95r : « Tened pues por cierto que ésta tal es la verdadera contemplación : porque de aquí toma el ánima conocimiento dela suma bondad, grandeza, y misericordia de Dios».

[64] Ibid., fol. 11v.

[65] *Alfabeto cristiano*, ed. Luis DE Usoz (London 1861) 110.

[66] Ibid., 145 : « ... que enviándoos Dios en la oración alguna buena inspirazión, os podáis detener en ella tanto, cuanto sintiéreis que vuestra alma le gusta».

[67] BATAILLON, *Diálogo*, 274 n. 64.

[68] *Fontes narrativi*, I, 74 n. 6.

[69] LETURIA, op. cit., II, 10-11 ; CALVERAS and DALMASES, op. cit., 47-52 ; IPARRAGUIRRE, op. cit., introduction to *Exercises*, 177.

[70] See the edition by C. BARAUT O. S. B. in *Garcia Jiménez de Cisneros : Obras completas* (Montserrat 1965) II, 334-408.

[71] *Imitation of Christ*, tr. R. Knox and M. Oakley (London 1960) 61, 93.

[72] *Ejercicios*, 53.

vary [73]. And one of the vocal prayers he says repeatedly is the *Anima Christi* [74]. Ignatius may indeed be said to have prolonged meditation on the Passion.

However, a brief look at the *Exercises* in the light of the Erasmians' criticisms indicates that in the process he transformed it.

In the first place he constantly reminds his retreatant of the divinity of Christ.

In the first colloquy, to Christ on the Cross, he draws attention to the Incarnation, reminding him that the dying Saviour is God become man [75]. In the second « week » the opening contemplation on the Incarnation involves alternating one's attention between Paradise, where the Trinity decides that the Word will take flesh, and this world, where the human race is in urgent need of redemption and where the Virgin conceives in Nazareth [76]. The concluding prayer may be directed to « [el] Verbo eterno encarnado » [77]. At certain points Ignatius emphasises Christ's divinity. One occurs in the « week » concerned with the Passion. The retreatant is asked to bear in mind the Godhead of Jesus in scenes where it appears to be hidden : « considerar cómo la divinidad se esconde, es a saber, cómo podría destruir a sus enemigos, y no lo hace, y cómo dexa padescer la sacratíssima humanidad tan crudelíssimamente » [78]. In the fourth « week » prominence is given to the divinity of Christ revealed at the Resurrection [79].

Secondly, compunction is an important theme throughout the *Exercises*.

In the first « week » the retreatant prays that he may experience it [80]. In the second he calls to mind before each contemplation that it was because he required forgiveness that God became man and died [81]. In the third he realises the dreadful suffering that his sins incurred for Christ and aspires to feel « dolor, sentimiento y confussión » [82]. As for the practical consequences of a love of Christ, the third concern of the reformers, it needs hardly to be said that they inform the whole of the retreat. The prayer before Christ crucified in the first « week » involves considering what one has done, is doing and ought to do in response to His love [83]. During the second « week » the retreatant's attention is drawn repeatedly to what is entailed by a Christian calling [84]. He prays

---

[73] Ibid., 116.
[74] In this connection see LETURIA, *Libros de horas, Anima Christi y Ejercicios espirituales de S. Ignacio*, AHSI 17 (1948) 3-50.
[75] *Ejercicios*, 53 : « Imaginando a Christo nuestro Señor delante y puesto en cruz, hacer un coloquio, cómo de criador es venido a hacerse hombre, y de vida eterna a muerte temporal, y así a morir por mis pecados ».
[76] Ibid., 101-109.
[77] Ibid., 109.
[78] Ibid., 196.
[79] Ibid., 223.
[80] Ibid., 48, 55.
[81] Ibid., 104, 113, 121, 159.
[82] Ibid., 193.
[83] Ibid., 53.
[84] Particularly, of course, in the exercises « del Rey », « de dos banderas » and « de tres binarios ».

throughout for grace to imitate Our Lord [85]. He learns that to follow Him involves suffering [86], that it means spiritual, perhaps actual, poverty [87] and the acceptance of insults and ignominy [88]. He prays that he may be allowed to serve Him on these terms [89], and considers how a natural disinclination to practise self-denial can lead to self-deception and a refusal to do so [90]. The particular and personal implications of commitment to Him are the subjects of the Election [91]. And in the third « week» he chooses to die with Christ [92].

Moreover, the Ignatian retreat is not meant to be a dour, hopeless experience. On the contrary, recognition that God became man and died for one personally will inspire gratitude and hope as well as shame. Ignatius expects the retreatant to experience moments of joy [93], especially in the fourth « week» when he prays for a share in Christ's exultation [94].

Lastly Ignatius certainly avoids the rigidity of method deplored by Valdés. He does prescribe set times for the exercises, but the retreatant is allowed a degree of freedom to adapt them to his own needs. It is he who decides the penances he wishes to observe [95]. He is encouraged to experiment with various postures to find the one most suitable for prayer [96]. In particular Ignatius leaves him free to respond to any special graces he may receive while praying. He is expected to pause in any exercise when the grace for which he is seeking is granted to him, and to abandon the rest of the exercise until he is satisfied [97].

Ignatius, in other words, may be said to have prolonged medieval devotion to the life and death of Christ by making it central to his *Exercises* ; but in doing so he reformed it of the defects it had acquired in his day which the illuminists and Erasmians criticised. In view of this it is surely misleading to suppose that he was opposed to Erasmus in his attitude to the devotion [98]. The evidence suggests that he would have agreed with him in condemning its distortion by hypocrisy and superstition.

Such similarities of view between Erasmus and Ignatius make it seem surprising that Ignatius should have been unsympathetic to Erasmianism in the 1520's. To explain them, however, it is not necessary to postulate a direct influence of the humanist on the

[85] Ibid., 104.
[86] Ibid., 95-98, 146, 166, 167.
[87] Ibid., 146.
[88] Ibid.
[89] Ibid., 147, 156, 157, 159.
[90] Ibid., 150-155.
[91] Ibid., 163, 169-189.
[92] Ibid., 203.
[93] Ibid., 6.
[94] Ibid., 221, 229.
[95] Ibid., 217.
[96] Ibid., 76.
[97] Ibid.
[98] See VILLOSLADA, op. cit., 95.

saint. To some extent they were influenced by the same authors. Erasmus, for instance, was indebted to *devotio moderna* teaching on prayer. He was educated in schools of the movement, and although he reacted against its educational methods, its tradition of piety was the most important single influence on his spirituality, excepting St. Paul. Ignatius in turn was very found of the *Imitation of Christ* and appears to have been influenced by the *Exercitatorio* of Cisneros which drew heavily on other *devotio moderna* works by Zutphen and Mombaer[99]. Furthermore, while Erasmus was writing the *Enchiridion* he was engaged on a commentary of the Pauline Epistles[100] and their teaching pervades his work. Ignatius in the early 1520's may not have been intimately familiar with the text of Paul[101], but the doctrine of the Epistles, particularly the theme of death with Christ to self, would have been mediated to him by à Kempis, Ludolph and Cisneros.

Acknowledgment that the two men had sources in common, however, complicates the problem. It makes it more difficult to understand why Ignatius found the *Enchiridion* uncongenial. To explain this apparent contradiction in the evidence it helps to bear in mind that in neither of the two accounts of his encounter with the work is there the suggestion that his objection to it was primarily doctrinal. The evidence of Gonçalves informs us that Ignatius refused to take it as his regular spiritual reading in place of the *Imitation*[102]. Ribadeneira relates that Ignatius abandoned it because it cooled his devotion[103]. His objection, in fact, was, in the first place, devotional. Why this should have been so may, I think, be adequately explained by the dissimilarities between the *Exercises* and the *Enchiridion*.

A number of themes central to the spirituality of Ignatius do not find expression in the *Enchiridion*.

First the ideal of disinterested love and service of Christ.

Erasmus insists that all Christians are meant to strive after perfection, and he does present selfless love of Our Lord as the best motive

---

[99] C. BARAUT, op. cit., I, 84 sqq. ; WATRIGANT, *La genèse des « Exercices» de saint Ignace de Loyola*, Amiens 1897 (sep. de *Etudes* vol. 71-73) ; and above n. 69.

[100] *Enquiridion*, 414.

[101] Not, that is, up to the time at Manresa ; in Alcalá the doctrine of the Epistles informed his teaching (see VILLOSLADA, art. cit., 411).

[102] *Fontes narrativi*, I, 584-585 : Ignatius, recalling the event in 1555, noted that criticism of Erasmus by preachers and people in authority had dissuaded him from taking the *Enchiridion* as spiritual reading. Gonçalves, however, introduces the anecdote to illustrate his fidelity to « el Gerçonzito ». It is possible that Ignatius came only gradually to see the significance of his initial dislike of the work as reserves about the wholesomeness of Erasmus' teaching became widespread in the Church. Of the incident at Barcelona, Villoslada writes (art. cit., 238) : « Se me antoja que San Ignacio, entonces, no dio al hecho del enfriamiento de su fervor tanta importancia como aquí parece atribuírle Ribadeneyra. Quizás no se acordó de esta experiencia psicológica hasta años adelante, cuando el nombre de Erasmo andaba de boca y sus libros empezaban a ser mirados como peligrosos y vitandos por las autoridades eclesiásticas » ; and op. cit., 51.

[103] *Vida*, loc. cit. above, n. 13.

for all devotions [104]. But when writing about the spiritual life in more general terms he never mentions such love explicitly, and he always makes provision for self-interest [105]. In the discussion at the end of the work of means of avoiding vice, he several times proposes that one consider death, Hell and Judgment, the results of sin, as well as the gifts of God [106]. Both themes, for instance, figure in the section on pride [107].

In this respect the spirituality of Ignatius differs. He does praise servile fear as a starting point in the life of the Christian [108] and at no point, of course, does his retreatant forget that he is a sinner. But meditation on sin and the castigation it deserves occupies the first « week » only. In the remaining « weeks » the retreatant's attention is focused on Christ ; gratitude is part of his response [109] but his love is encouraged to become increasingly compassionate and selfless [110]. The ideal of being ruled in one's interior and exterior life by a concern for God's glory informs the preparatory prayer before each exercise, the « Principio y Fundamento » which it echoes, and, of course, the second « week », including the Election [111].

Second, the two works differ in their conception of indifference and poverty.

These themes are of great importance in the *Exercises*. In the « Principio y Fundamento » the saint explains that man is meant to use Creation insofar as it helps him to praise, reverence and serve God, and thus save his soul, and to be detached from it insofar as it does not do so. It follows that, as a beginning, one must achieve indifference to one's possessions in the broadest sense [112]. Such indifference prepares for a subsequent moment of firm choice in accordance with the Divine will [113]. In the course of the four « weeks » the retreatant learns that to follow Christ involves choosing to be poor [114] and he prays that he may do so [115]. The call to poverty is, for Ignatius, intimately connected with the imitation of Our Lord [116].

This view of the matter, central to the *Exercises*, is not encountered in the *Enchiridion*. Erasmus does encourage indifference in the classical

---

[104] *Enquiridion*, 217.

[105] e.g. Ibid., 356 : « Si no quieres huyr de los vicios por amor de Jesu Christo..., hazlo a lo menos por tu proprio provecho. Y aunque sea en gran manera peligroso parar mucho tiempo en este estado ..., pero ya mucho mejor es los que no pueden assí levantarse a las virtudes *más ecelentes que llaman* heroycas, detenerse siquiera en estas virtudes polýticas y morales, ... que no dexarse caer de uno en otro en mil maneras de pecados ».

[106] Ibid., 375-409.

[107] Ibid., 399-401.

[108] *Ejercicios*, 370.

[109] During the second « week » he prays for grace to know, love and follow Our Lord « que por mí se ha hecho hombre ». Ibid., 104 ; see also 116.

[110] IPARRAGUIRRE, op. cit., 169-170.

[111] *Ejercicios*, 46, 23.

[112] Ibid., 23 : « Por lo qual es menester hacernos indiferentes a todas las cosas criadas, en todo lo que es concedido a la libertad de nuestro libre albedrío y no le está prohibido ».

[113] Ibid. : « solamente deseando y eligiendo lo que más nos conduce para el fin que somos criados ».

[114] Ibid., 146.

[115] Ibid., 147.

[116] See letter of Polanco, *ex comm.* to the « socii » of Padua in IPARRAGUIRRE, op. cit., 700-704 ; Italian original in MI, *Epistolae*, I, 572-577 (7 Aug. 1547).

sense of detachment from one's passions [117]. But he makes no mention in the context of the specifically Christian ideal of actually choosing to be deprived of good things in order to resemble Christ [118].

A third difference between the two works concerns the experience of direct divine guidance.

Karl Rahner has argued that it is for such an experience that the *Exercises* are intended to prepare one [119]. He has stressed the significance of the 15th. Annotation [120], and he has indicated how the rules for discerning spirits are related to the work of God in the soul of the retreatant [121].

This mystical dimension to the *Exercises* has no counterpart in the *Enchiridion*. Erasmus writes as a moralist rather than as a contemplative. The devotion to the Passion that he recommends, for instance, is meant to inspire virtuous behaviour, not mental prayer [122]. The same is true of the other exercises he advises to counter temptation : recollection of God's love and of the horrors of sin [123].

A fourth difference between the works is related to the third. Erasmus' moral teaching was influenced by the neo-Platonism of the Florentine Academy, particularly by Ficino and Pico. He drew from them an optimistic view of the freedom of the will, and of the potential goodness of man's nature.

It was this optimism which led the evangelical humanists to prefer the writings of Origen to those of Augustine, and it helps explain their differences with Luther [124]. Ignatius was almost certainly unacquainted with Renaissance neo-Platonism when he first encountered the *Enchiridion*. The same was no doubt true of a majority of the Spanish laity, including some who enjoyed the work [125]. Throughout his translation the Arcediano interpolates passages which modify statements of Erasmus that express an optimistic view of man' moral capacities, and emphasises his dependence on divine help [126]. Despite them, however, his version preserves the confidence in the freedom of the will and the power of reason characteristic of Erasmus.

It is unlikely that Ignatius would have found such confidence, absent from his beloved *Imitation of Christ*, very sympathetic. In this respect he was, like Luther, closer than Erasmus to late medieval tradition and popular religious feeling of the day.

The two works differ finally in the relative importance they attach to exercises that encourage love and fear, noted earlier.

---

[117] *Enquiridion*, 311.
[118] See below, 102-103.
[119] *The Dynamic Element in the Church* (London 1964) 84 sqq.
[120] Ibid., 90.
[121] Ibid., 95, 115 sqq.
[122] *Enquiridion*, 368-372.
[123] Ibid., 372 sqq.
[124] See prologue by A. H. T. LEVI to *Praise of Folly* (London 1971) 21 sqq.
[125] Such as the unlettered María Cazalla : BATAILLON, *Erasmo*, 209-211.
[126] See below, 101.

314

Erasmus' tendency to alternate consideration of God's gifts, including Redemption, with recollection of the suffering consequent on sin, is partly the result of his adoption of a neo-Platonic principle of spirituality : that love of God and love of self vary in indirect proportion to one another [127]. The same principle influences the writings of Valdés. In the *Alfabeto* he advises Giulia to set aside time each day to consider eight different subjects. The eight subjects are of two kinds. Four involve renunciation of self and of the world, the others are meant to increase her love of God [128].

Ignatius, however, does not prescribe two parallel sets of exercises. The structure of his work is simple and linear. Sin and redemption concern his retreatant throughout ; but having considered the former, he turns his attention more particularly to the latter and does not alternate between the two.

It will have become clear that when the teaching of the *Enchiridion* differs significantly from the *Exercises* it is usually in matters in which the influence of classical or Renaissance thought on Erasmus is very marked. Such influence explains why he accepts the viability of self-interest in the spiritual life, whereas Ignatius is more concerned with placing the most selfless ideals before one ; why he praises stoic indifference without transcending it as Ignatius does ; why he is more concerned with the practice of virtue than with divine guidance and more optimistic than Ignatius about man's moral capacities. Unlike the leading Erasmians in Spain — the Arcediano, Juan and Alfonso de Valdés, Virués, Vergara, Fonseca, Maldonado — Ignatius in the 1520's had no proper classical training. He would not have been as moved as they were by the prospect of reconciling pagan and Christian moral thought, the ideal of the *philosophia Christi*. This factor helps to explain why his devotion was not kindled by reading the *Enchiridion*.

A second, related factor was suggested many years ago by J. Huizinga : « In that robust sixteenth century it seems as if the oaken strength of Luther was necessary, the steely edge of Calvin, the white heat of Loyola ; not the velvet softness of Erasmus [...] ; his piety is too even for them, too limp » [129]. The analysis of differences between the *Enchiridion* and the *Exercises* confirms Huizinga's view. Ignatius makes heavy demands on the retreatant. He expects openness to the work of grace, total commitment to Christ and to the consequent self-denial and disinterested service of Him. Erasmus, by contrast, is restrained. He wants piety to become Christo-centric, but takes for granted that his reader's self-interest may be appealed to ; he is more concerned with inspiring compunction than openness to grace ; and he advises detachment from belongings and pleasures on rational as well as devotional

---

[127] *Enquiridion*, 354.
[128] *Alfabeto*, 101.
[129] *Erasmus of Rotterdam* (London 1952) 189 ; see VILLOSLADA, op. cit., 51-52.

grounds. Ignatius informs us that the *Exercises* were born of his own experience [130]. If so it is not surprising if he found the humanist spirit of the *Enchiridion* too moderate and undemanding to inspire him.

A third factor must have been, of course, that Ignatius wished to prolong the imaginative meditation on the Passion of which Erasmus and his followers disapproved. In this respect he was ahead of his time. If he had begun to compose the *Exercises* in the 1530's he would have found Erasmus' views on the subject more in accord with his own. By then the humanist had changed his attitude to the devotion and accepted it in a new form. Bataillon notes that he refers to it favourably in the *De praeparatione ad mortem*, but, I believe, underestimates the significance of Erasmus' words [131].

In the 1530's the controversial issue in religious writing both within and outside Spain was no longer the opposition between spirit and ceremony but justification by faith [132]. In the *De praeparatione* Erasmus states more than once that men are saved not by virtue of their own justice but by faith in the merits of Christ crucified [133]. And he praises contemplation of Christ on the Cross : it removes despairing fear [134]. He even goes so far as to recommend the daily practice of such contemplation. Bataillon implies in one passage that he counsels it only for children [135]; in fact, he urges adults to practise it each day until it becomes second nature, for it is invaluable in the hour of death [136]. If he praises extending the devotion to children it is because it will accustom them to practising it in later life [137]. The closing pages of the book are a moving meditation on the Passion, from Gethsemane to the last words of Jesus on the Cross.

An identical change of attitude may be observed in the writings of Valdés. In the *Diálogo* there are few references to the Passion, and implied criticism of devotion to it. In the *Alfabeto* on the other hand, he advises Giulia Gonzaga on several occasions to turn her attention to Christ crucified in order to overcome sinful inclinations [138]. He also states that contemplation of Christ crucified is the means of replacing fear by selfless love [139]. In one passage he goes further and asserts that such contemplation is the only means of knowing and loving God [140].

[130] *Fontes narrativi*, I, 504.
[131] BATAILLON, op. cit., 558, 590.
[132] E. ASENSIO, *Los estudios sobre Erasmo de Marcel Bataillon*, in *Revista de Occidente* (June 1968) 307 sqq.
[133] *Preparación y aparejo para bien morir* (Antwerp 1555) fol. 11v.
[134] Ibid., fol. 34r.
[135] BATAILLON, op. cit., 590.
[136] *Preparación*, fol. 23v.
[137] Ibid., 24v.
[138] *Alfabeto*, 120, 126.
[139] Ibid., 59.
[140] Ibid., 92.

Ignatius' *Exercises* make no explicit reference to justification [141]. But one of their results is to strengthen faith that God became man and suffered to save sinners fron Hell. Contemplation of Christ crucified is, in them, one of the means by which servile fear which could lead to despair is converted into joy, and by which one turns from love of self and grows in love of God. If Ignatius did not find his attitude to devotion to the Passion reflected in the *Enchiridion*, it was not because he disagreed with Erasmus' reserves about the practice, but because he was already in the process of renewing it, a stage Erasmus did not reach until the 1530's.

\* \* \*

If the argument I have advanced is correct, a number of conclusions follow about Ignatius' attitude to the thought of Erasmus, the distinction between Ignatian and Erasmian exercises, and the place of the saint in the Spanish movement of renewal.

First the inference that because he was not attracted to the *Enchiridion* Ignatius was an anti-Erasmian in the 1520's is evidently too simplistic.

If he had persevered with the book he would have found notions of which to approve, in particular the desire to preserve traditional devotions which in themselves were unexceptionable but to reform the motives for practising them, by encouraging death to self with Christ as understood by St. Paul. Had he persevered he would have found Erasmus' attitude to imaginative meditation on the Passion compatible with his own. He incorporated the devotion into the *Exercises* but eliminated from it all the faults noted by the Erasmians. Above all, he made it a mental prayer, which was so important to them. In a word, he could distinguish, at a time when many could not, the devotion from its aberrations. A point not noted sufficiently by Bataillon is that Erasmus was able to make the same distinction. In the *Enchiridion* he proposed a new form of the devotion, ascetical rather than spiritual. By the mid-1530's, when he wrote the *De praeparatione ad mortem*, he had definitely rediscovered the devotion, and reformed it to express belief in justification by faith. Ignatius, without stressing justification, had achieved a similar end much earlier : that of convincing his retreatant of his dependence on God's mercy.

Ignatius, however, as his earliest historians tell us, did not take to the work. This occurred mainly, it seems, for devotional reasons. He was not interested in the ideals of the *philosophia Christi*, not having had a classical training ; for the same reason he was not attracted by the restraint and moderation of its teaching. Nor did he find in it the ideal of a reformed devotion to the Passion of the kind he had begun to develop.

Secondly, on a more general plane, a number of points may be made about the history of spiritual exercises in Spain during the 1520's and 1530's. To oppose the Ignatian to the Erasmian system

---

[141] Except in the rules on orthodoxy, 366-369.

of meditation is, despite their obvious differences, to oversimplify a complex matter.

On the one hand, Ignatius did not just prolong meditation on the Passion, but made it a means of interiorising and christianising the spiritual life and therefore of countering the obsession with good works prevalent among his contemporaries. On the other, Erasmus, even in the *Enchiridion*, never condemned the devotion *per se*, and eventually returned to it. However, one must admit that the two systems had distinct characteristics, no doubt partly because they developed separately. They may, perhaps, be best distinguished structurally [142]. The arrangement of the Ignatian *Exercises* is linear : the retreatant meditates on only one theme at a time, sin in the first « week » and the life of Christ in the following three. That of the Erasmian exercises, on the other hand, is parallelistic. They consist of two sets of meditations : one deals with the life of Christ, the other with sin ; they run concurrently and at no point is one set replaced completely by the other. In this respect the Erasmian exercises were influenced by a neo-Platonic concept Ignatius ignored.

Thirdly : how unusual was Ignatius' attitude to Erasmus in Spain of the time ? It is difficult to define his position precisely ; he can be associated with no one group or programme of reform. This is no doubt partly because he was a man of independent spirit, guided from the start of his apostolate by a personal calling. One must also take into account the complexity of the reform movement and the wide variety of views it embraced. In his study of it, Marcel Bataillon described the movement as « the spiritual legacy of Erasmianism», a description later disputed by Eugenio Asensio in an article which is now famous [143].

Asensio argued that it was a more complex phenomenon than Bataillon suggested and that its roots could be found in medieval traditions of spirituality, particularly Franciscan piety and illuminism. He mentioned certain characteristics of the movement, such as openness to inspiration by the Holy Spirit, not found in Erasmus, and he pointed out that others, such as preference of mental to vocal prayer and criticism of attachment to externals, were shared by so many differing kinds of spirituality that they could not be called specifically Erasmian. In important respects, he argued, the teaching of Erasmus in the *Enchiridion* was irreconcilable with the Franciscan tradition: in its esteem for pagan wisdom, for example, its unheroic morality and its dislike for ascetic mortification. All these traditions, he concluded, enjoyed a certain solidarity as part of the renewal of popular religion at a time when the boundaries of orthodoxy were far from clear [144].

---

[142] Leaving aside the much discussed problem of the place of the Election in the retreat ; see IPARRAGUIRRE, op. cit., 202 n. 21.

[143] *El erasmismo y las corrientes espirituales afines*, in *Revista de filología española*, 36 (1952) 31-99.

[144] Ibid., 73 : « Los campos de ortodoxia y heterodoxia estaban mal deslindados. Todos cuantos defendían una religiosidad más intensa, más genuina y auténtica, parecían combatientes de la misma batalla. Fervores franciscanos y fervores erasmianos no se excluían».

Asensio's argument helps to explain the apparent anomaly in Ignatius' position. His dislike of the *Enchiridion* and the fact that he later professed to have escaped all Erasmian influence are difficult to reconcile with his interest in the renewal of the Church only if one supposes that it was customary for such an interest to lead to Erasmianism in the mid-1520's. It also suggests that Ignatius would have found more in common with Spanish Erasmians, who, like himself, were influenced by medieval traditions of piety, than he did with Erasmus himself. That this is so may, I think, be shown by a brief look at two sources of our understanding of Spanish Erasmianism at this time : the interpolations made by the Arcediano del Alcor in his translation of the *Enchiridion*, and the *Diálogo de doctrina cristiana* of Juan de Valdés. Both authors blend with the teaching of Erasmus themes characteristic of the Augustinian or Franciscan tradition of spirituality which also inform the *Exercises*. Two in particular merit examination : the affirmation of human sinfulness and of the power of grace on the one hand, and of the ideal of perfection on the other.

On several occasions the Arcediano mitigates Erasmus' confidence in the freedom of the will and in the power of reason to control the passions by emphasising that man depends on the grace of God to keep the moral law. At one point, for instance, Erasmus mentions several ways of repelling temptation, most of which involve vigorous activity on man's part. One of them, however, is prayer for grace, and it is this passing reference that the translator expands [145]. Elsewhere Erasmus urges his reader to persevere in virtue ; it is the Arcediano who insists that to do so requires the help of God [146]. And when Erasmus does point out that one can do no good without grace, the Arcediano is quick to stress the fact [147]. The same conviction of human moral weakness is found in the works of Valdés. A recurring theme in the *Diálogo* is that without the help of grace man is quite unable to observe the Law [148]. He takes this to the extreme of writing that the human will is not only helpless to do good of itself, it is always opposed to God's will [149]. From such premises follows a belief characteristic of Valdés : to keep the commandments one must *pray* [150] ; and this prayer involves complete withdrawal of confidence in one's own strength [151]. It is not a surprise to find that in his translation of the *Inquisitio de fide* he elaborates an allusion of Erasmus to man's dependence on God rather than self [152].

---

[145] *Enquiridion*, 359 : « Las más principales maneras para vencer y rechaçar al tentador son éstas : Contradezirle reziamente en tu coraçón, ... escupirle y arrojarle de ti, o ponerte a orar con gran fervor, *convirtiéndote todo a Dios con entera confiança y pidiéndole socorro y remedio con perseverancia*».

[146] Ibid., 195 : « antes con animosidad de gigante, *y sobrepujando por la gracia tus fuerzas humanas* te dispongas alegremente a passar la carrera *desta vida christiana*».

[147] Ibid., 373-374 : « considera ... si es buen consejo por un tan pequeño deleyte del pecado, ... caer de tan gran dignidad en tan gran baxeza, donde después por ti no puedes librarte, *ni diligencia humana, sin especial ayuda divina, baste para levantarte*».

[148] e.g. *Diálogo*, fol. 36v-37r.

[149] Ibid., 78r-78v.

[150] Ibid., fol. 26v, 32r.

[151] Ibid., fol. 48r-48v.

[152] Ibid., fol. 9v.

This pessimism about the moral strength of man is evident in the attitude of both writers to classical thought and moral doctrine. They draw a much firmer line than Erasmus between the realms of nature and grace. One of the rare occasions on which the Arcediano's translation contradicts the sense of the original occurs in a passage praising Platonism, in which mention is made of its similarities with Biblical teaching, and the reader is urged to study it : « E philosophis autem Platonicos te sequi malim propterea quod cum plerisque sententiis, tum ipso dicendi charactere, quam proxime ad Propheticam Evangelicamque figuram accedunt » [153].

This the Arcediano renders as : « De los filósofos, la verdad es que los platónicos son los que assí en muchas de sus sentencias como en el estilo y forma de dezir, se allegan en gran manera a las figuras de los profetas y del Evangelio, mas peligrosa cosa es saberlos » [154]. He not only omits the invitation to study Platonism, but he adds a warning against doing so. Later, in a passage in which Erasmus repeats his praise of Platonism and alludes to St. Augustine's esteem for it, the Arcediano interpolates a long warning that Augustine came to have misgivings about his own enthusiasm, that much in Plato is erroneous, and that he should not be read except by the very well instructed [155].

An explanation of these reserves is suggested by Valdés' views on pagan morality which emerge in the *Diálogo* during a discussion of the four cardinal virtues. One of the characters, the Archbishop, suggests that their name should be changed to *virtudes morales* on the grounds that for Christians it is the three theological virtues that are cardinal. One suspects that Valdés wishes to stress that the virtues man can acquire by his natural efforts are quite distinct from those which are conferred by baptism and depend on a special gift of grace. That this is so is confirmed by what follows. The Archbishop adds that Christians and Pagans possess the cardinal virtues in different ways : the Christian can attribute and direct them to God, but the Pagan can see their source and end only in himself and will fall into the error of pride. To be true, he says, they must be « baptised » [156]. Now the pride noted in the virtuous Pagan is, of course, the very same vice that Valdés wished to combat among his Christian contemporaries who sought justification in their good works. He appears to have feared that direct acquaintance with classical moral thought might encourage tendencies towards Pelagianism. So it is that the Archbishop lays down firm rules about the preparation of children for encounters with the classics [157]. It seems likely that such precautions would have met with the Arcediano's approval; that they underly his own remarks about the danger of reading Plato uncritically. One of his additions to the text of Erasmus expresses reserves about the orthodoxy of Origen [158].

It has already been noted that the general tone of Erasmus' spiritual teaching is one of moderation. Both the Arcediano and Valdés, on the other hand, like Ignatius, draw one's attention to the highest motives for loving God. Erasmus, for instance, counsels his reader to gain mastery

---

[153] See *Enquiridion*, 479.
[154] Ibid., 134.
[155] Ibid., 245-246, 480.
[156] *Diálogo*, fol. 50v-52v.
[157] Ibid.
[158] Ibid., 137, 479.

of the passion of wrath so that nothing can ever rouse his anger ; he adds that a stage more perfect than this involves directing one's fury exclusively to vice and dealing charitably with one's enemies. To these words the Arcediano adds a sentence which expresses the highest Christian ideal, willing acceptance of insults for love of Jesus, an ideal integral to the *Spiritual Exercises* [159]. Valdés in turn insists that all Christians, laymen as well as religious, are meant to observe the first commandment by trying to love God for His sake, and that those who do not, on the grounds that it is for the ' perfect ', will not be forgiven [160]. All are called to perfection [161]. His conviction that one should aspire to the highest ideals is the corollary of his confidence in the power of grace [162]. No doubt the same is true of the Arcediano.

The Erasmianism of the Arcediano and Valdés is characteristic of their contemporaries in Spain. Only certain works of the humanist were widely popular : his paraphrase of the New Testament and the *Enchiridion* in particular. It was the spiritual writer rather than the scholar or even the satirist that Spaniards acclaimed [163]. The themes in his works which most appealed to them were, broadly speaking, those which coincided with characteristics of the illuminist [164] tradition : encouragement of lay spirituality and of dissemination of the scriptures ; a preference of mental to vocal prayer ; and above all criticism of ritual and ceremony in the name of the spirit. When the tenor of his writings differed from or contradicted assumptions implicit in that tradition they supplemented or modified them, as our brief study suggests.

Erasmus was read avidly in Spain and became a figurehead of renewal because he articulated the principal aspirations of a generation with lucidity and eloquence and related them to the mainstream of civil life and culture [165]. The movement of reform itself, however, transcended Erasmianism, a fact which explains how individuals like Ignatius who were part of it could experience no direct influence of the humanist, and even find some characteristics of his spirituality wholly unsympathetic, while working to realise many of the changes for which he stood.

---

[159] Ibid., 407 :« Muy más perfecta y ecelente cosa será no solamente recebir con paciencia las injurias, mas aun dessearlas y holgarte con ellas por amor de Jesu Christo».

[160] *Diálogo*, fol. 23r.

[161] Ibid., 49r.

[162] Ibid., 36v-37r : « conoscemos por experiencia cómo nosotros por nuestra propria naturaleza no podemos hazer cosa perfectamente buena ; y que por el favor de Jesu Christo podamos hazer y cumplir todo lo que conoscemos ser bueno».

[163] BATAILLON, *Enquiridion*, 17.

[164] In the sense accepted by ASENSIO, art. cit., 72. In 1942 Villoslada pointed out the need for a precise definition of the term (art. cit., 235). He himself made it equivalent to heterodoxy. However some of the « recogidos» such as Osuna were never persecuted by the Inquisition. Karl Rahner has called for research into Spanish illuminism and Ignatius in the 1520's (op. cit., 93 n. 8). See too W. A. M. PETERS, *The Spiritual Exercises of St. Ignatius : Exposition and interpretation*, Jersey City 1968.

[165] ASENSIO, art. cit., 78.

## RESUMEN

Los años entre el nacimiento de san Ignacio y su salida de España en 1527 presentan un florecimiento del interés por la oración mental, manifestado en las muchas traducciones de libros de devoción y en el desarrollo de varias formas de espiritualidad. El A. distingue tres etapas anteriores a 1530. En la primera floreció la devoción a la Pasión. Hacia 1520 aparece el iluminismo que se opone a tal devoción y promueve un tipo de meditación despojado de discursos y del demasiado uso de la imaginación. En el tercero, hacia la mitad de los años 20, el debate se centra en los escritos de Erasmo. Su origen es Alcalá con la publicación del *Enchiridion* el a. 1526, precisamente cuando Ignacio llega a Alcalá. Uno de sus amigos, Miguel de Eguía, fue el impresor de la obra.

Tras examinar las opiniones hasta ahora emitidas sobre la reacción de san Ignacio a la lectura de Erasmo, el A. cree que hay que revisar el problema comparando el *Enchiridion* con los *Ejercicios* (escritos substancialmente antes de la llegada del santo a Alcalá), tratando de descubrir sus semejanzas y divergencias. Ante todo, juzga que los motivos del desagrado de san Ignacio ante el *Enchiridion* fueron de naturaleza devocional y no doctrinal. El examen detallado le lleva a detectar que temas centrales de los *Ejercicios* no hallan expresión en el *Enchiridion* : el ideal de amor desinteresado a Cristo ; los conceptos ignacianos de indiferencia y pobreza, que están intimamente ligados al deseo de imitar a Cristo en pobreza actual ; y la experiencia de la actuación directa de Dios en el alma, que no encuentra equivalente en la obra del humanista, promotora más bien de una conducta virtuosa que de una vida de oración. Otra diferencia, relacionada con la anterior, es la visión neoplatónica de Erasmo con su optimismo sobre el hombre, que no podía ser muy simpática a san Ignacio, congenial más bien con la *Imitación de Cristo*. La última es la diversa importancia y lugar dados por cada uno a los ejercicios que fomentan el amor y el temor. Estructuralmente los *Ejercicios* son lineales, una materia sigue a la otra : pecados, vida de Cristo. El *Enchiridion* presenta dos series de meditaciones en paralelo : la vida de Cristo y el pecado.

En el fondo, separa a los dos autores la ausencia de educación en el clasicismo antiguo por parte de san Ignacio. No movía a Ignacio, como a los humanistas, el proyecto de reconciliar el pensamiento moral cristiano y el pagano. Por otra parte, no rimaba la piedad demasiado racional y moderada de Erasmo con las exigencias de servicio y entrega total de san Ignacio. Ignacio deseaba que continuase la meditación de la Pasión, cosa que los humanistas desaprobaban al principio ; aunque más tarde se acercaron de nuevo a ella, cuando los escritos religiosos, por lo años de 1530, comenzaron a insistir más en la controversia sobre la justificación por la fe, que en la oposición entre espíritu y ceremonia religiosa. El paso a la verdadera devoción a la Pasión lo había dado san Ignacio antes.

Más simpatía habría encontrado san Ignacio, a juicio del A., en el contacto con los erasmistas españoles, que, como él, estaban influídos por la piedad medieval. Descubre estos rasgos propios de la interpretación española de Erasmo en la traducción del *Enchiridion* del Arcediano del Alcor y en el *Diálogo de la lengua* de Juan de Valdés.

En conclusión, el movimiento de reforma trasciende las fronteras del erasmismo. Esto explica que san Ignacio sin directa influencia de Erasmo, y aun sintiendo antipatía hacia algunas notas de su espiritualidad, realizara muchos de los cambios deseados por Erasmo.

# III

## ERASMUS, IGNATIUS LOYOLA, AND ORTHODOXY

ERASMUS of Rotterdam and Ignatius Loyola have both suffered injustice at the hands of their biographers. Erasmus is still sometimes described as a satirist whose wit covered a scepticism he would not avow, or as a humanist whose love of letters diluted his Christianity, but these and other legends which go back to his own day are gradually disappearing as more is learnt about his passion for the Fathers of the Church, his hostility to the paganizing effects of the Renaissance, and his acclaim as a writer on the spiritual life.[1] One book which helped to alter the traditional image of him was Marcel Bataillon's celebrated study, *Erasme et l'Espagne*, which revealed his enormous popularity in Spain during the 1520s, not, primarily, as a satirist, nor as a scholar, but as the author of the *Enchiridion militis christiani*.[2]

The renewal of Erasmus studies has contributed indirectly to current reappraisal of the figure of St. Ignatius, partly by revealing the extent to which our view of the early sixteenth century has been distorted by subsequent controversy between Protestants and Catholics. Ignatius is still thought of as a symbol of the Roman church after the Council of Trent, whereas he really belongs to an earlier period of reform. His formative years were the 1520s when the name of Luther, for instance, can have meant little, if anything, to him. By 1525 he had composed the substance of the *Spiritual Exercises* and had begun the quest for like-minded companions which was to issue fifteen years later in the Society of Jesus. Moreover, he spent most of the 1520s in Spain, when the writings of Erasmus were becoming popular.

Such facts have led recent scholars to question a tradition that Ignatius disapproved of Erasmus's works, and that he was an anti-Erasmian even in the 1520s. It may be traced back to the first official biography of the saint, written by Pedro de Ribadeneira and published in 1572, where one reads that Ignatius first came across Erasmus as a student in Barcelona (some time, that is, between early 1524 and mid 1526). Several people, including his confessor, urged him to read the *Enchiridion*, partly to improve his Latin, and he did so; but when he discovered that it was cooling his ardour he tossed it aside, and

---

[1] H. de Lubac, *Exégèse médiévale. Les quatre sens de l'Ecriture* (Paris, 1959–64), seconde partie, ii, pp. 454–80.

[2] M. Bataillon, *Erasme et l'Espagne* (Paris, 1937), Spanish translation *Erasmo y España* (Mexico, ²1966).

[Journal of Theological Studies, N.S., Vol. XXX, Pt. 1, April 1979]

116

conceived a distaste for Erasmus so great that he later banned all his works in the Society:

> In hac studiorum palaestra versanti
> pii quidam ac docti viri
> consilium dederunt ut Erasmi
> Roterodami . . . libellum de milite
> christiano legeret; cuius consilii
> confessarius etiam ad reliquos
> auctor accessit. Quod cum
> Ignatius simpliciter fecisset,
> observavit illius libelli lectione
> refrigescere in se spiritum
> Dei et devotionis sensim
> ardorem restingui. Qua re
> animadversa, librum de
> manibus omnino abjecit,
> et ita est aversatus, ut
> nec ipse amplius legerit
> illius auctoris libros, et
> passim in Societate
> nostra legi vetuerit.[1]

This event, as described by Ribadeneira, is not recorded in any earlier extant document concerning the saint. A different account, however, may be found in the writings of Luis Gonçalves da Cámara, a friend and assistant of Ignatius who jotted down biographical notes about him in 1555, when they were in daily contact. An entry for 28 February 1555 records that when Ignatius was in Alcalá de Henares (between mid 1526 and mid 1527) he was urged to read the *Enchiridion* by several people, including his confessor, but that having heard the author's orthodoxy disputed he declined:

> Quando el Padre en su principio
> estuvo en Alcala, muchos le
> persuadían, y aun su confesor,
> que leyese el Encheridion de
> Erasmo; mas oyendo decir que
> había diferencias y dudas sobre
> el autor, nunca lo quiso leer,
> diciendo que hartos libros
> había buenos de que no había
> duda.[2]

---

[1] P. Ribadeneira, *Vita Ignatii Loiolae, Societatis Iesu fundatoris* (Naples, 1572), ed. C. Dalmases, *Fontes narrativi de S. Ignatio de Loyola*, iv (Rome, 1965), p. 173.

[2] *Fontes narrativi de S. Ignatio de Loyola*, i (Rome, 1943), eds. D. Fernández Zapico, C. Dalmases, p. 669.

The interpretation of Ignatius's position implied by this early account is significantly different from Ribadeneira's. It indicates that in Alcalá he refused to read a controversial work of devotion, but it does not state that during his stay there he was, or became, an anti-Erasmian. It implies that he was concerned to be orthodox, but not that he had an opinion about the orthodoxy of Erasmus: in this matter, it suggests, he was uncommitted. It says nothing about his subsequent views, and it does not imply that he never read anything by Erasmus.

It is certain that Ribadeneira was familiar with the tradition Cámara recorded: his preparatory notes for the biography include a passage apparently based on the earlier account:

> Estando en Alcalá, como muchos
> le dixessen, y entre ellos su
> confessor, que leyesse el
> *Enchiridion* de Erasmo,
> nunca lo quiso hacer, diciendo
> que no faltaban otros libros
> buenos en que leer, de cuyos
> auctores no había ninguna duda.[1]

In the biography itself, however, this tradition is nowhere mentioned. One year after the biography appeared, in 1573, Cámara, who no doubt had read it, repeated his version with more facts, emphasizing that he had heard it from Ignatius himself.[2]

Some scholars accept the veracity of both accounts and assume that Ignatius was asked to read the *Enchiridion* twice, once in Barcelona, when he abandoned it, and later in Alcalá, when he refused it.[3] This involves supposing that for his version Ribadeneira had a separate source which has since been lost, a hypothesis made implausible by the fact that his text shares with Cámara's several similarities of phrasing and detail.[4] Moreover, the details in his account that differ from Cámara's are difficult to square with other historical evidence. Although there was a nucleus of Erasmians in Barcelona when Ignatius was there, the city was not a noteworthy centre of evangelical humanism. The *Enchiridion* does not seem to have been available in any library or bookshop in the city at the time;[5] and his teacher of Latin, Jeroni Ardèvol,

---

[1] *Fontes narrativi de S. Ignatio de Loyola*, ii (Rome, 1951), ed. C. Dalmases, pp. 417–18.

[2] *Fontes narrativi*, i, p. 585.

[3] C. Dalmases in *Fontes narrativi*, ii, p. 417 n. 15; iv, pp. 172–3 n. 12; P. Leturia, *Estudios Ignacianos* (Rome, 1957), i, p. 331 n. 3; p. 160; R. García-Villoslada, *Loyola y Erasmo* (Madrid, 1965), pp. 23–31.

[4] M. Batllori, 'Sobre l'humanisme a Barcelona durant els estudis de Sant Ignasi (1524–1526): Nebrija i Erasme', *Quaderni ibero-americani*, iii (1956), p. 229.     [5] Ibid., p. 230.

did not normally use the *Enchiridion*, or any of Erasmus's works, in his lessons.[1] Alcalá de Henares, on the other hand, was renowned, in 1526, as a centre of Erasmian enthusiasm, and the *Enchiridion* was a best-seller in the town.[2] In Barcelona Ignatius began to study Latin, and his knowledge of it was so rudimentary that a few years later, on arrival in Paris, he had to revise it from scratch:[3] it is improbable that he would have read the *Enchiridion* with the ease that Ribadeneira suggests.[4] In Alcalá, however, it was available in a vigorous Spanish translation.[5] Finally, Ignatius's regular confessor in Barcelona was an observant Franciscan: it is unlikely that he would have recommended Erasmus in view of his order's hostility to the humanist, in Spain as elsewhere.[6] In Alcalá his confessor was a secular priest who, according to Inquisition records, had Erasmian sympathies and friends.[7]

The evidence suggests that Ribadeneira drew the substance of his account from Cámara's, and changed some details of time, place, and content. But why should he have done so? It was in Alcalá that Ignatius first ran into trouble with the Inquisition, and several of his friends there, including his confessor, later became Jesuits.[8] In his biography Ribadeneira played down the gravity of the charges brought against Ignatius during his stay in the town: he may well have feared that Cámara's account would impugn the Society's orthodoxy.[9] In the 1560s anti-Erasmian feeling was strong in Italy and Spain.[10] In 1575 the use of Erasmus's works was severely restricted in the Society.[11] By altering the

---

[1] J. M. Madurell, C. Dalmases, 'Jeroni Ardèvol, maestro de San Ignacio, y la enseñanza de las Humanidades en Barcelona de 1508 a 1544', *Archivum Historicum Societatis Iesu*, xxxvii (1968), pp. 370–407.

[2] Bataillon, op. cit., pp. 206–25.     [3] *Fontes narrativi*, i, p. 464.

[4] See comments of J. C. Olin, 'Erasmus and St. Ignatius Loyola' in *Luther, Erasmus and the Reformation: A Catholic–Protestant Reappraisal*, eds. J. C. Olin, J. D. Smart, R. E. McNally (New York, 1969), p. 117.

[5] *El Enquiridion o Manual del caballero cristiano*, ed. D. Alonso (Madrid, 1932: reissued 1971).

[6] Cf. García-Villoslada, op. cit., p. 29.

[7] Bataillon, op. cit., p. 213 n. 16.

[8] Diego and Esteban de Eguía, brothers of the Alcalá printer Miguel, later joined the Society (*Fontes narrativi*, i, p. 110 n. 3); Manuel Miona, Ignatius's confessor in Alcalá, entered the Society in 1545 (ibid., pp. 446–7 n. 24, 585 n. 49); another contemporary of Ignatius in Alcalá, Miguel de Torres, who later fled to Paris with Miona, also became a Jesuit in the 1540s (ibid., p. 530 n. 5; Bataillon, op. cit., pp. 213, 475).

[9] See J. E. Longhurst, 'Saint Ignatius at Alcalá', *Archivum Historicum Societatis Iesu*, xxvi (1957), pp. 252–7; documents of the inquiries in Alcalá may be seen in *Scripta de Sancto Ignatio de Loyola*, ed. Luis M. Ortiz, Vicente Agustí, Mariano Lecina, i (Madrid, 1904), pp. 598–623; for Ignatius's own account see *Fontes narrativi*, i, pp. 440–52.

[10] Bataillon, op. cit., pp. 699–737.

[11] García-Villoslada, op. cit., pp. 269–70.

time and place of Cámara's account, and suggesting that Ignatius read the *Enchiridion* partly to improve his Latin, he dampened its significance. He may have been influenced also by the knowledge that his biography would be read by young Jesuits, many of them involved in missions to Protestants, who had not known Ignatius, yet wished to model their lives on his. The story that Ignatius actually read Erasmus, but recoiled in horror, shows him with an exemplary instinct for orthodoxy as the late sixteenth century defined it. It is also possible that Ribadeneira changed the location from Alcalá to Barcelona in order to take Ignatius's reserves further back in time. In his *Collectanea* he claimed that Ignatius burned all of Erasmus's writings long before they were placed on the *Index*,[1] a statement which is almost certainly untrue.[2] His assertion in the biography that Ignatius banned Erasmus's writings in the Society is also inaccurate: towards the end of his life Ignatius expressed reserves about using them in Jesuit schools, but it was only after his death that they were prohibited in the Society.[3] Such statements reveal how concerned Ribadeneira was to make Ignatius appear extremely orthodox, and from as early as possible in his career.

Other evidence suggests that Ignatius may well have read some of Erasmus's writings in the late 1520s and 1530s. Parallels have been noted between parts of the *Spiritual Exercises* and certain texts of the humanist. The 'Principle and Foundation', for instance, resembles a passage in the *Enchiridion*;[4] some of the 'Rules for the discernment of spirits' are anticipated in the preface to the *Paraphrasis in Evangelium Matthaei* of 1522;[5] and one of the 'Rules for thinking with the Church' recalls a line in the *Supputationes errorum in censuris Beddae* of 1527.[6] The sections of the *Exercises* in which these parallels have been found probably date in their final form from Ignatius's time in Paris and his early years in Italy (1528–41), when he would have had access to the writings of Erasmus and sufficient Latin to read them.[7]

Moreover, as Cámara's testimony indicates, Ignatius had Erasmian

---

[1] *Fontes narrativi*, ii, pp. 416–18.

[2] García-Villoslada, op. cit., pp. 239–40.                [3] Ibid., pp. 233–70.

[4] H. Watrigant, *La 'Méditation fondamentale' avant S. Ignace* (Enghien, 1907), p. 71; L. de Grandmaison, 'Les Exercices de Saint Ignace dans l'édition des "Monumenta" ', *Recherches de Science Religieuse*, xi (1920), p. 396; A. Codina, *Los orígenes de los Ejercicios espirituales de San Ignacio* (Barcelona, 1926), pp. 184–7.

[5] A. H. T. Levi, 'Erasmus, the Early Jesuits and the Classics', in *Classical Influences on European Culture, AD 1500–1700*, ed. R. R. Bolgar (Cambridge, 1976), pp. 223–38.

[6] G. Schurhammer, *Franz Xaver. Sein Leben und seine Zeit* (Freiburg, 1955), i, p. 122.

[7] *Exercitia spiritualia: textum antiquissimorum nova editio*, eds. J Calveras, C. Dalmases (Rome, 1969), pp. 4–35.

friends during his years in Spain; and later, in Paris, he continued to move in circles favourable to the humanist. In Alcalá he was a friend of Miguel de Eguía, the printer of many of Erasmus's works, including the *Enchiridion*.[1] His confessor, Manuel Miona, was close to Bernadino Tovar, a leading Erasmian in the town.[2] When the authorities restricted his apostolic activities, Ignatius was supported and encouraged by the Archbishop of Toledo, Alonso de Fonseca, a friend of Erasmus and a maecenas of his followers in Spain.[3] In Paris, Ignatius asked Miona (who had left Spain to evade the Inquisition) to continue as his director.[4] In 1529, during a visit to Flanders, he probably met the Spanish humanist Juan Luis Vives.[5] Later in the same year he decided to cease attending the reactionary Collège de Montaigu, and chose instead the Collège de Sainte-Barbe, which was permeated by the spirit of humanism.[6]

It would seem reasonable to conclude that in the 1520s and 1530s Ignatius was part of the movement of reform which Erasmus and other evangelical humanists inspired and led. There is, however, a further piece of evidence which might seem to indicate the contrary: the so-called 'Rules of Orthodoxy' at the end of the *Spiritual Exercises*. These rules, which probably date from 1539 to 1541,[7] contain praise of several aspects of medieval religious life which Erasmus was accused by his conservative critics of disparaging. Some scholars have interpreted them as a rebuttal of Erasmian views,[8] and it has been suggested that they were inspired indirectly by Josse van Clichtove, one of Erasmus's most hostile critics.[9] Such an interpretation, however, does not take

---

[1] *Fontes narrativi*, i, p. 442.

[2] Bataillon, op. cit., p. 213; see also A. G. Kinder, 'Juan Morillo—Catholic Theologian at Trent, Calvinist Elder in Frankfurt', *Bibliothèque d'Humanisme et Renaissance*, xxxviii (1976), pp. 345–6.

[3] *Fontes narrativi*, i, p. 450; Bataillon, op. cit., p. 214.

[4] *Obras completas de San Ignacio de Loyola*, eds. I. Iparraguirre, C. Dalmases (Madrid, ³1977), p. 126 n. 23.

[5] *Fontes narrativi*, i, p. 99; ii, pp. 557–8; García-Villoslada, op. cit., pp. 217–29; Olin, art. cit. pp. 123–5; the earliest surviving text of the *Spiritual Exercises* is in the handwriting of an English disciple of Vives, John Helyar: see Bataillon, op. cit., p. 590. [6] Levi, art. cit., pp. 228–9; Olin, art. cit., pp. 122–3.

[7] *Obras completas de San Ignacio*, pp. 191–2; recent general studies of the Rules include J. Salaverri, 'Significación teológica del "sentido verdadero que en la Iglesia debemos tener" según San Ignacio', *Manresa*, xli (1969), pp. 299–314; G. E. Ganss, 'Thinking with the Church: the Spirit of St. Ignatius's rules', *The Way*, Supplement 20 (1973), pp. 72–82; J. M. Granero, 'Sentir con la Iglesia', *Manresa*, xlvii (1975), pp. 291–310.

[8] Leturia, op. cit. ii, pp. 149–74; J. M. Granero, 'Sentir con la Iglesia', *Miscelánea Comillas*, xxv (1956), pp. 203–33.

[9] P. Dudon, *St. Ignatius of Loyola*, trans. W. J. Young (Milwaukee, 1949), pp. 146, 457–62; cf. García-Villoslada, op. cit., pp. 195–7.

into account the history of Ignatius's difficult relations with Church authority; nor does it do justice to the complexity of Erasmus's thought. The rules begin with praise of obedience:

> Depuesto todo juicio, debemos
> tener ánimo aparejado y
> prompto para obedescer
> en todo a la vera esposa
> de Christo nuestro señor
> que es la nuestra sancta
> madre Iglesia hierárchica.[1]

The same point is made later in rule 13, which includes the famous words:

> Debemos siempre tener,
> para en todo acertar,
> que lo blanco que yo veo,
> creer que es negro, si la
> Iglesia hierárchica assí
> lo determina.[2]

It has been suggested that Erasmus would have found both rules, especially the latter, unpalatable.[3] Since the sixteenth century it has been conventional to describe him as a reluctant Catholic who questioned, or was indifferent to, the claims of the Church of Rome.[4] Before the 1520s the issue of authority in the Church was less important in his writings than it later became. His initial concern was the abuse, rather than the principle, of papal and episcopal power. When he broke with Luther, however, it was one of the matters on which they differed; and, as Fr. de Lubac has shown, he took an orthodox line.[5] In the *Hyperaspistes*, for instance, he wrote to him:

> A vestro foedere me alienum esse
> semper professus sum, cum Ecclesia
> catholica pacem habeo, cui et censuram
> scriptorum meorum detuli, si quid
> inest erroris humani, nam malitiam aut
> impietatem procul ab illis abesse scio . . .

---

[1] *Obras completas de San Ignacio*, p. 287: 'Laying aside all private judgment, we must have a spirit prepared and prompt to obey in all things the true bride of Christ Our Lord, which is our holy mother the hierarchical Church.'

[2] Ibid., pp. 288–9: 'We must always hold, to be right in all things, that what I see as white I will believe to be black, if the hierarchical church determines it so.'

[3] Schurhammer, op. cit., loc. cit; cf. M. Rondet, 'Noir ou blanc selon l'Eglise', *Christus*, xv (1968), pp. 92–106; J. Iturrioz, 'Lo blanco y lo negro, según la determinación de la Iglesia', *Manresa*, xlii (1970), pp. 5–18.

[4] H. de Lubac, op. cit., pp. 464 sqq.

[5] Ibid., pp. 467–71.

An ideo sejunctus sum ab Ecclesia, quod
mihi cum duobus aut tribus theologis,
quos tu sopistas vocas, parum convenit?[1]

None the less, although this and similar statements indicate his allegiance to Rome, they differ in tone from the celebration of papal
authority characteristic of the later sixteenth century. Erasmus lived in
an age when the precise scope of papal authority was still open to
debate among theologians, and although, like his friend Thomas More,
he came to see union with Rome as the principle of Church unity, he
did not witness the 'centralisation around the papal office' by which the
traditional order was eventually preserved.[2]

Ignatius's position in the years preceding the formulation of the
'Rules' was not dissimilar. During the 1520s, before he came into contact
with Protestantism, the principle of authority in the Church does not
appear to have preoccupied him. The workings of authority were, if
anything, a thorn in his flesh when, in Jerusalem and Spain, his apostolate was hampered by restrictions which he feared would thwart his
calling. Until the late 1530s he hoped to leave Europe and spend his
days in Jerusalem, an ambition expressed in the vow that he took with
his companions at Montmartre in 1534. When, in 1538, they went to the
Pope, it was not in a counter-reformation spirit, but to ask for guidance,
their plans to travel east having failed.[3] Such was the origin of the fourth
vow of the Society of Jesus of special obedience to the Pope, which was
originally a means of discerning God's will for each professed Jesuit;
only gradually did the Society begin to realize its further implications.[4]
In rules 1 and 13 there is, moreover, no specific mention of the papal
office: Ignatius refers in general terms to obedience to the hierarchy.
Both Erasmus and Ignatius, in fact, had a view of the Church that was
medieval. They deplored its corruption and they longed for a reform
that would be led by, and begin with, the top. Its authority, however,
was something they took for granted, until schism provoked them into
defining their beliefs.

Four of the rules praise popular medieval devotions, including
attendance at liturgical prayer (3), pilgrimages, indulgences (6), the

[1] *Hyperaspistae Diatribes, liber primus* in *Opera Omnia* (Leyden, 1706), x, cols.
1267–8; quoted by de Lubac, op. cit., p. 469 n. 6.
[2] St. Thomas More, *Responsio ad Lutherum* (*Complete Works of St. Thomas
More*, vol. 5, part ii), (New Haven/London, 1969), p. 769; R. H. Bainton, 'The
Problem of Authority in the Age of the Reformation', in *Luther, Erasmus and the
Reformation*, pp. 14–25.
[3] Leturia, op. cit. i, pp. 201–21, 239–56.
[4] B. de Margerie, 'El cuarto voto de la compañía de Jesús, según Nadal',
*Manresa*, xlii (1970), pp. 359–76.

practice of corporal penance (7), and the veneration of relics (6) and images (8). Erasmus was critical of these devotions. His emphasis on the primacy of the interior life was a reaction against a popular concern with the externals of piety which he considered excessive. None the less he made it clear that he approved of popular devotions if they were practised for devout motives. In the *Enchiridion* he argued that the contemporary malaise in popular religion could be cured if men would practise the inner death to self preached by St. Paul, and thus be freed from the flesh that kills the spirit. For him the ideal was to be moved by pure love of Jesus, the one true end of piety.[1]

Ignatius's analysis of the malaise, and his solution, were not markedly different. He wished to preserve popular devotions, but to reform people's motives for practising them. His praise of the devotions in the 'Rules' is directed to the individual who has taken the *Exercises*; and one effect of the thirty-days' retreat is to interiorize the Christian life through meditation on Christ's life, death, and resurrection.[2] Throughout the *Exercises* the pure love of God is constantly mentioned as an ideal; and they offer a thorough training in mental prayer, which Erasmus always advocated.[3]

Erasmus's views on popular piety were connected closely with his criticism of the established religious orders. His concern with interior realities led him to reproach them for paying excessive attention to the externals of the religious life, and to praise the married state as an alternative vocation in which men and women could lead Christian lives without taking the three vows. Two of the 'Rules of Orthodoxy' concern this issue: both praise the religious life, and both imply that it is superior to marriage.

Rule 4 reads:

> Alabar mucho religiones,
> virginidad y continencia,
> y no tanto el matrimonio
> como ninguna destas.[4]

And Rule 5:

> Alabar votos de religión,
> de obediencia, de pobreza,
> de castidad y de otras
> perfecciones de

[1] T. O'Reilly, 'Saint Ignatius Loyola and Spanish Erasmianism', *Archivum Historicum Societatis Iesu*, xliii (1974), p. 305.

[2] Leturia, op. cit., p. 162; Batllori, art. cit., p. 227; P. Casperz, 'Liturgical Prayer and the Ignatian Exercises', *New Blackfriars*, liv (1973), pp. 72–80.

[3] O'Reilly, art. cit., p. 306.

[4] *Obras completas de San Ignacio*, p. 287: 'Greatly praise religious orders, virginity and continence, and not matrimony as much as any of these.'

124

> supererrogación; y es
> de advertir que, como el
> voto sea cerca las cosas
> que se allegan a la
> perfección evangélica,
> en las cosas que se alejan
> della no se debe hacer
> voto, así como de ser
> mercader o ser casado, etc.[1]

These two rules, however, do not express all Ignatius's ideas on the matter. He and the early companions with whom he founded the Society eventually took the three vows, but only after a long period of hesitation and discernment; when they did so it was the interior virtues entailed by them that they stressed, especially in the case of obedience.[2] They also omitted several features of the traditional religious life which Erasmus considered abused, including the choral office, a splendid liturgy, prescribed penances, and even a distinctive habit and a founder's name.[3] When Ignatius wrote the rules in question he was struggling to win official recognition of the Society's constitution, which was fiercely opposed by some cardinals who feared that it would be interpreted as an implied criticism of the established orders.[4]

In all these respects Ignatius and his followers were heirs of the early-sixteenth-century movement of reform in which Erasmus played a prominent part. Before Erasmus died, however, the movement was radically transformed by the eruption of Lutheranism in Germany. His stress on the interior life was followed among the Reformers by a rejection of many externals, and of the religious orders. Soon the issue was no longer the renewal of the traditional Church but its survival. It was in this new situation of crisis that the 'Rules of Orthodoxy' were composed. They were probably written to defend the nascent Society against suspicions of heresy at a time when its approval in Rome was in jeopardy.[5] Although they certainly distinguish Ignatius's views from

---

[1] Ibid.: 'Praise vows of religion, of obedience, of poverty, of chastity and of other supererogatory works of perfection; and it is to be noted that, as a vow is made concerning things which approach evangelical perfection, in the things which move away from it one ought not to make a vow, such as to become a merchant or married, etc.'

[2] M. Espinosa Polit, *La obediencia perfecta. Comentario a la carta de obediencia* (Mexico, [2]1962); J. C. Futrell, *Making an Apostolic Community of Love. The Role of the Superior according to Saint Ignatius of Loyola* (St. Louis, 1970); M. Bataillon, 'D'Erasme à la compagnie de Jésus. Protestation et intégration dans la Réforme catholique au XVIe siècle', *Archives de sociologie des religions*, xii (1967), pp. 68–9.          [3] Bataillon, art. cit., pp. 68–81.

[4] Ibid., pp. 68–73; H. O. Evennett, 'The New Orders', in *The New Cambridge Modern History*, ii, ed. G. R. Elton (Cambridge, 1958), p. 294.

[5] Bataillon, art. cit., pp. 66–73.

those of the Reformers, it is equally clear that he differed from men like Pedro Ciruelo,[1] Diogo de Gouvêa,[2] and Gian Pietro Caraffa,[3] who objected to the changes advocated in the old Church by the humanists. It was against the criticism of such conservatives that he had to defend his apostolate not only in Rome but in Venice, Paris, and Spain. In this respect his position in the Reformation debate resembled that of Erasmus, who objected equally strongly to the course taken by Luther and that advocated by the Sorbonne.

The many parallels that exist between Ignatius and Erasmus do not imply necessarily that Ignatius was a committed Erasmian. They may be explained by the fact that both men were shaped in part by common traditions, especially late medieval spirituality which Erasmus imbibed at school and Ignatius at Loyola and Montserrat. Their distrust of simply intellectual knowledge, for instance, and their esteem for the active life, for mental prayer, and for scripture are all traits of *devotio moderna* piety.[4] To this tradition, however, each one joined others that they did not share. Ignatius wished the Jesuits to be trained in the ancient languages, to know the Fathers of the Church and the Classics, but he was not centrally influenced by the Renaissance philology that meant so much to Erasmus: the Gospel meditations that form the core of the *Exercises* betray a reading of Ludolph of Saxony, not Lorenzo Valla. And although he may have been influenced by neo-Platonism,[5] the humanist ideal of reconciling pagan and Christian moral thought does not appear to have inspired him.[6] In the writings of Erasmus, on the other hand, one does not find the inclination to contemplative prayer,

---

[1] Ciruelo, a leading academic in Alcalá, and a participant in the conference on the orthodoxy of Erasmus at Valladolid in 1527, was noted for his theological conservatism: see Bataillon, *Erasmo y España* (Mexico, ²1966), pp. 247, 254, 262, 361; on his suspicion of Ignatius's apostolate in Alcalá see *Fontes narrativi*, i, p. 448.

[2] Gouvêa, principal of the Collège de Sainte-Barbe in Paris between 1520 and 1548, was one of the fiercest critics of Erasmus at Valladolid: Bataillon, op. cit., pp. 250–5; Levi, art. cit., p. 228; on his reservations about Ignatius's apostolate in Paris see *Fontes narrativi*, i, p. 468.

[3] On the history of Ignatius's difficult relations with Caraffa, the future Paul IV, in Venice and later in Rome, see G. Bottereau, 'La lettre d'Ignace de Loyola à Gian Pietro Caraffa', *Archivum Historicum Societatis Iesu*, xliv (1975), pp. 139–52; V. Codina, 'San Ignacio y Paulo IV. Notas para una teología del carisma', *Manresa*, xl (1968), pp. 337–62.

[4] A. Hyma, *The Christian Renaissance* (Hamden, 1965); R. R. Post, *The Modern Devotion* (Leiden, 1968); R. W. Southern, 'The Religious Bretheren of Deventer and its Neighbourhood' in *Western Society and the Church in the Middle Ages* (London, 1970), pp. 331–58.

[5] Levi, art. cit., pp. 232–3.

[6] O'Reilly, art. cit., p. 314.

126

nor the mystical confidence in the power and experiential nature of grace, that are characteristic of Ignatius.[1]

It must also be remembered that the two men belonged to different generations. Erasmus was in his twenties when Ignatius was born, and he died several years before the Society was founded. Most of his writings, composed before the break with Luther, dated quickly, partly because they lacked the precise definition of limits to reform which to Catholics in the 1530s and later mattered greatly. Their age difference, moreover, explains an apparent difference in their attitudes to scholasticism. In the 'Rules of Orthodoxy' Ignatius praises the scholastics, but the three he mentions by name (Thomas Aquinas, Bonaventure, and Peter Lombard) belong to the twelfth and thirteenth centuries.[2] He seems to have shared Erasmus's dislike of nominalism. In Paris, almost certainly, he did not study theology at the Sorbonne but at the Dominican convent in the rue Saint-Jacques, where the scholastic tradition was being renewed by a return to Aquinas.[3] Erasmus, one imagines, would have sympathized with this revival of Thomism, which was also occurring in Spain, for he made it clear more than once that he did not wish to reject scholasticism but to reform it, and he held St. Thomas in high esteem;[4] but it began rather late in his lifetime, and it did not bear full fruit until after his death.

Such differences may explain why Ignatius was not, apparently, an ardent supporter of Erasmus in Alcalá, even though he had Erasmian friends and was working for many changes that Erasmus desired; and also why he hesitated in the 1550s to recommend the use of his works in the Society's schools. His reserves differed greatly, however, from those of his contemporaries, like Melchor Cano and Paul IV, who considered Erasmus a heretic. In his last years Ignatius must have noted and deplored the ascendancy of this party which was hostile to all traces of the early reform movement, and which held the Jesuits, as well as Erasmus, in grave suspicion.[5]

Looking generally at what he achieved we may conclude that Ignatius realized many points of the reform programme that Erasmus advocated; but he incorporated into it qualifications which moderates like himself, faced with Protestantism and under pressure from the right, began to voice in the 1530s. He praised the Fathers, and encouraged their study,

[1] H. D. Egan, *The Spiritual Exercises and the Ignatian Mystical Horizon* (St. Louis, 1976); on the debt of St. Ignatius to the monastic tradition of contemplative prayer see T. O'Reilly, 'The *Exercises* of Saint Ignatius Loyola and the *Exercitatorio de la vida spiritual*', *Studia Monastica*, xvi (1974), pp. 301–23.

[2] *Obras completas de San Ignacio*, p. 288.

[3] García-Villoslada, op. cit., p. 162.

[4] Ibid., p. 175.     [5] Bataillon, op. cit., p. 703.

but he made use of scholasticism too.[1] He encouraged the critical study of scripture, but he urged that it submit to the mind of the Church, as Erasmus had done in his debate with Luther.[2] Through the *Exercises* he contributed to a revival of mental prayer that renewed rather than replaced the liturgy and popular devotions. And he founded a Society which broke with monastic tradition, and contributed to the reform of the older orders, yet defended the medieval justification of the religious life, and which made full use of the classics in its work of renewal. This synthesis, which bridged the early and late Counter-Reformation, took shape in the thought and work of several of his great contemporaries, but in him, and in the Society, it found complete expression. The aspects of the Counter-Reformation that Erasmus would have found repugnant go back to men like Noel Beda with whom it is misleading to associate Ignatius, *pace* his first biographer.

[1] See 'Constituciones de la Compañía de Jesús', sections 351, 446, 464, in *Obras completas de San Ignacio*, pp. 522, 539, 543.

[2] Ibid., sections 366–7, 447, pp. 524, 539–40.

# IV

# Melchor Cano and the Spirituality of St Ignatius Loyola

Our present understanding of the spirituality of St Ignatius has been shaped by the work of scholars earlier this century who published critical editions of his most personal writings and mapped the origins and early history of the *Spiritual Exercises*. Their research has made possible subsequent studies of his mysticism, and it has led to the recovery of neglected features of the *Exercises*, including their flexibility, individual dimension and openness to contemplative prayer[1]. It has also prompted questions about the relationship between Ignatian spirituality and other religious currents of the time, such as illuminism, and has raised the possibility that after the death of Ignatius the standard interpretation of the *Exercises* altered in subtle but telling ways because of disputes about their orthodoxy[2].

One of the most ardent early critics of the spirituality of Ignatius was the Dominican theologian Melchor Cano, who believed it was an offshoot of the kind of illuminism practised by the *alumbrados* or *dexados*, a group whose teachings were condemned in 1525 by the Inquisition of Toledo[3]. Cano's views of the *alumbrados* may be studied

---

[1] See the discussion by Philip Sheldrake in *The Way of Ignatius Loyola: Contemporary Approaches to the Spiritual Exercises*, edited by Philip Sheldrake S.J. (London, 1991), pp. 1-11.

[2] See Joseph Veale, «Ignatian Prayer or Jesuit Spirituality», *The Way Supplement* 27 (Spring 1976), pp. 3-14, reprinted in *The Way of Ignatius Loyola*, pp. 248-260.

[3] On Cano's attacks on the Society see Vicente Beltrán de la Heredia O.P., *Las corrientes de espiritualidad entre los domínicos de Castilla durante la primera mitad del siglo XVI* (Salamanca, 1941), p. 79 onwards. The edict of 1525 may be examined in the appendices to Antonio Márquez, *Los alumbrados: orígenes y filosofía*, 1525-1559 (Madrid, 1972; second edition 1980).

370

in detail in his lengthy critique of the catechism of Bartolomé de Carranza, but his reasons for associating Ignatius with the illuminists are not documented so fully[4]. Between 1556 and 1558 he wrote a number of letters in which he affirmed that the Society was a heretical force whose *Exercises* were undermining Church and State[5], but he declined to set out fully his reasons for this conviction, stating more that once that they were not «para carta»[6]. In one letter, dated 5 October 1558, he indicated that he had put his views in writing, and intended to show the document to the Pope, Paul IV, but this treatise was subsequently lost: Alfonso de Vargas, writing in 1641, claimed to have seen it in manuscript in Cano's own hand, but Fermín Caballero, in his biography of 1871, reported that it could not be traced[7]. In 1977, however, José Simón Díez drew attention to an unpublished manuscript in the British Library attributed to Cano and entitled, *Censura y parecer que dio contra el Instituto de los PP. Jesuitas*[8]. This document, which internal evidence permits us to date between 1552 and 1556, appears to be the one Cano mentioned[9]. The purpose of the present paper is not to give a full account of it, but to draw on the information it provides and on other sources in order to reconstruct Cano's view of the spirituality of St Ignatius, the *Spiritual Exercises* and the Society of Jesus.

# I

At the beginning of the *Censura* Cano states the principle that if the Society is the work of God its founders must be holy men, for God builds on rock[10]. He goes on to give reasons for supposing that

---

[4] *Qualification hecha por los Maestros Cano y Cuevas del catechismo [y de otros escritos] 1558-1559*, edited by J. Ignacio Tellechea Idígoras, *Fray Bartolomé de Carranza: documentos históricos*, volume VI (madrid, 1981), pp. 225-384.

[5] F. Caballero, *Conquenses ilustres, vol. 2: Melchor Cano* (madrid, 1871).

[6] See his letters to Miguel de Arcos and M. Venegas in Caballero, pp. 499-500.

[7] Caballero, pp. 110, 351, 354.

[8] José Simón Díaz, *Domínicos de los siglos XVI y XVII: escritos localizados* (Madrid, 1977), p. 110. I am grateful to Simon Tugwell O.P. for drawing my attention to this reference, and to Dr Michelle Brown for her help in obtaining a microfilm of the manuscript.

[9] British Museum Eg. 453 (fols. 91-105v, including title page). The manuscript, which is written in a clear hand, is divided into fifteen sections of unequal lenght. At one point [section 4] the author refers to an encounter with Laínez and Salmerón at the Council of Trent. This must have taken place during the second session of the Council [1551-2] which Cano attended (Caballero, p. 75). Since it is understood throughout the document that the General of the Society is Ignatius, it must have been composed before his death in July 1556.

[10] «Quanto a lo primero de la santidad de sus fundadores, se supone que Dios

the reputed holiness of Ignatius is more apparent than real. First he affirms that when Ignatius left Spain he was on the run from the Inquisition, who suspected him of being an *alumbrado*: «el General dellos es un Iñigo, el qual se escapó huyendo de España, porque le quería coger la Inquisición, porque se decía ser de los Alumbrados, o Dexados»[11]. And he implies that when the Roman authorities later cleared Ignatius of heresy they were ignorant of the evidence against him: «Fuese a Roma, y pidió ser juzgado del Papa; y no habiendo quien le acusase, fue dado por libre» [fol. 94r.].

The second reason Cano gives for being suspicious of Ignatius is more personal: he has met him several times, and on each occasion has found him wanting in integrity. Their first encounter ocurred when Cano, happening to be in Rome, decided to pay him a visit. He was taken aback when Ignatius, for no apparent reason, began to explain how he had been persecuted in Spain.

> Estando el autor una vez en Roma, deseó ver a Iñigo, y hablando con él, sin ningún propósito comenzó a hablar con él de su justicia, y de la persecución que le habían hecho en España y quán sin razón...

Ignatius also recounted certain revelations he had received from God: «y contó muchas y muy grandes cosas de las revelaciones que tenía de Dios, y eso sin haber ninguna necesidad» [fol. 94 r.-v.]. From these remarks Cano drew the conclusion that Ignatius was vain, and his revelations unworthy of credit, and he began to wish to know more about him and his companions. This first meeting is not dated, but if it was the origin of Cano's concern about the Society (as he implies) it probably occurred in 1542, the year when (according to one of his letters) he first began to think about the matter anxiously[12].

Their second encounter (as Cano recounts it) took place over a meal. While they were at table, Ignatius praised a member of the Society who had a reputation for holiness, but when this person was summoned he made a number of statements which seemed to Cano unorthodox, though he could also tell he was either simple or unwell:

---

como sumamente próvido planta sus cosas no sobre arena, o viento, sino sobre firmam petram» [section 3]. In all quotations from the manuscript, I. have made no changes in the orthography, apart from resolving abreviations and adding accents, and I have occasionally modified the punctuation.

[11] Compare the very similar passage quoted by Alfonso de Vargas: Caballero, p. 351.

[12] In his letter to Miguel de Arcos; written in 1556, Cano noted: «Sé que ha catorce años que pienso sobre ello» (Caballero, p. 499).

> Yendo otra vez a comer con él, alabó a un santo de su compañía, el qual siendo llamado le pareció al Autor ser loco. Y siendo preguntado de cosas de Dios, dixo muchas heregías, y aquello díxolo y hacíalo de idiota, que no sabía más.

Ignatius, who according to Cano found this incident embarrassing, explained to his visitor that the person in question was not a heretic, but someone with orthodox views who was not completely sound of mind:

> Y yéndose de allí el sobredicho Santo, quedándose afrentado el Iñigo, dixo al Autor: Ese no es herege, es loco, y creo tiene *lucida intervala*, como aora es conjunción de luna, no está tan católico. [fol. 94v.]

The reader sympathetic to Ignatius might surmise that he wished to make the point that when judging the orthodoxy of others one should proceed with discretion and kindness, a principle enunciated in the *Exercises* themselves. This incident, however, merely deepened Cano's suspicion and distrust.

The occasion of their third meeting was a joint visit to see and talk with Cardinal Farnese. A page who came to greet them asked whose name he should give his master, and Ignatius promptly reeled off a list of his titles:

> Ofrecióse otra vez que yendo a hablar al Cardenal Farnesio con él, salió un page, y preguntado, ¿quién diré que es? dixo bien alto: decid que es el Maestro Iñigo, o el General de los de la Compañía, o el confeoor de Madama, que por qualquier nombre destos os entenderá[13].

This behaviour showed Cano how conceited Ignatius was: «...de lo qual infirió el Autor había allí mucho viento» [fol, 94v. - 95r.]. Here the word «viento» recalls his earlier statement that God does not build on wind or sand [fol. 92v.].

Cano concludes his assessment of Ignatius with a story he was told by a Spanish cleric in Rome who enjoyed a reputation for holiness in spite of the fact (known to Cano) that he possessed two neglected benefices in Spain. When this cleric had an argument with a layman that ended in blows, Ignatius intervened to make peace between them, and arranged a settlement, acceptable to both sides, in which the layman agreed to receive a beating administered, on the cleric's behalf,

---

[13] The reference to Madama is to Margaret of Austria, daughter of Charles V (see *FN* 1, p. 749 n. 11).

by a member of the Society[14]. Cano, shocked, expressed the view that this solution was reprehensible, but was assured by the cleric that all had been arranged with the official permission of the Vicar of Rome. From this incident, and his own meetings with Ignatius, Cano concludes that he was ignorant of divine and human law, and imprudent and indiscreet as well as vain: «De todas estas cosas coligió el Autor ignorancia así del derecho divino como del humano... ¡Grande imprudencia y indiscreción, y gran vanidad de su trato!» [fol. 95v.].

## II

Apart from a vivid protrait of Ignatius, the *Censura* sets out clearly Cano's reasons for being suspicious of the *Spiritual Exercises*, in which he found several features that reminded him of the *alumbrados*. First, he deplored the fact that they offered everyone the same spirituality of a contemplative kind, irrespective of different temperaments and callings. Augustine (he writes) distinguished different types of sanctity corresponding to the various humours, but the Society is not so discriminating: «estos tienen para todos unos mismos exercicios de contemplación, como no todos sean aptos para ella» [fol. 103v.]. Here the word «contemplación» appears to be used not in the strictly Ignatian sense but with its traditional monastic associations. In his critique of Carranza's catechism, Cano levelled a similar charge against his fellow Dominican Luis de Granada, accusing him of having composed the *Libro de oración y meditación* in order to offer a contemplative spirituality to people living in the world, even though it would profit few of them. He believed it was not feasible to combine the active and contemplative lives, and he was concerned that people who tried to do so might neglect the works proper to their vocation. This had been the error of the *alumbrados*, who greatly prized prayer and contemplation, and who were led in their enthusiasm to abandon their responsabilities to home, work and family: Cano feared that through the *Exercises* the same upheavals would occur. In his view the Jesuits were closely related to the *dexados*, and valued contemplation and devotion just as highly. Satan could be expected to use these good things to lead souls astray once again, this time on a larger scale:

---

[14] The syntax of Cano's account at this point appears to allow for several, divergent readings. I have chosen the one that seems to make his case most effectively: «Sucedió que habiendo dado en Roma una bofetada a un seglar sobre no sé qué asunto, y no queriendo el injuriado perdonar, andando el Iñigo de por medio haciendo las amistades, uno de la Compañía acabó que diese al otro de palos, que él lo sufriría, y así serían amigos, porque así lo había él concertado» [fol. 95r.-v.].

374

> Se transfigura algunas veces en ángel de luz, y alumbra y da
> sentimientos espirituales, y aun ayuda desta suerte a muchos en
> el camino del cielo, para después dar con otros muchos en el
> camino y hoyo del infierno, como tenemos exemplo manifiesto
> en España, de los Alumbrados y Dexados que fueron primos
> hermanos destos; los quales por devoción y contemplación y
> otras cosas divinas hicieron tanto y más fruto que estos Padres,
> aunque el provecho dessos es más universal. [fol. 93r. -v.].

In a letter written on 21 September 1557 he was more specific.
His correspondent, Juan de Regla, had informed him that the Marqués
de Tavara was keen that the King should make the Ignatian retreat,
and Cano in his reply set out his reasons for thinking that this would
be disastrous. Since grace perfects nature, the spiritual exercises of a
Christian should improve him in the perfomance of his duties. If, after
his exercises, a cobbler or a cook plied his trade less effectively, he
would not be tolerated «por más que nos alegase que se da a devoción
y meditación». This, however, is the effect of the Ignatian *Exercises*:
they turn soldiers into women, and *caballeros* into hens, not lions.
Tavara himself had taken them, and instead of becoming a better
Christian he had become a poorer knight [«en ley de caballero des-
medrado»]. In this way the *Exercises* were threatening to undermine
the religious orders, the Spanish kingdom, and Christendom[15].

Cano's second reservation about the *Exercises* was prompted by
the importance he considered they accorded to affective spiritual experience. The person taking them [he writes] is given to understand
that during the retreat he will experience the work of grace in his soul
and be granted consolations. To make such a promise, he considers,
is presumption, an attempt to force the hand of God. He affirms also
that people taking the *Exercises* are encouraged to express in words
the sensible graces they have received, and in this way edify others.
This means, in practice, that during their meditations they are not only
nourishing themselves but preparing nourishment for others, an activity
that must leave their souls unsatisfied:

> Ofreciéndose la buena consideración luego se ofrece el cómo se
> ha de decir: lo qual hace que... el mantenimiento no harta del
> todo al alma, pues no es comida para ella sola, sino para sí y
> su compañero con quien trata.

Such readiness to speak of one's spiritual experience is a sign,
not of grace, but of the devil [fol. 105r.-v.]. In his comments on the
catechism of Carranza, Cano made a similar criticism of the *alum-*

---

[15] Caballero, p. 526.

*brados*. They, too, set great store by affective experiences of God's love, seeking in them the kind of assurance of personal salvation that the Lutherans sought in faith. He therefore objects to Carranza's appeals to experience, including his use of «sentir» [a verb used abundantly in the *Exercises*[16]].

Cano's third objection to the *Exercises* concerned their encouragement of indifference as a means of discerning God's will. In general, he felt, the Society erred by according an excessive and distorted importance to conformity with the will of God:

> éstos levantan tanto el conformarse con la voluntad de Dios *etiam in volito materiali*, que quieren decir que en ninguna causa nos entristezcamos, o a lo menos parece que se debe temer no vengan a esto.

This kind and degree of detachment [he affirms] runs counter to the example of Christ. It is an indication of false piety, and one of the signs of the Last Times [fol. 104v.]. The same error, according to Cano, characterised the *alumbrados*. They carried such conformity to absurd lengths, believing that in doing so they were giving God glory. In their case, too, this teaching gave rise to an apparent imperturbability, which St Paul had identified as a sign of «los tiempos postreros» [p. 272].

Cano's reservations about indifference underlay his views on the making of an election, which forms such an important part of the *Exercises*. At one point in the *Censura* he refers to the advice that God should be allowed to work directly in the soul, disposing it in the choice it wishes to make:

> tienen una cláusula no muy sana que dice: que quamvis licitum sit apto ad cor amplecti, consultius erit, quod anima eius maneat in equilibris, para hacer lo que Dios le inspirase [fol. 104r.].

The reasons for his criticism on this point may be inferred from his comments on two passages in the catechism of Carranza. The first stated that one should seek divine guidance in all decisions, even mundane ones. The second affirmed that people should not take solemn vows of chastity before reaching maturity, when they could evaluate their spiritual and corporal resources and, having done so, «escoger el estado que Dios les inspirare» [p. 267][17]. These two counsels are close

---

[16] See the data provided in Seppo A. Teinonen, *Concordancias de los Ejercicios Espirituales de San Ignacio de Loyola* (Helsinki, 1981).

[17] These quotations are drawn from Cano's critique of the catechism, not from the catechism itself.

376

in spirit to the Ignatian election, as practised by the saint himself and recommended in the *Exercises*. In both of them Cano discerned the imprint of the *alumbrados*, who sought direct guidance from the Lord in all areas of their lives: «los quales en todas las cosas humanas e divinas consultando por sí mesmos a Dios por el don de consejo que todos los justos tienen, pensavan seer alumbrados del Espíritu Sancto en todas sus consultas» [p. 268]. Cano objected to this way of discerning God's will because it undermined respect for reason, learning and authority [pp. 294, 268-9].

At one point in the *Censura* Cano gives an example of an election that he considered reprehensible. When Dr Pedro Ortiz was offered the Chair of Scripture in Alcalá he requested a lengthy period of time in which to discern God's will[18]. Eventually, he accepted it on three conditions that, in Cano's view, were outrageous because they ran counter to the instituted procedures of the university[19]. Cano later discussed the matter with the Jesuit Miguel de Torres, who explained to him that Ortiz had behaved as he did because he felt unable, in any other way, to discern God's purposes: «dixo que como el Espíritu Santo no le inspiraba lo que había de hacer, que acordó pedir aquellas condiciones, pareciéndole que si se las concedían, el Espíritu Santo quería fuese Catedrático». Torres, according to Cano, admitted that this procedure was «imperfect». For Cano it was totally misguided, a clear sign of the influence of illuminism: «He aquí muchos ramalazos de Alumbrados o Dexados» [fol. 96v.][20].

## IV

In the *Censura* Cano criticises not only the *Spiritual Exercises* but several other aspects of the life of the Society of Jesus. A number of his comments call into question the nature and extent of the Papal

---

[18] The treatise on the Election which Pedro Ortiz composed with his brother Francisco may be seen in J. Calveras S.J. and C. de Dalmases S.J., *Sancti Ignatii de Loyola Exercitia Spiritualia* (Rome, 1969 = MHSI, 100), pp. 627-645. It is prefaced [p. 627 n.°] by a note on the life of Pedro Ortiz, his friendship with St Ignatius, and his close association with the Society.

[19] «Pidió tres capitulaciones contra derechos divinos y humanos que tenía aquella Universidad: vivir dentro del Colegio, siendo como era Judío; pidió el primer asiento siendo como era contra leyes de la Universidad; pidió que no se le multasen, siendo las multas de los Bedeles». (Note: Ortiz was of *cristiano nuevo* descent.)

[20] There are many parallels between Cano's criticisms of the *Exercises* and those made by his contemporary, the Dominican Tomás de Pedroche, which have been published in *MHSI Polanco Chron. 111*, p. 503 onwards.

approval granted by Paul III, but most of them concern the spirituality of the first Jesuits which he considers, for various reasons, inauthentic.

He argues, first, that although the Society is doing apparent good throughout the Church, its spiritual fruits are out of season, and not destined to last. People who take the *Exercises* emerge from their retreat transformed; young novices preach ardent sermons after a brief period of training; and the Society's spiritual children grow to maturity with remarkable speed [fol. 97v.-100r.]. These are all signs of illuminism on a large scale, the work of the devil who dispenses spiritual gifts liberally in order to lead many astray.

He affirms, secondly, that the members of the Society are not men of proven virtue. This, he argues, is true of those who co-founded it with Ignatius: they lack patience, prudence and humility [fol. 94r; 95v.-96v.][21]. Others are wanting in chastity: he mentions several cases, referring twice to the branch for women founded by Isabel Roser, an experiment which (he claims) ended in sexual licence [fol. 97v; 100v.]. Such failures in chastity are a further legacy of the *dexados* who, beginning with a love of prayer, fell first into error and then into sexual sin.

He reproaches the Society, finally, for abandoning various features of the religious life which had always expressed and safeguarded the virtue of piety. One of these is the public recitation of the divine office, a costom rooted in the Old Testament, and continued by the traditional orders, which Luther had denounced in Germany. The Jesuits were now undermining it in Spain with less clamour but equal efficiency: «Y en España, forsan como el Diablo no puede entrar tan abiertamente con dichos, entra con hechos: porque esos padres de su instituto no tienen alabar a Dios en comunidad» [fol. 101v.]. Another is the practice of corporal penance, which previous founders treasured and developed, but which the Society has neglected: «estos ningunos [ayunos y asperezas] han añadido, ni de coro... ni de ayuno, ni de aspereza de vida, ni de vestido, ni de sueño, ni de cama, lo qual hace toda su santidad sospechosa» [fol. 102r.]. Lastly there is enclosure, a feature of the established orders which fosters holiness in religious who are observant, and protects the world outside from those who are not. The Jesuits have no place for it: «El otro culto de la piedad y

---

[21] The prominence accorded to Torres may be explained by the fact that it was his arrival in Salamanca in 1548 that provided the occasion for Cano's public denunciation of the Society. See Petro de Ribadeneyra, *Vita Ignatii Loyolae*, edited by C. de Dalmases S.J. (Rome, 1965 = MHSI 93), pp. 458-460. On the friendships of Torres in Alcalá during the 1520s, including his contacts with Miona and Tovar, see John E. Longhurst, *Luther's Ghost in Spain* (Lawrence, Kansas, 1969), p. 355.

378

Religión es clausura y encerramiento. Estos no tienen ninguno... de lo qual no se puede salir sino muy pressa salida para ellos, y muy gran perdición para la República Christiana» [fol. 102v].

These considerations lead Cano to apply to the Society the prophecy of St Paul: «Erunt in novissimis diebus homines speciem pietatis habentes, et virtutem eius abnegantes, penetrantes domos, qui captivas ducunt mulierculas» [fol. 101r.][22]. Their false piety is not merely a sign of their Satanic origin: it is a warning that if they are not stopped they will damage both the Church and the State, and bring about in Spain the calamities caused in Germany by the Protestants.

Cano's analysis of the spirituality of St Ignatius and his followers was challenged vigorously by several members of the young Society[23], and modern scholarship has been able to confirm that in many respects it was mistaken. It is true that the enquiries of 1526 into the apostolate of Ignatius in Alcalá were provoked by the edict against the *dexados* which had been issued the previous year[24], and there is evidence that his friends and contacts in the city included some (such as his confessor Miona) who also moved in illuminist circles[25]. There is, however, no indication that Ignatius himself belonged to the group that formed round Pedro de Alcaraz, Isabel de la Cruz and their sympathisers. In important ways, moreover, his teaching differed radically from theirs. The *Exercises*, for instance, offer a training in mental prayer and reveal a concern to interiorise the Christian life (both characteristics of the *alumbrados*), but they do not oppose mental to vocal prayer, nor do they criticise external forms of Church worship, and they give a central place to the Passion of Christ, a devotion that the *dexados* deplored[26].

However, Cano's analysis, though inaccurate in many ways, is valuable. It draws attention to several features of Ignatius' spirituality which he shared with the *alumbrados*, including an aspiration to combine contemplation and action, confidence in the sensible experience of God's love, and faith in the possibility of divine guidance in the ordinary decisions of life[27]. These parallels help to explain the controversy surrounding the *Exercises* in his lifetime, and some of the

---

[22] Cano's quotation from Scripture is an edited version of 2 Timothy 3:1-6.

[23] See FNI, 302.

[24] Milagros Ortega Costa de Emmart, «San Ignacio de Loyola en el 'Libro de alumbrados': nuevos datos para su primer proceso», *Arbor* 107 (1980), pp. 163-170.

[25] Luis Fernández Martín, «Iñigo de Loyola y los alumbrados», *Hispania Sacra* 35 (1983), pp. 585-680.

[26] On devotion to the Passion see Terence O'Reilly, «*Saint Ignatius Loyola and Spanish Erasmianism*», *Archivum Historicum Societatis Iesu* 43 (1974), pp. 301-321.

[27] See Antonio Márquez, «Origen y caracterización del iluminismo (según un parecer de Melchor Cano)», *Revista de Occidente* 21 (1968), pp. 320-333.

changes of emphasis that occurred after his death, such as the move away from the second method of making an election towards the third[28]. Cano's passionate conviction that the Society was a «novedad» [fol. 104v.], breaking with sacrosanct precedents, also helps us to understand the deep hostility aroused by the new order when its foundation was being approved[29], as well as the decision of Paul IV, once Ignatius had died, to impose on its members an obligation to chant the office in common. Perhaps it was this decision of the Pope, taken in September 1558, that encouraged Cano a few weeks later to consider sending him the *Censura*[30]. We do not know if Paul IV received it, but if he did it can only have fuelled his misgivings about Ignatius, and his resolve to reform the Jesuits.

## SUMARIO

Uno de los más ardientes y tempranos críticos de San Ignacio fue el teólogo dominico Melchor Cano, que creyó que su espiritualidad era una forma de aquel tipo de iluminismo practicado por los *alumbrados* o *dexados*. En una carta de 5 de octubre de 1558 recordaba que había puesto sus puntos de vista por escrito y que pensaba mostrarlos al Papa Paulo IV. Este documento, que posteriormente se extravió, parece que se ha conservado en un manuscrito de la British Library titulado *Censura y parecer... contra el Instituto de los PP. Jesuitas*.

En el curso de este escrito, Cano pone en cuestión la reputada santidad de Ignacio, mencionando tres entrevistas que con él tuvo en Roma. Describe también los aspectos de los *Ejercicios Espirituales* que él consideraba «iluministas», en particular sus estímulos hacia una espiritualidad contemplativa y afectiva, bajo la guía del Espíritu. Finalmente, arguye que la espiritualidad de la Compañía de Jesús, di-

---

[28] See Jacques Roi, «l'élection d'après Saint Ignace. Interprétations diverses», *Revue d'Ascétique et de Mystique* 42 (1962), pp. 305-323.

[29] Discussed in Marcel Bataillon, «D'Erasme à la Compagnie de Jésus. Protestation et intégration dans la Réforme Catholique au XVIᵉ siècle», *Archives de Sociologie des Religions* 24 (1967), pp. 57-81.

[30] See James Broderick S.J., *The Progress of the Jesuits (1156-79) (London, 1946), pp. 27-31.*

380

ferente en muchos aspectos de la de las Ordenes Religiösas ya establecidas, era una amenaza para la Iglesia y para el Estado. El tratado de Melchor Cano, aunque inexacto en muchos puntos, no deja de tener un cierto valor histórico, en cuanto que llama la atención sobre ciertos rasgos de la espiritualidad ignaciana que ayudan a comprender la controversia que provocó durante la vida del santo y en el período que siguió inmediatamente a su muerte.

## RESUME

L'un des plus ardents et précoces critiques de saint Ignace fut le théologien dominicain Melchor Cano, qui était convaincu que sa spiritualité était une forme de ce type d'illuminisme pratiqué par les *alumbrados* ou *dexados*. Dans une lettre du 5 octobre 1558, il déclarait avoir rassemblé par écrit toute une série d'observations qu'il avait l'intention de montrer au Pape Paul IV. Ce document, qui postérieurement fut égaré, semble avoir été conservé dans un manuscrit de la British Library sous le titre de *Censura y parecer... contra el Instituto de los Padres Jesuitas*.

Dans ce document, Cano remet en question la réputée sainteté d'Ignace, citant trois entretiens qu'il eut avec lui à Rome. Il y décrit également les aspects des *Exercices Spirituels* qu'il considérait «illuministes», en particulier ses encouragements à la spiritualité contemplative et affective, sous la conduite de l'Esprit. Finalement, il affirme que la spiritualité de la Compagnie de Jésus, différente dans de nombreux aspects des Ordres Religieux déjà établis, représentait une menace pour l'Eglise et pour l'Etat. Le traité de Melchor Cano, bien qu'inexact dans de nommbreux aspects, conserve cependant une certaine valeur historique, en soulignant certains traits de la spiritualité ignatienne qui aident à comprendre la polémique que le Saint souleva au cours de sa vie, ainsi que dans la période immédiatement postérieure à sa mort.

# V

Melchor Cano's *Censura y parecer contra el Instituto de los Padres Jesuitas*. A transcription of the British Library manuscript

For J.S. Cummins

The *Censura y parecer* that Melchor Cano directed against the Jesuits is a crucial source for the study of his views on the Society of Jesus and on its founder Ignatius Loyola. Despite its importance, however, it has been relatively neglected by historians, many of whom appear to have been unaware of its existence. The pages that follow trace the history of the text, discuss our present knowledge of the versions in which it has survived, and offer a description and an edition of a British Library manuscript in which it is preserved.[1]

## I

The earliest references to the *Censura* occur in letters written in Spain during the 1550's. In October 1557 Melchor Cano was elected Provincial at a chapter of the Dominicans in Segovia, but for various reasons Rome did not ratify the election and he returned to the house of San Esteban in Salamanca where he was prior. A few months later, in February 1558, he set out for Rome in order to attend the general chapter which was scheduled for 29 May,[2] and as the news of his journey spread through Castile it filled members of the Jesuit order with dismay. Rumour had it that he intended to confer with the Pope, Paul IV, about the Society of Jesus, and it was notorious that both men were implacably hostile to the young order. On 4 April Pedro de Ribadeneira wrote to the General, Diego Laínez, and warned him that he had heard "que el Mº Cano es provincial de su orden en Castilla, y que va a Roma a su capítulo, con determinación de desengañar al

---

[1]The research on which this article is based could not have been completed without the expertise and assistance of Dr. Barry Taylor of the Hispanic Section of the British Library, who supplied a description of Egerton MS. 453 and carefully checked my transcription, Professor J.S. Cummins, who kindly directed me towards the writings of Miguel Mir, Luis Martín and Andrés Mendo, and Mrs. Janet Hamilton, who answered my queries about the Latin passages in the *Censura*. To each of them I am deeply indebted.

[2]Fermín Caballero, *Melchor Cano*, Conquenses ilustres, 2 (Madrid: Colegio Nacional de Sordo-mudos y de Ciegos, 1871), 110-111.

papa en lo que toca a la Compañía, etc., y que para esto es menester mucho favor".[3] At about the same time the alarm felt in certain quarters was voiced by G. Battista Ribera who solemnly declared, "Imminet ruinae universae Societatis", and although the melodrama of the phrase made Diego Laínez laugh he was well aware of how grave the crisis was.[4]

Popular rumour about Cano's intentions was not mistaken. In the event he was obliged to abandon his journey at Rosas, because of diplomatic tensions between the Papacy and Spain. A few months later, in the October, he wrote from Valladolid to the royal confessor, Fray Bernardo de Fresnada, and explained that he was deeply disappointed, not only because in Rome he had hoped to regularise his election, but because he had planned to show the Pope what he had written about the Society, and thereby forestall the harm he feared it would do:

> Allende de lo que a mí tocaba yo pretendía comunicar con el
> papa los apuntamientos que tengo contra yerros desta
> nueva compañía, por descargar mi conciencia y tentar si por
> aquella vía se ponía algun reparo a tanto mal como yo
> temo desta gente.[5]

What did these notes or jottings (*apuntamientos*) contain? Ever since 1548, when Cano had begun to attack the Jesuits in public, the General in Rome had received from members of the Society in Spain a steady flow of information about his campaign, and in one of these bulletins there is evidence that as early as 1555 the contents of the *Censura* were familiar to Dominicans in Castile. On 14 February in that year Antonio de Araoz reported from Valladolid that some friendly colleagues of Cano had explained why he looked on Ignatius with such suspicion:

> Algunos Padres dominicos doctos, que quisieron saver dél sus
> fundamentos, me los dixieron, y son tan sin fundamento, que es

---

[3]Pedro de Ribadeneira, *Confesiones, Epistolae aliaque scripta inedita*, 2 vols (Madrid: La Editorial Ibérica, 1920-1923), vol. 1, 292

[4]Mario Scaduto, *L'epoca di Giacomo Laínez. Il Governo: 1556-1565* (Rome: La Civiltà Cattolica, 1964), 539-541.

[5]Caballero, 532-533.

lástima ver en tal porfía vn hombre de sus partes y letras. Estos Padres quedan bien satisfechos, y lo dizen á vozes. Dizen que dize de V. P.: Primero, que, ablándole, luego V. P. le descubrió y dixo reuelaçiones, y avn creo que le confesó que avía ydo huyendo de España. 2, que V. P. le alabó mucho á vno que comulgaba cada día, y que haziéndole venir delante dél, alló que era mentecapto, de que V. P. quedó bien corrido. 3, que asímismo V. P. le alabó mucho á çierto médico (creo era Inigo López), et tamen él supo que avía resignado ciertos beneficios, creo, curados á vn sobrino suyo, que estaba en Spaña. 4, que, yendo con V. P. á casa de vn cardenal, dixo V. P. á vn page, que dixiese al cardenal que estaba allí Ignatio, ó el confesor de madama, ó el prepósito de la Compañía: y también dize de vnos palos ó diferençias, y de çierto oficio que V. P. hizo en ello. Destas cosas infiere él vna conclusión arto de reyr y de llorar. También dize, creo que él, que la Compañía no fué aprobada canónicamente, y otras cosas indignas de dezirlas él, y de scribirlas yo. Gloria á Dios.[6]

The summary is secondhand and the tone derisory, but the points outlined clearly correspond to passages in the *Censura* as we know it now.[7]

The letter of Araoz was not the General's only source of information about the *Censura*. At some point (the precise date is not known) members of the Society managed to procure a copy of the text, perhaps from Dominicans critical of Cano, and they sent it secretly to Rome where it was filed away.[8] Pedro de Ribadeneira probably had it in mind when, years later, he alluded to the *Censura* in a manuscript entitled *De las persecuciones de la Compañía* which was left unpublished at his death. In the chapter on *la persecución de Melchor Cano* he wrote:

Viviendo él (a lo que entiendo) se escribió un papel contra nuestro Instituto y contra la santidad de N.B.P. Ignacio y

[6]*Epistolae Mixtae es variis Europae Locis ab anno 1537 ad 1556 scriptae,* 5 vols. (Madrid: Avrial, 1898-1900), vol. 4, 548

[7]The passages concerned may be seen in the *Censura* at ff. 94r-95v and 97r-97v.

[8]Antonio Astráin, *San Ignacio de Loyola, 1540-1556,* Historia de la Compañía de Jesús en la Asistencia de España, vol. I (Madrid: Sucesores de Rivadeneyra, 1902), 324 n.2

la de sus hijos, que entonces andaba, y después acá ha
andado, en manos de algunos frailes de Santo Domingo.

He went on to wonder if the document had been written by Cano himself,
or dictated to others who had added points of their own. He himself did
not know:

> No sé si este papel lo compuso el mismo M. Cano, o algún otro
> u otros frailes de su Orden escribiendo lo que decía, y
> añadiendo por ventura cosas recogidas de hablillas y
> cuentecillos impertinentes de gente ociosa.[9]

The death of Paul IV on 18 August 1559, and the election of his
successor Pius IV later that year, eased the situation of the Society as a
whole, and in Spain the change of atmosphere was confirmed when Melchor
Cano died suddenly in Toledo on 30 September 1560.[10] Copies of the
*Censura*, however, continued to circulate, and proved to be of interest,
naturally enough, to critics of the Jesuits who were eager to make a case
against the order. One of these was the Catholic apologist Gaspar Schopp
or Scioppius (1576-1649), the author of many anti-Jesuit tracts which were
eventually placed on the Index.[11] Under the pseudonym of Alfonso de
Vargas of Toledo he published a work in the 1630's in which he mentioned
a treatise of Melchor Cano entitled *Iudicio de Secta Jesuitarum*. This, he
affirmed, survived in a manuscript written by the author himself. He went
on to quote a passage from it, virtually identical with one in the *Censura* as
it has come down to us.

> Si me acerco a tratar de los fundadores de esta
> Compañía, es su general un cierto *Iñigo*, que huyó
> de España, cuando la Inquisición quería prenderle, por haberse
> dicho que era herege de la secta de los Alumbrados. Fue
> a Roma, pidió ser juzgado por el Papa, y como no había

---

[9]*Cartas de San Ignacio de Loyola*, 6 vols. (Madrid: Aguado, 1887-1889), vol. I, 525.

[10]Caballero, 135.

[11]J. Mercier, "Schopp (Gaspard)", *Dictionnaire de Théologie Catholique* vol. 14.2, cols.
1571-1574.

quien le acusase, fue absuelto.[12]

At about the same time the *Censura* was quoted extensively in another anti-Jesuit work published in Spain under the title *Juicio universal y parto singular de conceptos ocultos*. Its anonymous author included among his sources "el insigne *Tratado* del Sr. Obispo de Canarias". In this light but stinging jest the Society of Jesus is put on trial before a judge named *Juicio Humano*. The chief prosecutor is Melchor Cano, and the defendants are the five Jesuits singled out in the *Censura*: Iñigo, Salmerón, Laynez, Torres and Fabio. The prosecutor's case includes several passages, printed in italics, which are drawn from the *Censura*. They concern Pierre Favre's mission to Germany (cf. *Censura* f. 95v), the behaviour of Laínez and Salmerón at Trent (cf. f.96r), the legality of the Society's approbation (cf. f.97r-97v), its association with the sisters founded by the Countess of Guastalda (ibid.), and the sexual licence of some Jesuits (cf. f.100v).[13] This pamphlet, which was banned by the Inquisition, does not appear to have survived into modern times, but manuscript copies of the work are preserved in libraries in Coimbra and Vienna.[14]

A century later anti-Jesuit feeling came to a head in the events that led Pope Clement XIV to suppress the Society of Jesus in July 1773. A flood of literature hostile to the order appeared in print, and it seems to have included the *Censura*. On 20 June 1777 the Inquisitor General and bishop of Salamanca, Felipe Beltrán, prohibited a list of writings, among them:

Un papel impreso en quarto en quatro hojas útiles, con este título: *Censura y parecer que dio el P. M. Fr. Melchor Cano,*

---

[12]Alphonsi de Vargas, Toletani, *Relatio ad Reges et Principes Christianos de Stratagematis et Sophismatis Politicis Societatis Iesu ad Monarchiam Orbis terrarum sibi conficiendam* (printed in Germany). In the British Library there are several editions of the work. In those I have consulted the passage from the *Iudicium* is quoted in Latin; they date from 1636 and 1641, and the quotation occurs on p.21 and p.46 respectively. Fermín Caballero (352,401) examined another edition of 1641 in which the passage was cited in Spanish, and this is the text reproduced here.

[13]Caballero, 355-359.

[14]Caballero 356 n.1; José Simón Díaz, *Bibliografía de la literatura hispánica*, vol. XII (Madrid: C.S.I.C, 1982), 570.

*de la Orden de Predicadores, contra el instituto de los
Padres Jesuitas:* sin fecha, ni lugar de impresión.[15]

Early in the present century Miguel Mir claimed to have seen a copy of this
edition, but he did not indicate where he come across it, and no other copies
of it are recorded in modern bibliographies.[16]

The study of the *Censura* in recent times may be said to have begun
with the publication in 1871 of Fermín Caballero's biography of its author.
He was aware that the text of Cano's work had circulated in manuscript in
the seventeenth century and that it had been published in the eighteenth, but
despite an extensive search he was unable to trace it. He concluded that it
had been lost irretrievably, but he was not surprised:

> Al cuidado que pondrían los hijos de San Ignacio en que
> pereciese escrito tan ofensivo, debieron unirse los deseos de
> los mismos devotos del Obispo renunciante, interesados en
> que desapareciese un lunar que, a su juicio, empañaba
> la buena memoria del famoso escritor.[17]

In 1900 Caballero's pessimistic conclusion was challenged by Miguel Mir.
Writing anonymously in a collaborative work entitled *Crisis de la Compañía
de Jesús*, he announced that he had seen a transcription of the *Censura* in the
hand of don Ramón Cabrera, a member of the Spanish Academy. Although
he did not know the source on which the transcription was based he
surmised that it had come from the library of the dukes of Alba, a
conjecture made plausible by the fact that Cano was closely associated with
the Albas and managed to convince them that his view of the Jesuits was
correct.[18] Mir went on to publish Cabrera's transcription in full, with

---

[15]Caballero, 359.

[16]Miguel Mir, *Historia interna documentada de la Compañía de Jesús*, 2 vols. (Madrid:
Ratés Martín, 1913), vol.2, 620.

[17]Caballero, 360.

[18]On Cano and the house of Alba see John W. O'Malley, *The First Jesuits* (Cambridge,
Massachusetts, and London: Harvard University Press, 1993), 293-294; Scaduto, 564.

some minor amendments of his own.[19] Six years later, on 11 December 1906, the *Crisis* was placed on the Index.[20] Meanwhile, in 1902 the Jesuit historian Antonio Astráin had drawn attention to the manuscript version of the *Censura* in the archives of the Society of Jesus in Rome. He did not publish the text but he provided a summary of its argument which included some quotations. These indicated that the manuscript in Rome differed in many small but significant details from the one transcribed by Cabrera, an important point in view of Ribadeneira's reflections on its origins. Astráin, however, did not refer to the Cabrera manuscript, and was apparently unaware of its publication by Miguel Mir.[21] In 1913 a further version of the *Censura* appeared in Mir's posthumous work, *Historia interna documentada de la Compañía de Jesús*. It was based on two sources: the manuscript transcribed by Cabrera and the eighteenth-century pamphlet, a rare copy of which Mir said he had consulted. He did not refer to the earlier version in the *Crisis*, nor did he mention the manuscript in Rome, though he was evidently familiar with the work of Astráin. Ten years later, on 2 May 1923, the *Historia interna* was put on the Index.[22]

It might have been thought that the burst of interest in the *Censura* which occurred between 1900 and 1913 would inspire further research into the text and its history, but this is not, in fact, what happened. The

---

[19]*Crisis de la Compañia de Jesús* (Barcelona: Antoniana, 1900), 150-159. The book was published under the name of Segismundo Pey-Ordeix who indicated in the preface that he was not the author (9). Mir's reasons for choosing anonymity stemmed from his uneasy relations with the Society which he had left in 1891. On the background see Manuel Revuelta González, *La Compañía de Jesús en la España contemporánea*, 2 vols. (Madrid: Universidad Pontificia Comillas, 1984-1991), vol. 2, 694-701; *Memorias del P. Luis Martín*, edited by J.R. Eguillor, M. Revuelta and R. Ma. Sanz de Diego, vol. 2 (Rome: Institutum Historicum S.I., 1988), 553 n. 81; Miquel Batllori, "Mir y Noguera (Michel)", *Dictionnaire de Spiritualité* vol. 10.2, cols. 1273-1274. Despite the similar title, there does not appear to be a connection between the work published by Pey-Ordeix and Mir in 1900 and one by Andrés Mendo, *Crisi de Societate Iesu* (Lyons, 1666) which was also placed on the Index. It is catalogued in Antonio Palau y Dulcet, *Manuel del Librero Hispanoamericano*, vol. 4 (Oxford and Barcelona: Dolphin and Dulcet, 1956), 33.

[20]Revuelta González, vol.2, 699 n. 115.

[21]Astráin, 321-340, 368-370.

[22]Mir, vol. 2, 621-631; Revuelta González, vol. 2, 701 n. 120

publication of the *Censura* by Miguel Mir was mentioned in a number of encyclopaedia articles about Cano, beginning with one by the Dominican P. Mandonnet who in 1905 referred wittily to "la célèbre censure de Cano .... dont tant d'auteurs ont parlé, et que presque personne n'a vue".[23] References to Mir's work were also made in articles by John R. Volz in 1908 and E. Lamalle S.J. in 1949.[24] In more specialist studies, however, the *Censura* was often conspicuous by its absence. The Dominican Vicente Beltrán de la Heredia considered Cano's attacks on the Jesuits in one of the chapters of *Las corrientes de espiritualidad entre los dominicos de Castilla durante la primera mitad del siglo XVI* (Salamanca, 1941), but at no point in his analysis did he mention Cano's text. Nor did he do so twelve years later in an article on Cano in the *Dictionnaire de Spiritualité*.[25] Jesuit specialists were often reticent too. In 1945 Feliciano Cereceda devoted 48 pages to a detailed account of Cano's relations with the early Society but he did not refer to the *Censura* at any point even though it is apparent from his footnotes that he knew the *Historia interna* of Mir.[26] A year later Ignacio Iparraguirre, in the first part of his history of the *Spiritual Exercises*, referred in a footnote to the Roman manuscript and to Astráin's analysis of it, but he refrained from discussing the *Censura* in detail, and he made no mention of the editions of Mir. C. Gutiérrez also alluded to the manuscript of the *Censura* conserved in Rome, but he did not refer to the study of it by Astráin, nor did he mention Mir's editions of the text.[27] In view of this response by the specialists it is not surprising, perhaps, that the *Censura* does not figure in the standard bibliographies of Gilmont and Daman,

---

[23]"Cano, Melchior", *Dictionnaire de Théologie Catholique*, vol. 2, cols. 1537-1540.

[24]John R. Volz, "Cano, Melchior", *The Catholic Encyclopaedia*, vol. 3, 251-252; E. Lamalle, "Cano, Melchor", *Enciclopedie Cattolica*, vol. 3, cols. 533-534.

[25]"Cano (Melchior)", *Dictionnaire de Spiritualité*, vol. 7, cols. 73-76.

[26]*Diego Laínez en la Europa religiosa de su tiempo 1512-1565*, 2 vols. (Madrid: Cultura Hispánica, 1945-1946), vol. I, 369-417. There is a reference to Mir at 372 n.5.

[27]I. Iparraguirre, *Práctica de los Ejercicios de San Ignacio de Loyola en vida de su autor (1522-1556)* (Rome: Institutum Historicum S.I., 1946), 96; C. Gutiérrez, *Españoles en Trento* (Valladolid: C.S.I.C., 1951), 838-839.

Iparraguirre, and Polgár,[28] nor that it receives no mention in the studies of Hugo Rahner, Joseph de Guibert and Ricardo García-Villoslada.[29] The reasons for this lacuna require further investigation, but its consequences for scholarship are clear: although versions of the *Censura* have been known and accessible for nearly one hundred years, we do not yet possess a critical edition of the text.

## II

Our knowledge of the text of the *Censura* may be summarised as follows:

(i)   A manuscript in the hand of Ramón Cabrera, based possibly on an original in the library of the dukes of Alba. Published by Miguel Mir in 1900 and 1913.

(ii)  A printed pamphlet banned by the Inquisitor General in 1777. Seen by Miguel Mir and used by him in his edition of 1913.

(iii) A manuscript in the Roman Archive of the Society of Jesus (A.R.S.I. Hisp. 144, ff. 3$^r$-7v). Summarised by Astráin in 1902. Unpublished.

(iv)  A manuscript in the British Library (Egerton 453, ff. 91-105v). Catalogued by Pascual de Gayangos in 1877 but not analysed

---

[28]Jean François Gilmont and Paul Daman, *Bibliographie Ignatienne (1894-1957)*, (Paris-Louvain: Desclée de Brouwer, 1958); Ignacio Iparraguirre, *Orientaciones bibliográficas sobre San Ignacio de Loyola*, second edition (Rome: Institutum Historicum S.I., 1965); Lászlo Polgár, *Bibliographie sur l'histoire de la Compagnie de Jésus 1901-1980*, 3 vols. (Rome: Institutum Historicum S.I., 1981-1991).

[29]Hugo Rahner, *The Spirituality of St. Ignatius Loyola. An Account of its Historical Development* (Chicago: Loyola Press, 1980) (the German original was first published in 1947); Joseph de Guibert, *La spiritualité de la Compagnie de Jésus: esquisse historique* (Rome: Institutum Historicum S.I., 1953); Ricardo García-Villoslada, *San Ignacio de Loyola. Nueva biografía*, (Madrid: Editorial Católica, 1986).

until 1992.[30] Hitherto unpublished.

A detailed description of the British Library manuscript has been provided by Dr. Barry Taylor: Egerton MSS 452-456 are five volumes of 'papeles tocantes a los Jesuitas' formed by Tomás de Iriarte (1750-91), author of the *Fábulas literarias* and historian.[31] These tracts are copies, in a variety of 17th and 18th century hands, of documents dating from 1587 onwards. The latest date mentioned is 1789 (Eg. 452, item 7). The items in Eg. 453 have been reordered: the first item is numbered in a contemporary hand 'Miscelanea No. 6' and foliated in ink 207-224; items 2-4 are numbered 'No. 8', 'No. 3' and 'No. 7' respectively. The remainder are not numbered. Cano's *Censura* is the fourth item in Eg. 453. Page measurements: 215 x 150 mm; written space: 155 x 110mm. The text occupies ff. 92-105v, preceded by a title leaf (f. 91), on rougher paper, reading 'No. 7. Jesuitas Censura de M. Cano contra el Instituto de la C[ompañí]a'. The text is a fair copy, written in long lines, about twenty to the page, in a single 18th (possibly 17th) century hand. There are changes of ink or pen at f. 102r, line 3, after 'Hay' and f. 103v, line 7, after 'esto'. There are catchwords at ff. 93v, 94v, 95v, 96v, 97v, 99v, 101v, 103v. The evidence of the watermark (a monstrance with IC in the centre) and the slightly smaller size of ff. 100-101 suggest that the following leaves are geminate: 98/99, 100/101, 102/103, giving a collation for this document of seven bifolia.

In the transcription of the manuscript that follows certain norms have been observed: accents have been added, words have been separated or joined (e.g. *desto* is rendered as *de esto*) and punctuation has been modified in accordance with modern practice; words underlined in the original have been italicized; abbreviations have been resolved; *e* with a cedilla has been

---

[30]Pascual de Gayangos, *Catalogue of the Manuscripts in the Spanish Language in the British Library*, 4 vols. (London: British Museum, 1875-1893; reprinted 1976), vol.2, 178. The BL manuscript was included subsequently in the bibliographies of José Simón Díaz: *Bibliografía de la literature hispánica*, vol.7 (Madrid: C.S.I.C., 1967), 396; *Domínicos de los siglos xvi y xvii: escritos localizados* (Madrid, 1977), 110. It has been analysed in Terence O'Reilly, "Melchor Cano and the Spirituality of St. Ignatius Loyola", *Ignacio de Loyola y su tiempo*, edited by Juan Plazaola (Bilbao: Universidad de Deusto, 1992), 369-380 (reproduced in the present volume as essay IV). See also the discussion in O'Malley, 292-294.

[31]See the descriptions in Gayangos, vol.2, 177-180. Eg.379 is the correspondence of Iriarte and Eugenio Llaguno y Amirola, dated 1788 (Gayangos, vol.I, 331).

rendered as *ae*; scribal errors have been amended in the text and recorded in the footnotes; folio numbers have been indicated between brackets; scriptural references have been supplied.

## III

### (92r) Censura y parecer que dio el Padre Maestro Fray Melchor Cano de la Orden de Predicadores contra el Instituto de los Padres Jesuitas

1.    Toda esta materia se reduce a tres puntos. In primo adducuntur ea quae valent in favorem eorum. In secundo ista eadem tanquam suspecta rationibus convincuntur, aut saltem tanquam dubia. Tertio, así de su instituto y manera de vivir como de la divina Escritura y costumbre de la Iglesia en todas las Religiones que ha instituido se convence[1] el negocio de éstos no ir tan ordenado, y que por lo menos se debe sospechar y vehementemente temer que han de ser perjudiciales a España y a toda la Religión Christiana (92v).

2.    Acerca del primer punto in eorum favorem podemos traer que sus fundadores son buenos. Lo segundo, su institución aprobada por la Iglesia. Lo tercero, que no conocemos en ellos pecados. Lo quarto, que harán mucho provecho: videlicet, dan buen exemplo, son muy devotos, predican buenas[2] cosas, convierten almas, remedian pobres y hacen otras cosas muy buenas, de los quales frutos dice el Evangelio A fructibus eorum cognoscetis eos.[3]

3.    His suppositis pro eorum favore, el Autor frequentibus rationibus et conjecturis destruit atque confundit eorum ordinem eiusque dogmata. Quanto a lo primero, de la santidad de sus fundadores, se supone que Dios como sumamente próvido planta sus cosas no sobre arena o viento (93r) sino sobre firmam petram.[4] Ex quo sequitur que si esta religión es de Dios y no

---

[1]In the manuscript the word 'conoce' has been amended to 'convence'.

[2]In the manuscript 'bue' is an overwriting.

[3]Mt 7:16.

[4]Cf. Mt 7:24-27; Lk 6:47-9.

del Diablo que sus primeras piedras o fundamento han de ser muy santos y justos. Supónese lo segundo que el ver que una gente haga mucho provecho espiritual en el pueblo Christiano no convence ni concluye no ser artificio del demonio, pues como solícito engañador de los buenos, ya que no puede por especie de mal, se transfigura algunas veces en ángel de luz,[5] y alumbra y da sentimientos espirituales, y aun ayuda de esta suerte a muchos en el camino del cielo para después dar con otros muchos en el camino y hoyo del infierno, como tenemos exemplo manifiesto en España de los Alumbrados y Dexados que fueron primos hermanos de éstos, los quales por de - (93v) voción y contemplación y otras cosas divinas hicieron tanto y más fruto que estos Padres, aunque el provecho de éssos es más universal, pero pasaron poco a poco (siguiendo la falsa interpretación de aquello del Apóstol San Juan, 1. Canónica, 2: Unctio eius docebit vos de omnibus[6]) a pensar que eran impecables, y que no[7] habían de hacer sino lo que les venía a la imaginación, por haberse ofrecido todo a Dios. Y de aquí vinieron a pensar que ni la fornicación ni otras cosas semejantes eran pecados, sino que ofreciéndoseles adulterar pensaban que era dictamen del Espíritu Santo, y el ponerlo por obra acto meritorio. Destruyó esta heregía la Inquisición de España, de los quales Hereges aun hasta hoy hay algunos en la cárcel perpetua. De este supuesto se sigue (94r) que aunque veamos algunas gentes hacer provecho podemos justamente, atendiendo a otras cosas, sospechar, o temer el fruto.

4.    Viniendo pues a los fundadores de esta Compañia que llaman de Jesús, el General de ellos es un Iñigo, el qual se escapó huyendo de España porque le quería coger la Inquisición, porque se decía ser de los Alumbrados o Dexados arriba dichos. Fuése a Roma y pidió ser juzgado del Papa, y no habiendo quien le acusase fue dado por libre. Sus compañeros y Apóstoles son Torres, Fabro, Salmerón y Laínez.[8] Dicamus de singulis. Estando el autor una vez en Roma deseó ver a Iñigo, y hablando con él, sin ningún

---

[5]Cf. 2 Co 11:14.

[6]Cf. 1 Jn 2:27.

[7]Omitted in the manuscript which reads 'y que habían de hacer'.

[8]The manuscript reads 'Laines'. The early Jesuits mentioned here are Miguel de Torres (c. 1507-1593), Blessed Pierre Favre (1506-1546), Alfonso Salmerón (1515-1585) and Diego Laínez (1512-1565).

propósito comenzó a hablar con él de su justicia, y de la persecución que le habían hecho en España y quán sin razón, y contó muchas y muy grandes (94v) cosas de las revelaciones que tenía de Dios, y eso sin haber ninguna necesidad, lo qual fue ocasión al autor de que le tubiese por vano y no le diese crédito a sus revelaciones. Después de esto tomóle gana de descubrir más, así de su persona como de sus compañeros.[9] Yendo otra vez a comer con él, alabó a un Santo de su Compañía, el qual siendo llamado le pareció al Autor ser loco. Y siendo preguntado de cosas de Dios dixo muchas heregías; y aquello díxolo y hacíalo de idiota, que no sabía más. Y yéndose de allí el sobredicho Santo, quedándose afrentado el Iñigo, dixo al Autor: «Ése no es herege, es loco, y creo tiene *lucida intervala*; como aora es conjunción de luna, no está tan católico».

5.      Ofrecióse otra vez que yendo a hablar al Cardenal Farnesio[10] (95r) con él, salió un page, y preguntando «¿Quién diré que és?» dixo bien alto: «Decid que es el Maestro Iñigo, o el General de los de la Compañía, o el confesor de Madama,[11] que por qualquier nombre de éstos os entenderá». De lo qual infirió el Autor había allí mucho viento. Habló le otra vez a un Clérigo Médico que allí estaba, de gran Santo, el qual según se supo tenía propósito de estarse en Roma curando toda su vida; y escudriñando[12] más, se supo que el dicho Santo tenía dos beneficios curados en España, y encomendados a un Letor de Griego en Alcalá, que ni los servía ni podía. Sucedió pues que habiendo dado en Roma una bofetada a un seglar sobre no sé qué asientos, y no queriendo el injuriado perdonar,[13] andando el Iñigo de por medio haciendo las (95v) amistades, uno de la Compañía acabó que diese al otro de palos, que él lo sufriría, y así serían amigos, porque así lo había él concertado. Como el Autor reprehendiese eso respondió el sobredicho Santo que no se había hecho sin consejo de teología, porque se

---

[9]See Astráin, 325 n.1, who refers to a passage in the chronicle of Juan Polanco in which there is an allusion to a meeting or meetings between Cano and Loyola: J. Polanco, *Vita Ignatii Loiolae et rerum Societatis Jesu historica*, 6 vols. (Madrid: MHSI, 1894-1898), vol.1, 298.

[10]Cardinal Alessandro Farnese.

[11]Margaret of Austria.

[12]The manuscript reads 'escudrinando'.

[13]In the manuscript the final 'r' is an overwriting.

había demandado licencia al Vicario del Papa.[14] De todas estas cosas coligió el Autor ignorancia así del derecho divino como del humano; de beatificar al Médico con los beneficios curados en España y santificar al loco, ¡grande imprudencia y indiscreción, y gran vanidad de su trato!

6.     El Fabro tubo licencia del Papa para pasar a Alemania y llevar consigo dos clérigos muy necios, y sabido para qué es, para que dixesen misa entre los hereges: cosa de gran vani-(96r)dad. Los otros dos, Salmerón, Laínez,[15] que fueron al Concilio, hablando una vez con el Autor, dando las razones que tenía para parecerle mal su Orden, como entre otras dixese que era novedad, levantóse uno de ellos diciendo: «¿*Novedad? Mas ¡mierda!*». Enojado él de semejante desverguenza, fuéronse los teatinos, y volvieron después a pedirle perdón, fingiendo humildad, con echarle la culpa al injuriado.[16] El otro, Torres, siendo Retor de un Colegio de Salamanca, fue a verse con el Autor, y como beatificase a un Ortiz[17] de Alcalá dixo de él que murió como un[18] Santo, y que así había vivido; un hombre que murió a deshora después de haber muy bien cenado, y un hombre que convidándole con la Cátedra de Biblia de Alcalá pidió muchos días de término para (96v) que le respondiese el Espíritu Santo, y después pidió tres capitulaciones contra derechos divinos y humanos que tenía aquella Universidad: vivir dentro del Colegio, siendo como era Judío; pidió el primer asiento siendo como era contra leyes de la Universidad; pidió que no le multasen, siendo las multas de los Bedeles. Y como el Torres le escusase nunca dixo que aquello era malo, sino imperfecto. Insuper dixo que como el Espíritu Santo no le inspiraba lo que había de hacer que acordó pedir aquellas condiciones, pareciéndole que si se las concedían el Espíritu Santo quería fuese

---

[14]The incidents described occurred between 24 August and 2 September 1545 and involved two Spanish gentlemen, Bustamente de Herrera and Puerto Carrero, who was in minor orders. This was noted by Miguel Mir, *Historia interna*, vol.2, 623 n.4, who referred to the account by Ignatius himself in *Cartas de San Ignacio de Loyola*, vol.1, 203-204. See too Ricardo García-Villoslada, *San Ignacio de Loyola*, 540-541.

[15]The manuscript reads 'Laynes'.

[16]On this altercation see the accounts of Nadal, *Epistolae*, 4 vols. (Madrid: 1898-1905), vol.2, 45 and Polanco, vol.6, 640.

[17]Dr. Pedro Ortiz (d. 1548).

[18]In the manuscript 'un' has been added above the line.

Catedrático. He aquí muchos ramalazos de *Alumbrados* o *Dexados*. Hay otra cosa en *ésos* y en todos los de esta Compañía, que son lisongeros, y entran beatificando (97r) a aquellos con quien tratan y hablan, y unos a otros tienen gran cuidado de beatificarse y predicarse por Santos. Es aquello del Apocalipsi: que los cuernos eran como de cordero, y la lengua como de dragón.[19] Y como lo de Esaías: *Popule meus, qui te beatum praedicant, ipsi te[20] seducunt et decipiunt.*[21] Y el demonio quando acomete a los buenos por aquí empieza.

7.     A lo otro que se puede traer en su[22] favor, videlicet, que el Papa les confirmó su instituto, se responde que el Pontífice les confirmó el fin de su orden, scilicet el predicar por el mundo, que es oficio de Apóstoles, y así se llaman ellos los de la Compañía de Jesús, y sus votos. Primero confirmóles el fin sin medio para este fin, lo qual no hizo el sumo Pontífice con Santo Domingo (97v) ni San Francisco con haber hecho milagros, y haver visto la visión de la Iglesia de San Pedro que se caía, hasta que le traxeron reglas y constituciones para aquel fin; y entonces les confirmó sus órdenes. Hay también otra cosa, que el Papa confirmó el fin de éstos para sesenta y uno para pleno senatu, y por intercesión y soborno de Farnesio (cuya poca santidad todos conocen) y de Madama cuyo confesor era Iñigo. Iten, que en compañía de éstos se confirmó la compañía de las Religiosas de la condesa Guastalda, que paró después en acostarse juntos para ver si tenían las pasiones muertas.[23] Haec de eius confirmatione.

---

[19]Cf. Rv 13:11.

[20]The manuscript reads 'se'.

[21]Cf. Is 3:12: 'Popule meus, qui te beatum dicunt ipsi te decipiunt' (Clementine Vulgate).

[22]The manuscript reads 'en su su favor'.

[23]Ludovica Torelli (1499-1569), Countess of Guastalda, founded an order of sisters which was formally approved by Pope Paul III in 1535, five years before the Society of Jesus. See the article by Giuseppe M. Cagni in *Dictionnaire de Spiritualité* vol.15, cols. 1044-1048. Members of the Society helped with the spiritual direction of her later foundation (1557), a college for poor noble girls. See Ribadeneira, *Confessiones, Epistolae aliaque scripta inedita*, vol.2, 702, 710, 712. In my earlier article (essay IV in this volume) I mistakenly identified this as a reference to the sisters founded by Isabel Roser (377).

8.      A lo tercero y quarto que se trae en su favor, *videlicet*, que porque son buenos, que hacen mucho provecho; y a lo otro que se trae *a fructibus eorum*,[24] etc. (98r).   De lo mucho que se trae en favor sacó el autor mucha sospecha entre ellos, y explica aquella autoridad *attendite a falsis prophetis*,[25] etc. y que *cognoscetis eos*.[26]  Para conocerlos en los frutos es menester grande atención y consideración:  por eso dixo *attendite*.  El ser buenos ellos aora, y al cabo de[27] quarenta días de exercicios o[28] al cabo de quatro meses de la Compañia ser Santos y hacer luego Santos a aquellos con quien tratan, no hace por ellos;  antes ésos son los frutos de los quales dice Christo que les conoceréis, porque esa fruta es[29] sin sazón y muy temprana son los cornezuelos de los Ciruelos.[30]   Unde suspicandum est no sea artificio del Diablo, y la Orden de los Alumbrados más universal, y que el Diablo se transfigura en Angel de Luz[31] y los alumbra, y da gus-(98v)tos[32] espirituales para después mejor urdir su trama.  Porque el orden que Dios tiene en las cosas espirituales va conforme a las naturales: primero es el hombre niño, después varón, y entonces no engendra varones, sino niños; y así va poco a poco comenzando ab imperfectioribus subiendo ad perfectiora.  Así es en la vida espiritual: primero han de ser niños y después paulatim subiendo hasta venir a ser varones perfectos, y aun entonces no han luego de prima instantia y de improviso engendrar varones perfectos, sino niños.  En estos Padres es todo lo contrario:  pues fruto es del qual les conoceréis.  Es fruto antes de tiempo, nuevo, y sin sazón, y contra orden de naturaleza;  porque el mal interior no se conoce tan fácilmente; y aun entre (99r) ellos puede haber muchos engaños que no entiendan.  Es ardid del

---

[24]Mt 7:16.

[25]Mt 7:15.

[26]Mt 7:16, 20.

[27]In the manuscript 'd' has been corrected from 'q'.

[28]In the manuscript 'y' appears to have been amended to 'o'.

[29]Omitted in the manuscript which reads 'esa fruta sin sazón'.

[30]The manuscript reads: 'de los [7-letter word deleted] Ciruelos'.

[31]Cf. 2 Co 11:14.

[32]The manuscript reads: 'gus/gustos'.

Demonio.

9.　Allende de eso, el orden que han tenido todos los Santos que han fundado órdenes es que los Religiosos los vayan criando poco a poco, y esto no en poco tiempo sino en muchos años, en el tiempo del Noviciado, y entre los Novicios mucha mortificación de sí mismos, mucha disciplina, oración, abstinencia, mucho estudio; y después de siete u ocho años de estudio ad minus que salgan a predicar, y esto no luego a los pueblos grandes sino a las Aldeas.　Éstos a cabo de quatro meses de exercicios ya les parece son impecables, y así andan predicando en particular, y dando consejos, y hablando del Espíritu Santo, y beatificando las gentes:　ergo fruto es nuevo (99v) a quo cognoscetis eos.[33]　No es éste buen medio para instituto de Apóstoles[34] de Christo, que fue el dechado de todos los que habían de instituir Religiones Apostólicas.　Christo nos enseñó cómo se habían de hacer y instituir.　Él tubo en su escuela tres años a sus discípulos, y inviándoles a predicar a las Aldeas, y aunque no absolutamente sino ad omnem locum ad quem esset ipse venturus,[35] para que si hiciesen alguna bobería lo remediase el mismo Christo.　Insuper después de haberles dado Christo el Espíritu Santo, qui etiam docuit eos omnem veritatem,[36] no permitió que fuesen luego a predicar al mundo, ni que se dividiesen, sino que primero estubiesen juntos diez u doce años, confiriendo unos con otros, teniendo por Maestra a Nuestra Señora y por Ca-(100r)beza a San Pedro, y después de esto se dividiesen.　Éstos luego después de muy pocos días de exercicios luego hacen el oficio de los otros.　Luego fruta es temprana. *A fructibus, etc.*

10.　Otra fruta de los verdaderos Profetas es paciencia y humildad. Experiencia tenemos en la fingida de Salmerón y Laínez,[37] milagros en su cabeza ningunos, cosa hasta hoy nunca vista en los que han fundado Religiones aprobadas desde San Basilio hasta la última de los Mínimos.

---

[33] Mt 7:16, 20.

[34] The manuscript reads 'Aposto-'.

[35] Cf. Lk 10:1.

[36] Cf Jn 16:13.

[37] The manuscript reads 'Laynes'.

Después de esto hace grande sospecha el color, videlicet, que todos traen, que debe ser *exterminatio faciei*;[38] porque sabe el autor de cierta ciencia que a una muger para que refrenase las pasiones le dieron por consejo tomase el alcanfor, y a otra *ad exterminandam faciem* (100v) le dixo otro que bebiese agua de esparto. Y aumenta más la duda ver que todos ellos traen un color. Los ayunos y huevos[39] con hacer peor sangre no suelen quitar a todos el buen color. Estas cosas dichas parece que hacen algun tanto sospechosas las cosas de éstos. Insuper aconteció a uno que traía las manos por los pechos a una moza que confesaba, y dixo que lo hacía por ver si tenía las pasiones muertas; y otro besando a una muger dixo que no era pecado, porque San Pablo dixo: *Salutate priscam in osculo sancto.*[40] Las quales cosas todas parece que frisan con los *Alumbrados* y *Dexados*, o parece que tiran a los de la Orden de la Condesa Guastalda, prima hermana de éstos.

11. Vengamos ahora al punto tercero (101r) que prometimos al principio. El Apóstol San Pablo 1. ad Thimotheum 8: *Erunt in novissimis[41] diebus homines speciem pietatis habentes, et virtutem eius abnegantes, penetrantes domos, qui captivas ducunt mulierculas.*[42] Esta autoridad parece claro verificarse de aquesta gente al pie de la letra. Porque traen especie de piedad, ut oculis videtur, videlicet, in mortificatione et cultu divino, porque eso quiere decir piedad. Nam est in Deum et parentes ejus.[43] Tamen virtutem abnegantes. Una de las virtudes y fuerza del divino culto es que Dios se alabe con alabanzas públicas, y esto juntos en comunidad los Religiosos y fieles. La qual costumbre ha usado siempre la Iglesia desde su principio, y se levantan todos en tres vigilias y nocturnos a alabar a Dios. Y en la Iglesia que tubo Dios (101v) antiguamente, videlicet en la Sinagoga, David puso Cantores que alabasen a Dios,[44] y hasta aora las Religiones siempre han

---

[38]Cf Mt 6:16.

[39]The manuscript reads 'hueva'.

[40]Cf. Mt. 16:20; 2 Cor 13:12; Rm 16:3; 2 Tm 4:19.

[41]In the manuscript 'imis' has been overwritten from 'emis'.

[42]Cf 2 Tm 3:1, 5, 6. The reference in the text to 1 Tm 8 is erroneous.

[43]Cf. *Summa Theologiae*, 2-2 q.101; q.121.

[44]Cf. 1 Ch 16:4-6; 23:5-6; 25:1; 2 Ch 29:25.

llevado ese culto aprobado y por costumbre muy adelante; el qual quitó[45] Lutero en Alemania diciendo *quod ille erat labor asininus*. Y en España forsan como el Diablo no puede entrar tan abiertamente con dichos entra con hechos; porque esos Padres de su instituto no tienen alabar a Dios en comunidad; imo de su instituto ni rezar las horas Canónicas en particular, sino él que alias tiene obligación de rezarlas ratione ordinis. La otra, *penetrantes domos, captivantes mulierculas*,[46] con llevarles el ánimo con devocioncillas, y con hacer primero que juren *in verba Magistri*, desaficionándolas con beatifi-(102r)carlas y otras cosas, ne alios habeant conciliatores.

12.  Hay otra cosa, y esto no sé si es artificio del Demonio para después descubrirse, y es que se llegan a gente de toda broza, a casados y Obispos, ora residan, ora no; y así juntarán tantos que si después descubre la Inquisición algún mal no puede la Inquisición con tantos. Hay otra virtud de piedad y es[47] que todos quantos santos han hasta aora instituido Religiones siempre sobre los ayunos y asperezas de la Iglesia han puesto y añadido otros. Éstos ningunos han añadido, ni de coro como antes decíamos, ni de ayuno, ni de aspereza de vida, ni de vestido, ni de sueño, ni de cama, lo qual hace toda su santidad sospechosa. Hay más, que a esta orden se llega (102v) gente ambiciosa, videlicet, Judíos y Vizcaynos, los quales in hoc ordine amici facti sunt;[48] y el clérigo seglar, y el que tiene vendidos los frutos de sus beneficios por muchos años, al cabo de quatro meses de Teatino ya escribe cartas como el Apóstol San Pablo, y por falta de theología scatent erroribus. Hay otra cosa: que su instituto no es de estar encerrados en Colegios que tienen sino de andar por el mundo, y solos sin otro medio más que los dichos.

13.  El otro culto de la piedad y Religión es clausura y encerramiento. Éstos no tienen ninguno, sino que pueden salir adonde les pareciere, de lo qual no se puede salir sino muy presta salida para ellos y muy gran perdición para la República Christiana, porque tanto dura (103r) una Religión quanto

---

[45]In the manuscript the 'i' is an overwriting.

[46]Cf. 2 Tm 3:6.

[47]In the manuscript 'es' is an overwriting.

[48]Cf. Lk 23:12.

dura su clausura. Porque la clausura sirve[49] de conservar la santidad todo el tiempo que dura, y sirve después de perdida para tener los Religiosos encerrados como fieras para que no dañen a otros. Unde como estos Religiosos comiencen por donde los otros acaban y se pierden no puede dexar de durar poco, de lo qual se sigue, aora sean instituidos por Dios, ahora sea artificio del Demonio, que han de caer y ser perniciosos en la República Christiana, porque por el mismo caso que están tenidos por Santos han de querer llevar adelante tal opinión, y como por otra parte caygan han de querer dogmatizar sus errores. De lo qual se sigue claramente o que han de dañar a muchos de secreto con su mu-(103v)cha libertad y no diferencia de hábito y gran confianza que los demás tienen de su virtud o santidad, o que, teniendo fuerzas para salir en público, estragarán la simplicidad y Christiandad de España......[50] Añádese a esto que como el camino de Dios alius sic, alius autem[51] sic est, cum Beatus Augustinus distinguat contra quatuor qualitates humorum quatro maneras de Santos, éstos tienen para todos unos mismos exercicios de contemplación, como no todos sean aptos para ella: ergo signum est que no permanecerán mucho tiempo. Anádese a esto que con los mismos exercicios hay algunos no tan sanos,[52] porque post tot septimanas pollicentur gratiam y ternura de corazón y sentimientos espirituales, que parece obligar a Dios, que es (104r) un género de tentarle. Lo qual reprendió aquella muger *Judith* porque habían dicho los de Bethulia que se rendirían si de allí a seis días no les socorría Dios.[53] Insuper tienen una cláusula no muy sana que dice que quamvis licitum sit apto ad cor complecti, consultius erit quod anima eius maneat in aequilibrio, para hacer lo que Dios le inspirare.[54] Hay también otra cosa, de la qual se puede temor mal, que de la manera que Pelagio vino a levantar tanto el libre alvedrío que negó la necesidad de la gracia de Dios, y Lutero levantó tanto

---

[49]The manuscript reads 'dirve'.

[50]In the manuscript 'España' is followed by six points. It is not clear why.

[51]In the manuscript 'autem' is added above the line.

[52]The manuscript reads 'vanos'.

[53]Jdt 8:9-12.

[54]See Astráin, 369 n. 1, who surmises that Cano here had in mind two passages in the *Spiritual Exercises:* the fifteenth annotation [15] and the second point in the first way of making an Election [179].

la gracia de Dios que vino a negar el libre alvedrío, así también éstos levantan tanto el conformarse con la voluntad de Dios *etiam in volito materiali* que quieren decir que en ninguna causa nos entris-(104v)tezcamos, o a lo menos parece que se debe temer no vengan a esto, comoquiera que Christo se entristeció,[55] *quamvis cum ratione superiori* estuviese conforme a Dios, y *ibi* sintiese su miseria, aunque hubiese vencido a Dios por ella.[56] Y esto de no darse nada ni entristecerse por cosa ninguna es vida contenta, y lo que decía San Pablo: *erunt in novissimis diebus homines se ipsos amantes.*[57]

14.     Conclúyese que pues vemos una novedad como ésta, y una cosa hasta ahora nunca usada por los Santos, y una profesión de a cabo de siete años, y las de hasta ahora de año y día, y una gente que se defiende con decir que en habiendo qualquier defecto en los suyos le echan de su Compañía, y que debemos temer y atender, que si nos dixeran, *Hic est Christus in deserto*[58] en lugares (105r) y vidas que hasta ahora no han llevado los Santos, que no les creamos. Y si nos dixeren, *ecce hic est* in *penetralibus,*[59] y en nuestra vida secreta, cuyos exercicios *non*[60] *exhibent hominibus, ut pote legantur,* tampoco lo creamos. *Nam adventus ejus ut fulgur.*[61] Dios dondequiera que está luego se parece. *In secreto* decía Christo *locutus sum nihil.*[62] San Agustín Santo era, y tenía vida Apostólica más que éstos, *attamen cum mulieribus solus non*

---

[55]Cf Mt 26:38.

[56]The manuscript reading 'aunque hubiese vencido a Dios por ella' may include a scribal error, for it seems to imply that in Gethsemane Christ was prepared to go against his Father's will, an argument which would run counter to the point that Cano is making. The original text is not easy to reconstruct. Possibilities include: 'aunque no hubiese vencido a Dios por ella' <u>or</u> 'aunque hubiese vencido Dios por ella' <u>or</u> 'aunque hubiese bendecido a Dios por ella'.

[57]Cf 2 Tm 3:1-2.

[58]Cf. Mt 24:26.

[59]Cf. Mt 24:26.

[60]The manuscript reads 'nos'.

[61]Cf. Mt 24:27.

[62]Cf. Jn 18:20.

22

*loquebatur.* Y los Apóstoles se marabillaron de Christo de que *cum mulieribus solus loqueretur.*[63] Omito etiam que en tratando de Dios, la primera tentación del Demonio invisible es querer hablar luego de él en cierto modo, videlicet, que sienta el otro con quien habláis que así lo sentís. De donde se sigue que ofreciéndose la buena consideración luego se ofrece el cómo se ha de decir; lo qual hace que ya[64] el (105v) mantenimiento no harta del todo al alma pues no es comida para ella sola, sino para sí y su compañero con quien trata. Y esto sin entenderlo ellos mismos pasa por sus casas pues a cabo de quatro días andan luego diciendo sus sentimientos y ternuras, y comenzando sus pláticas y hablas por *«¡Y quán bueno es Dios, y quán amable!».*

15. De todas estas cosas infiere el autor que aunque ahora haya muchos buenos de éstos que a lo menos est timendum de lo adelante. Unde si alguno me preguntare si tratará con ellos le diré que no, y si me preguntare si tomará su instituto le diré que mucho menos.

---

[63]Cf. Jn 4:27.

[64]The manuscript reads 'que ya que'.

# THE SPIRITUAL EXERCISES AND THE CRISIS OF MEDIEVAL PIETY

IN THE LATE SIXTEENTH CENTURY Ignatius Loyola came to be seen as a symbol of the Counter-Reformation, and in particular of the points of belief and practice that distinguished Catholics from Protestants.[1] His first official biographer, Pedro de Ribadeneira, extolled him as the captain of the armies of the Church pitted against Antichrist, Martin Luther,[2] and the image, once established, received new life in the early nineteenth century when the term 'Counter-Reformation' was first used to denote the Catholic counter-attack on Protestantism.[3] Nowadays it is generally accepted that the militant side of Ignatius's character has been exaggerated. His formative years were the 1520s in Spain, when he probably had little, if any, knowledge of Lutheranism. In Paris during the 1530s he witnessed the irruption of the Reform into French life, but his thoughts at the time were set on living in Jerusalem. And even when, after 1540, his followers became involved in anti-Protestant work, it was only one of several activities in which the young Society engaged, and never the one to which he himself was most attracted.[4] Nonetheless he cannot simply be classified as part of the other strand in the early Counter-Reformation distinguished by Hubert Jedin, the movement to reform the late medieval Church.[5] Not only was it his ambition until 1538 to leave Europe and live in the Holy Land, but a certain mystery surrounds his attitude to one of the main forces in the early Catholic Reform, the evangelical humanists.

According to Ribadeneira, Ignatius was always hostile to the evangelical humanists, particularly Erasmus, whose *Enchiridion* he was invited to read in Barcelona in 1525 or 1526, and which he abandoned in disgust.[6] In modern times, however, this simple view of his position has been challenged. The evidence suggests that when writing the Barcelona story Ribadeneira changed and elaborated his sources in order to demonstrate that even in the 1520s Ignatius was orthodox in the late sixteenth-century sense of the term. It appears, moreover, that in Spain, France and Italy Ignatius moved in circles favourable to the evangelical humanists, and was opposed by conservatives who were also hostile to Erasmus. In addition, critical study of the *Exercises* indicates that during the 1530s he may well have read some of Erasmus's writings, including the *Enchiridion*, and that these left their mark on several passages in the text. Finally, it seems that in 1539 and 1540 approval of the Society was delayed in Rome because of certain Erasmian elements in its proposed constitutions.[7] One might conclude that Ignatius was well-disposed to the humanists after all, but this conclusion is made difficult to sustain by the history of the *Spiritual Exercises*.

In the period after the Council of Trent, the *Exercises* played a crucial role in shaping a confessional Catholic piety that ran counter not only to Protestant belief and practice but to the type of spirituality that Erasmus and his fellow humanists had advocated.[8] Erasmus, for instance, was strongly critical of the popular devotions of his day, such as the veneration of relics, the invocation of saints, processions, pilgrimages and rigorous acts of penance,[9] but in the late sixteenth century these were officially encouraged, helped by the *Exercises* in which they are warmly praised.[10] He was particularly critical of popular devotion to the Passion,[11] but Ignatius incorporated it into the *Exercises*, and later in the Tridentine Church it was accorded an honoured place. In general, Erasmus criticized the emphasis in late medieval piety on external acts and works, and inclined instead to a spirituality that was meditative and interiorized,[12] but the type of meditation popular in the late sixteenth century, and disseminated by the *Exercises*, encouraged intense activity, not only in the course of prayer, when all the powers of the mind were involved, but in its fruits. As Outram Evennett observed, the decree on Justification issued by the Council in 1547 ensured that

> the spirituality of the Counter-Reformation would be one in which activity of all kinds was to play a very large part; in which active striving after self-control and the acquisition of virtues would be vital; in which zeal for good works of mercy and charity, and labour for the salvation of souls, were to predominate.[13]

The substance of the *Exercises* was conceived at Manresa in 1522 and early 1523, and the text was elaborated over the next two decades, reaching its final form in about 1541.[14] If during these years the spirituality of Ignatius was incompatible with that of the Erasmian humanists, how could he have looked on them favourably? The pages that follow seek an answer to this question by examining the circumstances in which the *Exercises* were composed. Just before he began to write them, Ignatius endured a severe spiritual crisis which had all the characteristics of the malaise in popular piety that Erasmus and his fellow humanists had analysed.

*The crisis at Manresa*

It is well known that at Manresa in the summer of 1522 Ignatius passed through a period of acute doubt and temptation during which he feared that his sins had not all been forgiven, and that this inner torment, which lasted several months, drove him to the point of suicide before it was resolved. The roots of the crisis are not easy to trace, but they seem to go back at least to his conversion at Loyola after the famous battle at Pamplona nearly a year before. Ignatius later told Gonçalves da Câmara that before the crisis at Manresa his spiritual life was marked by an absence of inner conflict. This apparent peace, however, cloaked a serious misunderstanding of the nature of the Christian life. According to da Câmara, he paid no attention to

> any interior reality: he knew nothing of humility, charity, patience, of discretion which rules and measures these virtues. Instead his only thought was to perform great external works,

as the saints had done for God's glory.[15] This stress on externals rather than internals was the salient feature of the debased popular piety that Erasmus yearned to renew.[16] In the Spanish translation of the *Enchiridion*, which was published in 1526 and soon became a best-seller, we read these words:

> My own experience has taught me that this error of giving greater importance to things that are external and literal than to those which are interior and spiritual is a common plague afflicting all Christians. And it is all the more pernicious for seeming to resemble true devotion and sanctity.[17]

For Erasmus all the defects in popular piety flowed from this initial misconception, and Ignatius's behaviour after his conversion at Loyola had other characteristics of the malaise that Erasmus noted.

First, there was his attachment to formal vocal and liturgical prayer. According to his later companion, Diego Laínez, he was much given to vocal prayer before his crisis began, and Juan Polanco, who wrote an early account of his life, noted that in the same period 'he said a lot of vocal prayer, understanding almost nothing, and with little savouring of interior things'.[18] Ignatius himself recorded that it was his custom to spend seven hours daily in private devotions, and although he did not indicate how he filled these sessions, it is likely that they involved recitation of the Little Office of our Lady and of other prayers available in a Book of Hours. In addition he would go to church each day to attend sung High Mass, and would return later for Vespers and Compline.[19] Erasmus did not object to vocal prayer itself, but he lamented the neglect of mental prayer and urged a return to free meditation.[20]

Secondly, Ignatius was ardent in devotion to the Passion, a practice Erasmus criticized because often it focused on Christ's humanity to the exclusion of his divinity, and issued in despondence rather than compunction and hope. He considered it especially ironical that this commemoration of the main event in human redemption could coexist with popular fear of damnation and with an unhealthy devotion to the Virgin and the saints.[21] Ignatius was probably drawn to the devotion in the first place by the *Vita Christi* of Ludolph the Carthusian which he read at Loyola.[22] Later at Manresa he made a habit of reading an account of the Passion during sung High Mass, probably in his Book of Hours.[23] It was usual for such books to include extracts from the gospel narratives of Christ's death, and they give a clear idea of the excesses that the Erasmians deplored: alongside simple prayers of faith and hope in the saving merits of Christ, one finds in them constant appeals to the merits of the saints, a dolorous preoccupation with judgment, and a superstitious trust in magical prayers guaranteed to cure all ills.[24]

An indication that Ignatius's devotion to the Passion may have been initially affected by some confusion is given by the fact that it was able to coexist with an eccentric devotion to the Virgin Mary. After his conversion the Virgin appears to have played in his life something of the role of a Lady in the life of a faithful knight. It is well known how, on his way to Montserrat, he met a *morisco* who denied the virgin birth, and that he was tempted to fight him for having cast a slur on her honour;[25] and at Montserrat itself he kept a vigil of his arms before the Virgin's shrine in imitation of the knight Esplandián in the last book of *Amadís de Gaula*.[26] Diego Laínez later wrote that at this time Ignatius's devotion to Mary was unbalanced, or, as he put it, not '*secundum scientiam*'.[27] On the same journey to Montserrat Ignatius made a special vow of chastity, not, curiously enough, to God but to the Virgin. Despite this irregularity (Laínez concluded) God deigned to accept it, in view of his good intention.[28]

A further aspect of Ignatius's behaviour which Erasmus would have identified as a symptom of malaise was his practice of penance. His main aim after leaving Loyola was to do penance, and to this end he regularly flagellated himself once a day. At Manresa he was able to apply the discipline more often, and for several months he survived on a diet of bread and water.[29] According once again to Laínez, 'he thought holiness could be measured by austerities and that the man who practised the harshest penance would be the most saintly before God'.[30] This kind and degree of asceticism was abhorred by Erasmus, who discerned in it a temptation to rely on works rather than on grace, and who associated it with the monastic tradition, for which he had little liking. Ignatius in his early excesses was inspired by the example of the desert fathers and of the medieval saints, and his love of penance drew him to consider joining a monastic order. He thought of becoming a Carthusian and shelved the idea only when it occurred to him that he might not be allowed to practise all the austerities he had in mind.[31]

Ignatius's reasons for practising such harsh penance give us a further insight into his malaise: he later told Gonçalves da Câmara that at this time his motive was not so much to make satisfaction for sins already forgiven as by his rigours to please God; and although his interest in performing amazing feats often distracted his attention from his sins, he was never conscious that they had in fact been forgiven.[32] These remarks reveal the depth of his confusion: he hoped by good works to merit pardon, and underlying his striving was the image of a just God whom he felt it necessary to placate. That his later crisis at Manresa had its origin in this deep-rooted misconception is confirmed by two incidents that occurred during the crisis itself, the first at its onset, the second at its climax.

According to Ignatius's own account, his temptations began one day as he was entering a church to attend the usual services. He saw a vision of something like a snake, and he seemed to hear a voice within him saying, 'How can you put up with this life for the next seventy years?'[33] Complaints about the tedium of the Christian life were common in the late fifteenth and early sixteenth centuries, and Erasmus identified them as a further symptom of malaise caused by faulty motives: works rooted in fear and self-interest, he wrote, were oppressive; the remedy was to practise them for the love of Christ, whose yoke is sweet and whose burden is light.[34] Ignatius's reply to the devil at Manresa is noteworthy. He did not dispute that his life was extremely arduous; instead he replied with force, 'You miserable wretch! Can you guarantee me a single hour of life?'[35] And at this the temptation disappeared. His words, like his practice of penance, reveal a preoccupation with the Last Things.

It is significant also that when his crisis reached a climax it did so in the context of confession. At Montserrat he made a general confession of all the sins of his past life, which he prepared in writing beforehand: it lasted three days.[36] Thereafter at Manresa it was his custom to go to confession once a week.[37] During his crisis, however, he began to fear that there were sins he had omitted to confess, and that might not therefore have been forgiven. It was this fear that eventually took him to the verge of suicide.[38] Undoubtedly, his notion of confession was shaped by the many confessional manuals for penitents and priests which at the time were best-sellers. A general confession of three days' duration was the usual procedure that most advised, and they stressed the importance of recalling all sins. Technically, a penitent was obliged to confess mortal sins only; the problem was to distinguish these from the venial ones, and some idea of the anguish this could entail is suggested by the endless pages the manuals devoted to grading the gravity of faults.[39] The manuals give clear expression to the ills which Erasmus wished to correct and which led him, by contrast, to stress that inner remorse was far more important than the forms and formulae of confession itself.[40]

### Justification

There are many reasons for thinking that the sort of experience Ignatius endured at Manresa was not uncommon at the time. In the western Church of the day anxiety about the worth of human efforts in the spiritual life appears to have been widespread, and it has been suggested that this anxiety, which underlay debates about the nature of justification, may have been caused by the impact on popular religion of the tenets of Nominalist theology.[41] One of these tenets was the notion that, *pace* Aquinas, there was no necessary link between divine law and the aspirations of human nature, which meant that in practice the norms by which human perfection was to be attained were 'extrinsic to the internal exigencies of human moral aspiration and rational experience'.[42] Another was the principle that 'to the person who does what lies within him God will not deny grace' (*facienti quod in se est Deus non denegat gratiam*).[43] Anthony Levi has written:

> The current theology of the late fifteenth century . . . allowed man to earn his salvation by his own efforts, providing they were sufficiently intense. On the level of popular religion . . . the result was great moral tension. Since, in the ordinary theology of the late fifteenth century religious perfection was no longer considered to be intrinsic to moral achievement, it was clearly impossible to know whether one had satisfied the requirement of doing all that lay within one. There were no criteria in the realm of experience on which one could rely to know whether or not one was justified. The inevitable consequence was the growth of the religion of 'works'.[44]

The anguish to which this could give rise is apparent in the lives of two of Ignatius's contemporaries. In 1510 a Venetian nobleman, Paolo Giustiniani, entered Camaldoli, believing the monastic life to be for him 'the most effective form of spiritual action'.[45] The following Easter, his friend Gasparo Contarini, who had remained a layman, was brought to the point of despair by the recognition that he had not followed Giustiniani's example because he lacked the courage 'to leave the world and do penance for the satisfaction of my iniquities'. Later, after going to confession, he realized that, 'if I did all possible penance and much more besides, it would be of no avail to render satisfaction for past sins, let alone merit eternal happiness'.[46] His distress was provoked by what has been termed the 'sense of the nothingness of man's efforts at sanctity that seems to have pervaded the later Middle Ages'.[47] A similar sense of futility underlay the crisis of Martin Luther at the same period when, as a young Augustinian, he strove to observe the externals of his rule with scrupulous exactitude. After reading the

*Vitae patrum* he longed to imitate one of the desert fathers, 'who would live in the desert, and abstain from food and drink, and live on a few vegetables and roots and cold water'.[48] But in spite of frequent confession his efforts left his conscience unappeased, not only because they fell short of the perfection God demanded, but because he recognized that even 'if it were possible for man to do *quod in se est*, he could never know for certain whether he had, in fact, achieved this'.[49] In each of these cases the crisis was preceded by the conviction that the Christian life, in its highest form, involved heroic, penitential asceticism of the monastic kind, and in each of them the sense of personal failure that ensued led to near-despair of God's forgiveness in the context of confession. These features also marked the experience of Ignatius.

### The Spiritual Exercises

It was after the resolution of his crisis that Ignatius began to compose the *Spiritual Exercises*. According to his own account, the resolution was effected partly by a growth in his understanding of how to discern between the promptings of good and evil spirits, and partly by a series of visions and other experiences of a mystical kind during which he felt God teaching him as a master teaches a child.[50] In the period of tranquillity that followed, during the autumn of 1522, he began to write down the first draft of his work. If one examines the text in the light of his earlier misconceptions, one notes how completely his spirituality had altered, and that it had done so in ways of which Erasmus and other evangelical humanists would have approved.

First, the *Exercises* provide a thorough training in mental prayer, and draw the person taking them towards an intimate interiorization of the Christian life. The second annotation enunciates a principle implied throughout the text: 'It is not knowing much that fills and satisfies the soul, but feeling and tasting things internally' (*'no el mucho saber harta y satisface al ánima, mas el sentir y gustar las cosas internamente'*).[51] The words 'interno' and 'interior', and their cognates, occur fifteen times in the work.[52] The value thus attached to interiority is not seen as incompatible with the externals of devotion: the Rules for Thinking with the Church, for instance, contain praise of popular devotions and of liturgical and monastic prayer.[53] These rules, which were probably composed in Italy between 1539 and 1541,[54] may have been intended to defend the Society against the criticisms of conservatives;[55] whatever their origin they may be said to take for granted the interiorization of the devotional life that the rest of the text is designed to encourage.[56]

Closely connected with interiorization is the accent on experience. Retreatants are expected to be moved to consolation and desolation 'by various spirits', and if 'spiritual motions' of this kind do not occur it is an indication that something is wrong, as the sixth annotation makes plain.[57] During the retreat, moreover, they are expected to pray for intense inner experiences, such as remorse, tears, compassion, joy.[58] For Ignatius, such experience is intrinsic to the soul's quest, the symptom and sign of God's activity within it. This divine activity is, in turn, central to the retreat. Ignatius's sense at Manresa of being taught and guided by God is reflected most noticeably, perhaps, in the rules for making an Election,[59] and in annotation fifteen where the director is asked to be as sensitive as a balance, allowing God to act directly on the soul and the soul to interact with God.[60] It is here that the process of discernment (by which in part Ignatius's crisis was resolved) finds its role, enabling director and retreatant to interpret God's will directly. The fact that there are parallels between the rules for discernment set out by Ignatius and the ones recommended in various writings by Erasmus is not surprising: the importance that both men accorded to experience in the interior life made such guidelines indispensable.[61]

In the body of the *Exercises*, moreover, one notes all the elements of Ignatius's early and extreme behaviour, but now transformed. In the sections on penance it is pointed out that external acts of penance should be the fruit or expression of internal sorrow, and the virtue specifically counselled is moderation. The first purpose of penance is said to be the making of satisfaction for past sins: there is no mention of pleasing a wrathful God.[62] A similar stress on motive, especially inner compunction, is evident in the sections on the examination of conscience, which provide simple rules for distinguishing between venial and mortal sins.[63] Lastly, the devotion to the Passion that lies at the heart of the *Exercises* is one purged of all the defects that Erasmus and others had analysed: it centres on the divinity as well as the humanity of Christ, and gives rise to faith and hope of forgiveness.[64] In the colloquy at the end of the opening meditation on human sin, the retreatant is urged to call to mind Christ's saving love exemplified in the Cross, and both then and later, notably in the second week, his desire to act according to God's will is conceived as a *response* to divine love, not as a means of earning it.[65] As his gratitude deepens, his motives for following Christ are encouraged to become more selfless: he moves from consideration of his sins to contemplation of the risen Lord, a progression from servile fear to love, and from sorrow to joy, of the kind that Erasmus always counselled.[66]

One may conclude that in their origins the *Exercises* were in no way opposed to the spirituality advocated by Erasmus. They reflect concern with the crisis in popular piety that so disturbed him, and although Ignatius was not himself a humanist, and may have had reservations about some of Erasmus's views, the evidence suggests that he looked sympathetically on the movement of evangelical humanism of which Erasmus was, in Spain, the main spokesman. Furthermore, the fact that the *Exercises* embodied Ignatius's resolution of his crisis helps to account for the tremendous impact they later made on contemporaries. They addressed popular anxiety about the nature and process of justification, one of the most urgent pastoral problems confronting the early sixteenth-century Church.[67] They did not do so, however, in the terms of contemporary theology, humanist or scholastic, but in the language of the late medieval works of piety that Ignatius had read in Spain. This debt to the medieval past is one reason why, in the last analysis, Ignatius remains hard to classify. It was from Ludolph and Voragine that he originally drew his ambition to go to Jerusalem, and all the works that he read at Loyola and Manresa left their mark on the *Exercises*: evidently he was able to find in them elements compatible with his transformed vision of the spiritual life.[68] His crisis did not lead him to abandon popular piety but to renew it. This continuity with the Middle Ages was one factor that eventually distinguished his position from that of the early Protestants, but in Spain during the 1520s it was not a sign of anti-Protestantism or even of anti-Erasmianism. Later, however, as the Counter-Reformation became increasingly defensive, it enabled others to interpret the *Exercises* as a providential means of re-affirming Catholic tradition.

NOTES

[1] See I. Iparraguirre, 'La figura de San Ignacio a través de los siglos', in San Ignacio de Loyola, *Obras completas*, edited by I. Iparraguirre S.J. and C. de Dalmases S.J., fourth edition (Madrid, 1982), pp 3–38.

[2] Pedro de Ribadeneyra, *Vita Ignatii Loyolae. Textus latinus et hispanus cum censuris (M.I. Fontes narrativi IV)*, edited by C. de Dalmases S.J. (Rome, 1965), p 339 (henceforward referred to as *FN* IV).

[3] H. Outram Evennett, *The spirit of the Counter-Reformation* (Cambridge, 1968), p 4 onwards.

[4] See my article 'Ignatius Loyola and the Counter Reformation: the hagiographic tradition', *Heythrop journal*, 31 (1990), pp 439–470.

[5] On the distinction drawn by Jedin, and some of the reasons why it has proved unsatisfactory, see John W. O'Malley S.J., 'Catholic Reform' in Steven Ozment, *Reformation Europe: a guide to research* (St Louis, 1982), pp 297–319 (pp 302–3).

[6] *FN* IV, pp 173–4.

[7] The most recent discussion of this controverted subject provides a bibliography of previous studies, and a summary of the main points of view: Pascual Cebollada S.J., 'Loyola y Erasmo. Aportaciones al estudio de la relación entre ambos', *Manresa* 62 (1990), pp 49–60.

[8] See Irwin Iserloh, Joseph Glazik and Hubert Jedin, *Reformation and Counter-Reformation* (London, 1980), pp 446, 555–564. The best study of the nature of Counter-Reformation piety is still Evennett, pp 23–42.

[9] On the general features of humanist spirituality see John W. O'Malley S.J., 'The Jesuits, St Ignatius and the Counter-Reformation. Some recent studies and their implications for today', *Studies in the spirituality of Jesuits* 14 (1982) Part One, pp 1–28 (pp 15–26), and the introduction by A. H. T. Levi to Erasmus of Rotterdam, *Praise of folly and letter to Martin Dorp 1515*, translated by Betty Radice (Harmondsworth, 1971), pp 7–50.

[10] Exx 358, 359.

[11] O'Malley, 'The Jesuits, St Ignatius, and the Counter-Reformation', p 16; Terence O'Reilly, 'Saint Ignatius Loyola and Spanish Erasmianism', *Archivum Historicum Societatis Iesu* 43 (1974), pp 301–321 (pp 301; 306–8; 315).

[12] Levi, p 21.

[13] Evennett, pp 31–32.

[14] On the history of the text see Sancti Ignatii de Loyola, *Exercitia spiritualia* (MHSJ 100), edited by J. Calveras S.J. and C. de Dalmases S.J. (Rome, 1969), p 4–33.

[15] *Fontes narrativi de S. Ignatio de Loyola et de Societatis Iesu initiis*, volume I, edited by D. Fernández Zapico S.J. and C. de Dalmases S.J., with the help of P. de Leturia S.J. (Rome, 1943), p 382 (henceforward *FN* I).

[16] On the spirituality of Erasmus, and his critique of popular piety, see Carlos Eire, *War against the idols: the reformation of worship from Erasmus to Calvin* (Cambridge, 1986), and the introduction by John W. O'Malley S.J. to Erasmus, *Spiritualia* (Collected works of Erasmus, volume 66) (Toronto, 1988).

[17] Erasmo, *El Enquiridion o manual del caballero cristiano*, edited by Dámaso Alonso, with an introduction by Marcel Bataillon (Madrid, 1932), p 257: 'he visito por esperiencia que este error *de estimar las cosas exteriores y literales más que las interiores y espirituales*, es una común pestilencia que anda entre todos los christianos. La qual tanto es más daños a quanto más cerca anda, al parecer, de santidad y devoción.' (The words in italics were added by the translator, Alonso Fernández de Madrid.) On the crucial importance of this passage in the history of the movement of reform in Spain, see Marcel Bataillon, *Erasmo y España. Estudios sobre la historia espiritual del siglo XVI* (Mexico and Buenos Aires, 1966), p 200.

[18] *FN* I, p 78; 159. The short accounts by Laínez (1547) and Polanco (1547–8) are the earliest biographies of Ignatius that we possess.

[19] *FN* I, pp 390; 396; 402.

[20] Bataillon, p 144; pp 572 sqq.; 589–90.

[21] O'Reilly, 'Saint Ignatius Loyola and Spanish Erasmianism', pp 306–8; Bataillon, pp 577, 590.

[22] *Exercitia spiritualia*, pp 38–43; Bataillon, p 589.

[23] *FN* I, p 390.

[24] Pedro de Leturia S.J., 'Libros de horas, *Anima Christi* y Ejercicios Espirituales de San Ignacio', in *Estudios Ignacianos*, edited by I. Iparraguirre S.J., two volumes (Rome, 1957), volume 2, pp 99–148; on Erasmian criticism of the *libros de horas* see Bataillon, p 577.

[25] *FN* I, pp 382–4.

[26] *FN* I, p 386; see Pedro de Leturia S.J., *El gentilhombre Iñigo López de Loyola en su patria y en su siglo*, second edition (Barcelona, 1949), pp 256-8.

[27] *FN* I, p 76. The phrase calls to mind Romans 10, 2 (Vulgate) and the passage in the opening section of the bull *Regimini militantis Ecclesiae* (MHSJ *Constitutiones*, volume I, pp 24-32), in which each member of the Society is urged to 'use all his energies to attain this goal which God himself sets before him, always according to the grace which each one has received from the Holy Spirit and the proper grade of his vocation, lest any might be carried away by a zeal without knowledge' ('*ne quis forte zelo utatur, sed non secundum scientiam*').

[28] *FN* I, p 76. According to Polanco it was the vow, rather than the devotion, that was not '*secundum scientiam*': *FN* I, p 158.

[29] *FN* I, pp 78; 159; 380.

[30] *FN* I, p 74.

[31] *FN* I, p 378.

[32] *FN* I, p 382: '*y así determinaba de hacer grandes penitencias, no teniendo ya tanto ojo a satisfacer por sus pecados, sino agradar y aplacer a Dios*'. This statement is accompanied by a note by da Câmara explaining its significance: '*tenía tanto aborrecimiento a los pecados pasados, y el deseo tan vivo de hacer cosas grandes por amor de Dios, que, sin hacer juicio que sus pecados eran perdonados, todavía en las penitencias que emprendía a hacer no se acordaba mucho dellos*'.

[33] *FN* I, p 390: '¿*Y cómo podrás tu sufrir esta vida 70 años que has de vivir?*'.

[34] *Enquiridion*, pp 211; 217; 247; 277; 288-9; 291; 409.

[35] *FN* I, p 390; see too the testimony of Laínez, pp 78-80.

[36] *FN* I, p 386.

[37] *FN* I, p 392.

[38] *FN* I, pp 392-6.

[39] See J. Calveras, 'Los "confesionales" y los ejercicios espirituales de San Ignacio', *Archivum historicum Societatis Iesu* 17 (1948), pp 51-101. The anguish caused by the requirement to confess all sins was depicted vividly by Calvin: *Institutes of the Christian religion*, edited by John T. McNeill, two volumes (Philadelphia, 1960), volume I, pp 641-3. See too Thomas N. Tentler, *Sin and confession on the eve of the Reformation* (Princeton, 1977).

[40] Bataillon, pp 143; 291.

[41] Levi, pp 16-21.

[42] Levi, p 17; see also the same author's 'The breakdown of Scholasticism and the significance of evangelical humanism', in *The philosophical assessment of theology: essays in honour of Frederick C. Copleston*, edited by Gerard J. Hughes (Tunbridge Wells, 1987), pp 101-128.

[43] On this principle, and the pactum theology of justification, see Alister E. McGrath, *Iustitia Dei: a history of the Christian doctrine of justification*, two volumes (Cambridge, 1986), volume I, pp 83-91.

[44] Levi, *Praise of folly*, p 20.

[45] Dermot Fenlon, *Heresy and obedience in Tridentine Italy: Cardinal Pole and the Counter Reformation* (Cambridge, 1972), p 6.

[46] Contarini's letters to Guistiniani were edited by Hubert Jedin in 'Contarini und Camaldoli', *Archivo italiano per la storia della pietà*, 2 (1959), pp 51-117. They have been translated into English with an introduction and bibliography by Elisabeth G. Gleason, *Reform thought in sixteenth-century Italy* (Chico, 1981), pp 21-33.

[47] Charles Trinkaus, 'The religious thought of the Italian Humanists and the Reformers: anticipation or autonomy?', in *The pursuit of holiness in late medieval and Renaissance religion*, edited by Charles Trinkaus and Heiko Oberman (Leiden, 1974), pp 339-366 (p 350).

[48] Quoted in G. Rupp, *The righteousness of God* (London, 1953), p 103.

[49] Alister E. McGrath, *Luther's theology of the cross: Martin Luther's theological breakthrough* (Oxford, 1985), p 132. For a recent general comparison of Luther and Loyola see Rogelio García Mateo, 'Ignacio de Loyola: ¿antilutero? Consideración ecuménica de su confrontación histórica', *Manresa* 57 (1985), pp 251-9.

[50] *FN* I, pp 398-400.

[51] Exx 2. Erasmus expressed similar sentiments in the *Enchiridion:* see Henri de Lubac S.J., *Exégèse mediévale. Les quatres sens de l'écriture*, four volumes (Paris, 1959-1964), volume 4, p 440.

[52] See the information provided in Seppo A. Teinonen, *Concordancias de los Ejercicios Espirituales de San Ignacio de Loyola* (Helsinki, 1981).

[53] Exx 355; 358-60.

[54] *Exercitia spiritualia*, p 33.

[55] Marcel Bataillon, 'D'Erasme à la Compagnie de Jésus. Protestation et intégration dans la Réforme Catholique au XVIe siècle', *Archives de sociologie des religions* 24 (1967), pp 57-81 (pp 72-3).

[56] See Leturia, *Estudios ignacianos*, volume I, p 162.

[57] Exx 6.

[58] For instance: Exx 4; 48; 56; 65; 203; 221.

[59] Exx 169-189 (especially 175, 176).

[60] Exx 15.

[61] See A. H. T. Levi, 'Erasmus, the early Jesuits and the classics', in *Classical influences on European Culture, AD 1500-1700*, edited by R. R. Bolgar (Cambridge, 1976), pp 223-236; Marjorie O'Rourke Boyle, 'Angels black and white: Loyola's spiritual discernment in historical perspective', *Theological studies* 44 (1983), pp 241-257.

[62] Exx 82-87.

[63] Exx 24-44.

[64] See O'Reilly, 'Saint Ignatius Loyola and Spanish Erasmianism', pp 309-310.

[65] Exx 53.

[66] I have studied this progression in detail in 'The *Exercises* of Saint Ignatius Loyola and the *Exercitatorio de la vida spiritual*', *Studia monastica* 16 (1974), pp 301-323 (pp 307-314).

[67] See Alister McGrath, *The intellectual origins of the European Reformation* (Oxford, 1987), pp 24-28.

[68] The literary sources of the *Exercises* are discussed in *Exercitia spiritualia*, pp 34-60.

# VII

## THE STRUCTURAL UNITY OF THE EXERCITATORIO
## DE LA VIDA SPIRITUAL

The *Exercitatorio de la vida spiritual* [1] is a text of great interest to scholars concerned with the history of spiritual exercises, partly because it was the first manual of methodical prayer to be published in Castilian, and also because of its own intrinsic merits. It not only prolonged the *devotio moderna* tradition of meditation but added to it substantially: «il marque... un grand progrès dans ce genre de systématisation pratique de l'enseignement de la vie d'oraison».[2]

Its author, García de Cisneros,[3] did not lay any claim to originality. He published it anonymously, and described it as a «compilation»: the last paragraph opens with the words, «Fenesce el presente tractado... El qual compilamos assí en vulgar».[4] And modern research has established the truth of his remark: most of the contents are indeed drawn from previous writings on prayer.[5]

Although the sources that have come to light are numerous, they may be divided into three groups. The first and most influential comprises writings of the *devotio moderna*, as one might expect. Of the sixty nine chapters in the treatise fifteen are taken from Zutphen (seven from the *De reformatione virium animae* and eight from the

---

[1] First printed in 1500 at Montserrat. See the critical edition by C. BARAUT O.S.B. in *García Jiménez de Cisneros, Obras Completas*, t. 2 (Montserrat, 1965), which will be followed here.
[2] H. WATRIGANT S.J., *Quelques promoteurs de la méditation méthodique au quinzième siècle*, in *Collection de la Bibliothèque des Exercices*, LIX (Enghien-Paris, 1919), 69.
[3] 1455/6-1510. See G. M. COLOMBÁS O.S.B., *Un reformador benedictino en tiempo de los Reyes Católicos, García Jiménez de Cisneros, abad de Montserrat* (Montserrat, 1965).
[4] *Exercitatorio*, ch. 69, L. 169, 174-175.
[5] See WATRIGANT, *art. cit.*, and *La genèse des exercices de saint Ignace*, in *Études Religieuses*, LXXI (1897), 506-529; LXXII, 195-216; LXXIII, 199-228; A. ALBAREDA O.S.B., *Intorno alla scuola di orazione metodica stabilita a Monserrato dall'abate Garsias Jiménez de Cisneros (1493-1510)*, in *Archivum Historicum Societatis Iesu*, XXV (1956), 341-353; COLOMBÁS, *op. cit.*; BARAUT, *op. cit.*

288

*De spiritualibus ascensionibus*), one from the *Hortus rosarum* of a Kempis, and eleven from the *Rosetum* of John Mombaer:[6] a total of twenty-seven, or just under one half of the entire work. The second group consists of writings in the Franciscan tradition. Three chapters are drawn from the *de triplici via* of St. Bonaventure, and parts of two others from his *Soliloquium de quatuor mentalibus exercitiis*. The *Meditationes vitae Christi* are used in two chapters, and another work attributed to Bonaventure, the *Stimulus amoris*, in three. Dom Baraut has shown that a further Franciscan source, the most influential after the writings of Bonaventure, is the *Tractat de contemplació* of Francesc Eiximenis (d. 1409), which supplies the substance of no less than six chapters.[7] The third important group of sources is composed of Carthusian works, including the *Mystica theologia* of Hugh of Balma, from which six chapters are drawn. The *Vita Christi* of Ludolph is also quoted, though less extensively. The *Alphabetum divini amoris* of Nicholas Kempf (d. 1497), a Carthusian contemporary of Cisneros, is the source of seven chapters. In other words, Cisneros was indebted most to writings that formed and popularised the conception of spiritual exercises which he made his own and introduced into Spain. The only ones of significance not included in the three groups are by John Gerson (d. 1429), whose teaching had much in common with the anti-speculative, practical and affective tendencies of Groote and his disciples.[8]

Cisneros' dependence on previous writers for the matter of his book, has prompted some critics to write of it as wholly unoriginal. Ignacio Iparraguirre, for instance, considers that, «el libro no es más que un zurcido de retalos de diversas obras clásicas en el medio ambiente de la *devotio* moderna»,[9] and a Benedictine, F. Vandenbroucke, judges it, «not... an original work; it is only a compilation in which Cisneros' touch can rarely be discerned».[10] This latter opinion contrasts sharply with the view expressed by Allison Peers who, apart from including a chapter on Cisneros in his *Studies of the Spanish Mystics*, translated the *Exercitatorio* into English.

6 For a list of sources and some indication of their influence see C. BARAUT, *La bibliothèque ascétique de García de Cisneros*, in *Studia monastica*, IX (1967), 327-339.

7 See the article by C. BARAUT, L'Exercitatorio de la vida spiritual *de García de Cisneros et le* Tractat de contemplació *de Francesc Eiximenis*, in *Studia monastica*, II (1960), 233-265.

8 BARAUT, *op. cit.*, t. 1, 87.

9 I. IPARRAGUIRRE S.J. (ed.), *Obras Completas de San Ignacio de Loyola* (B.A.C. Madrid, 1963), 177.

10 F. VANDENBROUCKE O.S.B. and J. LECLERCQ O.S.B., *The Spirituality of the Middle Ages* (London, 1968), 540.

He was impressed by the fact that, although composed of extracts from other works, it read coherently, as if it were original, and seemed to be marked by an author's personality.[11] Few critics writing since Peers have carried his view further. Dom Colombás, who is by no means unsympathetic to Cisneros, holds that Peers did not take sufficient account of the derivative nature of the work. It is clear, though, that when he made his comments Peers was acquainted with Watrigant's researches.[12] In a recent study, however, Dom Baraut has stressed the intelligence with which Cisneros combined his source materials, and found evidence of unity in the treatise which helps to explain Peers's impression. He argues, first, that the sources were chosen with care: they are of the highest quality and of a wide variety, representative of the main tendencies in medieval spirituality.[13] His second point is that the passages used are translated and edited with a sense of purpose. The rendering of some extracts in Castilian is rather free: phrases, and sometimes entire paragraphs, are altered without, however, grave infidelity to their sense. On occasion, to make the meaning of a text quite explicit, or to relate it clearly to others, extra passages, either borrowed from some other source or composed by the compiler, are inserted into it. It is not uncommon for a source to be abbreviated to keep the work concise, or for the sequence of its subject matter to be altered.[14] Thirdly, a thorough analysis enables him to demonstrate that many sections of the work are by the compiler himself. These sections are usually just a few lines in length, though some are quite substantial: more than half the prologue, for instance, appears to be original, and one chapter (ch. 10) for which no immediate source has been found, may well be so. Of these original passages, the most significant, in his view, provide details of the subjects of exercises and of the actions to be carried out before, during and after them.[15] He concludes that the skill with which its sources are combined prevents one from reading the work as a mere compilation:

«Cisneros ha tenido una participación personal bastante más extensa e importante de lo que hasta ahora se suponía en la elaboración del *Exercitatorio de la vida spiritual*... La armonía que

---

[11] E. ALLISON PEERS, *Studies of the Spanish Mystics*, t. 2 (London, 1930), 16-17. The English translation by Peers was published at Montserrat in 1929 under the title, *Book of Exercises for the Spiritual Life*.
[12] COLOMBÁS, *op. cit.*, 237.
[13] BARAUT, *op. cit.*, t. 1, 94.
[14] *Ibid.*, 94-115.
[15] *Ibid.*, 117-123.

> reina entre los diversos materiales... y la unidad que su autor
> supo imprimir al conjunto disimulan de tal suerte su carácter
> compilatorio, que sería fácil tomarlo por una obra original.»[16]

We now know the degree of discrimination with which Cisneros
chose, edited and arranged the excerpts from previous writers that
form his treatise. The extent to which to which the work possesses
a coherent *structural* unity is, however, still a matter of debate. Dom
Baraut, in a fine analysis of the teaching on prayer that it contains,[17]
tends to observe rather closely the divisions that Cisneros himself introduced into the subject matter. The sixty-nine chapters that follow
the prologue are organised in four parts of unequal length: the first
three contain exercises for each of the classical Three Ways, purgative,
illuminative and unitive, while the fourth, longer than the others together, deals with various aspects of the contemplative life, and provides
meditations on the life and Passion of Christ. The question of form
is, in fact, still at the stage it reached when Watrigant concluded his
pioneer studies of the subject . He realised that Cisneros was an intelligent compiler, but felt that he had not succeeded in welding his
sources together to form a new whole. He wrote:

> «il ne s'assimile pas tout à fait les riches éléments qu'il a trou-
> vés: il les laisse dans leur état rudimentaire, sans leur donner
> une vie bien autonome. Sa gerbe est belle, mais le lien qui retient
> les épis est plutôt extérieur.»[18]

Did he merely gather texts of disparate content and purpose and
arrange them according to broad themes to form a kind of «spiritual
anthology»?[19] Or did he, on the contrary, arrange them carefully, in an
interlocking sequence, to realise a well-defined end? It is with this
problem that the pages that follow are concerned.

### DEFINITIONS OF PURPOSE

The beginnings of a solution are suggested by an initial examination of the first three parts of the treatise.[20] One's first impression is
likely to be that at points the arrangement of the contents is rather

---

16 *Ibid.*, 124.
17 *Ibid.*, 48-84.
18 WATRIGANT, *Quelques promoteurs...*, 68.
19 The phrase is VANDENBROUCKE'S, *op. cit.*, *loc. cit.*
20 I shall consider the first three parts of the treatise separately from the fourth, which
is thematically distinct.

erratic. All the same one cannot but note the frequency with which order and method in the spiritual life are praised. The reader is urged to practise exercises at regular times each day (ch. 8, 9), and to confirm his confidence in the value of mental prayer, the benefits gained through «los çiertos y ordenados exercicios» (Ch. 3, L. 2-3) are enumeerated.

At one point it is stated clearly that exercises must be chosen with care to realise a well-defined end:

> «El que quiere aprovechar en sus exerciçios conviénele establescer un fin, y para alcançar aquél ordenar sus medios, que son los exerciçios, y en aquéllos esté fixo» (Ch. 5, L. 46-48).

In the prologue, Cisneros defines the end to which his own exercises are directed. It is to bring the soul to union with God, «ayuntar el ánima con Dios», a union also termed «verdadera y no conoscida sabiduría» and «el amor divinal» (Prol. L. 18-20, 27). The means by which the soul will be prepared for union are also specified: they are meditation, prayer and contemplation according to the Three Ways. Their orderly nature is explicitly and repeatedly noted:

> «En este libro... tractaremos cómo el exercitador y varón devoto se ha de exercitar según las tres vías... Y cómo por çiertos y determinados exerçicios, según los días de la semana, meditando, orando, contemplando, ordenadamente podrá subir a alcançar el fin desseado» (L. 7-18).

Definitions of purpose expressed in identical or similar terms recur frequently in the following thirty chapters. In the third, for instance, after praising exercises of a well-ordered kind, Cisneros reminds the reader that he will provide such exercises later in the work (Ch. 3, L. 57-60).

At the end of Chapter 7, in words that echo those of the prologue, he announces that the time has come to keep this promise:

> «Conviene agora que digamos y pongamos en prática, cómo conviene al religioso exercitarse según las tres vías... porque exercitándose por ellas, y por la oración y contemplación, pueda ordenadamente venir al fin desseado que es ayuntar el ánima con Dios» (Ch. 7, L. 80-84).

At the start of ch. 19 he rounds off his treatment of the purgative way, by recalling that by its exercises «el nuevo discípulo de Christo se dispone a subir al fin desseado, que es venir poco a poco a ayuntar su ánima con Dios» (Ch. 19, L. 5-6), and his discussion of the unitive way in ch. 26 opens with a similar phrase (Ch. 26, L. 6-11). In ch. 19 too he introduces a fresh image to convey his understanding of the Three Ways: the progression from the purgative through the illuminative Way is compared to two kisses of increasing intimacy bestowed by the soul on its Lord, Christ: after kissing His feet in the recollection of sins one may kiss His hands in thanksgiving for His gifts (Ch. 19, L. 15-18). The image, used by Hugh of Balma who himself drew it from St. Bernard, recurs later in ch. 27: union with God is described as a third kiss, on the mouth, and Cisneros reminds the reader that he has made mention of the comparison before (Ch. 27, L. 108-113). Lastly, at the very end of the third part, he alludes to the definition of purpose originally made in the prologue, and indicates that in the intervening pages this purpose has been realised:

> «Hasta aquí hemos puesto en prática las dichas tres vías, y cómo por ellas meditando y orando podrás ordenadamente venir al fin desseado, que es ayuntar el ánima con Dios» (Ch. 30, L. 128-130).

Statements of this kind, in which Cisneros' personal touch may be discerned, suggest that he compiled the first three parts with a plan clearly in mind. Considered alone, however, they do not tell us much about the details of that plan. After all, the notion that by the Three Ways one attains union with God is a traditional and of itself quite unexceptional notion. In three passages, though, which deserve more critical attention than they have been granted, the relation between the end and the means of its attainment is made more precise. In ch. 4 one reads of spiritual exercises: «havemos de... ordenarlos según que mejor nos podrán traer a este fin, que es el amor de Dios y la pureza del coraçón» (Ch. 4, L. 35-37). The role of this double objective, which Cisneros drew from Cassian,[21] becomes clearer in the next chapter, in which it is written:

> «El fin de nuestros exerciçios... es alcançar la pureza del coraçón y la perfecta caridad de Dios. El uno, esto es, la caridad o la bienaventurança, es fin último. El otro fin, que es secundario y dispositivo, es la pureza del coraçón, que nos dispone para alcançar la perfecta caridad y bienaventurança» (Ch. 5, L. 48-54).

---

[21] Cisneros acknowledges his debt to Cassian, and also to the *De spiritualibus ascensionibus* of Zutphen: ch. 4, L. 38-39.
[22] *Exercitatorio*, ch. 36-38.

The purpose defined in these two passages seems very different from the one announced in the prologue. The relation between perfect love of God, on the one hand, and union with Him, on the other, is not immediately clear. It becomes clear, however, in the course of the first three parts. At one point the beginning of union, in contemplation, is described as the experience of perfect love.[22] In the prologue itself, the virtue specifically associated with the unitive Way is charity (Prol. L. 21-30). And in the last chapter the two definitions are explicitly brought together: one attains a pure heart, and perfect love of God, by the Three Ways:

> «en esta vida ninguna de las dichas tres vías que havemos tractado... perfetamente podemos acabar, mas exercitándonos por ellas subimos a la pureza del coraçón y caridad perfeta, según que en esta vida se puede alcançar» (Ch. 30, L. 101-105).

In a third passage Cisneros provides a further definition of his purpose which, when related to the other two, explains in more detail exactly how the exercises of the Three Ways prepare the monk to love God perfectly. In occurs in the one chapter of the entire work for which no immediate source has been found, the tenth, which, by virtue of its significance, must now be examined in some detail.

THE GRADES OF FEAR

In Chapter 10 Cisneros discusses the part that fear plays in the life of the Christian, and distinguishes the various kinds of fear he may experience according to the state of his relationship with God. It opens with praise of fear as the beginning not only of faith and charity but also of wisdom, the term used in the prologue as a synonym of union:

> «Bienaventurado es aquel a quien es dado el temor de Dios. Ca el temor es fundamento de la fe, principio de la caridad, y comienço de la sabiduría divina» (Ch. 10, L. 7-9).

Four distinct grades of fear are then defined, following several authorities, the most important one being Peter Lombard.[23] The first is *temor humano* or *mundano*, which leads the individual to commit sin because he is afraid of the pain or poverty he might otherwise

---

[23] See BARAUT, *op. cit.*, t. 2, 132, n. 1.

incur (L. 28-31). The remainder differ in that they do not result in sin but, on the contrary, in resistance to temptation. *Temor servil* for instance, inclines one to avoid sin because of the pain that may attend it in this life, or later in Hell (L. 32-33). It is made clear that, although better than the sort that leads to vice, this fear lacks charity, and is therefore not a sufficient motive to save one's soul. However, its value lies in the fact that it is the means by which charity first enters and grows in the soul:

> «El que haze bien por temor de la pena no ama a Dios... Empero havemos de considerar, que aunque con este temor no esté juntamente la caridad, es carrera y puerta para ella» (L. 37-40).

As charity develops it expels servile fear (L. 42-45). Eventually the soul reaches the stage of *temor filial o casto*, a fear from which concern with one's own interest has been removed. Now one resists temptation because one loves God and does not wish to give Him offence or be separated from Him:

> «tememos que no offendamos al esposo, o que no se tarde, o que se vaya y carezcamos de su presençia. Este temor nasce de verdadero amor de Dios» (L. 46-49).

The soul that has attained this fear is compared to a son (L. 74-75) and to a spouse (L. 47). The last kind of fear distinguished by Cisneros exists in the person who has experienced servile fear, and in whom the charity which will eventually become filial fear has begun to evolve without, however, being yet strong enought to eradicate all self-interest. It is termed *temor inicial*, and is an intermediate stage between imperfection and perfection:

> «Deste temor inicial dize sant Bernardo que tiene dos ojos: uno derecho con el qual mira arriba y teme ser apartado de Dios si peca, y otro siniestro con el qual mira abaxo, temiendo ser dañado en las penas del infierno» (L. 78-81).

The person who experiences it, in other words, is moved both by the fear of Hell which informs servile fear and the love of God in filial fear. It is the state of beginners in the spiritual life (L. 81-83).

At the end of the chapter Cisneros explains why he has gone to the trouble of distinguishing in such detail the grades of fear. It is his wish that the monk should progress from the stage of servile fear to that of filial:

> «Estos temores havemos aquí declarado porque puedas conoscer en quál especie dellos estás, y dexes el temor de siervo y te allegues al filial» (L. 89-91).

If these words may be applied to the three parts as a whole we now have a definition of purpose difficult, at first sight, to reconcile with the previous two. The place it occupies in the overall scheme becomes comprehensible, however, in tho light of the meaning Cisneros attaches to the term «fear». He is influenced by the use of the word in the Bible, where it is closer in sense to what we understand by «love» than to «terror».[24] The progression he has in mind is really from the kind of love of self that excludes a true concern for God and His purposes *(temor servil)* to a love of God for His own sake, selfless and generous to the point of transcending self-interest. The scriptural passage that informs the theory of grades of fear occurs in the first letter of St. John, where one reads:

> «Timor non est in charitate: sed perfecta charitas foras mittit timorem, quoniam timor poenam habet: qui autem timet, non est perfectus in charitate.»[25]

For the evangelist, spiritual growth involves the expulsion of fear (in the sense of «terror») by perfect love. It will be recalled that the second of Cisneros' definitions of intent which we examined mentioned perfect love as being the ultimate end of the exercises of the Three Ways. In view of this, is it not possible that the exercises are structured in terms of the three kinds of fear, servile, initial and filial? It is my belief that they are.

### THE PURGATIVE EXERCISES

The first part of the *Exercitatorio* opens with a number of chapters which introduce the reader to the notion of spiritual exercises, and to the ways in which he can prepare to practise them. He learns the essential preconditions of prayer (Ch. 1, 4), the characteristics

---

[24] See J. LECLERCQ O.S.B., *The love of learning and the desire for God* (New York, 1962), 81-82.
[25] 1 John 4:18.

of well-conducted exercises, and the results that may be expected from them (Ch. 3, 5, 8, 9). The remaining chapters concern the meditations of the purgative way, which are set out in detail according to the days of the week. The seven subjects are sin, the moment of death, Hell and the Last Judgement, the agony of Jesus in the garden of Gethsemane, His mother's sufferings and, finally, Paradise (Ch. 12-18). The last chapter of all explains how and when a monk will know that he has practised the exercises for a sufficiently long time and may pass on to those of the second part. A month is the usual and probable period (Ch. 19). As for the purpose of the Way, it is said to be to inspire repentance:

> «el exercitador llora sus pecados y offensas que con Dios ha hecho, de manera que assí llorando implore la misericordia de Dios. Ca esta vía es para alimpiar la consciençia, la qual... pertenece a los que comiençan» (Ch. 12, L. 41-44).

After reading the introductory section, and before embarking on the first of the purgative exercises, the monk makes a meditation entitled, «De las cosas que nos traen temor y que siempre devemos temer» (Ch. 11). A brief look at the points for reflection it contains indicates that the kind of fear they are meant to arouse is *temor servil*. More than half draw one's attention to the suddeness of death, the severity of the Last Judgement and the torments of Hell (Ch. 11, L. 32-62). Others deal with the insecurity and mutability of the present life, both of which result from sin, man's vulnerability to temptation and his continual uncertainty about whether he is justified in the eyes of God or not (L. 8-15). One long passage, inserted by Cisneros into the text, presents examples of the severity with which sin is castigated. He points out that both Lucifer and Adam fell from a state of glory through only one sin, and refers to the death of Christ as a supreme instance of God's justice in operation (L. 17-29). These thoughts are evidently intended to lead the monk to repent heartily for all his sins so that he may be spared the dreadful punishments that otherwise await him. The fact that only one moment of error was enough to condemn Lucifer and Adam, for instance, prompts the idea that he, with so many sins to his name, is hardly likely to receive different treatment (L. 17-18), and similar considerations are suggested by the Crucifixion:

> «Pues esta justicia fue executada tan cruda y espantosamente en el madero verde y lleno de virtudes, y tanto amado del Padre,

¿qué será en nosotros que somos maderos secos de virtudes y llenos de pecados?» (L. 26-29).

All these reflections emphasise that sin entails the loss of one's happiness and well-being, and by doing so they appeal to servile fear. The chapter devoted to the initial purgative exercise is the longest in the first part, for the meditation it contains is really a model of the kind Cisneros wishes his monk to practise throughout the Way, and so includes instruction on the techniques and forms of prayer to be adopted. The meditation itself develops in three stages, in the first of which, the «vía asperativa», another appeal is, I believe, made to *temor servil*. Before recalling in some detail the sins he has committed in the past (Ch. 12, L. 93-105), the monk considers how much God is displeased by sin, and the punishment it deserves (L. 81-92). Several examples of divine wrath are mentioned; the principal ones are precisely those inserted by Cisneros into the previous chapter: the falls of Lucifer and Adam, and the Passion of Jesus:

> «Considera... cómo el Hijo de Dios tu redentor por el pecado sufrió tan amargosa muerte, porque el pecado no quedasse sin ser punido, ni la justicia de Dios sin satisfación» (L. 84-86).

Yet, since servile fear is praised in chapter 10 because it can introduce one to the love of God, it is not surprising that the growth of such love is encouraged throughout the model exercise. When he has finished examining his conscience, the monk addresses God directly in prayer, and expresses shame at not having responded properly to the many gifts He has offered him (L. 122-129). In the preamble to this prayer he is asked to feel sorrow for his faults, not because they have merited Hell-fire, but because they have offended God's goodness:

> «como tú, pecador... rebolvieres estas cosas en tu pensamiento y te sintieres herido del temor, y en lo interior lleno de dolor, no por las penas del infierno que meresces, mas porque has offendido a tu muy benigno Dios...» (L. 115-119).

Such an awareness of God's love for men and of His mercy complements the opening stress on His justice and wrath, and marks the evolution of a confident, loving response to Him on the part of the monk which becomes more important in the «vía compuntiva», the second stage of the meditation. Now he confesses his failings to the Lord in general terms. His sorrow is inspired not so much by the knowledge that he deserves to suffer for them as by the fact that they have resulted in the loss of His friendship and involved repudiating His love:

> «O Señor, duélome: Porque perdí vuestra amistança. De haber vuestra bondad menospreciado» (L. 144-146).

He convicts himself of ingratitude:

> «De mi gran desagredesçimiento, ca muchas vezes me perdonastes los pecados, e yo mezquino otra vez y otra los torné a renovar» (L. 159-161).

And when in the course of the prayer that follows, he is tempted to despair, he rejects the suggestion that he should kill himself, recalling that His Lord is abundant in mercy (L. 178-184).

Love of God finds further expression in the third stage, the «vía elevativa», in which the monk turns to God with great confidence (L. 194) and begs Him for forgiveness. As he does so he considers the perfections of God and praises them in five Latin words, «Domine, bone, pulcherrime, dulcis, misericors» (L. 200-204). An image provided in the text to explain why he should render praise of this kind informs us that his motives are still likely to be self-interested. Just as jesters praise their lord before making known their requests, so he should extol God before asking Him to pardon his sins (L. 205-210). And yet this concern with self coexists with a growing appreciation of how lovable God is: as he recites the five words he reflects on His goodness to all members of Creation, the angels and saints, the animals and mankind in general, and nature too (L. 210-224). The Passion is now referred to as the means by which the pardon he so greatly desires may be attained (L. 246-251). Finally, after imploring the intercession of Mary and all the saints, he adores God and thanks Him for all His gifts (L. 300-306).

In the course of the model exercise, then, there is a progression from reflections on the justice of God that appeal to fear of being damned to prayers full of confidence in His mercy which encourages one to love Him gratefully: a progression, in fact, from servile fear towards initial. In the remaining meditations of the Way the content of the «vía asperativa» varies with the subject matter, but the last two stages are substantially the same: at the end of each the monk is urged to feel compunction and then to conclude with the prayers of the «vía elevativa».[26]

By the end of the week, both servile fear and the incipient love of God it makes possible should be familiar themes in the monk's devotions. That this is so is confirmed by considering the seven meditations as a whole: those of Tuesday, Wednesday and Thursday are designed to encourage primarily servile fear, while those of the latter half of the week are meant to strengthen faith in God's love. On Tuesday the theme is death, which entered the world through sin. The monk considers its unpredictability, the illness that will precede his own last moments, and the anguish he will then experience when the sins for which he made no reparation come to mind: «Quánto dolor será a ti, quando vieres que por una tan pequeña delectación perdiste aquellos eternos gozos» (Ch. 13, L. 36-37). On Wednesday likewise he reflects that he could spare himself all the terrible torments of Hell by repenting while he still has the chance (Ch. 14, L. 37-41). On Thursday the Last Judgement makes him ponder that people who do not accept God's offer of forgiveness while it is available will suffer the indignation of Christ:

«Mira: Cómo allí mostrará nuestro redentor las señales de su passión, y cómo por aquellas señales los maltratarán, porque lo menospreciaron» (Ch. 15, L. 33-35).

In the exercise of Friday the emphasis alters noticeably. Christ's Passion, considered only in its early stage in Gethsemane, is once more described as an exemplar of divine justice (Ch. 16, L. 42-43), but this is no longer the interpretation of it that predominates. The monk's attention is now drawn to the fact that Christ, as God, suffered to save him, personally, from Hell:

«Deves pensar:... cómo allí se le representaron todos tus pecados, y quánto dolor rescibió por cada qual dellos, offresciéndole por ti satisfación de justicia» (L. 8, 27-29).

On Saturday he considers how Christ's sufferings, particularly those of the Passion, affected His mother Mary, an exercise which involves imagining what it must be to love Him selflessly. One passage concerns the scene in the upper room after Christ's death, where the

---

[26] *Exercitatorio*, ch. 13, L. 69-87; ch. 14, L. 63-68; ch. 15, L. 47-53; ch. 16, L. 74-82; ch. 17, L. 66-69; ch. 18, L. 52-60.

apostles, who had foresaken Him, encountered Mary, who had been faithful. They are described as asking her to forgive them:

> «Mira qué dolor huvo:... quando los discípulos estaban delante con gran vergüença y confusión porque lo havían desanparado, en especial sanct Pedro que lo havía negado, todos hiriéndose en los pechos, demandando perdón a nuestra Señora» (Ch. 17, L. 31, 48-51).

The monk is meant to identify himself with them, especially Peter, and to judge his own sinfulness as they did: by the criterion of unselfish love. So it is that he feels compunction for having, with Peter, repudiated Christ, a compunction that springs from love rather than servile fear:

> «estimulada tu consciencia... conviértete al Señor demandándole perdón de todos tus pecados que tantas vezes le has negado, y a nuestra Señora con todos los otros sanctos» (L. 66-69).

It is on a note of hope and love that the whole series of meditations ends. On Sunday the subject is Paradise, and the monk turns over in his mind the fulfilment of mind and body experienced there. Significantly it is himself that he imagines blissful and forgiven, and not just the saints (Ch. 18, L. 40-51). And his closing prayer is not a request to be spared the pains of Hell, but sorrow for his sins because they involve risking the loss of such joys:

> «hermano... suspira fuertemente porque te has mucho alongado por tus culpas y pecados desta tan excellente morada» (L. 52-55).

By the time the monk has practised these exercises for a month (i.e. four times) his love of God should have deepened. It is a love that proceeds from servile fear, a love that is, in fact, its converse, for just as such fear derives from attachment to one's own well-being, so the love encouraged, particularly in the final meditation, is essentially *gratitude*: for being spared Hell-fire and for the offer of Heaven.

This interpretation of the structuring of part I explains the apparently anomalous position and content of one chapter, the exercise to inspire the monk with fervour (Ch. 6): although a meditation, it is quite removed from those of the purgative Way and from the exercise on fear that precedes them. It is an interesting chapter, for its source was reworked extensively by Cisneros. He drew his inspiration from the *Rosetum* of Mombaer, but of its sixteen points for reflection only two, the last two, are copied literally from the original.[27] A close look at them reveals the care with which they were chosen. Some are evidently intended to stimulate servile fear (e.g. Ch. 6, L. 71-113), while others stress the goodness, favours and mercy of God (e.g. L. 17-39). Admittedly it is surprising that the latter theme should be given such prominence so early in the work: as we have seen, it is not taken up in the purgative exercises themselves until the end of the first stage of the model meditation, and does not take precedence over that of justice until late in the week. An explanation is, however, suggested by Cisneros himself. In the conclusion to the exercise he writes:

> «El fin destas consideraçiones en dos cosas consiste. Primeramente, en el sentido de la propia imperfeción; lo segundo, en desseo de venir en más alta perfeción y muy mayor fervor» (L. 130-132)

The implication is that although he believed servile fear, and the awareness of one's need for grace provoked by it, to be a necessary basis for the spiritual life, he did not wish to overstress it lest his monk should be discouraged from seeking divine forgiveness at all. By reminding him from the start that God is merciful as well as just he not only encouraged him to persevere with the exercises but prepared him for the almost exclusive appeal to servile fear in the first part of the model meditation. He insists, significantly, that the exercise should be practised frequently (L. 136-140). If it is seen in this light its placing among the preparatory chapters seems most appropriate.

### THE SECOND PART

The second part begins at the point at which the first ends: its main exercises are the meditations of chapter 23, all of which concern the gifts received by the monk from God, and they are intended, as we shall see, to inspire him with thanksgiving, and thereby to confirm his grateful love of God.

However, before considering in detail how this part relates to the three grades of fear, it is necessary to resolve a certain confusion concerning its contents. The nature of the illuminative Way, and how one is prepared for it by the purgative, are subjects dealt with early on in two chapters (Ch. 20, 22). In this Way the soul grows in kno-

---

[27] BARAUT, *op. cit.*, t. 1, 117-120.

wledge and love of God, enabled to do so by the removal of previous impediments due to its sins (Ch. 22, L. 3-7). It comes to know Him better by realising how indebted it is to His generosity which has showered it with gifts:

> «Entonçes el ánima a ssí misma pregunta, diziendo: ¿Quién es el mi amado? Responde ella misma: Aquel es que tantos bienes y tantos beneficios me ha fecho» (L. 7-9).

The principal exercise proposed is, as one would expect, meditation on the gifts one has received from God, which the monk is to practise each evening after Compline (Ch. 23, L. 2-6).

The other exercises included in the second part are not so easily related to the purpose of the Way. For instance, why did Cisneros include a long and detailed method of examining one's conscience in this section (Ch. 21)? He does explain that he wishes each monk to recall his faults after Compline (Ch. 21, L. 2-4), but why did he not place this chapter in the first part which is so concerned with compunction and where it would be most appropriate? The meditations on God's gifts are followed by a series of prayers based on the phrases of the *Pater Noster* (Ch. 24) which also seem misplaced. Cisneros, admittedly, recommends the prayers to people in the illuminative Way (Ch. 24, L. 16-20), but does not indicate how they contribute to the realisation of its ends. A recurrent theme in them, as we shall see, is longing to be united with God, which he elsewhere associates with the unitive Way (Ch. 27, L. 114-115). Since reflection on God's gifts is not an important part of them, why were they not placed in the third part of the work where they would have been eminently suited? As for the last chapter of all (Ch. 25), it appears to be quite unconnected thematically with any of the others. It contains a sequence of reproaches to religious who neglect their exercises. A better place for it would surely have been the initial, introductory chapters of Part I.

Faced with these problems, Dom Colombás concluded that the chapters of the second part were chosen in a largely haphazard fashion, and obeyed no carefully thought-out plan:

> «El *Exercitatorio* dedica seis capítulos... a esta que él llama "segunda parte", si bien no todos estos capítulos traten propiamente de la tal vía. Por lo demás, su ordenación no responde a plan alguno bien establecido.»[28]

---

[28] COLOMBÁS, *op. cit.*, 257.

I do not think myself that Cisneros' deployment of subject matter observes no rules. To discover the thinking behind this second part we must pay closer attention to his understanding of the Three Ways, which was rather complex. He held, in common with most medieval writers, that they could be used to describe the whole course of the spiritual life, from imperfection to perfection. In the *Exercitatorio* the progress encompassed by them is from repentance in the purgative Way to the onset of contemplation, the start of union with God, in the unitive.[29] But he was also influenced by another, Bonaventurian tradition which did not make this equation between the Ways and spiritual growth. It finds expression in the closing paragraph of chapter 12:

> «Has de saber que, aunque cada una de aquestas vías tiene nombre determinado y propio modo de proceder, no por esso se excluye que en cada una dellas... no te exercites en todas tres, conviene a saber, en la purgativa, illuminativa y unitiva, reconosçiendo tus miserias, haziendo gracias y ensanchando tu ánima a adorar y magnificar a Dios» (Ch. 12, L. 318-323).

If my earlier analysis of the model meditation is correct, it can be no accident that these words follow it immediately, for its stages between them do involve the practice of all three themes: penitence, reflection on God's gifts that sin abuses, and praise. It contains the Three Ways within itself, in microcosm, as it were.

Cisneros' views are developed in the second part. At the end of the meditations on God's gifts he urges the monk to include thanksgiving in all his prayers and not just in those of the illuminative Way, for it is one of three themes necessary for prayer to be perfect (Ch. 23, L. 255-260). He goes on to explain that the theme given prominence will vary according to the progress one has made, and in this conection uses another tripartite division familiar to previous writers:

> «Y en cada una destas partes el exercitador puede começar la oración, ca no es sienpre necessario começar en el reconoscimiento de las miserias, mas según el estado del ánima, conviene a saber: los principiantes, en el reconoscimiento de las miserias; los aprovechantes, en el hazimiento de gracias; los perfetos... en desseos y sospiros unitivos, conviene a saber de amor» (L. 261-267).

---

[29] For discussion of how Cisneros understands the Three Ways see Baraut, *op. cit.*, t. 2, 218 n. 1, and Peers, *op. cit.*, 23, 24, 26.

Here the three ranks of Christian, beginner, progressive and perfect, describe the gamut of the spiritual life, as the Three Ways do in certain passages.[30]

His understanding of the traditional classifications of spiritual progress makes sense of his deployment of sources. We have seen that all three themes are present in each of the purgative meditations: the one emphasised throughout, though, is repentance, the most important for beginners. In the second part, similarly, the principal exercise involves thanksgiving, the theme appropriate for progressives, but repentance and longing for God are also expressed, in the examination of conscience and in the prayers on the *Pater Noster* respectively. Furthermore, the four initial chapters, considered as a whole, may be said to fall into three sections. The first two (Ch. 20 and 21) stress the relevance of compunction to the illuminative Way by explaining how the purgative Way prepares the soul to enter it (Ch. 20), and encouraging sorrow for sin (Ch. 21). The next chapter explains the primacy of thanksgiving at this stage (Ch. 22), and is followed by exercises that arouse it (Ch. 23). Chapter 24, in turn, opens with a few words on growth in love of God (Ch. 24, L. 134-135) which introduce prayers that express it. In each case a brief reflection on the theme at hand and its connection with the Way is followed by practical, relevant exercices. Far from being erratic, Cisneros' editing seems both careful and intelligent. Admittedly we have not yet explained the inclusion in this section of chapter 25: to do so we must first examine the second part as a whole in terms of the grades of fear, an analysis we are now in a position to undertake.

### THE ILLUMINATIVE EXERCISES

As we noted earlier,[31] the fact that the principal exercise of the part is thanksgiving for God's gifts will tend to confirm the monk in the *temor inicial* he should have been approaching at the end of the purgative Way. If filial fear of God is the ultimate end of the three parts, as I believe, one would expect this incipient love to be encouraged to grow and to become more selfless. This is in fact what occurs. In the chapter that precedes the meditations of chapter 23, Cisneros gives the monk to understand that although grateful love

---

[30] See BARAUT, *op. cit., loc. cit.*
[31] See above, 301.

of God is good it is rooted in self-interest, and for this reason must give way to love of Him for His own sake:

> «Empero, devemos considerar que no devemos principalmente amar a Dios por sus beneficios, mas por su bondad sin medida y por sí mismo» (Ch. 22, L. 13-15).

In the exercises that follow the monk is helped to observe this precept by various means. In each one, for instance, after rendering thanks, he praises God in the words of the Psalmist (Ch. 23, L. 26-31). As he retires, the exercise complete, he privately intones a number of phrases in Castilian, most of which express adoration of the divine perfections. Their purpose is to inspire him with love (L. 39-46, 231-233). Some express a longing to be united with God, and most significantly, to love Him as a son:

> «¿Quándo te amaré con filial amor? ¿Quándo te abraçaré con todas mis entrañas?» (L. 47-48).

On two separate occasions, moreover, Cisneros urges him not to rush to complete the exercises but to dwell on each stage slowly and to treasure the burgeoning love within him, even if it involves abandoning the remainder of the meditation (L. 53-69, 230-231). The growing concern with God rather than with self is made apparent by a further detail: whereas the reflections in the purgative exercises involve the monk adressing and berating himself as a prelude to prayer, those of the second part are directed personally to God and are themselves prayers.

The theme of love of God becomes more and more dominant as the second part develops. In the introduction to the meditations on the *Pater* one reads that its seven petitions will be interpreted in the anagogical sense: that is, they will be related to life in Heaven, the ultimate end of man (Ch. 24, L. 20-23). Since the next life is the state of union with God, and presupposes the attainment of perfect love, it is not surprising that the meditations give expression to a longing for *temor filial*. The desire to love God as a son occurs early in the preparatory prayer:

> «O padre muy dulçe, vos sois acquel que engendráys fijos spirituales... Pues assí es, Señor, si yo soy verdaderamente hijo vuestro, mostradme cómo os pueda amar de amor verdadero y abraçar con todas mis entrañas» (L. 24-29).

306

As he reflects on each of the petitions, the monk prays that he may love God more than any earthly thing (L. 54-62), that the Lord alone may reign in Him (L. 64-72), that he may become perfectly one with Him (L. 80-86), and never be separated from Him (L. 124-126). The prayers based on the seventh petition are the most interesting of all. The monk prays that he may be delivered from all evil, «sed libera nos a malo». By «malo» he means particularly the pain experienced in the next life by sinners; the progress made since the purgative Way when similar requests were prompted by self-interest may be measured by the fact that it is not Hell-fire alone that concerns him but Purgatory too, and not because he wishes to be spared punishment but because he wishes to be with God:

> «Y no pido yo esto, padre amado y bueno, por huyr los tormentos, mas porque mucho tiempo detenido en el purgatorio no sea enbargado el cumplimiento de mi deseo, conviene a saber, de acatar la tu magestad llena de gracias» (L. 130-133).

The fear expressed in this prayer is *temor filial*, fear of being separated from God because one loves Him. It develops further in the third part.

CHAPTER 25

In the light of this analysis we may now explain why Cisneros included chapter 25 in the second part and not, for instance, in the first. Its purpose is obviously to jolt the lazy or negligent religous into practising spiritual exercises and to warn the more committed against temptations to laxity. It may, in this sense, be classed with the chapters designed to inspire fervour, of the first part. It differs from them, however, in one notable trait: it includes no direct appeal to servile fear. On the contrary, one of its recurrent themes is that the negligent religious abuses God's generous gifts. God has given him the peace and opportunity to pray (Ch. 25, L. 7-9), placed him in an exalted position (L. 35), given him a greater chance to do good than others (L. 40-41), honoured him with the role of mediator between Him and the laity (L. 46-48); and he has a right to be called one of His special friends and servants (L. 23-24). It is pointed out that he deserves to forfeit God's love, to be denied signs of it (L. 29-30), including consolation in prayer (L. 44-45), and to be passed over in favour of others (L. 37-39): the loss envisaged is not primarily that of physical or material well-being, but of spiritual gifts and privileges.

Such arguments would not appeal to the monk gripped by servile fear. They are directed to one who can appreciate something of the great love God has shown him, and the horror of being deprived of that love. As such their position in the second part is quite appropriate.

## THE UNITIVE EXERCISES

The organisation of the third part is more self-explanatory than that of the previous two. It opens with a chapter in which the nature of the unitive Way is defined:

> «vía unitiva... es aquella por la qual el exercitador ya purgado y alumbrado amorosamente es unido a su creador, alegrándose de sus perfeciones, y desseando aplazer a él solo prompta y alegremente» (Ch. 26, L. 12-15).

The meditations that follow (Ch. 27), arranged according to the days of the week, all concern God's perfections, as one might except. Their title indicates that he who practises them will be enabled to climb six steps that lead to union, «subir seys grados que convienen para ayuntar el ánima con Dios» (Ch. 27, L. 5-6). The remaining three chapters, logically enough, deal with union, and one of them, the last, describes the six steps mentioned.

How does this part relate to the grades of fear? Briefly, the filial fear encouraged in the illuminative Way is now expected to develop further until it becomes the prime characteristic of the monk's spirituality. Cisneros, in common with the body of orthodox spiritual writers, did not hold that one could love God selflessly in this life, and points this out in the course of the third part (Ch. 30, L. 101-105). Filial fear is an ideal he sets before his reader, to which he wishes him fervently to aspire. From the introductory chapter on it is placed before him. The Way is defined as the transposing of love from creatures to Creator (Ch. 26, L. 30-33). It is said to involve loving Him above all actual or conceivable things (L. 58-62). In one passage he is explicitly instructed to love God for His sake rather than out of self-interest in any form:

> «Y este amor con que buscas al tu amado ha de ser... principalmente por su bondad, según aquello del psalmista, que dize... yo, Señor, puramente os amo, no por los dones de los çielos, ni tanpoco por los dones de sobre la tierra, mas por vuestra sobe-

rana bondad y por vos mismo, sobre todas las cosas que son en el çielo y en la tierra» (L. 23-29).

These precepts are echoed in the prayers on three of the divine perfections (omnipotence, wisdom, goodness) recommended at the close of the chapter. The monk expresses the joy inspired in him, a joy that transcends egoism:

> «O Señor y amado mío, yo me gozo porque vos soys potentíssimo, no por el bien que dello me viene principalmente, assí como buscando mi provecho, mas porque esta es vuestra perfeción» (L. 74-76).

The meditations of the next chapter (Ch. 27) are all designed to prompt and facilitate the growth of such love. In each a sequence of points for reflection is followed by ardent prayers which remain unvaried. The monk tells God that He is all he desires (Ch. 27, L. 49-50), and asks for grace to love nothing else (L. 77-88). To those who prefer a simpler method, Cisneros recommends short prayers of the kind he introduced into the illuminative Way. The two examples given express a longing to be joined with God, and to love Him with specifically *filial* devotion:

> «O Señor, ¿quándo os podré abraçar con çierto y entero amor? O amador ardentíssimo, ¿quándo os amaré con filial amor?» (L. 100-101).

The two chapters that follow the meditations are concerned with «verdadera sabiduría», the term used in the prologue for the experience of union. Although they do not treat the grades of fear directly, they do help one to see how the progression from servile to filial fear has prepared the monk for union. «Wisdom», or contemplation, in the sense used here is very different in some respects from the exercises of the three parts. For instance, it involves less activity on the part of the monk, being a gratuitous gift of God. The understanding, so active in the exercises, becomes passive:

> «la nuestra ánima se ha aquí, assí como receptiva y no como activa quanto el entender, ca allí donde reyna sola affeción de amor, el seso ni el entendimiento no tienen cosa que hazer» (Ch. 28, L. 17-20).

Instead of preceding the experience of love, as it does in the meditations, it now if anything follows it (Ch. 29, L. 5-8). Cisneros is, however, adamant that one may prepare and dispose oneself to receive it, and the analysis of it which he provides includes references to techniques of preparation adopted earlier in the Three Ways. Beginners in prayer, for example, are said to benefit by reflecting on creation and God's activity in it — as the monk does, especially in the illuminative Way:

> «los nuevos y no tan altos contemplativos, ante que sean en la inflamación deste amor, en la qual toda contemplación se acaba y tiene fin, han menester primeramente pensar en las creaturas y obras de Dios» (L. 25-28).

Other preparations include the short ejaculatory prayers recommended earlier in chapter 22, and in the exercises of chapter 26, as Cisneros actually notes (L. 60-64). Elsewhere it is hinted that before receiving «wisdom» the soul must have eradicated its attachment to self — and this, as I have argued, is the purpose of the Three Ways (Ch. 28, L. 26-29). Moreover, although it is the discontinuity between meditation and contemplation that receives emphasis, a certain continuity between the two is evident also, particularly in the matter of selfless love. The love of God experienced in contemplation is a response to His perfection, and is not self-interested:

> «ca ni en cosa más baxa que Dios se reposa, ni aun en él por respecto de algún deleyte o provecho, mas por solo amor de aquel que sólo es soberanamente amable» (L. 36-38).

The six steps which lead from the beginnings of contemplation to complete union are also described in terms of increasingly perfect love. The second step renders the soul incapable of finding delight in anything apart from its Lord (Ch. 30, L. 28-34). The fourth makes it willing to accept any sort of suffering except sin rather than be separated from Him (L. 43-48). To the six steps the author of chapter 30 adds two more, «seguridad» where the soul loses all fear of being torn apart from God against its will, and «complido reposo»:

> «ca pues ninguna tribulación ni daño corporal ni temor pueden espantar la tal ánima, síguesse que ella está en complida paz y reposo, y tan grande que no se puede dezir por ninguna lengua» (L. 93-96).

VII

The precise connection between the evolution of filial fear on the one hand and union on the other becomes clearer in the light of a passage already quoted from chapter 5:

> «El fin de nuestros exerciçios... es alcançar la pureza del coraçón y la perfecta caridad de Dios. El uno, esto es, la caridad... es fin último. El otro fin, que es secundario y dispositivo, es la pureza del coraçón, que nos dispone para alcançar la perfecta caridad» (Ch. 5, L. 48-53).

We noted earlier that in this context «perfecta caridad» is a synonym of «union» or «true wisdom».[32] It follows that purity of heart is achieved by the movement from servile towards filial fear: for this movement disposes the monk to receive «wisdom», as we have seen. A couple of passages in the third part confirm that this equation is correct. The unselfish love to which the monk should aspire is qualified as «puríssimo»:

> «Y este amor con que buscas al tu amado ha de ser puríssimo, conviene a saber, principalmente por su bondad» (Ch. 26, L. 23, 24).

By way of illustration a line from Psalm 72 is quoted in Latin, and then translated to include another reference to purity (L. 25-29).

The progress made between the purgative and unitive Ways is indicated, finally, by one tiny but remarkable detail. In the exercises of the first part, designed to arouse *temor servil*, the monk sees himself as a prisoner on trial before a severe judge, and he feels afraid (Ch. 12, L. 70-73). In those of the third part, by contrast, he tries to feel love instead, and sees himself as a son or bride (Ch. 27, L. 7-10), the two images used in chapter 10 of *temor filial*.[33]

This analysis of the first three parts of the *Exercitatorio* has shown, I think, that they are arranged according to a preconceived plan, which may be discovered by examining Cisneros' theory of spiritual direction. He believed purity of heart to be a precondition of union with God, the purpose of the contemplative life. He conceived of its attainment in terms of a progression through three kinds of fear, and ordered the exercises of the three Ways accordingly. The result is a programme of prayer which takes the monk who follows it from preoccupation with self *(temor servil)*, through grateful love

[32] *Ibid.*, 293.
[33] *Ibid.*, 294.

of God *(temor inicial)*, to love of Him for His own sake *(temor filial)*, which is brought to perfection in the experience of union.

## THE FOURTH PART

The fourth part of the *Exercitatorio* is nine chapters longer than the previous three, but despite this, and the wide range of subjects it treats, is not subdivided by Cisneros at all. Passages relating the choice of material to his general aims are included in the text, as we shall see, but they are fewer in number than before, and less clear. The reader is likely to be confused about its place in the treatise as a whole:

> «to many... the chapters containing the meditations based upon them (the Three Ways) are the principal part of the book. They think of it as a threefold collection of exercises, together with some supplementary chapters of less practical value, forgetting that these last occupy half the book».[34]

Allison Peers believed that it fell into three subsections, of unequal length: eighteen chapters on contemplation (Ch. 31-48), eleven on the life of Christ (Ch. 49-60), and nine on perseverance in prayer (Ch. 61-69). His classification is convincing on a first reading. But he did not explain how these subsections were related to each other and to the work's overall purpose: and on closer examination they appear so disparate and disorganised in content that it is hard to accept them as carefully thought-out.[35]

The first eighteen chapters, for instance, deal with very varied topics: some concern contemplation itself (Ch. 36-39) and its preconditions (Ch. 31-35); others defend the monastic life against detractors (Ch. 40-43); others again include discussion of techniques of mental prayer (Ch. 46-48). True, one could argue that they all pertain to the «contemplative life», but even so they constitute an assembly of apparently random texts on the subject. The following eleven chapters do treat the life and death of Christ, but after a fashion that is very far from straightforward. After an introductory passage on how to contemplate the Gospel (Ch. 49), there is a partial summary of its principal events, beginning with the Prophets (Ch. 50-52). For some reason not made explicit this is at once followed by a

---

[34] PEERS, *op. cit.*, 26.
[35] *Ibid.*, 13-14.

second summary in Latin (Ch. 53). The next chapter, on the Last Supper, develops into a disquisition on receiving Communion (Ch. 54, 55). The subsequent four all treat the Passion: only one, though, contains the narration of events (Ch. 58). The other three consist of praise of the devotion (Ch. 56), an explanation of six ways of contemplating the events (Ch. 57), and prayers based on the Passion in general (Ch. 59). After this lengthy treatment of Christ's death, His Resurrection and Ascension, and Pentecost, are dispatched in one short summary (Ch. 60), with which the narration ends. One's initial impression is that the sequence of these chapters obeys no precise plan. The concluding nine chapters deal with the contemplative life in general terms. They form the most convincing of Peers' categories. Remarks about perseverance in prayer (Ch. 61-64) and guidelines for the contemplative (Ch. 65-68) are followed by a concluding summary (Ch. 69). They seem, however, to be a continuation of the opening section, and at first sight there appears to be no good reason why they should not have been included in it. The seeming absence of a concern with form was noted by Dom Colombás:

> «Y así, sin esforzarse lo más mínimo para llegar al número setenta de sus capítulos, en este capítulo 69 pone fin Cisneros a su *Exercitatorio*. Ha dicho cuanto quería decir; la estética de los números no le importa nada.»[36]

How are we to explain the apparent disorderliness of this fourth part, and reconcile it with the concern for precision noted in the previous three? Peers thought an explanation lay in its subject matter:

> «It must be admitted that, in these chapters which deal with contemplation, and even more in the fourth section... Cisneros is considerably less clear than elsewhere. He is drawing not so much upon his own imagination or experience as upon authorities.»[37]

We have seen, though, that by no means all the chapters deal with contemplation. Those on the monastic calling and the Gospel were surely familiar to the Abbot. Three main problems must concern us if we are to understand his intentions. First, and foremost: how is it connected with the purpose of the treatise outlined in the prologue? Secondly, does it have an underlying form, as the first three parts

---

[36] COLOMBÁS, *op. cit.*, 267.
[37] PEERS, *op. cit.*, 24.

do, or is it just an anthology? Thirdly, and more specifically, how are the exercises it contains related to the earlier ones, and are they, like them, structured?

## PURPOSE

Cisneros himself provides an answer to the first question. At the end of the third part he writes:

> «Hasta aquí havemos puesto en prática las dichas tres vías, y cómo por ellas meditando y orando podrás ordenadamente venir al fin desseado, que es ayuntar el ánima con Dios. Por ende, haziendo fin en esta vía unitiva, conviene agora que brevemente toquemos en qué manera contemplando podrás venir al dicho fin» (Ch. 30, L. 128-132).

His words may be interpreted in two ways. He may mean that the section of the work concerned with the Three Ways has come to an end, and that he will, instead, talk of contemplation. The phrase «haziendo fin en esta vía unitiva» suggests this. It is, however, an ambiguous phrase. The «unitive Way», as understood in the third part, denotes the meditations on God's perfections, and these, it is true, are not developed further in the fourth. But it also denotes the experience of contemplation, or union, for which the exercises prepare the monk, and his concluding words, «conviene agora que... toquemos en qué manera contemplando podrás venir al dicho fin», suggest that this subject, already discussed in chapters 28-30, will be carried further. A second reading would therefore be that the exercises of the unitive Way are concluded, but not the treatment of contemplation: in which case the fourth part should be seen as a continuation, in one sense, of the third, and as belonging to the unitive Way. This reading is confirmed by a glance at the definition of purpose set out in the prologue:

> «En este libro... tractaremos cómo el ejercitador y varón devoto se ha de exercitar según las tres vías... Y cómo... meditando, orando, contemplando, ordenadamente podrá subir a alcançar el fin desseado» (Prol., L. 7-18).

The means of realising the end are threefold: yet at the close of the third part Cisneros claims to have dealt with only two, meditation and prayer. Contemplation remains. At the end of the fourth part,

314

on the other hand, he includes it in his summary of what has been achieved:

> «havemos tractado cómo el varón devoto se deve exercitar meditando, orando y contemplando, para ayuntar su ánima con Dios por las tres vías» (Ch. 69, L. 5-7).

This passage not only confirms that the last part belongs to the schema of the Ways: it implies that we may expect to find in our study of it the same consistency of purpose, applied in detail, that we noted in the carlier sections.

### FORM

Our approach to the second problem, the overall form of the part, is greatly aided by the solution of the first. Early in chapter 31, Cisneros repeats his undertaking to discuss contemplation:

> «tractaremos aquí brevemente de la dicha contemplación, como quier que della hayamos harto dicho arriba» (Ch. 31, L. 10-12).

Only some of the chapters following are about it, however, as we noted above: the exercises on Christ's life are really meditations, as Allison Peers pointed out:

> «though... he details his six degrees of higher prayer (in chapter 30), he fills most (sic) of the chapters which follow with meditations suited to those who are still in the lower states of prayer».[38]

But is Cisneros inconsistant? Critics have not paid enough attention to the adverb he used at the end of the third part and repeats here: «brevemente». He cannot be referring to the fourth part as a whole, and a close examination of the text that follows confirms, I think, that he is not.

Cisneros keeps his promise to deal with contemplation in the first thirteen chapters only, and does so in three distinct stages. Chapters 31-35 define it in broad terms: by distinguishing the knowledge, or wisdom, it confers from the natural kind (31, 33), describing the sort of temperaments suited to it (Ch. 32), and explaining how asceticism is an indispensable preparation for it (Ch. 34, 35). He then

---

[38]  *Ibid.*, 28.

describes it more precisely and directly as perfect love (Ch. 36-38). Finally, he defines its purpose and its value for society by defending it against criticism (Ch. 40-43). These chapters between them fill but a third of the fourth part. Those remaining have a different purpose: to describe more specifically how one may prepare for contemplation by meditation. Towards the end of chapter 38, in which the discussion of contemplation as love comes to a head, he reminds the reader that he has already explained how to dispose oneself to receive it: «Y en qué manera puede ser alcançado este amor, demostrémoslo en alguna manera» (Ch. 38, L. 32-33). He is referring, of course, to the exercises of the Thre Ways. In the chapter following two kinds of silence and solitude are described, external and internal. The reason for its inclusion at this point does not become clear until chapter 44 when, having finished his reply to detractors of the contemplative life, he resumes discussion of «silence», with an explicit reference back to the previous passage (Ch. 44, L. 3-5). Now it is the practical matter of how to attain inner silence, how to prepare for contemplation, that concerns him (L. 6 sqq.). He concludes that it is perfectly attained only by a gift of grace, for which one must dispose oneself:

> «Aqueste don de gracia verdaderamente es atribuydo a aquellos solos que diligente y ardientemente lo buscan, y para esto se disponen» (L. 32-34).

The next four chapters merely develop this conclusion. In chapter 45 one learns that meditation is the specific means of preparation:

> «Y por ende digo que la tal elevación del ánima devota... es hecho por fuerte y sancta meditaçión o por ardiente amor» (Ch. 45, L. 10-13).

But meditation on what subject? In chapter 46 Cisneros seeks an answer in the writings of the saints and rejects several possibilities: Richard of St. Victor is too speculative (Ch. 46, L. 22-27), St. Gregory is not specific enough (L. 32-35); the theme of the mystical marriage. developed by St. Bernard and Henry Suso, is not suitable for beginners (L. 53-64); and St. Jerome's suggestion cannot be adopted because it has already been made use of in the first three parts (L. 36-52). Eventually, in chapter 47, a satisfactory subject is found: the life and Passion of Christ (Ch. 47, L. 4-29). Once it has been extolled, the discussion of modes of preparation comes to an end, as Cisneros makes plain in his concluding remarks:

> «Y por evitar prolixidad, dexados otros muchos modos que tovieron otras muchas devotas personas en los exerciçios y materias de la contemplaçión, diremos agora della algunas cosas» (L. 42-43).

True to his promise, the next chapter expounds in summary three doctrines of Richard of St. Victor about contemplation itself. The third brings the discussion back once again to the practical realm:

> «el exercitador en su contemplaçión sintiéndose frio se deve escalentar con arte especial... tomando alguna materia para se ençender... según que arriba havemos dicho en las meditaciones de las tres vías» (Ch. 48, L. 61-65).

Having noted that such material has already been supplied in the Three Ways, Cisneros promises to supply more, on the life of Christ (L. 66-71). With this reference to both sets of exercises the chapter ends.

Seen in this light the arrangement of part four makes sense. It is not really helpful to subdivide it along the lines suggested by Peers, though it does fall into three parts. It opens with thirteen chapters in which the ends, nature and conditions of contemplation are examined, as announced at the close of the third part. They are followed by seventeen chapters on ways of preparing for contemplation in mental prayer: six of these are concerned with general principles, the sifting of possible methods, and the choice of one in particular, which is then set out in the form of exercises (Ch. 50-60). The concluding section resumes the subject of contemplation, but deals with aspects of it that the monk will need to bear in mind if he is to persevere and develop in his vocation.

## THE LIFE OF CHRIST

Let us now examine more closely the ten chapters devoted to Christ's life. They include the only exercises set out in the fourth part. As we have noted, Cisneros connects them with those of the Three Ways on more than one occasion. They have the same purpose: to prepare the monk for contemplation. The question naturally arises: is there a structure to them too? I will argue that there is and that it is also based on a theory of spiritual direction. But before discovering that theory and its application, it will help, as a preliminary, to examine the stages in which the Gospel is narrated.

It is not generally noted that the story of Christ's life is related in three parts. At the close of chapter 48, Cisneros promises a summary of events up to the Last Supper (Ch. 48, L. 70, 71), which he provides in chapter 52: it ends with the entry into Jerusalem which preceded the meal. This first part is followed by a chapter in Latin (Ch. 53) that effectively divides it from the second, which concerns the Passion. Chapter 54 evokes the Supper, while chapter 58 continues the narration up to the piercing of Christ's corpse by Longinus (Ch. 58, L. 206-213). The concluding part covers the days between the Resurrection and Pentecost (Ch. 60).

In the preamble to chapter 49, Cisneros mentions an idea which is quite central to his approach to the life of Christ. He refers to Him as a mediator by whom men come to know and love God, and implies that He can fulfil this role because He shares both natures:

> «Deves saber que nuestro redentor Dios y hombre, medianero entre Dios y los hombres, es la carrera por la qual al conoscimiento de la divinidad y amor juntamente deves sobir» (Ch. 49, L. 4-6).

The point is made more explicitly later:

> «más façil es a nosotros el conoscimiento de la humanidad, assí como más inprimida en nuestra mente, que el conoscimiento de la divinidad que es muy más apartado della» (L. 87-89).

The frequency with which statements of this doctrine recur throughout the treatise suggests that it was most important to the compiler, as Dom Baraut says.[39] As early as chapter 8 one reads that the life and death of Christ is a «door» by which one passes through His human nature to the divine:

> «Y en señal desto fue abierto su costado con fierro, porque claramente conosçiéssemos que no podíamos entrar al amor de su divinidad sino por las puertas de las llagas de su humanidad» (Ch. 8, L. 24-26).

The image is re-introduced in the very first chapter of the fourth part: the way to contemplation is described as meditation on Christ's

---

[39] BARAUT, *op. cit.*, t. 1, 82.

deeds, and those who spurn it are called thieves, attempting to enter the sheepfold but refusing to use the «door» (Ch. 31, L. 24-31). Later, in chapter 47, when the life of Christ is finally chosen as a subject for meditation, the teaching is reiterated with an allusion to St. Bonaventure (Ch. 47, L. 19-29), which is subsequently repeated (Ch. 48, L. 66-70).

The doctrine finds its full expression in chapter 49, in which the monk is taught three ways of contemplating the Gospel events. The first involves concentrating on the human nature of Christ and considering His exemplarity as man. It is a matter of «following» Him in the imagination, and rejoicing in His presence, for any of the reasons that prompted men to do so while He was on earth (Ch. 49, L. 19-46). It prepares one for contemplation by encouraging detachment, after the example of the Apostles who gave up all they held dear to be with Him (L. 47-59). The second, more advanced, involves bearing in mind both natures of Jesus:

> «Conviene a saber, contemplando no solamente açerca de la humanidad de Christo, mas... en Christo hombre conviene hallar a Dios» (L. 65-67).

In scenes that reveal His divinity, such as those that include miracles, one should make an act of faith in His humanity, and *vice versa* (L. 74-80). The last way is the passage from His humanity to His divinity:

> «es por la humanidad de Christo al affecto spiritual levantarse contemplando... y assí por el conoscimiento de la humanidad, al conoscimiento y amor de la divinidad venir por ayuntamiento de Dios» (L. 96-100).

The chapter is taken entirely From the *De spiritualibus ascensionibus* of Zutphen except for three sentences, apparently by Cisneros himself, in which these three ways of contemplating are said to correspond with the three ranks of Christian defined earlier in the work, beginners, progressives and the perfect (L. 62-63, 94-95, 120-121).

By placing a full exposition of this teaching just before the Gospel account, Cisneros evidently intended his monk to learn from and practise it in some way as he performed the exercises. He nowhere indicates, however, exactly how it relates to them. One might suppose that he leaves the individual to choose the way of contemplating that suits him most, depending on the progress he has made. Certain passages in the exercises themselves, though, suggest that there may be a direct correlation between the three ways of contemplating and the arrangement of material in chapters 50 to 60. For instance, the narration of the Passion in chapter 58, is prefaced by a few brief remarks about points to bear in mind while considering it. The last is to recall throughout the two natures of Christ, God and man. One is at once reminded of the second way of contemplating. Cisneros himself refers back to it:

> «Y nota que en todo este modo de contemplaçión de la passión del Señor, según que arriba diximos, sienpre has de pensar a Christo no solamente honbre solo ni Dios solo, mas una persona que es Dios y hombre verdadero» (Ch. 58, L. 39-42).

In the meditations that follow, the principle is applied. After considering the human weakness of Jesus in Gethsemane, the monk reflects that He was divine — in accordance with the earlier teaching:

> «Y sometiéndote a él por consentimiento de la razón, cree y piensa ser él verdaderamente Hijo de Dios, Principio de todas las cosas, Salvador de los hombres, Gualardonador de todos» (L. 83-88).

Next he reflects on the trials before Anas, Caiphas and Herod, after which he thinks of Jesus as «Innocentíssimo, mitíssimo, amantíssimo, nobilíssimo» (L. 117-120). These adjectives recall others used of Christ in chapter 49:

> «Si piensas a Christo hombre, dende te verná dulce affición y gran confiança, porque es mansuetíssimo, benígnissimo, nobilíssimo, suavíssimo, todo bello, gracioso y hermoso» (Ch. 49, L. 83-85).

The question arises: if Cisneros makes allowance for the second way of contemplating, what of the first and the third? Now the Passion, as we noted above, is the second stage of the Gospel narration: it is preceded by an exercise on the previous life of Christ, in chapter 52. If one reads this with chapter 49 in mind many parallels between it and the first way of contemplating do, I think, become plain. First, the humanity of Jesus is especially emphasised, notably in the Nativity scenes, when one's natural sympathy for the innocent and vulnerable is appealed to:

> «Contempla: cómo Dios pequennyto gime y llora en el pesebre... Duélete del niño, porque seyendo tan tierno es llagado, y por ti derrama su sangre» (Ch. 52, L. 6, 7; 20, 21).

VII

Secondly, the first way of contemplating involves following Jesus, and watching and listening to Him in the imagination, as if one were truly present. Similarly, in chapter 52 the monk is asked to kiss the manger in imagination (L. 15), greet the Holy Family, Anna and Simeon in the Temple (L. 36-37), follow the child and His parents to Egypt (L. 41, 42), and accompany Jesus in His public life:

> «[Contempla]... cómo muchas vezes gran pueblo seguía a Christo... Síguelo tú, y está cerca dél porque oyas sus palabras, mirando la cara del Señor y de los apóstoles, y sus coloquios» (L. 81-84).

Thirdly, one's attention is drawn continually to the exemplarity of Christ's acts. His patience when exiled as a child teaches one how to bear suffering (L. 40-42); the obscurity of his early years teaches the virtues of silence and humility (L. 44-48); His resistance to temptation in the desert shows one how to deal with it (L. 61-64). This too is a characteristic of the first way, which is at one point described as «aqueste exerciçio... esto es, ocuparse açerca de las costumbres y enxemplos de Christo nuestro redentor» (Ch. 49, L. 48, 49).

If this interpretation is correct it may explain why a second summary appears in Latin in chapter 53. The meditation of chapter 52 is said to be «para exercicio de los nuevos contemplativos» (Ch. 52, L. 2, 3). The first way of contemplating is also for beginners (Ch. 49, L. 62, 63). Chapter 53, on the other hand, is for «los más exercitados y enseñados» (Ch. 53, L. 3). One needs to remember that the monk, when he reaches these chapters, will already have practised the exercises of the Three Ways. It is quite possible that he will wish to pray in a more advanced way than chapter 52 offers. For such a person, I suggest, Cisneros provides chapter 53: it is in litany form, and contains praise of Christ as well as petition; as such it expresses a particularly ardent and affective love of God.

It would be tempting to seek the third way of contemplating in the third stage of the narration. Chapter 60, however, is factual and brief to the point of excluding almost all discussion of, and textual reflection on, the events related. In one passage the journey of the resurrected Lord to Galilee is interpreted as an image of the soul's ascent to perfection in the future life, but without emphasis on the notion of union with God (Ch. 60, L. 37-61). Cisneros does make allowance for the third way, but earlier, in the chapter immediately following the account of the Passion. In a preamble to ardent prayers to Christ crucified one is urged to pass through His wounded side to attain His heart, there to be transformed:

> «no solamente mete tu mano en su costado, mas enteramente por la puerta o llaga del costado entra hasta el su coraçón. Y allí por ardentíssimo amor del tu amado crucificado, todo en él transformado, con los clavos del amor divinal fixo... ninguna otra cosa busques, ninguna otra cosa dessees, ni en ninguna otra cosa quieras ser consolado salvo que tú con Christo puedas morir en la cruz» (Ch. 59, L. 26-33).

One is reminded of chapter 8, in which it is said that the wound in the side is a sign that we can attain love of the divinity only by passing through the wounds or «doors» of Christ's humanity (Ch. 8, L. 24-26). This passage from the human to the divine is, of course, the distinguishing characteristic of the third way of contemplating (Ch. 49, L. 96-104).

IMITATION, DEATH AND UNION

The transfer of attention from the humanity of Christ to His divinity is accompanied by a parallel progression from imitation of His virtues, through death with Him, to union. This progression is evident in the six ways of considering the Passion outlined in chapter 57. The first two are respectively to imitate and suffer with Him: the latter involves «sharing» the Crucifixion out of compassion:

> «de la yel y vinagre y mirra que a él dieron seamos embriagados, y sólo las llagas del Señor sintamos... y no sea nada en nosotros que no se desaga de dolor de compassión y sea largamente affligido» (Ch. 57, L. 62-66).

The fifth involves transformation into Christ crucified (L. 143-153), the sixth, even fuller union:

> «Y tanto quanto más se allega a él, tanto más por devotíssimo amor en sí desfallesce y se desfaze, y quanto más desfallesce de sí mismo por amor y devoçión, tanto más se ayunta con su amado muerto por él» (L. 159-163).

There is certainly some correspondence between these six ways and the narration of the Passion in chapter 58, which is divided into six parts. In the preamble one is urged to imitate Christ in carrying the Cross:

> «en lo que leyeres, pensares y contemplares, contempla como si te dixiese Christo: Esto hize por ti porque tú sigas mis pissadas y te humilles y seas paciente, y tomando tu cruz me sigas» (Ch. 58, L. 31-33).

In the second part of the account it is compassion for Him that is stressed (L. 115, 116). In the fourth the theme of imitation becomes important again, but now it is imitation as a result of compassion:

> «estudia y acostúmbrate de manera que, por mucha costumbre de padescer por Christo, tengas el ábito de la virtud según la semejança de la ymitaçión suya» (L. 195-197).

At the end of the fifth, one is encouraged to embrace the Cross, to share it, to die with Him (L. 215-222).

In the course of the Passion narration alone, then, the monk progresses from a desire to imitate Jesus the exemplary man to a yearning to share His death. If we consider the other chapters in the same light, a similar pattern emerges. In those before chapter 58 imitation of Jesus is the principal theme. It informs chapter 52, as we have seen, and even more so chapter 56, in which the dying Saviour is praised as a paradigm of the virtues (Ch. 56, L. 45-50). By contrast, in the chapter which follows the account of the Passion, it is union with, and transformation into, Him that is expressed, in the passage quoted earlier (Ch. 59, L. 25-35). In the whole section on the Gospel, between chapters 50 and 60, the theme of imitation is emphasised at first; it gradually becomes that of death with Christ, which is in turn succeeded by that of union.


CONCLUSION

It would be foolish to argue that the fourth part of the *Exercitatorio* is as cohesive and self-consistent as one expects an original work to be. It is a compilation. And yet, as I hope to have shown, it is far from being a mere collection of texts on a common theme. Nor is it just an appendix or supplement to the first three parts, but a necessary continuation and completion of them, more particularly of the third. It is foreshadowed in the prologue, which is echoed at its close.

The exercises it contains are structured according to a theory of spiritual direction, like those of the Three Ways. Between them the two sets of exercises included in the work inform us that Cisneros particularly approved of two methods of preparing for contemplation: the gradual eradication of servile fear by love, and aspirations to union with God through imitation and compassionate love of Christ.

In several passages he relates these two methods to each other. In chapter 38 he describes a love of God so great that it does not care about death or even paradise. Such a love is, of course, the end set before the monk in the first three parts of the work: now, though, it is defined in terms of death to self:

> «en el estado del tal amor ya dicho, sería dicho muerto y cru-cificado al mundo, porque... dormiría a las vanidades deste siglo y velaría a los bienes eternos» (Ch. 38, L. 4-26).

Later, in chapter 68, near the end of the fourth part, the monk is urged to practise his exercises on death, judgement, Hell and the vanity of this life, even when he is very advanced, until love casts out all fear (Ch. 68, L. 13-35). The very last chapter of all includes an allusion to the image of the three kisses, first used of the Three Ways in chapter 19 (Ch. 69, L. 115-119). It also contains an appeal to the monk to aspire to pure and filial love, in words which could well have prefaced the first three parts:

> «El fin de la meditaçión, oraçión y contemplaçión no sea por tu provecho, no por evadir las penas o por esperança de ganançia o del premio celestial... porque este tal sería amor merçenario. Mas medita, ora y contempla por puro y filial amor...» (L. 55-60).

The most remarkable confirmation of Cisneros' consistency of purpose is provided by a few lines that occur early in chapter 8, where one reads that to attain truly devout prayer and a desire to be joined to God by the Three Ways one should reflect on two subjects:

> «Primeramente, las materias que traen temor, por las quales el ánima comiença la carrera spiritual para se allegar a Dios. Lo segundo, deve pensar a menudo la vida y passión de nuestro redentor» (Ch. 8, L. 19-22).

The first subject, «las materias que traen temor», is not mentioned in the *Mystica theologia* of Hugh of Balma, which is the source of the remainder of the passage.[40] Cisneros himself inserted it, for a reason which will be clear in the light of our analysis of the text. He wished to refer, not just to the meditations of the first part, which very evidently inspire fear in the sense of «terror», but to the exercises of the entire Three Ways. He thus transformed a general precept of Hugh of Balma into a description of the overall plan of the *Exercitatorio*. If he had concluded the work after the third part he would have left one of the two subjects he considered necessary in prayer completely untreated.

These two subjects, and the theories connected with them, are the twin poles of his teaching and explain the structure of his treatise. It is a remarkable work. Allison Peers believed that it read like an original literary creation, even when one knew it to be a compilation. Dom Baraut partly accounted for this impression by demonstrating the technical accomplishment with which its sources were combined. I hope to have produced evidence of its thematic unity, and of the compiler's originality as a writer of spiritual exercises. Of course, the theories of spiritual progress which he adopted were not of his devising: he drew them from previous authors in the tradition of methodical prayer, notably Zutphen. He managed, however, to adapt them to his personal ends, to use them as a basis for his wide choice of texts, and by doing so to make them completely his own.

---

[40] *Ibid.*, t. 2, 124 n. 2.

# VIII

## THE EXERCISES OF SAINT IGNATIUS LOYOLA AND THE EXERCITATORIO DE LA VIDA SPIRITUAL

St. Ignatius Loyola began to compose his *Spiritual Exercises* in 1522 and is thought to have completed their substance before 1527, when he left Spain for France. In 1522 he could not read Latin, and the only meditation manual available in Castilian was by García de Cisneros. Did he know the Benedictine's work, and if so did it influence his? These questions have been debated, often with passion, since the early seventeenth century.[1] The relevant evidence may be briefly summarised.

It is certain that Ignatius visited Montserrat in March 1522, a few months before he began writing his exercises. He himself recorded the visit in an account of his life which he later dictated to Luis Gonçalves da Cámara.[2] He was travelling to Barcelona at the time, where he hoped to embark for Italy and the Holy Land, and decided to visit the shrine of the Virgin on the way. Afterwards he changed his plans, for reasons he does not specify, and remained in the neighbourhood for ten or eleven months.[3] On first reaching the monastery he made a general confession of his sins, and kept an all-night vigil before the shrine during which he dedicated himself to the service of Christ. The next morning he left the mountain and travelled to Manresa, a small village a few miles distant.[4]

---

[1] See A. M. ALBAREDA, *Sant Ignasi a Montserrat* (Montserrat 1935), 21-22; G. M. COLOMBÁS, *Un reformador benedictino en tiempo de los Reyes Católicos, García Jiménez de Cisneros, abad de Montserrat* (Montserrat 1955), 455-462.

[2] This account, edited by C. de DALMASES, S. J., may be seen in *Obras Completas de San Ignacio de Loyola* (BAC Madrid, 1963), 84-159. The visit to Montserrat is described on p. 97. On the spirituality of the monastery at the time see A. M. ALBAREDA, *Intorno alla scuola di orazione metodica stabilita a Monserrato dall'abate Garsias Jiménez de Cisneros (1493-1510)*, in *Archivum Historicum Societatis Iesu XXV* (1956), 254-316.

[3] For discussion of his possible reasons for changing plan see ALBAREDA, *op. cit.*, 75-79; P. DE LETURIA, *¿Hizo San Ignacio en Montserrat o Manresa vida solitaria?*, en *Hispania Sacra* (1950), 251-318, reprinted in *Estudios ignacianos* vol. 1 (Rome 1957), 113-176.

[4] *Autobiografía*, 99 sqq.

Ignatius makes no reference to reading the *Exercitatorio* or of further contact with the monastery. It seems probable, however, that he later returned to the mountain and lived there as a solitary for a time.[5] Other evidence suggests that the priest who heard his confession introduced him to methodical prayer, and continued to see and advise him at intervals. The monk charged with welcoming pilgrims was a Frenchman, Jean Chanones, who had entered the monastery ten years previously in 1512.[6] When canonisation enquiries were made at Montserrat in 1595, one religious, Laurentius Nieto, testified that Chanones had given Ignatius some exercises to practise, and that Ignatius returned from time to time to report on them and on his experience in prayer generally. Two others, Ioachim Bonanat and Michael de Santa Fe, declared that the exercises in question were by Cisneros.[7] Although none of this evidence was first-hand, contemporaries appear to have accepted it, including the saint's biographer, Ribadeneira. In a letter of 1607 to Francisco Girón he wrote that in his opinion it was highly likely («muy probable») that Ignatius read Cisneros' book and, instructed in certain parts of it by Chanones, made it an initial basis for prayer. That this had occurred was, he noted, «cosa antigua y recibida entre los Padres de Nuestra Señora de Monserrate», and he had been told of it by a monk of the house, Juan de Lerma.[8]

Most modern scholars accept that Ignatius was introduced to *devotio moderna* methods of prayer at Montserrat and that he knew the *Exercitatorio*.[9] If so, we have good *a priori* grounds for supposing that his exercises were influenced by the work. The likelihood that they were is heightened by research into the stages in which he composed them, which suggests that they first took shape in his mind shortly after he met Chanones.[10] Before he went to Montserrat he read

---

[5] I here follow the conclusions of Leturia, *art. cit.*, 316-317; see also the earlier study of the question by Albareda, *op. cit.*, 80-100, and the interesting discussion of the Saint's way of life on the mountain by J. LECLERCQ, *A propos du séjour de saint Ignace à Montserrat*, in *Christus* L (1966), 161-172.

[6] See H. WATRIGANT, *Quelques promoteurs de la méditation méthodique au quinzième siècle*, in *Collection de la Bibliothèque des Exercices* lix (Enghien-Paris 1919), 82-83.

[7] J. CALVERAS and C. DE DALMASES, *Sancti Ignati de Loyola: Exercitia spiritualia* (*MHSI*, vol. 100) (Rome 1969), 4-52.

[8] *Ibid.*

[9] e.g. P. DE LETURIA, *Génesis de los Ejercicios de San Ignacio y su influjo en la fundación de la Compañía de Jesús (1521-1540)*, in *Estudios ignacianos*, vol. 2, 10-11: «sabemos que Chanones introdujo a su hijo espiritual en los métodos del *Ejercitatorio* de fray García de Cisneros (esto es cierto), y aun que le entregó el librito, perla de la abadía (lo que es sumamente probable)»; see also CALVERAS and DALMASES, *op. cit.*, *loc. cit.*, and the introduction of I. IPARRAGUIRRE to his edition of the Ignatian excercises in *Obras Completas*, 177.

[10] LETURIA, *art. cit.*, H. PINARD DE LA BOULLAYE, *Les étapes de la redaction des Exercices de S. Ignace* (Paris, 1950); CALVERAS and DALMASES, *op. cit.*, 27-33.

two books that helped to form his spirituality: the *Legenda aurea* of Jacopo de Voragine and the *Vita Christi* of Ludolph the Carthusian. At some point before the autumn of 1522, perhaps after reaching Montserrat, he read a third book which became his favourite devotional manual, the *Imitation of Christ*. It was at Manresa, however, that the *Exercises* themselves were first conceived. Between April and July he was beset with severe spiritual trials and temptations. They were followed in August or September by a clarification of understanding and purpose after a mystical experience by the river Cardoner, and the *Exercises* were written, it is thought, over the next four months. No copy of this first draft has survived. It was probably just an outline and not meant to be used as a manual for others, and over the following decade it was continually revised. It is generally agreed, however, that it contained almost all the principal sections of the version we now possess, and that their purpose and overall structure were already apparent. Writing of the circumstances that gave rise to «este esbozo definitivo, fundamental, de Manresa», Fr. Iparraguirre has remarked:

> «Todo, el cuaderno de Loyola, el substrato de sus lecturas y prácticas anteriores, desaparece. Ya han cumplido su fin. Surge, en cambio, en plena iluminación sobrenatural, el esquema sustancial, personal, característico de sus propios ejercicios.» [11]

External evidence, then, suggests that Ignatius read the *Exercitatorio* and that he did so at a critical time in his life when his own exercises were taking shape. One might expect internal evidence to confirm this. However, the results of comparisons between the two texts have so far been surprisingly inconclusive. The first two modern studies of the subject appeared in article form in 1897, one by the Jesuit Henri Watrigant, the other by Dom Jean Martial Besse, a Benedictine.[12] Both scholars found verbal coincidences in the two works. Watrigant noted echoes of the *Exercitatorio* in four of Ignatius' Annotations, in three of the Additions and in the last rule for thinking with the Church.[13] Besse remarked on several similarly word-

---

[11] IPARRAGUIRRE, *op. cit.*, 182; on the probable contents of the draft of Manresa see CALVERAS and DALMASES, *op. cit.*, 31.

[12] H. WATRIGANT, *La genèse des Exercices Spirituelles de St. Ignace de Loyola*, in *Études publiées par les pères de la Compagnie de Jésus*, 1897, vol. 71, 525-529, vol. 72, 198-210; J.-M. BESSE, *Une question d'histoire littéraire au XVIe siècle: «L'Exercice de Garcias de Cisneros et les Exercices de Saint Ignace»*, in *Revue des questions historiques*, LXI (1897), 22-51.

[13] I here follow the summary by E. ALLISON PEERS, *Studies of the Spanish Mystics*, vol. 1 (2nd. ed. London 1951), 9; vol. 2 (1st. ed. London 1930), 32.

ed phrases about the pains of Hell, the Last Judgement and the fall of the angels and of the first man.[14] Each concluded that Ignatius knew Cisneros' work, although Watrigant made the point that if all external evidence in the matter were lacking it would be difficult to prove this on textual grounds alone, a reservation later repeated by Arturo Codina.[15] The most balanced assessment was probably made by Allison Peers who held that all the parallels noted were either common currency in devotional writing or could be explained by supposing that Ignatius read Cisneros' sources. He wrote:

> «We cannot help feeling that in a purely literary controversy it (the internal evidence) would be regarded as quite inconclusive.»[16]

The paucity of internal evidence discovered does not necessarily imply, of course, that Ignatius did not read Cisneros after all. None of the books that influenced him may be identified by coincidences of phrasing alone, and the parallels noted by Besse and Watrigant are more substantial than the traces left in his work by the *Vita Cristi*, for instance, which he certainly read.[17] It is, however, surprising. Dom Colombás suggests that the lost draft of Manresa bore a much closer resemblance to the *Exercitatorio* than the later versions.[18] And Allison Peers argued that

> «No sensible and unprejudiced investigator will doubt that St. Ignatius' debt to Cisneros goes far beyond what any internal evidence can reveal to us. Even were there not a single verbal similarity to show, the formative influence of the book would still be indisputable.»[19]

One factor which must be borne in mind, of course, is the extent to which all Ignatius' sources were transformed by his own experience of prayer. In the words of Watrigant, «Tout le livre a été *vécu* avant d'être écrit».[20] The importance of this factor, however, has sometimes been exaggerated.[21] Hugo and Karl Rahner, for example, draw a firm

---

[14] *Ibid.*, 2, 32.
[15] A. CODINA, S. J., *Los orígenes de los Ejercicios espirituales de S. Ignacio de Loyola* (Barcelona 1926).
[16] PEERS, *op. cit.*, 2, 32.
[17] *Ibid.*, 1, 9-10.
[18] Colombás, *op. cit.*, 469-471.
[19] PEERS, *op. cit.*, 2, 34.
[20] WATRIGANT, *art. cit.*, vol. 71, 511.
[21] See the astute remarks of Dom COLOMBÁS, *op. cit.*, 461-462.

distinction between the *Exercises* and all previous devotional literature, and deny that there is any substantial similarity between them
and the medieval tradition of methodical prayer. Their case, in the
view of John Bossy,

> «seems largely inspired by the desire to safeguard spiritual expe-
> rience as a region of certainty transcending any historical or
> psychological conditions, and a historian may think twice before
> commenting on it. But, faced with Karl Rahner's assurance that
> Ignatius really belongs not to his own time but to an archaic
> past or an unrevealed future, he is bound to feel uneasy».[22]

A certain tendency to emphasise Ignatius' originality has perhaps
influenced studies of the *Exercitatorio*. Its derivative nature has been
detected and stressed to reveal the saint's independence more clearly.
Fr. Iparraguirre, for instance, holds that Ignatius read it, but he does
not consider the influence it may have had as a work in its own right,
since it is for him, essentially, an edited collection of texts: in his
view it merely introduced Ignatius to the best of medieval piety.[23]
The conclusion of my earlier article, however, that Cisneros' work has
a distinctive purpose and form, suggests that a re-examination of the
internal evidence would be worthwhile. In the following pages I shall
compare the two writings in general terms at first, and then more
particularly examine their structural similarities.

GENERAL COMPARISON

Certain broad differences between the two books spring to mind
straight away. First, the Ignatian exercises are not read and learned
off by heart by the person taking them: they are explained orally by
one man, termed «el que da los exercicios», to another, «el que los
rescibe» (*Ex.* 8). Second, they are meant for lay people and religious
living in the world, and not for monks. Nor are they integrated into
a monastic routine. On the other hand, if practised in full, they do
involve withdrawal from normal secular activity for about a month
(*Ex.* 4,20). Third, they contain none of the long discussions of the
nature and purpose of prayer found in Cisneros: instead they are

---

[22] In his postcript to H. OUTRAM EVENNETT, *The spirit of the Counter-Reformation* (Cambridge 1968), 126-127.
[23] IPARRAGUIRRE, *op. cit.*, 177.

complemented merely by brief explanatory notes and directions. The work is a practical manual rather than a treatise. Fourth, Ignatius divides his exercises into «weeks» just as Cisneros provides meditations for seven days in each of his Three Ways. However, whereas the Benedictine prescribes one exercise a day, Ignatius, on average, prescribes five. Like Cisneros he allows his retreatant to adapt the system to his own needs. He nowhere stipulates how often a day's exercises should be repeated: it will depend on the rate of progress made (*Ex*. 4). Cisneros likewise lets his monk repeat the meditations of each Way until he is ready to move on.[24] Ignatius nonetheless expects the retreat to be over in about a month (*Ex*. 4), whereas Cisneros sets no time limit at all and clearly expects his exercises to last several months.[25] Ignatius's exercises are practised more frequently than his predecessor's, but over a shorter period.

A closer look at the principal exercises of Ignatius reveals further diferences between the two works. At first sight, for instance, the themes of his first «week» remind one of the Benedictine's purgative Way. It includes two meditations on sin designed to inspire compunction and one on the punishments of Hell (*Ex*. 45-61, 65-71). However, there is none on death, the Last Judgement or Paradise, to each of which Cisneros's monk devotes a complete exercise. Nor do Gethsemane and the sufferings of Mary figure in this «week».

The second, third and fourth Ignatian «weeks» treat the life of Christ. They begin at a later point than Cisneros's meditations on the same subject (there is no reflecion on the Old Testament Prophets), and they end earlier, at the Ascension rather than at Pentecost. On the other hand, the three sections into which Ignatius divides the Gospel story correspond almost exactly with the divisions of Cisneros' narration, an important parallel. The second «week» covers events from the Annunciation to Palm Sunday, the third is devoted to the Passion, and the fourth begins with the Resurrection and ends with the Ascension. In other respects, though, the Ignatian account of the Gospel is unique. The second «week» contains four exercises which seem to be of the saint's own devising: the exercise «del Rey» (*Ex*. 91), the two meditations of the fourth day (*Ex*. 136, 148), and the «election», which begins on the fifth day (*Ex*. 163).

So far, then, as the content of the two works is concerned, a number of preliminary conclusions suggest themselves. The exercises

---

[24] *Exercitatorio*, ch. 19, L. 8-13.
[25] The purgative exercises alone are expected to take one month: *ibid*.

of Cisneros' purgative Way are represented in the first Ignatian «week», but in a modified form. However those of the illuminative Way (on God's gifts) and of the unitive (on His perfections) appear to have found no place in the work at all. The narrative structure of the exercises on Christ's life is similar in both cases, but Ignatius includes new material in his second «week» for which there seems no immediate counterpart in Cisneros at all.

If the two texts are compared in terms of structure, however, they turn out to have much more in common than this preliminary survey has suggested. It is my belief that the two theories of spiritual progress that inform the *Exercitatorio* are integral to the *Spiritual Exercises* too. I will consider them in turn, starting with the notions of servile, initial and filial fear.

### THE GRADES OF FEAR

Throughout the first «week» Ignatius appeals to *temor servil* in his retreatant. In the first meditation, for instance, the retreatant strives to realise that his sins have deserved damnation:

> «será demandar vergüenza y confussión de mí mismo, viendo quántos han sido dañados por un solo pecado mortal, y quántas veces yo merescía ser condenado para siempre por mis tantos peccados» (*Ex.* 48).

To this end he considers three examples of serious sin. Two are precisely those introduced by Cisneros into his exercise designed to inspire fear: the falls from grace of the angels and Adam (*Ex.* 50, 51). The third involves imagining Hell, and reflecting on the individual mortal sins that have led men there (*Ex.* 52). All three are intended to provoke a train of thought we noted earlier in the first purgative exercise of Cisneros: if one sin was enough to incur damnation for others, what do my many sins merit? The retreatant compares his sins with the sin of the angels (*Ex.* 50); he considers the terrible results of the single sin in Eden (*Ex.* 51); and he reflects that many are in Hell for committing fewer sins than he:

> «el... pecado particular de cada uno que por un pecado mortal es ido al infierno, y otros muchos sin cuento por menos pecados que yo he hecho» (*Ex.* 52).

In the fifth meditation he turns his mind directly to the sufferings of Hell, and, to make it more immediate, applies his senses to it in imagination (*Ex.* 66-70). Cisneros too describes Hell in images which appeal to touch, hearing, sight and smell.[26] Ignatius indicates explicitly that his purpose is to arouse servile fear:

> «... pedir interno sentimiento de la pena que padescen los dañados, para que si del amor del Señor eterno me olvidare por mis faltas, a lo menos el temor de las penas me ayude para no venir en pecado» (*Ex.* 65).

According to Cisneros, servile fear serves the valuable purpose of preparing the soul to grow in the love of God, and earlier we noted that his purgative exercises contain appeals to such love throughout. The same is true of Ignatius's first «week». In the course of the initial meditation the retreatant realises that sin offends the *goodness* of God:

> «... trayendo a la memoria la gravedad y malicia del pecado contra su Criador y Señor, discurrir con el entendimiento, cómo en el pecar y hacer contra la bondad infinita justamente ha sido condenado para siempre» (*Ex.* 52).

The reference to God as «Creator» is important. Earlier he reflects that the angels were created in grace, and Adam and Eve in justice, and that it was by their own free choice that they destroyed this original harmony and order (*Ex.* 50, 51). The meditation closes with a colloquy, or prayer, before the crucified Christ, in which, by referring to Christ as «Creator», Ignatius indicates that, as God, He was the same Being that man originally offended, and that He became human to save him:

> «Imaginando a Christo nuestro Señor delante y puesto en cruz, hacer un coloquio, cómo de Criador es venido a hacerse hombre, y de vida eterna a muerte temporal, y así a morir por mis pecados» (*Ex.* 53).

The exercise's concluding note is one of faith in, and response to, God's merciful love, and not servile fear.

---

[26] *Ibid.*, ch. 14.

Faith in divine mercy is the predominant theme of the second meditation. The retreatant recalls his past sin, and compares himself with ascending orders of Creation (mankind, the angels and the saints) and Creation itself with God (*Ex.* 56-58). He ends by realising his utter wretchedness by contrast with divine perfection (*Ex.* 58, 59). To this point the exercise is just an expansion of a notion expressed in the previous one: that sin offends God's goodness. After the fourth point, however, it changes dramatically in theme. The retreatant realises that the converse of his sinfulness and lack of merit is that God must love him more than he can conceive: otherwise he would have been damned long ago. He considers His mercy as it finds expression in the various parts of Creation, the angels, the saints and nature itself (*Ex.* 60). One is reminded of the third part of Cisneros's purgative exercises in which nascent love of God is expressed in praise of His goodness as it is revealed in Creation.[27] The colloquy which brings the excercise to a close voices heartfelt gratitude:

> «Acabar con un coloquio de misericordia, razonando y dando gracias a Dios nuestro Señor, porque me ha dado vida hasta agora, proponiendo enmienda con su gracia para adelante» (*Ex.* 61).

By the end of the second meditation, the retreatant's sorrow for sin is likely to be rooted in an awareness that it offends divine goodness, rather than in fear of its castigation. The incipient love of God this implies is consolidated by the following two exercises in which he repeats the two meditations (*Ex.* 62), and then resumes the repetition (*Ex.* 64), dwelling on the parts that most affected him. The overt appeal to servile fear in the final meditation on Hell is thus made only once he is convinced of God's mercy. Its wording implies that such fear is a second-rate motive for avoiding wrong, and that love is eminently preferable (*Ex.* 65). And although the evocation of the pains of the damned does arouse servile fear, the colloquy includes a reference to the Incarnation, to the means by which the sinner may be forgiven and saved, and gives expression to profound thanks (*Ex.* 71).

During the day, then, the thematic emphasis shifts from servile fear towards initial, a progression evidently meant to be confirmed each day until the «week» ends.[28] Precisely the same development is

---

[27] *Ibid.*, ch. 12, L. 210-224.
[28] See *Exercicios*, 4.

evident in Cisneros's purgative exercises. The one distinction is that Ignatius, if anything, gives more prominence to God's saving love, and less to His justice, than his predecessor. He never refers to the Passion, for instance, as an exemplar of the punishment due to sin: in the very first exercise it is interpreted as proof of divine mercy (*Ex.* 53). Before the second meditation the retreatant sees himself as a prisoner about to appear before his Judge (*Ex.* 74). This image of servile fear also occurs in Cisneros, as we have noted.[29] However, whereas his monk bears it in mind throughout the purgative Way, Ignatius does not recommend it until his retreatant has made the colloquy to Christ crucified at the end of the first meditation, and is on the point of beginning the exercise which, more than any other in the first «week», encourages faith in God's mercy. Before the first meditation, by contrast, which appeals to servile fear, the retreatant sees himself as a knight who has abused the kindness of his King (*Ex.* 74).

In the second «week», as in Cisneros's illuminative Way, the retreatant's grateful love of God is intensified, thus confirming him in the stage of *temor inicial*. The basic theme of the first contemplation will be quite familiar to him: it is human sinfulness, now envisaged in general terms as the predicament of all mankind since the Fall. He considers:

> «cómo las tres personas divinas miraban toda la planicie o redondez de todo el mundo llena de hombres... viendo que todos descendían al infierno» (*Ex.* 102).

It is juxtaposed with another, already alluded to in the first and last meditations of the previous «week»: God's mercy, made evident in the Trinity's decision that the Son should become man to save men (*Ex.* 102). His attention is drawn specifically to the reality of the Incarnation as an event in space and time, conveyed by reflecting on Mary in Nazareth receiving Gabriel's message.

In the course of the exercise he moves from theme to theme, contrasting one with another, the better to grasp the significance of God's merciful love. The composition consists in a confrontation of the sinful race, on the one hand, with events in Nazareth on the other, of the universal problem with its unique solution; while the main points of the exercise involve observing and listening to the pro-

---

[29] *Exercitatorio*, ch. 12, L. 70-74.

tagonists of the drama on all three levels (*Ex.* 103, 106-108). The
response expected of the retreatant is grateful love of Christ, based
on a vivid understanding of the notion that He became man for his
sake, personally. The third preamble is a prayer for help to know,
love and follow Him, «que por mí se ha hecho hombre» (*Ex.* 104).

The second contemplation, on the Nativity, is different in
character. It does not involve considering directly the large-scale
implications of the event. Instead, it is the immediate, domestic situation of the Holy Family that receives attention. In the third point
the retreatant reflects on the toil they underwent so that Christ could
be born in poverty, and then anticipates His subsequent suffering,
including the Passion. Once again he notes that it was for his sake
that all this occurred:

> «mirar y considerar lo que hacen, así como es el caminar y tra-
> bajar, para que el Señor sea nascido en summa pobreza, y a cabo
> de tantos trabajos, de hambre de sed, de calor y de frío, de
> injurias y afrentas, para morir en cruz; y todo esto por mí»
> (*Ex.* 116).

The third preamble of the first contemplation is repeated in the
second, and, indeed, remains constant throughout the «week», excepting only the fourth day (*Ex.* 113, 159).

When in the third «week» the retreatant contemplates the Passion he continues to recall that it took place «por mí» (*Ex.* 203). In
the first exercise, on the Last Supper, he prays that he may be granted sorrow for his sins. His request differs from similar ones made
in the first «week» in that it is now quite dissociated from servile
fear. It is prompted instead by love of Christ whom he has helped to
crucify:

> «demandar lo que quiero: será aquí dolor, sentimiento y confus-
> sión, porque por mis peccados va el Señor a la passión» (*Ex.* 193).

The shame he feels is, in a sense, the converse of gratitude: Christ
died to save him, but it was his sin that caused Him to do so. However, it expresses also a more selfless love. In the second contemplation, on events before, and including, the Agony in the Garden, his

prayer changes into a plea of compassion, a desire to actually share Christ's pain:

> «demandar lo que quiero... dolor con Christo doloroso, quebranto con Christo quebrantado, lágrimas, pena interna de tanta pena que Christo passó por mí» (*Ex.* 203).

The theme informs the second addition, about his thoughts as he rises after sleep (*Ex.* 206). This development in the third «week» is no doubt prepared in the second, when he prays repeatedly for grace to love Christ more. It indicates a growth in the love of God present in *temor inicial*, and marks a further stage in the progression away from self-interest towards *temor filial*.

It is in the fourth «week» that filial fear becomes a principal theme in the *Exercises*, as it does in the unitive Way of the *Exercitatorio*. The retreatant prays for grace to rejoice at the Resurrection. He no longer considers that, or how, it benefited him, and his joy is not moved by self-interest. He is concerned with Christ and the joy *He* felt. On rising he considers the contemplation he is to make, «querriéndome affectar y alegrar de tanto gozo y alegría de Christo nuestro Señor» (*Ex.* 229). His prayer during the exercise is for grace «para me alegrar y gozar intensamente de tanta gloria y gozo de Christo nuestro Señor» (*Ex.* 221). In the words of William Peters, S.J.:

> «This joy has one cause only, namely, the joy and happiness of the Lord together with His glory... The exercitant's own redemption is passed over in silence as a possible source... No matter what his own sufferings are and, consequently, how great his need of comfort is, his is a most unselfish joy.» [30]

## FROM SERVILE TO FILIAL FEAR

The progression from servile fear to filial is reflected in changes in the practical instructions which Ignatius includes at every stage of the exercises. In the first «week», when servile fear develops into initial, the retreatant closes the doors and windows of his room to exclude the light, and breaks the darkness only to read, eat or pray vocally from a book. He practises penance, restrains his sense of

---

[30] William A. M. PETERS, S. J., *The Spiritual Exercises of Saint Ignatius, exposition and interpretation* (Jersey City 1968), 147.

humour and concentrates his thoughts on subjects that inspire sorrow for sin: the topics mentioned, death and judgement, occupy Cisneros's monk in the purgative way (*Ex.* 78-82). In the second and third «weeks», by contrast, when initial fear becomes increasingly selfless, he decides himself when to use light or practise penance: presumably he will vary between gratitude and sorrowful compassion, depending on the subject at hand (*Ex.* 130, 206). In the fourth, the stage of filial fear, on the other hand, he is encouraged to make full use of light, of warmth if it is winter, of coolness in summer, insofar as he finds these a help, to reflect on joyful subjects and to cease his practice of penance (*Ex.* 229).

The development is reflected also, as in the *Exercitatorio*, by a change in images used of the retreatant's relationship with God. In the first «week», as we noted earlier, he sees himself as a royal servant and as a criminal (*Ex.* 74). In the second he imagines himself serving the Holy family as a slave, «haciéndome yo un probecito y esclavito indigno» (*Ex.* 114). In the meditation on two standards Christ is said to summon both His servants and His friends (*Ex.* 146). Finally in the fourth «week» the retreatant is just a friend. He considers Christ's role as a comforter, «comparando cómo unos amigos suelen consolar a otros» (*Ex.* 224). In the last contemplation love is defined as an exchange between equals:

> «el amor consiste en comunicación de las dos partes, es a saber, en dar y comunicar el amante al amado lo que tiene o de lo que tiene o puede, y así, por el contrario, el amado al amante» (*Ex.* 231).

And later, after considering how generous God has been to him, he decides to offer Him in return all he is and has (*Ex.* 234). The relationship has developed from one of inequality, informed by vestiges of self-interest, to one of reciprocity, moved by true love.[31]

Ignatius, then, does use in his exercises the theory that underlies Cisneros's three Ways, although he combines it with contemplations on the Gospel, an innovation which can distract attention from its use in the work. The exercises close with praise of both servile and filial fear in which, significantly, Watrigant has discerned echoes of the *Exercitatorio* (*Ex.* 370).[32] One passage, which occurs early in the

---

[31] This development in imagery is noted by PETERS, *ibid.*
[32] See PEERS, *op. cit.*, t. 2, 32 n. 10.

314

work, offers final confirmation of this debt. In the tenth annotation, on the rules for discerning spirits, he writes:

> «... comúnmente el enemigo de natura humana tienta más debaxo de especie de bien, quando la persona se exercita en la vida illuminativa, que corresponde a los exercicios de ia 2.ª semana, y no tanto en la vida purgativa, que corresponde a los exercicios de la 1.ª semana» (*Ex.* 10).

Some critics have pointed out that he does not use Cisneros's term «via» but «vida», and imply that the meaning he gives to «purgativa» and «illuminativa» is quite distinct from the way they are used by the Benedictine.[33] The preceding analysis, however, suggests otherwise. The first «week» contains only some of the subjects meditated in Cisneros's purgative Way, but nonetheless it has the same purpose of arousing *temor servil* and transmuting it into *temor inicial*. The second is not, at first sight, about «los beneficios de Dios», but it inspires the same grateful love, or *temor inicial*, that Cisneros encourages in his illuminative Way: for Ignatius the Incarnation is *the* gift of God. And although the saint makes no mention of a «vida unitiva» he does expect initial fear to become filial fear in the last two «weeks», a development which occurs in Cisneros's third part, the unitive Way.

## THE LIFE OF CHRIST

Let us now consider if Ignatius was also influenced by Cisneros's second theory of spiritual progress. It will be recalled that in his fourth part the Benedictine recommends three ways of contemplating the Gospels. The first is to reflect on the humanity of Christ and to imitate His example and follow Him; the second involves bearing in mind His two natures, human and divine; the third is contemplation of His divinity. Two passages in the *Exercises* suggest that Ignatius

---

[33] IPARRAGUIRRE, *op. cit.*, 198 n. 11, points out the difference in terms, but adds that in some of the early directories the Exercises are interpreted according to the traditional doctrine of the Three Ways. WATRINGANT, *art. cit.*, 202, notes similarities in the writers' understanding of the purgative Way, but holds that they differ in their notion of the illuminative. PETERS, *loc. cit.*, suggests that Ignatus preferred «vida» to «via» because it was more expressive.

knew of this theory and adopted it. The first occurs in the opening exercise of the third «week»:

> «considerar lo que Christo nuestro Señor padesce en la humanidad o quiere padescer... considerar cómo la Divinidad se esconde, es a saber, cómo podría destruir a sus enemigos, y no lo hace, y cómo dexa padescer la sacratíssima humanidad tan crudelíssimamente» (*Ex.* 195, 196).

These two points are repeated in each exercise of the «week». Cisneros, of course, associates the second way of contemplating with the Passion, the subject of the third «week», and also notes that during it Christ's divinity seemed to be occluded.[34]

The second occurs later, in the opening exercise of the last «week», when the retreatant reflects on the manifestation of Christ's divinity at the Resurrection. Now His humanity is not stressed:

> «considerar cómo la Divinidad, que parescía esconderse en la passión, paresce y se muestra agora tan miraculosamente en la sanctíssima resurección» (*Ex.* 223).

It would appear, then, that the second and third ways of contemplating inform the third and fourth «weeks» respectively. What of the first way? Cisneros applies it to the Gospel events before Palm Sunday, and the same events are contemplated in Ignatius's second «week». Is there a connection between the first way and this «week»? I believe that there is.

Firstly, Cisneros expects the monk who practises the first way of contemplating to imagine himself present at the events he contemplates.[35] In the second «week», likewise, the retreatant looks on the people involved in a scene, listens to them and watches what they do (*Ex.* 106-108, 114-116). At one point he actually helps and serves them in their needs (*Ex.* 114). He applies his five senses to them in imagination (*Ex.* 121-126), an exercise which involves touching and kissing the places where they walk and sit down (*Ex.* 125).

Secondly, Cisneros urges his monk to follow Christ and imitate His virtues.[36] The same themes are to the fore in the second «week». In the prefatory prayer, for instance, the retreatant asks to know

---

[34] *Exercitatorio*, ch. 49, L. 70-80.
[35] *Ibid.*, ch. 49, L. 19-46.
[36] Ibid.

316

Christ «para que más le ame y le siga» (*Ex.* 104), and in the first colloquy he repeats the request «para más seguir e imitar al Señor nuestro» (*Ex.* 109). The books recommended at this stage include «libros de imitacione Christi» (*Ex.* 100). Like his predecessor, Ignatius interprets certain actions of Christ as paradigms of virtue: he takes the life He led in Nazareth in obedience to His parents as an exemplar of the state of life of most Christians, for whom perfection consists in observing the commandments. The occasion of His loss in the Temple, on the other hand, when He left His parents to serve God, represents the state of evangelical perfection, embraced normally by priests and religious (*Ex.* 134, 135). His exemplarity is considered also in the exercise «del Rey», in which the portrait of the human king, subsequently applied to Christ, is idealised: the dignity and virtue implicit in his call for help suffice to validate it (*Ex.* 94). The theme recurs later, during the meditation on two standards, in the image of Christ as an exemplary leader of men (*Ex.* 143-146).

Thirdly, Cisneros argues that the main fruit of the first way of contemplating should be detachment from one's own possessions and self-interest:

> «el término de aquesta primera contemplaçión... será a ti que assí como los apóstoles por esse affecto traydos todas las cosas del mundo... dexaron, assí tú en este grado perseverarás de manera, que el coraçón tuyo aquella suavidad ocupe y todo lo atraya assí, apartándolo de todo amor carnal».[37]

The themes of renunciation and poverty are central to the second «week», in particular to the four exercises for which, as was noted earlier, there seems no immediate precedent in Cisneros. The retreatant first encounters them in the exercise «del Rey». He learns that to follow Christ involves suffering:

> «quien quisiere venir conmigo, ha de trabajar conmigo, porque, siguiéndome en la pena, también me siga en la gloria» (*Ex.* 95).

He reflects how just and reasonable it is to accept the summons, and then considers that some people will not only offer themselves in service but desire to go further and actually imitate Him by bearing

---

[37] *Exercitatorio*, ch. 49, L. 53-59.

THE EXERCISES AND THE EXERCITATORIO 317

insults and poverty (*Ex.* 96-98). On the fourth day, in the meditation
on two standards, Christ's summons is defined in more detail. He
learns that it will certainly involve poverty, and the readiness to
undergo opprobrium and ignominy (*Ex.* 146). This time he does not
merely consider different possible responses to the call: he is expected to beg God to accept him as a follower of Christ on these terms
(*Ex.* 147).

It is unlikely that the retreatant will face up to the challenge of
such detachment without certain misgivings, and it is to help him
deal with these that Ignatius asks him to make the meditation on
three groups of men.[38] The problem of all the men in question is
identical: they have acquired great wealth, yet wish to save their
souls and be reconciled with God (*Ex.* 150). Their position is analogous
to the retreatant's: like them he wishes to serve God, but realises
that this will involve a spirit of poverty, and perhaps even actual
poverty (*Ex.* 146). Of the three different solutions proposed by the
men, two involve self-deception. The first two men wish to attain
spiritual detachment from their riches («querría quitar el affecto que
a la cosa acquisita tiene») but they postpone doing so until the moment of death (*Ex.* 153). The solution of the second group is morally
worse: they attempt to reconcile deference to God's will with continued possession of their money:

> «Él 2° quiere quitar el affecto, mas ansí le quiere quitar, que
> quede con la cosa acquisita, de manera que allí venga Dios donde
> él quiere, y no determina de dexarla, para ir a Dios, aunque
> fuesse el mejor estado para él» (*Ex.* 154).

As he considers these two examples the retreatant confronts possible
evasions of Christ's call within himself. The third group acts in the
way of which Ignatius approves. It wishes to eradicate its attachment
to wealth so that whatever it ultimately does with it will be prompted
by God's will, and nothing else. As a preparation, it strives to attain
true detachment in indifference:

> «quiere quitar el affecto, mas ansí le quiere quitar, que también
> no le tiene affección a tener la cosa acquisita o no la tener, si no
> quiere solamente quererla o no quererla, según que Dios nuestro
> Señor le pondrá en voluntad» (*Ex.* 155).

---

[38] See IPARRAGUIRRE, *op. cit.*, 169: «Práctico San Ignacio como siempre va apartando el
alma de los escollos que más fácilmente podía encontrar en esta ardua navegación hacia la
meta de su ideal: ...de los de la voluntad, mediante los tres binarios...»

The theme of detachment explains not only the character of the two exercises of the fourth day but also their position in the «week» as a whole. On the second day the retreatant considers the presentation of Christ in the Temple and the flight into Egypt (*Ex.* 132), on the third, Christ's hidden years at Nazareth and His disappearance in Jerusalem at the age of twelve (*Ex.* 134). The fifth day, by contrast, opens with an exercise on His departure from Nazareth at the age of thirty, and His subsequent baptism in the Jordan by John (*Ex.* 158). Day 4, then, marks a division between Christ's private and public life, His childhood and maturity. There is a clear parallel between the call of the Father to which He responded by embarking on His ministry and His call to the retreatant, examined particularly on the fourth day. Ignatius stresses it by drawing attention to the detachment practised by Christ at this turning point in His life. For instance he mentions His departure from home and His farewell to His mother, even though the event is nowhere described in the Bible (*Ex.* 273). His intenton appears to be to emphasise the spiritual poverty and solitude His vocation entailed. The next day the retreatant considers His trials and temptations in the desert, when He suffered the actual poverty of hunger (*Ex.* 161). On the seventh day he contemplates the calling of the Apostles: «El séptimo día, cómo sancto Andrés y otros siguieron a Christo nuestro Señor» (*Ex.* 161). One wonders why special reference is made to St. Andrew. A look at the points for reflection set out in the appendix indicates why: Ignatius wishes the retreatant to consider the distinguishing characteristic of Andrew's calling, a growth in understanding of the detachment required of himı

> «tres veces parece que son llamados San Pedro y San Andrés: primero a cierta noticia... secundariamente a seguir en alguna manera a Christo con propósito de tornar a posseer lo que habían dexado... terciamente para seguir para siempre a Christo nuestro Señor» (*Ex.* 275).

It will be recalled that in the *Exercitatorio*, learning detachment through the first way of contemplating is explicitly associated with the experience of the Apostles when they followed Christ.[39]

Parallels of such a kind are convincing evidence that Ignatius adopted the three ways of contemplating known to Cisneros. Even his

---

[39] *Exercitatorio*, ch. 49, L. 53-59.

most original exercises may be related to this triple method as we have seen. One innovation of his that has not been examined, however, is the «election». It too, I believe, is connected with the theme of detachment, and so with the first way of contemplating.

The meaning Ignatius gives to «detachment» is more complex than Cisneros's, for whom it designates simply the sacrifice one must make as a Christian. The third group of men considered on the fourth day strive for indifference to their wealth, but only as a prelude to positive acceptance or rejection of it, depending on God's will. The same two «stages» are evident in the «Principio y Fundamento» (*Ex.* 23), a statement of basic principles which prefaces the first «week». It opens with a definition of man's *raison d'être*: to adore and serve God, using the created order insofar as it helps him to do so, and thus save his soul:

> «El hombre es criado para alabar, hacer reverencia y servir a Dios nuestro Señor, y mediante esto salvar su ánima; y las otras cosas sobre la haz de la tierra son criadas para el hombre y para que le ayuden en la prosecución del fin para que es criado. De donde se sigue que el hombre tanto ha de usar dellas, quanto le ayudan para su fin, y tanto debe quitarse dellas, quanto para ello le impiden.»

The practical consequences of this are then outlined. One must aspire to indifference; «Por lo qual es menester hacernos indiferentes a todas las cosas criadas...». However, indifference is not its own end, but a preparation for firm choice: «solamente deseando y eligiendo lo que más nos conduce para el fin que somos criados» (*Ex.* 23). Ignatian «detachment», understood in this sense, is central to the work's purpose as it is defined in the first Annotation:

> «quitar de sí todas las affecciones desordenadas y después de quitadas... buscar y hallar la voluntad divina en la disposición de su vida para la salud del ánima» (*Ex.* 1).

The two «stages» are once again evident, the first involving the removal of disordered attachments, the second a reorientation in life.

Now the «election» is intimately connected with the problem of the choice that follows indifference, with the process of reorientation. In the first «week» the retreatant is primarily concerned with the eradication of disorder. He learns that original sin upset God's plan for man, and that his own sins have brought disharmony into his relations with God and Creation.[40] He prays for grace to know «el dessorden de mis operaciones, para que, aborresciendo, me enmiende y me ordene» (*Ex.* 63). In the second «week», likewise, he considers examples of disordered love of self which make him aware of similar disorder within himself (*Ex.* 149-156). At the same time he gradually becomes involved in reordering his desires according to God's will, of which he gains an increasingly clear understanding. In the first «week», for instance, he considers what he has done, is doing and ought to do for Christ (*Ex.* 53). In the exercise «del Rey» he learns of the sacrifices involved in following Him, and these are defined in greater detail in the meditation on two standards. When, on the fifth day, he starts to contemplate Christ's public life he is brought face to face with God's summons to him personally, as we have seen: and it is at this point that the «election», if one is to be made, begins.[41] Its connection with the stage of reorientation is made quite explicit in a preamble in which particular attention is paid to the choice that follows indifference, in words which echo those of the «Principio y Fundamento». One's motive in choosing the course of action that pleases God must conform with man's *raison d'être*, «el fin para que soy criado»:

> «En toda buena elección, en quanto es de nuestra parte, el ojo de nuestra intención debe ser simple, solamente mirando para lo que soy criado, es a saber, para alabanza de Dios nuestro Señor y salvación de mi ánima» (*Ex.* 169).

### IMITATION, DEATH AND UNION

The process of removing disorder and of re-ordering, of indifference followed by choice, is closely connected with another theme, imitation of, and death with, Christ. Its influence on the exercises concerned with the Gospel will already be evident. The desire to imitate Jesus which permeates the second «week» becomes one to suffer and die with Him in the third. It is a theme which throws further light on the saint's debt to the *Exercitatorio*, in which the transition from imitation to union through death with Jesus is connected with the doctrine that one attains to His divine nature by meditating on His humanity. Ignatius, unlike the Benedictine, makes

[40] *Exercicios*, 51, 58, 60.
[41] *Ibid.*, 163.

no explicit reference to union towards the end of his exercises on the Gospel. He alludes to it in the fourth «week», however, in the image of lover and beloved, which he applies to the relationship between God and the retreatant in the last contemplation (*Ex.* 230).

## CONCLUSION

If my analysis of Ignatius's exercises is correct it provides firm evidence that he read the *Exercitatorio* and was influenced by it. His retreatant, like the monk, grows in love of God, passing from servile to filial fear. He does so in the course of contemplating Christ's life: like the monk he first pays attention to His human nature, then to the hypostatic union, and ultimately to His divinity, and in the process his desire to imitate the second Adam becomes a willingness to die and be united with Him. Ignatius draws on both Cisneros's theories of direction and combines them.

There are, of course, important differences between the two works. In the first place Ignatius is more consistent and precise than his predecessor. For instance, he directly relates the three ways of contemplating Christ to the three stages of the Gospel narration, while Cisneros relates them to the first two only. Also, he gives equal prominence to each part of Christ's life, whereas Cisneros devotes most of his exercises to the Passion.

In the second place, the end to which the exercises are directed is in each case quite distinct. For Cisneros, steeped in monastic tradition, it is union with God in contemplation. Ignatius, on the other hand, prepares his retreatant to return to an active life in the world, and his exercises have a practical dimension throughout. In the colloquy before Christ crucified at the end of the very first meditation he considers what he ought to do for Him and what he has done and is doing; the «Principio y Fundamento» explains how loving God is connected with serving Him by the correct use of Creation; while the «election» caters for very particular decisions arising from recommittal to Christ.

It would be mistaken, of course, to claim that Ignatius does not encourage contemplation. On the contrary, the replacement of servile fear by filial is a preparation for it, as the *Exercitatorio* makes apparent.[42] But he is concerned to relate it to the conditions of the

---

[42] According to Peers, «There is no attempt in the *Exercises* to teach... anything beyond meditation», *op. cit.*, t. 1, 15. Peters, 37-40, takes the contrary view, and the evidence presented here confirms it.

active life. In the last contemplation just before the retreat ends, he prompts the retreatant to reflect on God's presence in all created things (elements, plants, animals, man) and in himself, and to consider how He works through them all (*Ex.* 230-237). In his autobiography he defines devotion as «facilidad de encontrar a Dios»: this exercise helps the retreatant to find God in his everyday, active life.[43] An earlier passage in the *Exercises* confirms the point. In the general examination of conscience one reads:

> «Los perfectos, por la assidua contemplación y iluminación del entendimiento consideran, meditan y contemplan... ser Dios nuestro Señor en cada criatura según su propria essencia, presencia y potencia» (*Ex.* 39).

Now «perfectos» is the term used by Cisneros of people who have attained contemplation in the unitive way, and our earlier analysis suggested that the fourth «week», which includes the last contemplation, is the equivalent of that Way.

In the third place, the overall plan of Ignatius's work is distinctively his own. Its two stages, the eradication of disorder in human affections and their subsequent re-ordering, are not found in Cisneros. The two theories Ignatius borrowed from him, however, are integral to the realisation of this plan. The ideal set forth in the «Principio y Fundamento», that one should love God and all things for His sake only, presupposes the attainment of filial fear or pure love. Before each exercise the retreatant prays that the ideal may be realised in his life:

> «La oración preparatoria es pedir gracia a Dios nuestro Señor para que todas mis intenciones, acciones y operaciones sean puramente ordenadas en servicio y alabanza de su divina majestad» (*Ex.* 46).

The use of the adverb «puramente» is perhaps an allusion to *amor puro*. It is, moreover, possible that the connection between the notion of order and pure love was itself suggested to Ignatius by the *Exercitatorio*. At one point Cisneros writes: «el amor es todo el fin de nuestras cogitaciones en el hombre bien ordenado».[44] Later the point is made again more fully; «por amor de Dios se ha de hazer y ser orde-

---

[43] Autobiographical account, 159.
[44] *Exercitatorio*, ch. 29, L. 69-70.

nado todo lo que hazemos».[45] Finally, by combining the two theories and leading the retreatant to this reorientation through contemplation of Christ, Ignatius stresses the central role of the Incarnation in the retreatant's spirituality, an emphasis most suited to one actively involved in the world.

It is possible, no doubt, that Ignatius drew the two theories that inform the *Exercitatorio* directly from Cisneros's sources. As Henri Watrigant wrote in 1897:

> «pour établir... définitivement que l'auteur des *Exercices* est redevable à Cisneros... il faudrait prouver qu'Ignace n'a pas puisé directement aux mêmes sources que le Bénédictin».[46]

However, it is most unlikely that he did so. His borrowings are integral to the structure of his exercises, as I hope I have shown; and it is generally agreed, as we noted earlier, that by 1522 the quintessence of his work was already conceived in his mind. He did not then understand Latin, and could not have read the treatises of Zutphen and Mombaer, even though they were available at Montserrat. It may be that Dom Jean Chanones discussed them with him. But the principles that inform his book were evidently lived and practised first, and the only exercises published in Castilian at the time were in the *Exercitatorio*.

---

[45] *Ibid.*, ch. 37, L. 9-10.
[46] WATRIGANT, *art. cit.*, 204-205.

# IX

## Saint Ignatius Loyola and Castles in Palestine

The meditation on the Kingdom in the *Spiritual Exercises* of Saint Ignatius Loyola is a text of great interest to students of Jesuit spirituality, and of its influence on devotional poetry, because of its key position in the *Exercises* themselves and because of its influence in the evolution of the Society of Jesus.[1] One of the enigmas involved in its interpretation concerns the composition of place. In the original Spanish version the retreatant is asked, rather surprisingly, to imagine Christ preaching in the 'castles' of Palestine:

> El primer preámbulo es compositión
> viendo el lugar; será aquí ver
> con la vista ymaginativa
> sinagogas, villas y castillos, por donde
> Xpo nuestro Señor predicaua.[2]

It has been suggested by the distinguished scholar Ignacio Iparraguirre that here Ignatius had in mind the Crusader castles which he would have seen during his visit to the Holy Land in 1523.[3] According to an early tradition the meditation was composed at Manresa in the autumn of 1522 when the first rough draft of the *Exercises* was committed to paper.[4] If Fr. Iparraguirre's explanation is correct, the word 'castillos' was not present in this draft, which has since been lost. However, there is another explanation which makés an earlier dating possible, and which also implies that by 'castillos' Ignatius did not mean 'castles' in the conventional sense at all.

It has often been pointed out that the meditation on the Kingdom contains many allusions to Scripture,[5] and the composition of place certainly recalls the words of St. Matthew's Gospel, chapter 9, verse 35:

> Et circuibat Iesus omnes civitates,
> et castella, docens in synagogis

> eorum, et praedicans evangelium
> regni, et curans omnem languorem,
> et omnem infirmitatem.

Here the term 'castellum' is used, not in the classical sense of 'fortress' but in the later medieval sense of 'small town' or 'village'.[6] In his commentary on Matthew 9:35 St. Jerome indicates that 'castella' are the insignificant districts that Christ did not neglect:

> Cernis quod aequaliter et villis,
> et urbibus, et castellis, id est,
> et magnis et parvis Evangelium
> praedicaverit, ut non consideraret
> nobiliam potentiam, sed
> salutem credentium.[7]

His words were echoed by subsequent commentators, including Bede and Rabanus Maurus.[8] In one of the two early Latin translations of the *Exercises* the Spanish word 'castillos' is rendered by 'oppida'.[9] In the other, the earlier, the Latin used is 'castella'.[10]

In the Spain of St. Ignatius the commonly accepted meaning of 'castillo' was, of course, 'castle', 'stronghold',[11] but there is evidence that it was also used more loosely to mean a small, walled town or village. In *La Gran Conquista de Ultramar*, a fourteenth-century text published in Salamanca in 1503, the word 'castil', an archaic form of 'castillo', is said to have been used by Moors of tiny country communities ('villetas chicas'):[12]

> E las villetas chicas,
> que llaman 'castiles',
> teníanlas los moros,
> e obedescían a las grandes villas
> e querían muy mal
> a los cristianos.

That this usage survived, and was not confined to a cultural minority, is indicated by the Spanish-Latin dictionary of Nebrija (1492), in which 'castillo' is defined as 'villeta cercada'. The Latin suggested for 'castillo' is 'castrum'; 'castillo pequeño' is 'castellum'.[13]

'Castillo' was certainly understood in this secondary sense by fifteenth and sixteenth-century translators of the Vulgate text. Although no vernacular version of the complete New Testament was permitted in Spain, there were translations of the Epistles and Gospels of the liturgical year.[14] The Gospel for Easter Monday opened with the words of Luke, chapter 24, verse 13:

> Et ecce duo ex illis
> ibant ispa die in castellum
> . . . nomine Emmaus.

In the version of Gonzalo García de Santa María (Salamanca, 1493) 'castellum' is rendered by 'çastillo':

> En aquel tiempo dos
> de los discipulos de Jesu
> yuan el mesmo día
> al castillo por nombre Emaus.[15]

In the version of Ambrosio Montesino (Toledo, 1512) the same usage prevails:

> En aquel tiempo. Dos de los
> discipulos de Iesu yuan
> el mismo día de la resurrectión
> a un castillo
> llamado Emaus.[16]

And St. John of the Cross, writing later in the century, also refers to Emmaus as a 'castillo':

> Y a tanto llegaba esta dificultad
> de entender los dichos de Dios
> como convenía, que aun hasta
> sus mismos discípulos que
> con él habían andado estaban
> engañados, cual eran aquellos
> dos que después de su muerte
> iban al castillo de Emaús . . . [17]

It is possible that when he was at Manresa Ignatius had a copy of the Epistles and Gospels in the translation of Montesino.[18] He was certainly familiar with another work translated by Montesino, the *Vita Christi* of Ludolph the Carthusian, which he began to read at Loyola in the summer of 1521.[19] Many years ago Fr. Arturo Codina drew attention to a passage in Ludolph in which Christ is described as preaching in 'castillos':

> De continuo andaba
> por todas las cibdades
> e castillos predicando
> e haciendo miraglos.

He noted the parallel with the meditation on the Kingdom, but was reluctant to admit a direct dependence.[20] There is, however, another passage in the work which calls to mind Ignatius's exercise: it opens with a quotation from Matthew 9:35, interpreted along the lines of St. Jerome:

> *E cercava el señor*
> destruyendo la negligencia de todos
> *todas las cibdades y castillos*
> (esto es) todos los lugares

mayores y menores: lo qual
es contra los afecionados
a unos lugares y personas
mas que a otras. Por lo qual
dize teofilo, 'No solamente
predicava el señor en las ciudades
mas aun en los castillos:
porque deprendamos no menospreciar
los pequeñuelos pueblos
ni buscar siempre las grandes
cibdades: mas sembrar
la palabra de dios quando
fuere menester en los barrios
desechados y viles'.[21]

Here, quite clearly, 'castillos' is used to mean a small rural town.

It is likely that it was the Spanish translation of Ludolph which introduced Ignatius to the word 'castillo' in a scriptural context. And although we do not know the original form of the meditation on the Kingdom, there is no reason to doubt that 'castillos' figured in the first drafts of the composition of place. The Ignatian retreatant is not expected to imagine Jesus in military strongholds, but, on the contrary, among the powerless and unimportant.


## NOTES

1 Saint Ignatius of Loyola, *Obras completas*, ed. I. Iparraguirre and C. de Dalmases, 3rd ed. (Madrid, 1977), pp. 230-1; C. de Dalmases, 'Las meditaciones del reino y de dos banderas y la vocación a la compañía de Jesús, según el P. Nadal', *Manresa* 20 (1948), 311-320; the fundamental study of Ignatian spirituality and devotional poetry is still L. Martz, *The Poetry of Meditation* (Yale, 1954); see also A. J. Divver, *Seventeenth-Century French and English Devotional Poetry and the Ignatian Paradigm* (Ann Arbor, 1972).

2 St. Ignatius of Loyola, *Exercitia spiritualia: textum antiquissimorum nova editio*, ed. J. Calveras and C. de Dalmases (Rome, 1969), p. 216

3 St. Ignatius, *Obras completas*, p. 231 n. 74: 'San Ignacio se refiere a los castillos edificados en tiempo de las Cruzadas que él vio durante su permanencia en Tierra Santa'.

4 St. Ignatius, *Exercitia spiritualia*, pp. 15, 31, 61.

5 *Ibid.*, p. 58.

6 See the entries under 'castellum' and 'castrum' in Charles du Fresne, Seigneur du Cange, *Glossarium mediae et infimae latinitatis*, 10 vols. (Niort, 1882-7); and under 'castellum' in A. Sleumer, *Kirchenlateinisches Worterbüch* (Limburg, 1926).

7 P. L. xxvi, col. 60.

8 Rabanus Maurus, P. L. cvii, col. 886, follows Jerome word for word; Bede, P. L. xcii, col. 50 makes the contrast between town and country even sharper: 'Qui urbibus videlicet et castellis, id est, magnis et parvis Evangelium praedicavit . . .'

9 In the *Versio vulgata* of 1546-7: St. Ignatius, *Exercitia spiritualia*, p. 216.

425

10  In the two surviving copies of the *Versio prima* (1541, 1547): *idem,* p. 217; most English versions follow the Latin translations: that of W. H. Longridge (London, 1919) p. 77, has 'villages'; that of T. Corbishley (London, 1963), p. 42, has 'hamlets'.

11  See the entries under 'castillo' in J. Corominas, *Diccionario crítico etimológico de la lengua castellana* (Madrid, 1954); M. Alonso, *Enciclopedia del idioma,* 3 vols. (Madrid, 1958), vol. 1.

12  See the entry under 'castil' in Academia Española, *Diccionario histórico de la lengua española,* 2 vols. (Madrid, 1933-6), vol. 2.

13  Antonio de Nebrija, *Dictionarium ex hispaniensi in latinum sermonem* (Salamanca, 1492); in Nebrija's Latin-Spanish dictionary *Dictionarium ex sermone latino in hispaniensem* (Salamanca, 1492), 'castellum' is defined as 'la villa cercada'.

14  See the article by E. M. Wilson on Spanish versions of the Bible before 1600 in *The Cambridge History of the Bible: The West from the Reformation to the Present Day* (Cambridge, 1963), pp. 125-9.

15  Gonzalo García de Santa María, *Evangelios e epistolas con sus exposiciones en romance* (Salamanca, 1493), ed. 1. Collijn and E. Staaf (Uppsala and Leipsig, 1908), p. 95.

16  Ambrosio Montesino, *Epístolas y evangelios para todo el año* (Toledo, 1512), fol. cxxiii.

17  *Subida del monte Carmelo,* libro segundo, capítulo 19, párrafo 9, in *Vida y obras de San Juan de la Cruz,* ed. L. Ruano (Madrid, 1973), p. 526; Luis de Granada uses 'castillo' for 'castellum' when translating Matthew 21:2: *Obras,* ed. J. Cuervo, 14 vols. (Madrid, 1906-8), vol. 10, p. 354. In English translations of Scripture up to the sixteenth-century 'castellum' was often rendered as 'castle': see *A Dictionary of the Bible,* ed. J. Hastings, 5 vols. (Edinburgh, 1900), vol. 1, p. 358; and the entry under 'castle' in the *The Shorter Oxford English Dictionary,* 2 vols. (Oxford, 1944; reprinted with corrections 1969).

18  St. Ignatius, *Exercitia spiritualia,* p. 55.

19  *Ibid,* pp. 38-43.

20  A Codina, Los orígenes de los ejercicios espirituales de S. Ignacio de Loyola (Barcelona, 1926), pp. 147-8, 226-7.

21  *Vita Cristi Cartuxano,* 4 vols. (Alcalá de Henares, 1502), vol. 2 fol. 1(v); the Spanish is a very faithful rendering of the Latin original: see Ludolphum de Saxonia, *Vita Jesu Christi,* ed. A. C. Bolard, L. M. Rigollet and J. Carnandet (Paris and Rome, 1865), p. 220.

# X

## THE ERASMIANISM OF *LAZARILLO DE TORMES*

Towards the end of his life Marcel Bataillon came to believe that *Lazarillo de Tormes* showed the literary influence of *The Praise of Folly*, but he continued to hold the view, first advanced in *Erasme et l'Espagne*, that it was not Erasmian in its spirituality.[1] Its anticlerical satire, he argued, is directed against hypocrisy, not against the failing that most concerned Erasmus, misunderstanding or ignorance of the Gospel: 'la sátira erasmiana...no reprocha a los sacerdotes vivir mal, "sino creer mal" '.[2] Nor, he contended, does it satirise attachment to the mere externals of religious practice, an abuse that Erasmus particularly attacked: 'Ni una sola vez... hay el menor asomo de un erasmismo que oponga el espíritu a las ceremonias, el alma al hábito'. He concluded that if its anonymous author was an Erasmian he had managed to hide it well.[3]

In formulating this opinion Bataillon did not, it seems, attach significance to certain similarities that have been noted between the story and the Gospel parable of Lazarus and Dives.[4] Several features of the story immediately call the parable to mind. In both the protagonist, Lazarus, is deprived through avarice of the necessities of life; in both his oppressor, or masters, are not named; and in both he is brought by hunger to the point of death. We may assume that these general parallels would have struck contemporary readers, for the Gospel text and its exegesis were all well known. It was read at Mass at least once every year, and for those who did not know Latin it was available in a popular translation.[5] Patristic commentaries were quoted in the Breviary[6] and summarised cogently in two well known works: the *Vita Christi* of Ludolph the Carthusian, which was highly praised by Juan de Valdés,[7] and the *Paraphrasis in Evangelium Lucae* of Erasmus himself.[8] It may be argued that if the story is read in the light of the parable and its exegesis it suggests that the Erasmianism of the author, although in some respects unconventional, was not confined to admiration of Erasmus as a writer but extended to his view of religion and society.

### I

In the course of the parable Dives, who lived well, goes down to Hades where he thirsts, while Lazarus, who lay at his gate, rises to Heaven. This illustrates the paradox, central to the Gospel, that 'he who exalts himself will be humbled, and he who humbles himself will be exalted' (Matthew 23.12; Luke 14.11, 18.14), a paradox which informs the Sermon on the Mount where the hungry are declared blessed 'for they shall have their fill' while the rich are cursed and promised hunger (Luke 6.21, 25; also Luke 1.52, 53). Ludolph quotes the Fathers on this abrupt change of Fortune (*L*, fol cvii); Erasmus goes further and makes it the principal lesson of the parable; for him it is a graphic illustration of the truth that in the Kingdom of Heaven 'the needy will abound in every good thing and the rich will be tormented and suffer hunger' (*P*, cols 414-15). This reversal of roles is not present in the story, where Lázaro comes to resemble his masters, none of whom is spectacularly ruined.[9] But the paradox that the reversal illustrates is not absent: it is alluded to early in the work, and supplies an important theme.

Lázaro describes his initiation with the blind man as a religious conversion or healing:

> y como me viese de buen ingenio, holgábase mucho, y decía: "Yo oro ni plata no te lo puedo dar, mas avisos para vivir muchos te mostraré". Y fue ansí, que después de Dios éste me dio la vida, y siendo ciego me alumbró y adestró en la carrera de vivir.
>
> (1. 101-07)

As Peter cured the cripple in the name of Christ (Acts 3.6) so the blind man enabled Lázaro to tread the path of life. This opened his eyes, which had been shut in childhood innocence (1. 97-98) and illumined him. It was, like baptism, a second birth in which he became the spiritual son, not of God but of his blind master. After this passage replete with scriptural allusions[10] Lázaro gives a summary of his moral code:

> Huelgo de contar a V.M. estas niñerías para mostrar cuánta virtud sea saber los hombres subir siendo bajos, y dejarse bajar siendo altos cuánto vicio.
>
> (1. 108-10)

These words evoke the paradox that informs the parable, but only to invert it. Virtue for Lázaro is to rise in society, and to fall is vice. This worldly ethic is a parody of Christ's teaching: he who exalts himself, it implies, should be praised, and he who humbles himself faulted.

The paradox that Lázaro, with apparent ingenuousness, inverts is stated three times in the New Testament, on each occasion directed against the pharisees. In Matthew it follows a warning to call no man 'Master' or 'Father' (Matthew 23. 8-12), and in Luke, where it precedes and follows the parable, it is directed against two faults in particular: ambition for social success and blindness to one's own moral failings (Luke 14. 7-11; 18. 9-14). As the story unfolds it becomes clear that both these faults characterise Lázaro. Ambition explains his capacity as an adult to endure 'el caso', his unhappy married situation. And from early in the story he is shown to be unaware of his failings which include, ironically, faults deplored in his first master. In the last adventure of the first *tratado*, the blind man is crippled by the boy he enabled to walk: this trick, which parallels the initiation on the bridge in Salamanca, proves that Lázaro has learnt, literally, that 'el mozo del ciego un punto ha de saber más que el diablo' (1. 95-96). The blind man's adage

is recalled during the adventures of the *tratado* by repeated allusions to 'diablo' (1.
138, 152, 161, 227),[11] and the reader comes to see that he is, indeed, an 'old devil',
but by the end his spiritual son is equally, even more, diabolic and, ironically,
seems unaware of it. Lázaro's flight from the blind man (the only one of his three
formative masters that he actually abandons) recalls his earlier words: '¡Cuántos
debe de haber en el mundo que huyen de otros porque no se veen a sí mesmos!' (1.
42-43).[12] His eyes have been opened to the need to live on his wits, but closed to
his own loss of innocence: he has become spiritually blind. In retrospect his period
with the blind man recalls the scriptural warning against the blind leading the
blind, a passage glossed by Erasmus in appropriate terms:

> He who wishes to guide another must himself be free from the defilement of any
> evil. How can someone who is enmeshed in his own error teach another? But (you
> say) it is hard to endure the obstinate malice of some people... Is it reasonable to
> expect the disciple to be better than his master?... Why are you so quick to see the
> defects of your neighbour yet blind to your own faults?... You condemn your
> brother for what he eats or drinks yet you plot his ruin and death? Listen you
> unjust hypocrite, if you wish to be truly just, cast out the beam from your own eye
> first... .[13]

The full significance of Lázaro's initiation, and of his moral code, becomes
clear in the work as a whole, particularly in two passages directed, like his
definition of virtue and vice, to *Vuestra Merced*. In the first, at the end of the
prologue, he indicates the lesson he hopes will be drawn from his tale:

> consideren los que heredaron nobles estados cuán poco se les debe, pues fortuna fue
> con ellos parcial, y cuánto más hicieron los que, siéndoles contraria, con fuerza y
> maña remando, salieron a buen puerto.
>
> (Pr. 37-40)

This claim, it has been shown, recalls the tradition of praising the virtue and deeds
of the self-made man, and in particular a late medieval literary convention in which
a 'homo novus' was allowed to praise his achievements in a speech. It has been
suggested that Lázaro'a self-justificatory letter was intended to burlesque the
convention.[14] If so, his definition of morality may have been carefully framed to
indicate the criterion by which his pretension should be measured. Like a 'homo
novus' he aspires to the nobility that springs from virtue, but his understanding of
virtue is shown to contradict the letter and spirit of the Gospel. For Erasmus,
moreover, the precept that Lázaro inverts, and the parable that illustrates it, are
both directed against the self-righteous belief that one may be justified by one's
works (*P*, cols 119-21, 400-01, 422). Lázaro, of course, does not aspire to salvation
but to a certain kind of social success. Nonetheless he does presume, like a
pharisee, to be justified by his efforts or 'virtues'. In this he is shown clearly to run
counter to the teaching of Christ.

The second passage appears at the end of the work, where Lázaro states that
when the Emperor entered Toledo (i.e. in 1525 or 1538) 'estaba en mi prosperidad
y en la cumbre de toda buena fortuna' (7. 80-81). The past tense seems to indicate
that he is referring not to the time of writing but to the date of his marriage, with
the implication, perhaps, that Fortune's wheel has since turned further and begun
to decline. Since he is still married and prosperous the change would seem to lie
not in his circumstances but in the recurrent and widespread gossip that threatens

to make life unbearable, and that may have provoked *Vuestra Merced* to request an explanation.[15] This closing hint of a decline in Fortune would not have surprised a reader familiar with the parable, and its reversal of roles, which is interpreted by Ludolph and Erasmus as a warning to the rich that Fortune is fickle, and that those who, like Lázaro, come to resemble Dives will, eventually, suffer (*L*, fol cvii; *P*, cols 415-16). It also raises the possibility that Lázaro shares to some extent in the author's irony, and that his narrative is imbued with a slightly self-mocking tone.[16] But there is no suggestion that Lázaro himself realises how his story, and his moral code, invert the parable.[17] This final irony is foreshadowed in the Gospel: Dives asks for a sign to be sent to his relatives, not realising, as Abraham says, that they have warning enough in 'Moses and the Prophets'. The story portrays a society in which the teaching of Scripture, though pertinent, has been marginalised. The responsibility for this does not lie with Lázaro, however, but elsewhere.

## II

It is in the second *tratado* that allusions to the parable become most intense. The child's hunger reaches a new climax when he longs, like Lazarus, for crumbs of his master's bread, and he languishes at the door of his master's box, just as Lazarus lay at the rich man's gate, until he reaches the point of death. As Lazarus is released from agony by angels who carry him to Abraham's bosom, so Lazarillo is rescued by a tinker (described as an angel) who gives him access to 'mi paraíso panal' (2. 107, 129). And in both cases the name of Lazarus (meaning 'helped by God') is given its full etymological significance: in the parable its meaning is proved by the intervention of the angels,[18] and in the story the relief of hunger is marked by frequent allusions to God's help.[19] Both end, moreover, with a reference to resurrection. Dives' request for someone to be sent back from the dead, which is refused on the grounds that such a messenger would be rejected, was taken in exegesis as an allusion to the resurrection of Jesus that the Jews greeted with incredulity.[20] Lazarillo describes his final beating and illness as 'three days passed in the belly of the whale' (2. 353) a text applied to the Resurrection by Jesus himself,[21] and when he eventually recovers it is only to be dismissed by his master. In addition, the motif in the parable of hungering for bread is developed into the key image of the eucharist. At their first meeting the priest asks the boy if he can serve Mass and accepts him when he replies that he can (2. 3-7). Later he is portrayed at the Offertory preoccupied with the collection (2. 53-58). On Saturdays, when he feasts on mutton, he gives the child the scraps:

> Aquélla le cocía y comía los ojos y la lengua y el cogote y sesos y la carne que en las quijadas tenía, y dábame todos los huesos roídos, y dábamelos en el plato, diciendo: "Toma, come, triunfa, que para ti es el mundo".
>
> (2. 38-42)

This description recalls the actions and words of Jesus at the Last Supper, quoted in the Canon:

> accepit Jesus panem, et benedixit, ac fregit, deditque discipulis suis, et ait: Accipite, et comedite; hoc est corpus meum.[22]

But instead of the life-giving lamb of God the child receives only the gnawed bones of a sheep. Later Lazarillo is shown adoring the bread in the box (termed, significantly, an 'arca' or 'arcaz')[23] in which he sees 'la cara de Dios', and he longs to 'receive' it (2. 118-19, 150-52, 160-63). Finally, just as the Mass ends with a blessing so does the *tratado*, when the priest, with characteristic avarice, blesses not the boy but himself (2. 381).

In such ways the author reminds the reader of the main event in the sacramental life of the Church and implies that the priest has missed, ironically, the very point of his vocation. This kind of criticism was characteristic of Erasmus who often recalled the importance of the eucharist, and deplored the widespread ignorance of its meaning. In the *Enchiridion* he writes that to say Mass and neglect another's needs is to observe the ceremony but not its spirit:

> Tú por ventura dizes cada día missa, y junto con esto bives assí para ti solo, que no curas mucho de los males y daños de tu próximo. Desta manera aun te estás en la carne, que es en lo exterior del Sacramento. Pero si diziendo missa, procuras de ser tú aquello que recibes ... y si ya ninguna cosa amas sino en Christo, si todos tus bienes tienes por comunes a todos tus próximos, y si los daños y inconvenientes agenos te duelen y desseas remediarlos como los tuyos propios ... desta manera yo te digo que con mucho fruto dizes missa, porque lo hazes espiritualmente.[24]

The author suggests in a remark of Lázaro (2. 9-11) that the priest is typical of many, and thus implies the wider effects of such a dereliction of duty which deprives the needy not only of bread but of spiritual sustenance too. According to Ludolph the poor should be fed in two ways, with bread and doctrine, but the priest offers neither to the child.[25] The satire is reinforced by the allusions to the parable: the man who should preach it and exemplify its teaching actually re-enacts the part of Dives. Of all Lázaro's masters it is the priest who, in his avarice, gluttony and lack of pity, most resembles the traditional portrait of the rich man (*L*, fols cv-cvi).

The full significance of the *tratado* becomes clear at the end of the work which reveals its bearing on 'el caso'. The behaviour of Lázaro the adult is foreshadowed by that of the child who, as in the first *tratado*, comes to resemble his master. When he adores the bread he is mirroring the priest's avarice, a vice that, as Erasmus notes in the *Enchiridion*, involves 'worshipping' one's possessions and letting them usurp the place of Christ:

> a sólo el vicio de la avaricia llama sant Pablo ydolatría, y no ay otro que más nos aparte de Jesu Christo, ni es possible, finalmente, a ninguno servir juntamente a Dios y al dinero.
>
> (*En*, p. 395)

The moral disorder in the life of the priest recurs in Lázaro at the end, when the gifts he receives from the archpriest include, ironically, 'bodigos' (7. 34). In order to maintain such gifts he is prepared to proclaim his wife's virtue with an oath on the sacred Host (7. 73-74). He can subordinate the eucharist itself to his needs for, like the priest, he has made them, not Christ, his priority.

## III

The parable is pertinent also in the portrait of the squire, who exemplifies a further failing of Dives mentioned in exegesis: his pride. Ludolph describes his vainglory and love of display, and Erasmus argues, following St. Gregory, that he was conscious of his reputation and socially ambitious. Both find their evidence in the statement that he 'dressed in purple and fine linen'.[26] The squire, like Dives, is preoccupied with his status and keen to rise in society, and he is satirised specifically for his pride (3. 347-49). Attention is often drawn, moreover, to his clothes and posture (3. 44, 49-52, 165-70, 180-84, 200-01, 252-53). These details serve to indicate the importance in his life of appearances. They also prepare for the scene in which Lazarillo on looking through his clothes discovers an empty purse and realises his poverty (3. 332-38). The parable's motif of hunger and death is developed too in the depiction of the house as sorrowful, empty and dark. The description, which is built up slowly, culminates in the amusing incident of the funeral procession, but continues to be important once the joke is over.[27] It runs as a *leitmotif* through the whole *tratado* and thus helps to give unity to its many episodes. It also acts as a reminder of the squire's quandary: when others, including Lázaro, see him in town they imagine a house full of belongings, only to discover that he owns nothing (3. 21-23, 36-41, 190-93, 199-207, 560-61).

The explanation of the squire's behaviour lies in his notion of *honra* which is, in his view, a matter of outward decorum quite unconnected with virtue (3. 265-68, 375-78, 530-35). This notion of honour is criticised in a crucial reflection of Lazarillo:

> ¡Oh Señor, y cuántos de aquéstos debéis vos tener por el mundo derramados, que padecen por la negra que llaman honra lo que por vos no sufrirían!
>
> (3. 207-09)

Bataillon conceded that one might discern in this remark an allusion to Rule IV of the *Enchiridion*: 'que el fin de todas nuestras obras, oraciones y evociones 'ha de ser tan sólo Jesuchristo' ('Un problema', p.332). It recalls a later passage also in which Erasmus criticises the false honour that accrues to the avaricious:

> por respeto de tus riquezas te honrrarán los que no saben estimar ni hazer honrra, sino a cosas vanas... . La verdadera honrra es ser alabado y honrrado de los que son en sí dignos de toda honrra. La summa honrra es aplazer a Jesu Christo. La honrra cierta no ay por qué se deva a las riquezas, sino a las virtudes.
>
> (*En*, p. 393)

The squire, moreover, like the earlier masters, leaves his mark on Lázaro in a way which helps to account for 'el caso'. In his presence the child practises dissimulation (3. 56-59, 82-86, 116-17) and so, on a larger scale, does the adult in order to preserve his marriage (7. 65-76). When he becomes independent, and pays attention to his clothes, Lázaro dresses, like the squire, as 'un hombre de bien' (6. 11-18) and becomes, like him, preoccupied with obtaining a good position which he preserves by unscrupulous means. But in one respect Lázaro is different: he does not equate 'honra' and 'opinión'.[28] At the end his reputation is in shreds but he is prepared nonetheless to accept the archpriest's assurance that his honour is intact. He can do this because 'honra' for him is identified with naked self-interest: 'Ella entra muy a tu honra y suya, y esto te lo prometo. Por tanto, no mires a lo que pueden decir, sino a lo que te toca, digo a tu provecho' (7. 47-49). This equation of honour and 'provecho', which enables Lázaro to reach 'la cumbre de toda buena fortuna' (7. 80-81), is similar to his earlier definition of virtue as the capacity to rise in society. And it recalls a passage of the *Enchiridion* in which Erasmus, wishing to satirise 'la ambición y cobdicia de la onrra' invokes the paradox of the parable:

> piensa ... quán aparejado está a caher el que se sube a los resbaladeros, quán peligrosa es la cayda de lo alto y cómo toda onrra trahe consigo gran carga.... . Mira también que a quien se humillare como un pequeñito, a aquél socorrerá la misericordia de Dios; y el que se ensalça para ser muy acatado, él mesmo se pone impedimento y estorva el socorro de la gracia divina.
>
> (*En*, p. 398)

By the contrast between Lázaro and his third master the author implies an understanding of honour that is characteristically Erasmian. It is not a matter of appearances, *pace* the squire, but of integrity. The virtue in which it consists, moreover, is not the sort practised by Lázaro but the paradoxical ideal preached in the Gospel of which both he and the squire seem unaware.

## IV

The satire of the first three *tratados* is directed against the contrast between professed belief and actual behaviour. This, according to Ludolph, is also the point of the parable, which was intended to undermine the hypocrisy of the pharisees and to show that men see only the exterior, but God sees into the deepest heart (*L*, fol cii). But *Lazarillo* goes further and implies that each of the three masters ignores, or is ignorant of, the teaching and spirit of Jesus, and that this is true also of Lázaro who comes to resemble them. In this respect it reflects an important concern of Erasmus and his followers in Spain.

This Erasmianism, however, is not uniform throughout the story. It does not appear in the sketches of the Mercederian, the Canon of Toledo or the archpriest of Sant Salvador, and it is conspicuous by its absence in the longer portrait of the pardoner in the fifth *tratado*. He is satirised for unscrupulous hypocrisy, but there is no sustained allusion to the Gospel teaching he flouts, and Bataillon was doubtless correct to describe it as no more than an anticlerical satire in the medieval tradition.[29] But the fifth *tratado* differs in many other ways from the earlier part of the work. It contains no mention of hunger; Lazarillo's role is reduced in it to that of a mere observer; and all allusions to the parable cease. These differences have received various explanations, the most convincing being that of Lázaro Carreter for whom *tratados* 4, 5 and 6, which bridge the gap between Lázaro's formative years and his adult life, were written hastily and are technically unsuccessful: 'son ... de necesidad arquitectónica, pero resulta obvio lo atropellado de su construcción'.[30] Like many of the tales in *tratados* 1-3, the main part of *tratado* 5 is clearly medieval in origin,[31] but unlike them it has not been refashioned and integrated fully into the work.

Discontinuity within the work is one reason why its Erasmianism has been so controversial. Another reason seems to be that it differs in some respects from writings of the period in which Erasmus is the sole or dominant influence. It contains no direct quotation from the works of the great humanist, and a number of themes characteristic of 'el erasmismo militante', notably the 'monachatus non est pietas', receive no mention.[32] It has been argued, moreover, that some Erasmians would have disapproved of its scriptural jokes.[33] This no doubt indicates the author's literary skill and independence which enabled him to refashion a wide range of derivative material in an original way.[34] It may also reflect a certain diversity in the Spanish movement of reform. Many Spaniards who admired Erasmus drew inspiration also from other traditions, some hard to reconcile with his teachings, and were not his disciples in a narrow or exclusive sense. Their enthusiasm for him, and their unity, stemmed from a common understanding of the nature of corruption in society and the Church.[35] The evidence suggests that the anonymous author of *Lazarillo*, who admired the literary artifice of *The Praise of Folly*, also shared in the widespread concern for renewal that found expression in the *Enchiridion*.

[1]Marcel Bataillon, 'Un problème d'influence d'Erasme en Espagne. *L'Eloge de la Folie'* in *Actes du Congrès Erasme (Rotterdam, 27-29 octobre 1969)* (Amsterdam and London, 1971), pp. 136-47, translated as 'Un problema de influencia de Erasmo en España. *El Elogio de la Locura'* in *Erasmo y el erasmismo* (Barcelona, 1977), pp. 326-46. All references to *Lazarillo* are to the edition by R.O. Jones (Manchester, 1963).

[2]*Erasmo y España*, second edition (Mexico, 1966), p. 610.

[3]*Erasmo y España*, p. 610. For the contrary view see Manuel J. Asensio, 'La intención religiosa del *Lazarillo de Tormes* y Juan de Valdés', *HR*, 27 (1959), 78-102; Francisco Márquez Villanueva, 'La actitud espiritual del *Lazarillo de Tormes'* in *Espiritualidad y literatura en el siglo XVI* (Madrid, 1968), pp. 67-137.

[4]See A.D. Deyermond, *Lazarillo de Tormes. A Critical Guide* (London, 1975), pp. 27-32.

[5]Fray Ambrosio Montesino, *Epístolas y Evangelios con sus sermones y doctrinas* (Zaragoza, c.1515). Nine editions before 1558 are recorded by A. Palau y Dulcet, *Manuel del librero hispanoamericano*, second edition (Barcelona, 1948-77). I have used the edition of Seville, 1540: the parable is translated as the Gospel of the First Sunday after Trinity and recommended as an alternative Gospel on Thursday of the Second Week of Lent.

[6]In all the pre-Tridentine printed Breviaries that I have seen the readings are from the homily on the parable by St. Gregory: J-P Migne, *Patrologia Latina*, 76, cols 1301-11.

[7]Ludolph the Carthusian, *Vita Christi Carßuxano*, 4 vols (Alcalá, 1502), iii, fols ci-cxii (*L*); Juan de Valdés, *Diálogo de doctrina christiana* (Alcalá, 1529), edited by Domingo Ricart (Mexico, 1964), p.112.

[8]Bataillon, *Erasmo y España*, p. 164; in *Opera omnia*, 10 vols (Leyden, 1703-06), vii, cols 414-17 (*P*).

[9]It may be, as some have suggested, that its absence is pointedly ironic: see B.W. Wardropper, 'The Strange Case of Lázaro Gonzales Pérez', *MLN*, 92 (1977), 202-12, and more convincingly A.D. Deyermond, 'Lazarus and Lazarillo', *Studies in Short Fiction*, 2 (1964-65), 351-57 (p. 355).

[10]Deyermond, *Lazarillo de Tormes*, p.24.

[11]Anthony P. Perry, 'Biblical Symbolism in the *Lazarillo de Tormes*', *Studies in Philology*, 67 (1970), 139-46.

[12]Fernando Lázaro Carreter, *Lazarillo de Tormes en la picaresca* (Barcelona, 1972), p. 109.

[13]Erasmus, col. 349. The passage glossed is Luke 6. 39-42.

[14]R.W. Truman, 'Lázaro de Tormes and the "Homo novus" Tradition', *MLR*, 64 (1969), 62-67; '*Lazarillo de Tormes*, Petrarch's *De remediis adversae fortunae*, and Erasmus's *Praise of Folly*', *BHS*, 52 (1975), 33-53.

[15]L.J. Woodward, 'Author-reader relationship in the '*Lazarillo de Tormes*', *FMLS*, 1 (1965), 43-53 (pp. 50-51).

[16]R.W. Truman, 'Parody and Irony in the Self-Portrayal of Lázaro de Tormes', *MLR*, 63 (1968), 600-05.

[17]Deyermond, *Lazarillo de Tormes*, p.29.

[18]On the etymology of the name see Cornelius à Lapide S.J., *Commentaria in Scripturam Sacram*, 21 vols (Paris, 1868-76), xvi, p. 220.

[19]L.J. Woodward, 'Le *Lazarillo*—oeuvre d'imagination ou document social?' in *Théorie et pratique politiques à la Renaissance: XVII colloque international de Tours* (Paris, 1977), pp. 333-47 (pp. 333-36).

[20]Cornelius à Lapide, p. 228; Ludolph, fol. cx.

[21]Matthew 12. 40. On the image of death and resurrection see Deyermond, *Lazarillo de Tormes*, pp. 29-32.

[22]Matthew 26. 26. For a different view see Víctor G. de la Concha, 'La intención religiosa del *Lazarillo*', *RFE*, 55 (1972), 119-34 (p. 263).

[23]'Arca' was also used in the sixteenth century for 'Ark' of the Covenant: see the entry in Martín Alonso, *Enciclopedia del idioma*, 3 vols (Madrid, 1958).

[24]*El Enquiridion o Manual del caballero cristiano*, edited by Dámaso Alonso with an introduction by Marcel Bataillon (Madrid, 1932), pp. 249-50 (*En*).

[25]Ludolph, fol. cxi, following Gregory, col. 1309-10.

[26]Ludolph, fol. cv; Erasmus, *Paraphrasis*, col. 415; Gregory, col. 1305.

[27]Marcel Bataillon, *Novedad y fecundidad del Lazarillo de Tormes* (Salamanca, 1973), pp. 42-45.

[28]*Lazarillo de Tormes*, edited with an introduction and notes by Francisco Rico, second edition (Madrid, 1980), p. liv.

[29]*Erasmo y España*, p. 610; *Novedad y fecundidad*, p. 17.

[30]Lazaro Carreter, pp. 154-56 (p. 154). See also F. Courtney Tarr, 'Literary and artistic unity in the *Lazarillo de Tormes*', *PMLA*, 42 (1927), 404-21; Albert A. Sicroff, 'Sobre el estilo del *Lazarillo de Tormes*', *NRFH*, 11 (1957), 157-70; Raymond S. Willis, 'Lazarillo and the Pardoner: the artistic necessity of the fifth *Tratado*', *HR*, 27 (1959), 267-79.

[31]See Deyermond, *Lazarillo de Tormes*, pp. 83-87.

[32]Bataillon, *Erasmo y España*, p. 610; *Novedad y fecundidad*, p. 17 n. 1. See also Concha, p. 272.

[33]Lázaro Carreter, pp. 184-85.

[34]Lázaro Carreter, pp. 64-65.

[35]Eugenio Asensio, 'El erasmismo y las corrientes espirituales afines', *RFE*, 36 (1952), 31-99 (p. 73); José Luis Abellán, *El erasmismo español. Una historia de la otra España* (Madrid, 1976), pp. 60-69.

# The Ode to Francisco Salinas

When Menéndez y Pelayo wrote about the Ode to Salinas in his *Historia de las ideas estéticas en España*, he described it in the words of Milà y Fontanals as 'bella paráfrasis cristiana de la estética de Platón', and he affirmed that its medieval sources lay in Plotinus, Boethius, the Pseudo-Areopagite and Bonaventure.[1] Since then the patient work of scholars such as Spitzer and Rico has revealed that the classical and Christian notions of harmony which inform it are remarkably diverse and complex.[2] Improved knowledge of the poem's background, however, has not made its interpretation any easier: on the contrary there exist strong differences of opinion about the nature and causes of the ecstasy it describes.

For some, including Dámaso Alonso, the climax of the ode is an experience of union with God described in verses 5 to 8;[3] and Professor Woodward has argued that 'the resonances in this poem . . . are Christian and not pagan'.[4] For others, however, it is about an aesthetic experience; the thought behind it is classical; and it is not mystical in the Christian sense at all. Fr Angel Custodio Vega, the editor of Fray Luis, has defended this view in forthright terms: 'En toda esta poesía no hay el menor asomo del cielo o de cosa espiritual, sino un éxtasis estético, sublime y deleitoso, como toda contemplación de la naturaleza en sus manifestaciones de grandeza y hermosura . . . Todavía es muy pronto para los traspasos místicos'.[5]

Some who hold the latter view also argue that Fray Luis was not a mystic, and quote in evidence a passage from his commentary on the *Canticle* in which he expressed misgivings about writing on mystical experience:

> Est enim magna res, et plane supra hominis vires, et denique ejusmodi, ut vix possit intelligi, nisi ab iis, qui eam non tam

doctoris alicujus voce quam ipsa re, et suavi amoris
experimento a Deo didicerunt, de quorum numero non esse
me, et fateor et doleo.[6]

These words, it is true, express an unsatisfied longing for full union
with God, but it would be mistaken to conclude from them that
Fray Luis was not a mystic. In the Middle Ages, and in the
sixteenth century, another term for mystical prayer was contemplation, and as Ruth Burrows, a recent writer on the subject, has
pointed out, contemplation can be bereft of what Fray Luis calls
'the sweet experience of love': a contemplative may be conscious
only of dryness, or of nothing, and may even be unaware that his
prayer is mystical.[7] Furthermore, a longing for union has always
been considered central to contemplative experience. In the
monastic tradition of the Middle Ages contemplation was defined as
a yearning for the life of Heaven, and this eschatological image
certainly informs the great poems of Fray Luis.[8]

However, the interior life of Fray Luis (about which we know
little) is not really pertinent to the interpretation of his writings, for
in a work of the imagination an author is not confined to describing
his personal experience. Fray Luis' own words bear this out:
despite his misgivings he did attempt to describe 'the sweet
experience of love' in his commentary on the *Canticle* and
elsewhere.[9] The appropriate question is not 'Was he a mystic?', but
'Do his poems draw on images and themes associated traditionally
with contemplation?'. In the *Ode to Salinas* there are, I believe, three
motifs which indicate that its subject is mystical prayer. They
concern music, wisdom and friendship.

I

In medieval spirituality a connection was often made between
contemplation and music. It was well expressed by Richard of St
Victor, an Augustinian recommended by Fray Luis as an authority
on union with God.[10] In the *Benjamin Major* he advises the
contemplative who cannot pray to summon a minstrel:

At this psalmody and spiritual harmony the contemplative
soul accustomed to spiritual experiences will begin to
dance . . . and leap up as it were towards spiritual being and
be raised up above the earth and all earthly things and pass
over wholly in ecstasy of mind to the contemplation of
heavenly things.[11]

Emilio Orozco has shown that this tradition was well known in
sixteenth century Spain, but he does not believe that it informs the
poem, for he does not consider Fray Luis a mystic.[12] However, if
we make no assumption about the poet's spiritual life, we find that
the poem recalls the tradition clearly.

The ecstasy described in the poem is inspired by two musicians
and is described in two stages. The first verse alludes to Salinas
playing. Line 5 implies that he is playing a keyboard instrument,
and we recall that he was famed as a Cathedral organist. The three
verses that follow note the effects on the poet's soul. His memory is
restored (verse 2), he comes to know himself (verse 3), and he is
caught up into heaven (verse 4). Verse 5 introduces a second
musician, God himself, the great artist, who is playing a lyre and
whose church is the Universe. The three verses that follow describe
the effects: union (verse 6), and rapture (verses 7, 8).

The organ and the lyre were both associated specifically with
contemplation. A passage in the *Book of Kings* tells how Elisha,
when asked for a prophecy, summomed a minstrel: on hearing the
music he began to prophesy (IV Kings 3:15). This text was
interpreted to mean that music could dispose a soul for
contemplation, and the instrument supposed to have been played
was the Old Testament lyre or psaltery. The medieval tradition
was summed up by Denis the Carthusian:

> Eliseus videns sibi lumen propheticae gratiae non fulgere,
> voluit se ad illud per elevationem animi praeparare: ideo fecit
> psaltem coram se ludere et cantare, quoniam melodia illa cum
> laude Dei ad elevationem disponit, praesertim in quibusdam,
> qui ex naturali dispositione ad hoc magis dispositi sunt:
> quorum nonnulli ex discantu et consonantia melodiae
> celerrime et intense moventur ad fletum, compunctionem, et
> contemplationem.[13]

The tradition survived into the period of the Counter Reformation.
In a commentary of 1623, for instance, a Jesuit exegete who
lectured at Alcalá described Elisha's rapture in terms that resemble
the poem:

> Cum caneret psaltes ad musicos numeros, soporati sunt
> Helisaei sensus, et animus magis a corporeis impedimentis
> solutus, sicut in somno contingit, seipsum ad coelestium rerum
> contemplationem afflatumque divinum excitavit.[14]

110

He also drew a parallel between Elisha and St Francis who, according to legend, was caught up in ecstasy on hearing a lyre.[15]

In the Middle Ages it was the organ, not the lyre, that accompanied the singing of psalms, and after the Council of Trent the organ was the only instrument permitted within a church. Commentators on *Kings* often pointed out that Elisha's experience prefigured that of later contemplatives whose prayer was accompanied by an organ:

> ... non erat aliquis modus quo anima sua ab exterioribus curis rediret ad seipsam quam per armoniam: ideo fecit quod caneret citharista coram eo. Et ista fuit intentio Ecclesiae ordinantis varietatis cantuum in divinis officiis, et organa musica, ut variae armoniae diversimode corda hominum ad devotionem incitent.[16]

These traditions would have been familiar to Fray Luis and his circle, and it may well be that his poem was intended to call them to mind. In his treatise on the Incarnation he writes that music has a natural power to raise the soul to heavenly things[17] and in the *De Musica* Salinas himself argues that music can dispose a soul for contemplation:

> Religiosiores autem a musica nos reddi manifestum est: valde enim erigimur ad rerum caelestium contemplationem modulationibus et canticis quae in templis audiuntur, quod in sacris solennibus experimur in quibus maiori cum artificio et suavitate cantatur.[18]

We do not know when the poem was composed, and we cannot be certain that it alludes to the *De Musica*, or vice-versa, but clearly it draws on a body of ideas quite familiar to the small group of friends among whom it first circulated.

## II

One name given to contemplation in the Middle Ages and in the sixteenth century was 'wisdom'. Peter Lombard associated it with the gift of wisdom bestowed by the Holy Spirit, and his teaching was developed by St Bonaventure and St Thomas.[19] In the first Spanish manual for contemplatives, the *Exercitatorio de la vida spiritual* (1500), the reader is urged to pray for the wisdom that

'comes down from above' (Jm. 1:17; 3:15, 17),[20] and the commentaries of St John of the Cross often describe contemplation as
'sabiduría secreta'.[21]

In the *Ode to Salinas* wisdom is an important theme. The first
effect of the music, described in verses 2 and 3, is to teach the poet
self-knowledge, or wisdom in the Socratic sense. Such knowledge of
self is but a prelude to the vision of God, described in verse 5. The
image of the divine Musician, which had classical roots, was
commonly applied in Patristic writings to the wisdom of God, who
brings all the elements of the Universe into harmony:

> Just as a musician, tuning his lyre and skilfully combining the
> bass and the sharp notes, the middle and the others, produces
> a single melody, so the wisdom of God, holding the universe
> like a lyre, draws together the things in the air with those on
> earth, and those in heaven with those in the air, and combines
> the whole with the parts, linking them by his command and
> will, thus producing in beauty and harmony a single world
> and a single order within it.[22]

The interdependence of these two kinds of wisdom, Socratic and
contemplative, was established for the West by St Augustine,
whose *Soliloquium* was quoted by St John of the Cross to make the
same point:

> de esta noche seca sale conocimiento de sí primeramente,
> donde, como de fundamento, sale estotro conocimiento de
> Dios. Que, por eso, decía San Agustín a Dios: 'Conózcame yo,
> Señor, a mí, y conocerte he a ti'; porque, como dicen los
> filósofos, un extremo se conoce bien por otro.[23]

In the *Ode* the poet does not merely behold wisdom; he is united
with it (verse 6) and called into rapture (verses 7 and 8), and the
experience transforms him. His interior senses are awakened to the
Divine reality, and mortified to the world, and he is enabled to
appreciate the true relation between the worlds of sense and spirit
(verses 9 and 10). In a word he becomes wise.

As verse 10 reminds us, the gift of wisdom is imparted to him as
he listens to the playing of Salinas, whose keyboard touch is described
in line 5 as 'sabio'. This reference to wisdom is one of many parallels
and contrasts between verses 1 and 5. In the context of the poem as
a whole it implies, I think, that Salinas himself has experienced the

close union with God that transforms the poet.[24] His wisdom, moreover, is associated with his playing, an image that helps to explain his effect on Fray Luis, whose ecstasy is inspired not simply by music but by the music of his friend, music that is 'rare' ('extremada' 1.4) and even 'divine' (1.6).

III

The connection between contemplation and friendship was a recurring theme in the writings of St Augustine, for whom the loving union of friends could itself lead to an experience of union with God. It has been argued by Professor Woodward that this tradition informs the poem. His evidence lies in verse 9 interpreted as a eulogy of Salinas who, in line 42, is termed 'gloria del apolíneo sacro coro'. In line 43 'amigos' should read 'amigo' (as it does in some editions) for the friend 'loved above all treasure' is Salinas. These words, it is argued, would be 'exaggerated and almost unpleasant flattery' if it were not for the context of spiritual friendship that links the love of a friend to the love of God.[25]

This reading of verse 9 is, however, open to question. In all the early manuscripts and editions line 43 reads 'amigos' not 'amigo', and the singular form was not introduced until 1761. This modification, moreover, shortened the line from 7 syllables to 6, and as a result it does not scan. Mayáns y Siscar, who made the change, justified it on the grounds that it was appropriate: 'El original dice amigos. Pero debe leerse *amigo*, porque habla con Francisco de Salinas'.[26] However, if Salinas already enjoys the experience the poem describes it makes better sense to suppose that he is not included in the general invitation of verse 9. It is also unlikely that he is being praised in line 42, which probably refers to the angels who stand in the presence of the Lord: they are the choir of Apollo whose glory is the 'aqueste bien' of line 41, union with God. It was indeed conventional to compare the angels in Heaven with contemplatives on earth: the image occurs in the *De Musica* itself.[27]

But although Professor Woodward's interpretation rests on evidence that is unconvincing, it includes a profound insight into the poem that may be justified on other grounds. Salinas is mentioned only twice in the *Ode*, at the start and at the end, but between these two points there are several lines that call him to mind and that imply a deep spiritual friendship. The substance of the poet's ecstasy is a transforming vision of the relation that should exist between the worlds of sense and spirit. To convey this he constantly alludes to the interplay between the five senses of the body and the corresponding senses of the soul.[28] On occasion, as in verse 10, all the senses are mentioned together, but usually the poem focuses on two. One is the sense of hearing, as might be expected, the other is the sense of sight, and from the start the two are closely linked. In verse 1 the striking description of the change in the air and in the light is a reminder that Salinas was blind: 'he can hear his music but not see its effects'.[29] Knowing this shapes one's interpretation of the verses that follow in which the soul's experience is described as a recovery of spiritual sight. In verse 2 it is said to recover the memory of its origin and identity, and this process is described as an illumination: the soul is 'enlightened' ('esclarecida' 1.10). The type of darkness it has left is mentioned in verse 3: excessive love of passing beauty, a form of spiritual blindness. This healing of memory and reason leads in verse 5 to the cleaving of the will to God, described as the opening of the interior eyes to a vision. When, in verse 9, the poet reflects on his experience, he remarks that now 'todo lo visible es triste lloro' (1.45), meaning 'visible' to the physical sense.[30]

These references to sight indicate that the musician, and his affliction, are never far from the poet's mind. They also convey the theme that true vision is interior and spiritual; its corollary, that physical blindness does not really matter, was doubtless a reassuring message for one who could not see. And this lesson is mediated to the poet by Salinas himself, a crucial paradox that takes us to the poem's heart: the musician exemplifies the truths that his music helps to reveal. By the way in which he plays Salinas mediates spiritual sight to a dear friend because, though physically blind, he is spiritually wise, a contemplative like Fray Luis himself.

# XII

## Courtly Love and Mysticism
## in Spanish Poetry of the Golden Age

In memoriam
A. A. Parker

One of the striking characteristics of the mystical poetry of St John of the Cross and St Teresa of Avila is its use of a passionate language of love, charged with desire, drawn largely from the courtly love tradition.[1] This, as Denis de Rougemont saw (1940), raises questions of a philosophical kind. Why did the mystics describe their love of God in the language of human love? And does the fact that they did so throw light on the relation between mysticism and sexuality? In *The Philosophy of Love in Spanish Literature* (1985) the late Alexander Parker advanced some possible answers. As a critic, though, he was more concerned with the literary problems raised. Why did the Spanish mystics, like a number of their medieval forebears, describe their experience in the language of *courtly* love, a tradition whose religious basis in medieval society was in many ways so uncertain (Terry 1988: 170)? And when courtly terms appear in mystical poetry, what is their function? How should the reader interpret them?

It was with these questions in mind that Parker turned to the courtly poetry of the *cancioneros*, in which he found two features that seemed to him important. First, there was its dominant note, which he considered to be the pain of unfulfilled love, a pain not only endured but embraced as a sign of true devotion. In human terms, he reflected, this cult of suffering did not make sense, and he remarked, 'if this is taken as a statement of

[1] This article is a revised and extended version of a memorial lecture in honour of A. A. Parker (1908–89) which I gave at Queen Mary and Westfield College, London, in February 1990, during my year as a Visiting Research Associate in the Department of Hispanic Studies. I am greatly indebted to the following friends and colleagues who made helpful comments on earlier drafts: Mr Bernard Bentley, Dr Roger Boase, Professor Alan Deyermond, Professor Ian Macpherson, Dr Barry Taylor, Professor John Varey, Dr Jane Whetnall. I am grateful also to the Dean and the Faculty of Arts of University College Cork who awarded me a grant towards the expenses of research.

XII

actual human loving, then without question it is morbid'; but he added, 'the reason why this poetry makes no rational sense for human love is because it uses the concepts and language of something different: it makes sense all the time in terms of divine love within the tradition of medieval Christianity' (Parker 1985: 21). Courtly love should be interpreted, he believed, as an attempt to revalue human love by describing it in religious terms: 'In the "Ages of Faith" there was theoretically no dispute about the order of values: divine love had priority over human love and the latter was undervalued. It may be held that the Courtly Love phenomenon was part of a reaction against this undervaluation, an attempt to give human love a value in its own right' by transferring to it concepts and words traditionally applied to the love of God (22).

Secondly, there was its idealism. The transfer of concepts from religion to courtly love did not occur, he felt, only at the level of language but also at the level of ethics. The notion that erotic passion could be purified by suffering was, he held, 'an artificial attitude to life', but

A poetic convention divorced from reality points to some sort of aspiration or ideal. If fifteenth-century poets found satisfaction in posing as suffering martyrs of love are we not justified in concluding that they would have liked to be such? In other words, that this convention was a kind of wish-fulfilment, an attempt to envisage a pure and perfect love by conceiving it as a self-sacrificing and therefore ennobling devotion? (17)

These two features, he concluded, explained why the Spanish mystics used the language of courtly love to express their own experience of the love of God. First, since the language of the *cancioneros* was 'religious' it recovered its proper context when used by the mystics, in whose writings concepts such as 'mortification', 'long-suffering', and 'unending desire' made sense. And secondly, because the ideal of love to which the courtly poets aspired was religious in origin it was practicable only in religious terms. In real life the mystics aspired, like the poets, to a perfect love purified by suffering, in their case the suffering of the Dark Night. 'The courtly convention', he wrote, 'points, however confusedly, to a genuine aspiration and ideal, and it is based, however confusedly, upon the concept of suffering as a valuable experience. The literature of mysticism is what dispels the confusion and clarifies the aspiration by achieving it in actual experience' (80).

This theory has the lucidity that marked Parker's finest work. Yet is it well-founded? The question arises because a number of scholars, among them Roy Jones, Keith Whinnom, and Ian Macpherson, have questioned the interpretation of *cancionero* poetry on which it rests. It may be argued that in the light of their criticisms the theory does require some modification and development, but that this revision does not affect its main argument, which merits a central place in any consideration of the poetic analogy between profane and sacred love. The pages that follow examine again the two features of the courtly lyric to which Parker drew attention, and having done so reconsider a mystical poem in which he saw his theory exemplified, the *Llama de amor viva* of St John of the Cross.

I

Parker's conviction that the poetic language of the *cancioneros* was fundamentally religious was disputed in 1981 by the late Keith Whinnom who examined two kinds of religious language that occur in the poems: the use of courtly terms that also have a theological meaning, such as *fe*, *gloria*, and *pasión*, and allusions to the doctrines of the Church and to its feasts, notably the Passion. He concluded that both were of local significance only: 'coincidencias léxicas', as he put it, and 'picantes juegos de palabras' (Whinnom 1981: 23). There are, one might add, further problems. In many lyrics religious terms and parallels do not occur at all: in what sense is *their* language religious? More basically: given the diversity apparent in *cancionero* lyrics, are there not 'dangers inherent in generalizations made about the genre as a whole' (Macpherson 1989a: 101)?

Parker responded to Whinnom's views in an appendix to *The Philosophy of Love*, at the end of which he made an important distinction. 'My concern in this study', he wrote, 'has not been the range of meaning possible in particular *cancionero* poems, but the origin and nature of the convention itself' (1985: 38). This distinction between a poetic convention and its use in individual poems is a crucial one. If a convention may be described as the material or data out of which a poem is constructed,[2] then in *cancionero* poetry of a courtly type these were precisely defined. The vocabulary was restricted to a small number of abstract terms; the situation of the lover was, in principle, one of suspended or unfulfilled desire; and his anguish was depicted through certain recurring topics, such as the conflict within him between passion and reason, his sadness and silence, his paradoxical sense of dying yet living, and his longing for, yet renunciation of, a *galardón*. The immediate cause of individual lyrics, however, was not these data, which all 'courtly' poems began with, but the virtuosity of the writer.

When reading the lyrics now, we find many in which the poet seems to be showing his skill simply by complying with the rules and writing in the manner of his predecessors; but in others we sense him struggling with a problem that B. W. Ife has described as one that 'writers constantly face [...] how can I speak the poetic language of my age without saying what has

---

[2] See the excellent discussion by B. W. Ife (1986).

56

already been said?' (1986: 514).[3] The variations that occurred within the convention were consequently immense: the vocabulary was given extended range by a certain *conceptismo* and by the use in some lyrics of sexual *double-entendres*; the lover's painful experience of suspended desire was depicted in many different situations, even marriage; and the topics of courtly love were given new life by means of various techniques, such as the introduction of imagery from popular sources and the use of ingenious, initially baffling, chains of logic. The language of the convention was common to all the lyrics that used it; its formulation in any particular lyric was always unpredictable.

This distinction may be applied usefully to the study of religious language. In the *Cancionero general* (1511) of Hernando del Castillo there are a number of courtly terms, themes, and topics that have parallels in devotional writings of the late Middle Ages, including one of the most popular, *The Imitation of Christ*, a work that greatly influenced some of the Spanish mystics of the sixteenth century, among them John of Avila, Ignatius Loyola, and Teresa of Avila. Yet these elements of the convention are used in individual poems in a great variety of ways. In some the religious parallels seem to be no more than 'concidencias'; in others that are developed with considerable skill.

First, in the *Imitation* as in the *cancioneros* we find the notion of suffering love so important to Parker. The *cancionero* lover (in the convention) not only accepts the suffering that his lady chooses, he embraces it because obedience proves his love. This notion, which informs countless lyrics, may be illustrated by two examples, one by Soria, the other by Cartagena:

> Pudo tanto mi querer
> siendo vos desgradescida
> que ooy porque ooye corvida
> contento con padescer. (11CG; fol. 146ʳ)[4]

> Si mi mal no agradesceys
> aunque me dañe y condene
> digo que muy bien hazeys
> pues mas que todas valeys
> que mas que todos yo pene. (11CG; fol. 123ʳ)

---

[3] The point is made with a vivid illustration: 'No one looks for the significance of Bach in the fact that he often wrote in counterpoint; his genius lay in how he exploited the potential of a conventional musical language. In the same way, Quevedo's choice of an archaic poetic language is always less significant than what he was able to do with that language.'

[4] The system of classification followed here is the one established in Dutton 1982, and the edition of the *Cancionero general* referred to is Castillo 1958, a facsimile of the Valencia, 1511 edition. Quotations from the *Imitation* are from Kempis 1975, an edition of the version of St John of Avila. See too Bernard-Maître 1956.

The same notion occurs in the *Imitation* where one reads, in the translation of John of Avila, that if a person loves God he must be ready to suffer: 'no vive ninguno en amor sin dolor. El que no está aparejado a sufrir toda cosa y estar a la voluntad del amado, no es digno de ser llamado amador' (Kempis 1975: 93). He must accept suffering because it is God's will for him: 'quiere Dios que aprendas a sufrir la tribulación sin consuelo y que te sujetes del todo a Él' (78). Love impels him to obey, and to endure tribulation willingly, for 'gloriarse en la tribulación no es dificultoso al que ama' (64).

Secondly, there are the paradoxes of pain and joy through which the suffering of the *cancionero* lover is portrayed. Lope de Sosa writes:

> Aunque es de gran padescer
> la tristeza del amor
> tenella es tanto plazer
> como sentilla es dolor. (11CG; fol. 123$^r$)

And for Jorge Manrique, love

> Es plazer en que ay dolores
> dolor en que ay alegria
> un pesar en que ay dulçores
> un esfuerço en que ay temores
> temor en que ay osadia.
> Un plazer en que ay enojos
> una gloria en que hay passion. (11CG; fol. 98$^r$)

In the *Imitation* the same paradoxes occur: 'En la cruz es la salud y vida [...] En la cruz está la infusión de la suavidad soberana [...] En la cruz está el gozo del espíritu' (Kempis 1975: 77). The reader learns that to suffer for love is to find heaven on earth: 'Cuando llegares a esto, que la tribulación te sea dulce por amor de Jesucristo, piensa que te va bien, porque hallaste paraíso en la tierra' (81). He therefore prays for suffering, knowing that it will bring him health, 'porque el padecer y ser atormentado por ti es gran salud para mi alma' (118). One of the paradoxes most common in the *cancioneros*, the death that gives life, is common too in the *Imitation* where the reader is told: 'Si murieres juntamente con Él, vivirás con Él' (78), and later: 'Sabe de cierto que te conviene morir viviendo: cuanto más muere cada uno a sí mismo, tanto más comienza a vivir a Dios' (82).

Thirdly, there is the link between suffering and merit, often affirmed in the *cancioneros*. It occurs, for instance in lyrics by Jorge Manrique and Soria:

> padesci no meresciendo
> y meresci padesciendo
> los bienes que no demando. (11CG; fol. 97$^v$)

> Tanto quanto meresceys
> peno yo por mereceros

> y pues no meresco veros
> mirad que tal me teneys. (11CG; fol. 129ʳ)

And the hope it can inspire is expressed by Rull:

> No canseys de tal passion
> pues vosotros merescistes
> que sufriesse el coraçon
> lo que vosotros hezistes.
> Llorad y sofrid muy tristes
> no cessays
> que algun tiempo gozareys. (11CG; fol. 149ᵛ)

In the *Imitation*, similarly, the reader is told, 'no está nuestro merecimiento [...] en muchas consolaciones y suavidades, mas en sufrir grandes pesadumbres y tribulaciones' (Kempis 1975: 82), and he is encouraged to embrace pain: 'Cuanto más te dispones a padecer, tanto más sabiamente haces, y más mereces' (117). Because he suffers, he may have hope: 'cuanto más se sujeta a la cruz de su voluntad, tanto más la carga de la tribulación se convierte en confianza de la divina consolación' (79); for suffering is always rewarded: 'no hay cosa, por pequeña que sea, padecida por amor de Dios, que pase sin galardón' (118).

Finally, there is the concept of constancy in love, according to which the true *cancionero* lover seeks no reward, for his love is disinterested and it is enough for him to do the lady's will. It is expressed in well-known lines by Jorge Manrique:

> El toque para tocar
> qual amor es bien forjado
> es sofrir el desamar
> que no puede comportar
> el falso sobredorado. (11CG; fol. 98ʳ)

And by Cartagena and Juan Álvarez Gato:

> Que pago de mi aficion
> no lo pido ni se espera
> pues me muestra la razon
> que en querer que por vos muera
> me days pago y gualardon. (11CG; fol. 123ʳ)

> Ninguno sufra dolor
> por correr tras beneficios
> que las fuerças del amor
> no se ganan por servicios. (14CG; 108ᵛ)[5]

---

[5] The reference is to the second edition of the *Cancionero general* (Valencia, 1514), edited by Antonio Rodríguez-Moñino in Castillo 1959.

In the *Imitation*, similarly, one reads: 'los que aman a Jesús por el mismo
Jesús y no por su propria consolación, bendícenlo en la tribulación y angus-
tia tan bien como en la consolación' (Kempis 1975: 75); and perfect love is
said to consist in this: 'en ofrecerte de todo tu corazón a la divina voluntad,
no buscando tu interés en lo poco ni en lo mucho, en lo temporal ni en lo
eterno' (130). In *Don Quixote*, several generations later, the same concept of
love is discussed by the knight himself in chapter 31 of the first part:

> es gran honra tener una dama muchos caballeros andantes que la sirvan, sin
> que se estiendan más sus pensamientos que a servilla por sólo ser ella
> quien es, sin esperar otro premio de sus muchos y buenos deseos sino que
> ella se contente de acetarlos por sus caballeros.

It is Sancho who points out the religious parallels: 'con esa manera de amor
[...] he oído yo predicar que se ha de amar a Nuestro Señor, por sí solo, sin
que nos mueva esperanza de gloria o temor de pena.' His words win Don
Quixote's approbation (Cervantes 1972: 316).

These parallels in the two notions of suffering love, which could be
multiplied, are evidence for the view that the courtly convention used what
Parker called 'the concepts and language of religion' (1985: 21), by which
he appears to have meant not only the use of religious terms and allusions,
but something more basic, underlying them: the value and meaning
accorded to suffering love itself. Yet it is also true, as Whinnom indicated,
that in many lyrics the religious parallels are undeveloped or without
significance; and in some that do use religious terms and images the
religious language is an example of what Northrop Frye has called
'superficial and inorganic convention', which a poet uses 'merely because
it has often been used before in the same way' (1957: 104, 103). Jane Tillier
has shown how, in certain poems, the use of the word 'pasión' in a
religious sense, and explicit references to the Passion, serve the purpose of
comparing or contrasting the lover's anguish with Christ's. One of her
examples is a fine lyric of Diego de San Pedro ('Cuando señora entre nos',
11CG, fol. 114ᵛ) in which 'pasión' has a double meaning: his own 'passion'
and that of Jesus. It may be taken as an instance of poetic originality, if this
is understood as consisting 'not so much in the creation of something
wholly new' as in the 'repristination [...] of something old' (Livingston
Lowes 1919: 98). But she has also pointed out that 'one would obviously be
unwise to attempt to find a religious echo, a reference to Christ's suffering,
in every secular use of "pasión"' (Tillier 1985: 66). One must always
distinguish between the convention itself and its use in a particular lyric.

It would be equally misleading to suppose that the *cancionero* poets were
themselves responsible for the parallels in the language of love: long before
the fifteenth century the traditions of secular and religious love had met
and intertwined. The beginnings of the process may be observed in those
parts of the Old Testament in which nuptial imagery is applied to religious

experience, and in the medieval period, as Tony Hunt has pointed out, it was carried further by exegesis of the *Song of Songs*, particularly in the commentaries of St Bernard and other Cistercians: 'the new synthesis provided by the *Song* [...] contributed signally to the blurring of sacred and profane [...] whereas in the eleventh and twelfth centuries secular writers frequently borrowed from the *Song* [...] in the thirteenth century religious writers borrowed from secular poetry' (Hunt 1981: 193). By the late fifteenth century the two traditions had come to echo and mirror each other so extensively that it is no exaggeration to say, as Parker did, that they 'spoke the same poetic language' (1985: 20).

One area of Golden Age writing in which this common language may be observed is poetry on the death of Christ. When seeking an analogue in medieval religious tradition for the suffering love of the *cancioneros*, Parker found it in the Flemish mystic Ruysbroeck, who called the love of God 'an irresistible desire [...] in which the object of desire is neither attainable nor can it be abandoned' (21).[6] It may be argued that he would have found closer analogues in devotional meditations on the Passion, which showed how the suffering of Jesus revealed the true nature of divine love, and in which the individual Christian was encouraged to take up his own cross in the *imitatio Christi*. This literature flourished in late fifteenth and early sixteenth-century Spain, when the courtly concept of suffering love was most popular.

A topic in the *cancioneros* that also occurs in late medieval writings on the Passion is the notion that the sorrow of the unhappy lover may be a cause of his death. In the courtly tradition it was embodied in the legend of Macías, and expressed in the lyrics of many poets, including Garci Sánchez de Badajoz:

> [...] yo soy aquel
> a quien mas fue amor crüel
> crüel que causó el dolor
> que a mi no me mató amor
> sino la tristeza de él. (11CG; fols 119$^v$–20$^r$)[7]

In devotional writing it stemmed from exegesis of the words of Jesus in Gethsemane, 'My soul is sorrowful unto death' (Matthew 26. 38). According to St Jerome, His mortal sorrow was caused by selfless love of those who, by rejecting Him, would be responsible for His passing. In the later Middle Ages this interpretation was followed by St Thomas Aquinas in the *Summa Theologica*, and popularized by the *Legenda aurea*, the *Meditationes vitae*

---

[6] Originally quoted in de Rougement 1940: 151.

[7] The lyric in which these lines occur ('La mucha tristeza mía') is edited by Patrick Gallagher (1968: 116–18), which is the text followed here. The lines quoted occur on p. 117.

*Christi* and the *Vita Christi* of Ludolph of Saxony (O'Reilly 1982: 364–65; Ludolph of Saxony 1502–03: IV, fol. 59).

Another topic that the two traditions shared is the conflict within the lover between passion and reason. J. M. Aguirre (1981: 65–67) has studied its incidence in the *Cancionero general* where it informs many lyrics, among them one by Gonzalo Carrillo:

> En mi que ventura sigo
> de tristes penas y afan
> el amor y el seso estan
> en gran debate consigo.
>
> El amor lo que procura
> contradize la razon
> y lo que el seso assegura
> no lo consiente passion. (14CG; fol. 108$^v$)

Similarly, in writings on the Passion, the anguish of Jesus in Gethsemane was attributed to an inner conflict between His reason and His sensibility. According to chapter 75 of the *Meditationes vitae Christi*, His reason consented to the Father's will and was prepared to die, but His flesh and his senses suffered at the prospect of death; in the end it was His divine will which ensured that reason was followed (St Bonaventure 1864–71: XII, 602). The same point was made in the *Vita Christi* of Ludolph: 'como verdadero hombre temía la muerte y según la voluntad de la sensualidad quería no morir'; nonetheless 'sometió [...] su voluntad a la conformidad de la voluntad divina' (1502–03: IV, fol. 50$^v$).

A further common topic is the lover's silence, which in both traditions formed an important part of his suffering. In the *cancioneros* he endures his anguish without complaint in order to prove the integrity of his love. It is well-expressed in an anonymous lyric:

> No espero remedio yo
> que se iguale con mi mengua
> pues no descubrio mi lengua
> lo que mi alma sintio. (11CG; fol 130$^v$)

And in poems by Soria and Jorge Manrique:

> Encubroos el mal que siento
> porque hallo
> que mas sirvo quando callo. (11CG; fol. 148$^r$)[8]
>
> Si el esfuerço que (he) tenido
> para callar y sofrir

---

[8] Dutton 1982: II, 75 (ID 3468) gives the alternative reading 'Encubraos'. The original reads 'Encubros'.

> tuviera para dezir
> no sintiera mi bevir
> los dolores que ha sentido. (11CG; fol. 97ᵛ)

In devotional writings, similarly, the silence of Jesus in His Passion was considered an indication of His love: the *Legenda aurea* states that because Eve sinned 'by speaking', Jesus chose to make reparation 'by being still and not speaking',[9] and Ludolph of Saxony observes that 'quando no responde calla [...] como cordero que por toda la grey quiere ser sacrificado' (1502–03: IV, fol. 104ʳ).

The closeness of the two languages of love offered courtly writers the possibility of making a wide range of religious allusions, if they chose to do so. Dorothy Severin has written of Diego de San Pedro, for instance, that he provides 'a prime example of how rhetorical categories can be transported from poetry to prose and from a religious to a profane genre' (1989: 178). This may be observed above all in *Cárcel de amor*, where the religious references operate at several levels. At the most obvious level, Leriano's death, like that of a Christian martyr, reproduces the suffering of Christ: he is betrayed by a friend, denounced by false witnesses, and tried before an unjust judge; when he chooses to die, he drinks a bitter cup, says 'acabados son mis males' (an echo of the 'consummatum est') and is mourned by his widowed mother. At a second level, the allusions to the *Imitatio Christi* occur also in the courtly language by which Leriano and Laureola communicate with each other and with the narrator: Leriano has 'faith' in his beloved; he strives to 'merit' her favour, either by 'serving' her or by 'suffering'; and if she will requite his love, she will, he avers, 'redeem' him. This is the terminology of suffering love in devotion to the Passion.

Beneath these two levels of religious allusion there is a third: the situation of Leriano himself, a lover torn between passion and reason. He chooses to obey the wishes of Laureola, to respect her freedom, and to serve the King; but his desire and sensibility suffer at the prospect that his love may never be fully returned. As he tells her in one of his letters, 'no me culpes, que aunque la voluntad se satisfaze, el sentimiento se querella' (San Pedro 1982: 151; see also Parker 1985: 22–24, and Terry 1988: 170). When this conflict cannot be resolved, he is plunged into the *tristeza* that leads to his death. At this level the parallels with Christ's anguish are not explicit, but they are present, and underlie the other levels at which they are made quite clear. These three levels of allusion and parallel were made available to San Pedro by the courtly convention itself, and *cancionero* lyrics in which suffering love is a serious theme usually operate at one or more of these levels too: not all use religious terms or compare the lover's pain to Christ's,

---

[9] Anon. 1900: I, 73. The poetic topic of silence is a broader and more complex subject than can be indicated here; see Egido 1986.

but the language of suffering love on which they draw has latent religious echoes, which some of them develop and others ignore.

A religious poem that illustrates the connections is the *Pastorcico* of John of the Cross. The secular lyric that inspired it is italianate in its metre, its pastoral mode, and its third-person depiction of the lover, but the sorrow of the lover at the prospect of being parted from his lady, the play on 'ausencia' and 'presencia', and the despair with which he lies stretched out at the end, are all courtly (Blecua 1949; O'Reilly 1982: 363–67). St John, by a few deft changes, and by adding an extra verse, made it into a religious poem about the death of Christ; yet what is striking, as Parker pointed out (1985: 20), is not the features he changed but those he left untouched because they already had religious echoes.

The image of the lover as young shepherd, for instance, which was rooted in the traditional lyric as well as Italian pastoral, was mirrored in the Scriptural image of Jesus the good shepherd, full of divine love. The image of the wound of love, long-established in secular poetry, also existed in the devotional tradition, where the cry of the lover in the *Song*, 'You have wounded my heart' (Song of Songs 4. 9) was applied to the wound in Christ's side on Calvary (Cornelius a Lapide 1868–76a: 66–67).[10] Even the closing image of the lover and the tree, which St John added, derived from both traditions. On the one hand it drew on exegesis of the *Song* in which the lover ascending a tree (Song of Songs 7. 8) was interpreted as a foreshadowing of Christ mounting the Cross. On the other it had antecedents in secular poems, such as Garcilaso's *Second Eclogue*, in which it is beneath a tree that the suffering lover seeks refuge, or the sonnet of Hernando de Acuña, 'Apenas el aurora había mostrado', in which a melancholy shepherd 'a un árbol arrimado' complains that his beloved, by deserting him, has brought him close to death.[11] In the source poem the religious parallels were latent and invisible, mere 'coincidencias' in Whinnom's phrase; but St John was able to bring them alive simply by transposing them to a religious context, because the poetic languages were so close.

Apart from *cancionero* and Passion poetry, there were at least two other areas of Golden Age writing in which the languages of love overlapped, both of them important to the mystics. One was the *Song of Songs* itself. Although, as Jane Ackerman has shown (1984), the imagery of the *Song* was generally used in the Golden Age of sacred love rather than profane, there are many parallels between its poetic language and secular love poetry in

---

[10] On the image of the wound of love see Riehle 1981: 44–45, and Gougaud 1927: 75–130.
[11] On the antecedents in Garcilaso and in the divinization of his poetry by Sebastián de Córdoba, see Alonso 1958: 43–48 & 193–96, and 1962: 245–47 & 263. The sonnet by Hernando de Acuña is included in Empaytaz 1976: 31. See also Boase 1980.

Castilian. Like the *cancionero* lyric, the *Song* is about courtship, and the suffering caused by suspended or unfulfilled desire; and like the courtly poets, the lovers in the *Song* proclaim that they are dying of love, that love is a fire, and that it transcends death (Song of Songs 2. 5; 5. 8; 8. 6). In other ways, however, the *Song* differs. Its subject is a reciprocated love compatible with marriage, and in this respect it is closer to the chivalresque romances. Its background, moreover, is the countryside, which provides its main images, and here it shares common ground not only with the pastoral convention but with the traditional lyric, in which one finds its central motifs of the garden, the deer and the fruits of love.[12] One instance of this common ground is Gil Vicente's play *Don Duardos*, written in the 1520s and based on a romance of chivalry, *Primaleón*. Its subject is a courtship that ends well, in a reciprocated love fulfilled in marriage, and this is portrayed in images drawn from the traditional lyric, among them the garden, which throughout the play is a symbol of the lady as well as the context of her love. So close are the parallels with the *Song* that a recent critic has been led to suggest a direct influence (Zimic 1981; see also Parker 1985: 29–31, 220 n. 41).

St John of the Cross, more than any other poet, was aware of these parallels, and he drew on them often, especially in the *Cántico espiritual*. At one point, for instance, the bride mentions that her skin used to be dark until her beloved looked on her with love:

> no quieras despreciarme;
> que, si color moreno en mí hallaste,
> ya bien puedes mirarme
> después que me miraste,
> que gracia y hermosura en mi dejaste
>
> (San Juan de la Cruz 1981: 598–99)

The image occurs in the *Song* where the bride says 'I am dark but beautiful' (Song of Songs 1. 4) and 'Do not look on me for I am dark, because the sun burnt me' (1. 5). It also occurs in the traditional lyric where the *morenica* laments her own dark skin, burnt by the sun (Cummins 1977: 99–101; Wardropper 1960; Gornall 1986–87). St John is sensitive to both sources, not only in the poem, where he selects 'morena' for the Latin words 'nigra' and 'fusca', but in the commentary where, from various possible exegetical traditions, he chooses to interpret the dark skin of the bride as a sign of failure and weakness, which were also its associations in traditional verse.[13]

The languages of love also overlapped in the vocabulary of warfare, which was often used in the *cancioneros* to describe the experience of love.

---

[12] See Cummins 1977, and, on the imagery of the *Song*, Landy 1983.
[13] San Juan de la Cruz 1981: 868–73. See Morales 1971: 185–86; and on the exegetical background, Cornelius a Lapide 1868–76a: 492–98.

In many lyrics love is said to strike and wound the lover, and to burn him like fire, while passion and reason struggle within him until he is vanquished and becomes love's captive. Such images of conflict drew on an association of love and war long-established in classical literature which was given new life in the literature of courtly love and chivalry (see Rougemont 1940: 248–50, and Boase 1980: 22–27). In the mystical tradition the same imagery was applied to the experience of divine love. The image of the spiritual life as a battle, which was common in Scripture, and prolonged in the early Church by writers like Prudentius, was renewed in the late Middle Ages when the language of chivalry was applied, in turn, to the love of God. Francisco de Osuna, for instance, wrote in 1530:

> el amor no pelea sino con halago, no tiene otras amenazas sino blandas palabras; y las saetas y golpes son beneficios y dones; el encuentro es ofrecimiento de gran eficacia; y su artillería son suspiros; y su prender es abraçar; y su matar es dar la vida por el amado.[14]

Both traditions were brought together in the mystical writings of Teresa of Avila, in which we find not only the images of wounding (in her description, for instance, of the Transverberation) but the chivalric metaphors of battle, notably in the *Moradas del castillo interior*. As a child she was a keen reader of the romances of chivalry, and according to her early biographer, Ribera, she tried to write one, while the religious writings that most influenced her as an adult were precisely those in which courtly and chivalric images were transposed to the Christian life: the translation of Ludolph of Saxony by Ambrosio Montesino, the treatises of Alonso de Madrid and Bernardino de Laredo, and the *Tercer abecedario espiritual* of Osuna. In these two kinds of literature, secular and sacred, the poetic language of love that she encountered was one and the same (see Concha 1978).

## II

The notion that the *cancionero* poets aspired to a perfect love purified by suffering was questioned on literary grounds by Roy Jones and Keith Whinnom. They held, as Parker did, that the longing of which the poets wrote was sexual desire, but they also argued that the goal of the poets was not a perfect love but sexual union, attained by protestations of fidelity, flattery and special pleading. Jones wrote, 'We should not read into these poets' reticence any suggestion that they elevated frustration into a principle. They

---

[14] Quoted in Etchegoyen 1923: 276 (see also 232–44).

made their requests in veiled terms, but the veils are transparent enough';
and he took as an example the lines of Juan del Encina:

> La muerte es vitoria
> do bive aficion
> que espera aver gloria
> quien sufre passion.[15]

The ostensible meaning of the courtly terms here is theological: a religious
language is being applied to human love. As Jones put it, 'he declares his
hope that his passion, like Christ's, will be rewarded with entry into glory'.
But he went on to argue that 'gloria' had another, more telling, meaning
too: sexual pleasure, as it does, for instance, in *Celestina* (Jones 1966: 535–36;
Whinnom 1968: 22).[16] Keith Whinnom later took the matter further by
drawing attention to the rich vein of comic and obscene literature in which
courtly terms were given an erotic meaning, and he instanced the verb
'morir', which in the courtly tradition meant 'to suffer', but in comic and
obscene verse 'to have a sexual climax' (1981: 34–46). He went on to affirm
that the two meanings were not completely separate. In the *cancionero* line
'muero porque no muero' he accepted the courtly sense, but felt that always
present was the erotic meaning, 'I am dying because I cannot have intercourse with my lady'. The two meanings, he believed, could not be kept
rigidly apart.[17]

This theory presents problems for the interpretation of mystical verse.
Both Teresa and John, for instance, glossed 'muero porque no muero' in a
mystical sense: 'I am dying because I cannot die and be with God.' If the
same line can have three levels of meaning, how do the three levels inter-
relate? Parker argued that the meaning of courtly terms was determined by
the social context: a verb like 'muero' could have one meaning in a secular
context, but quite another in a contemplative convent or monastery (1985:
19–20). There is, however, a literary problem involved. If Whinnom was
correct, and the courtly and erotic senses were always closely linked, how
could the erotic meaning be absent at the religious level too? How could the
mystics have ignored the accepted meanings of the lyrics they divinized?
The resolution of this problem is important for our reading of mystical
poetry for it raises the question: what kind of human love is mystical
longing being compared to?

---

[15] From the *villancico* 'Más vale trocar' (ID 3825) in Juan del Encina 1928: fol. 89ᵛ–90ʳ.

[16] For an example of the erotic sense of 'gloria' in the *Celestina* see Rojas 1976: 191 ('Bien
me huelgo que estén semejantes testigos de mi gloria').

[17] Whinnom 1981: 37: 'No estoy dispuesto a sostener que, cuando los poetas cancioneriles
se quejan: "Y muero porque no muero", están diciendo abiertamente: "Siento dolores morta-
les porque mi amada no me permite el alivio sexual", sino que detrás de la paradoja del
vivo muerto [...] yace también esta sugerencia erótica.'

A solution may lie in the notion of literary categories. At the end of *La poesía amatoria* Whinnom noted that the erotic use of courtly terms is explicit only in obscene and comic works, and he concluded: 'Though we need to ponder the matter more, it is clear that the poets were working within aesthetic and linguistic conventions that were distinct and well-defined' (1981: 88)[18] Here, it may be argued, we are dealing with three literary categories which, though separate, shared the same terms. First there is the poetry of courtship, in which the convention of courtly love is used in a great variety of ways. In many lyrics, especially perhaps in the early *cancioneros*, courtly terms are employed in their conventional sense to denote a suffering love embraced because it is of value. In many others, especially perhaps in the *Cancionero general*, the convention is played with endlessly, and even undermined, often by *double-entendres*. Such is the case with the poem of Encina quoted earlier, in which the courtly meaning of 'gloria' is still present, but as an ironic counterpoint. Second, there is poetry that is obscene or burlesque, in which courtly terms like 'gloria' and 'morir' are used with the unequivocal meaning of sexual pleasure. In such lyrics the courtly meaning, when present, is evoked as a joke, for this is no longer a poetry of courtship, but of sexual experience (see the useful anthology Alzieu, Jammes, & Lissorgues 1984). Third, there is religious poetry in which courtly terms are used, but with a religious or theological meaning. In this poetry the courtly meaning is present, but in a secondary sense, providing an image of human love to which religious experience is compared.

In all three categories the same terms occur, but in each their meaning is distinct, which is why it is possible for a poet to quote one category within another. Diego de San Pedro, for instance, quotes the religious meaning of 'pasión' alongside the courtly ('Cuando señora entre nos', 11CG, fol. 114ᵛ, cited above), just as Encina alludes to the erotic meaning of 'gloria' alongside its courtly sense. Such *double-entendres* are possible only because the three categories are separate. It follows that the courtly meaning of 'muero' does not necessarily imply the erotic one, any more than the erotic meaning necessarily implies the religious, or vice versa. Equally important is the fact that in each category the courtly meaning is present, though to different effect. At the obscene level it is present as a joke, as the language that is being undermined. At the religious level it is present as an image of human love: in the glosses of Teresa and John, for instance, the language of human courtship evokes the mystical courtship of the soul and God celebrated in the *Song of Songs*. These distinctions are crucial when we come

---

[18] 'Aunque convendría que ponderásemos más el problema, se ve que los ´poetas trabajaban dentro de distintas y bien definidas convenciones estéticas y lingüísticas.'

to consider the *Llama de amor viva*, the poem that Parker took as his example of the tranposition of courtly language to mystical experience.

## III

The *Llama*, like the other major poems of St John, confronts us with what has been termed 'the central paradox' of his poetry: 'how could a mystic who seeks God by way of negation have created such marvellous and sensual witnesses to his search?' (Thompson 1990: 224). According to the commentary, the poem describes the state of the soul on emerging from the Dark Night. It knows that its worst suffering is over, and it enjoys the peace and joy of union with God evoked especially in the last two stanzas, yet it is still suffering with desire for the complete union possible only after death, which St John describes, in the nuptial imagery of the *Song*, as the consummation of the spiritual marriage (*Llama de amor viva*, version B, 1: 27, in San Juan de la Cruz 1980: 937) To convey this complex state, St John turned to the poetic language of the *cancioneros*, and, in Parker's words, 'took over the conventional courtly love language of the flames of love, of wounding, and of suffering as a living death' (1985: 81).

Recently, in a carefully-argued study (1989b), Ian Macpherson has suggested another interpretation of the opening images: their meaning, he holds, is not courtly but erotic. 'Rompe la tela' (in the fifth line of stanza one) does not mean primarily 'rend the veil' or 'break the barrier in the lists' but 'break the hymen', as it can in obscene verse; and 'encuentro' (in the same line) is not used primarily with its literal meaning of 'encounter', nor in the chivalric sense of 'a clash of arms', but as a synonym for intercourse. Here the point at issue is not the presence within the poem of an analogy between sexual and mystical union (which was long-established in the religious tradition) but the mode of its articulation: if this approach is correct, the poem alludes to the act of intercourse in the language of erotic secular verse (Macpherson 1989b: 197–200)[19]

Macpherson supports his interpretation with two arguments. First, he affirms, the erotic meanings of 'romper la tela' and 'encuentro' were so well established in the Golden Age that they could not be avoided: 'it is difficult to imagine that any sixteenth-century reader of San Juan even slightly experienced in the ways of courtly poetry would have been able to read San Juan's line as if it existed in a literary vacuum' (1989b: 200). If, however, the distinctions made earlier are accepted, it follows that St John was writing, not in a literary vacuum, but within firm literary categories that enabled

---

[19] On the traditional analogy between sexual and mystical union, see Parker 1985: 86–89.

him to use courtly terms in an amorous context without invoking their obscene connotations, unless, that is, he wished to. But did he wish to?

Macpherson's second argument is that St John deliberately invoked the obscene meanings in order to rehabilitate them: 'from a literary and linguistic point of view, one of his major achievements in *Llama de amor viva* is, through the process of *divinización*, to reclaim such concepts and vocabulary from the adulterated and often frivolous contexts frequently assigned to them by the secular poetry of the time' (1989b: 201). It would be possible to find support for this approach in Parker's view of St John as someone who 'never intended to be a "professional" poet or to imitate his predecessors', and in whose poetry he noted a striking 'freedom from precedence, rules and fashions', and a 'marvellously unconscious disregard for the conventional decorum of rhetorical theory' (1985: 85, 101). There are, however, two reasons for hesitating.

First, although St John often broke with the conventions of secular poetry, he was more closely bound by those of sacred writing, especially exegesis of the *Song of Songs*. Jean Leclercq has shown that in his commentary on the *Song* St Bernard gave clear descriptions of human courtship and lovemaking in order to establish the analogy between human love and divine. Yet even Bernard did not describe intercourse in intimate detail, and in this he differed from the erotic poetry of his day (Leclercq 1981: 75). At one point in Bernard's commentary, for instance, the bridegroom assures the bride, 'Even in the vineyard there will be time for that which we both sigh after', and here the Latin reads, 'id quod pariter optamus' (*Sermones in Canticum*, 61: 2). Jean Leclercq remarks: 'The text does not tell us what *id* refers to here. In such language, spangled as it is with words from the Vulgate which are often hazy, vague, mysterious, the actual consummation of love is never mentioned in overbold or common terms; it is always wrapped in poetry' (1981: 76).

St John, in his other major poems, observed the same constraints. In the *Cántico espiritual* the actual union of the lovers is an event that occurred in the past, or to which they aspire in the future, and it is referred to in the same imprecise terms as those used by St Bernard. This is the case, for instance, in the stanza that reads:

> Allí me mostrarías
> aquello que mi alma pretendía,
> y luego me darías
> allí tú, vida mí,
> aquello que me diste el otro día.
> (San Juan de la Cruz 1981: 604–05)[20]

---

[20] On the 'overwhelming impression of mystery' that the *Cántico* conveys see Thompson 1977: 84–91.

In the fifth stanza of the *Noche oscura*, similarly, sexual union is alluded to directly, but not the physical details. The word 'transformada' in the last line is a metaphor for union, but also, as Parker pointed out, a technical term used in mystical vocabulary to denote the transformation of the soul into God (1985: 98–99). In St John's day, the religious and the obscene were demarcated clearly by the Church: obscene literature was banned by the Index and the Inquisition, and secular songs, though often allowed in church, were not so approved if they were lewd or 'profane' (see the evidence quoted in Whinnom 1968: 19; Whinnom 1981: 22). To suggest that in the *Llama* St John went against these conventions, is to suggest that he broke with the practice he followed in other poems and spheres, and this is surely unlikely.

Secondly, in his commentary on the poem St John makes no mention of the possible erotic meanings of the words used. Macpherson, who acknowledges this, agrees with the late Dámaso Alonso that 'the poems were composed in the intense glow of inspiration', but that 'the commentaries were a rationalized analysis *a posteriori*, which the poet manipulated to make the inspired poems mean what he, as a theologian, later wanted them to mean' (Parker 1985: 96).[21] On this point Parker disagreed with Alonso strongly, and he argued, in some fine pages, that the relationship between commentary and poem was not arbitrary but necessary, and could be established by sensitive reading. 'Our only test', he wrote, 'for the legitimacy of the commentaries as vehicles for the intrinsic meanings of the images must be, first, that the revelation of the meanings prove entirely illuminating within the context, and, secondly, that they in no way go counter to the poetic emotion and tone' (1985: 96). After applying this principle to a number of lines in the *Cántico espiritual* he concluded: 'it seems impossible that the poet composed these poems in the fire of poetic intuition, and only later worked out meanings for them [...] The symbolism and allegory revealed by the commentary are no pedestrian addition rendering it lifeless; on the contrary, they make the poetry glow with a heightened radiance of mind and heart' (1985: 230).

Parker's guiding principle may be applied to the images of pain with which the *Llama* opens. St John asks: why is the flame said to wound? And he answers: 'El amor, cuyo oficio es herir para enamorar y deleitar, como en la tal alma está en viva llama, estále arrojando sus heridas como llamaradas ternísimas de delicado amor' (1: 8). This is the imagery of love as conflict, rooted in the traditions of divine as well as human love. In St John's comments on the other images, similar meanings occur. Divine love is described as wounding the soul, just as sunlight strikes glass: 'llegará a

---

[21] This summary of Alonso's view is quoted by Macpherson (1989b: 194) in a passage that could be taken to imply that Parker agreed with it.

herir el amor de Dios hasta el último centro y más profundo del alma [...]
Bien así como el cristal limpio y puro es embestido de la luz' (1: 13). The
verb used, 'embestir', which had military associations in John's day, recurs
repeatedly in the text.[22] Similarly, the noun 'encuentro' is normally used
in its chivalric sense of a clash of arms. St John writes: 'veamos ahora por
qué [...] a este embestimiento interior del Espíritu le llama *encuentro*'; and
he continues: 'hace él en ella estos embestimientos divinos y gloriosos a
manera de encuentros, que, como son a fin de purificarla y sacarla de la
carne, verdaderamente son encuentros con que siempre penetra' (1: 35).

The literal meaning accorded to 'rompe la tela' varies. In some passages
the 'tela' is the fabric of life itself, sundered by death. The soul is said to
cry, '*rompe la tela* delgada de esta vida y no la dejes llegar a que la edad y
años naturalmente la corten' (1: 36). The image used in this sense had a
classical background that may have been mediated to St John by Garcilaso;
it also had Scriptural origins in the traditional exegesis of Isaiah 38. 12: 'my
life is cut off, as by a weaver'.[23] Elsewhere the 'tela' is compared to a
spider's web ('tela de araña') and is said to bind and imprison the soul,
which longs to break free (1: 32; 1: 31).

In other passages again the meaning of 'tela' appears to be chivalric. The
*tela*, or barrier, placed in Spain between jousting knights, was designed to
prevent injury. Pérez de Castro, writing in 1639, noted the dangers: 'En el
juego de lanzas sólo puede la cordura prevenir los riesgos: uno el que no
lleven hierro con que herir [...] otro evitar los choques de los caballos, sin
duda peligrosos a los ginetes, y este riesgo [...] le cautelaron con las vallas
interpuestas' (quoted in Leguina 1904: 29). The 'valla' was also called a
'tela': the term is used in this sense by Díez de Games in the fifteenth
century: 'los franzeses justan por otra guisa que non façen en España; justan
sin tela, a manera de guerra [...] por el topar', and he adds: 'es muy
peligrosa justa' (Díez de Games 1940: 237).[24] An encounter that broke the
barrier would therefore be unusually violent, and those involved would risk
death. St John picks up these connotations precisely when he defines the
'tela' allegorically as the barrier between life and death: 'parece que [...] está
tan cerca de la bienaventuranza, que no la divide sino una leve tela [...]
cada vez que la absorbe y embiste le parece que le va a dar la vida eterna,
y que le va a romper la tela de la vida mortal' (1: 1; see also 1: 32, 33, 36).
In all these various passages there is, to quote Parker again, 'a perfect fusion
of both the human and the mystical levels of experience', and the

---

[22] See, for instance, 1: 19, 22, 25, 35; 2: 9. On the meaning of 'embestir' in the sixteenth
century, see Corominas 1954.

[23] On the classical background, and the possible influence of Garcilaso, see Alonso 1958:
30, and on the exegesis of Isaiah 38. 12, see Cornelius a Lapide 1868–76b: 478.

[24] In the glossary at the end of this edition, the word 'tela' is defined as 'valla que se
ponía a lo largo del campo para evitar que los caballeros se topasen' (363).

associations of the word on both levels become relevant to the image (1985: 98).

The *Llama de amor viva* is not only a fine example of the application to mystical experience of *cancionero* terms; it also reveals how that experience ultimately transcends courtly concepts. In conventional *cancionero* lyrics the flame that wounds the lover is love, unrequited and therefore painful, but in St John's poem the flame is the beloved, who reciprocates love fully, and the wound is the longing for ever greater union. The poetic subtext here is not courtly, but the *Song of Songs*, whose influence becomes clearer in stanzas three and four when the bridegrooms appears. His presence is announced by a change of gender in stanza four, when masculine adjectives denote that the singular subject is no longer 'llama'. At first 'manso' and 'amoroso' (l. 19) appear to make no sense on the literal level, but they are explained in the commentary as referring to the divine Word, the beloved mentioned at the end of verse three (4: 1–12). Another mysterious image brings the poem to a close, the breathing of the lover that enamours the bride (ll. 22–24), an image probably drawn from traditional exegesis of the *Song*, in which the bridegroom's breath is the Holy Spirit (4: 16, 17).[25] This is the kind of breakdown in the literal sense that led Parker to refer to the fire in the poem as 'non-human, solely transcendental', and to affirm that 'to read St John's poetry as human love-songs [...] leaves the larger part of its imagery unintelligible' (1985: 99, 97). It is a technique that St John probably drew from patristic and medieval exegesis of Scripture, which held that absurdity in the literal sense indicated the presence of allegory (Smalley 1983: xiv).[26] It also reminds the reader that because the experience that the mystics describe is said by them to exceed all images, the poetic analogy between profane and sacred love, however telling, can never be exact or complete.

WORKS CITED

Ackerman, Jane Ellen, 1984. 'The Presence of the *Canticle of Canticles* in Sixteenth and Seventeenth Century Hispanic Poetry' (unpublished doctoral dissertation, Univ. of Kentucky).

Aguirre, J. M., 1981. 'Reflexiones para la construcción de un modelo de la poesía castellana del amor cortés', *RF*, 93: 55–81.

---

[25] On the exegetical background see Leclercq 1981: 80–81.

[26] I am grateful to Professor Bernard Hamilton for drawing my attention to this reference.

Alonso, Dámaso, 1958. *La poesía de San Juan de la Cruz*, 3rd ed. (Madrid: Aguilar).

——, 1962. *Poesía española*, 4th ed. (Madrid: Gredos).

Alzieu, Pierre, Robert Jammes, & Yvan Lissorgues, editors, 1984. *Poesía erótica del Siglo de Oro* (Barcelona: Crítica).

Bernard-Maître, Henri, SJ, 1956. 'Saint Ignace de Loyola et les anciennes traductions espagnoles de l'*Imitation de Jésus-Christ*', *Ons Geestelijk Erf*, 30: 25–42.

Blecua, José M., 1949. 'Los antecedentes del poema del *Pastorcico* de San Juan de la Cruz', *RFE*, 33: 378–80 (reprinted in his *Sobre poesía de la Edad de Oro* (Madrid: Gredos, 1970), pp. 96–99).

Boase, Roger, 1980. 'Imagery of Love, Death and Fortune in the Poetry of Pedro Manuel Ximénez de Urrea (1486–c.1530)', *BHS*, 57: 17–32.

Castillo, Hernando del, 1958. *Cancionero general* (Valencia, 1511), ed. in facsimile by Antonio Rodríguez-Moñino (Madrid: Real Academia Española).

Castillo, Hernando del, 1959. *Cancionero general*, 2nd ed. (Valencia, 1514), in *Suplemento al Cancionero general*, ed. Antonio Rodríguez-Moñino (Madrid: Castalia).

Cervantes Saavedra, Miguel de, 1972. *Don Quijote de la Mancha*, ed. Martín de Riquer (Barcelona: Juventud).

Concha, Víctor G. de la, 1978. 'Las lecturas de santa Teresa', in his *El arte literario de santa Teresa* (Barcelona: Ariel), pp. 47–81.

Cornelius a Lapide, 1868–76a. *Commentaria in Canticum Canticorum*, in *Commentaria in Scripturam Sacram*, 21 vols (Paris: Vives), VIII, pp. 1–260.

——, 1868–76b. *In Isaiam prophetam*, in *Commentaria in Scripturam Sacram*, XI.

Corominas, J., 1954. *Diccionario crítico-etimológico de la lengua castellana* (Madrid: Francke Bern).

Cummins, John G., ed., 1977. *The Spanish Traditional Lyric* (Oxford: Pergamon).

Deyermond, Alan, & Ian Macpherson, editors, 1989. *The Age of the Catholic Monarchs, 1474–1516: Literary Studies in Memory of Keith Whinnom* (Liverpool: UP, 1989).

Díez de Games, Gutierre, 1940. *El Victorial: crónica de don Pedro Niño, Conde de Buelna*, ed. Juan de Mata Carriazo (Madrid: Espasa Calpe).

Dutton, Brian, et al., editors, 1982. *Catálogo-índice de la poesía cancioneril del siglo XV*, 2 vols (Madison: HSMS).

Egido, A., 1986. 'La poética del silencio en el Siglo de Oro: su pervivencia', *BH*, 88: 93–120.

Empaytaz, Dionisia, ed., 1976. *Antología de albas, alboradas y poemas afines* (Madrid: Playor).

Encina, Juan del, 1928. *Cancionero* (Salamanca, 1496), ed. in facsimile by Emilio Cotarelo (Madrid: Real Academia Española).

Etchegoyen, Gaston, 1923. *L'Amour divin. Essai sur les sources de Sainte Thérèse* (Bordeaux: Féret et Fils).

Frye, Northrop, 1957. *The Anatomy of Criticism* (Princeton: UP).

Gallagher, Patrick, 1968. *The Life and Works of Garci Sánchez de Badajoz* (London: Tamesis).

Gornall, John, 1986–87. '"Por el río del amor, madre": An Aspect of the Morenita', *JHP*, 10: 151–60.

Gougaud, Louis, 1927. *Devotional and Ascetic Practices in the Middle Ages* (London: Burns, Oates).

Hunt, Tony, 1981. 'The *Song of Songs* and Courtly Literature', in *The Court and Poet: Selected Proceedings of the Third Congress of the International Courtly Literature Society (Liverpool 1980)*, ed. Glyn S. Burgess (Liverpool: Francis Cairns), pp. 189–96.

Ife, B. W., 1986. Review of Julián Olivares, *The Love Poetry of Francisco de Quevedo* (Cambridge: UP, 1983), *MLR*, 81: 513–16.

Jones, R. O., 1966. 'Bembo, Gil Polo, Garcilaso: Three Accounts of Love', *Revue de Littérature Comparée*, 40: 526–40.

Kempis, Tomás de, 1975. *Imitación de Cristo*, translated by St John of Avila, ed. Francisco Martín Fernández (Madrid: Editorial Católica).

Landy, Francis, 1983. *Paradoxes of Paradise: Identity and Difference in the Song of Songs* (Sheffield: Almond Press).

Leclercq, Jean, 1981. *Monks on Marriage: A Twelfth-Century View* (New York: Seabury).

Leguina, Enrique de, 1904. *Torneos, jinetes, rieptos y desafíos: apuntes reunidos* (Madrid: Fernando Fe).

Livingston Lowes, John, 1919. *Convention and Revolt in Poetry* (London: Constable).

Ludolph of Saxony, 150?–03. *Vita Cristi Cartuxano*, 4 vols (Alcalá de Henares: Stanislaus de Polonia).

Macpherson, Ian, 1989a. 'Juan de Mendoza, *El bello malmaridado*', in Deyermond & Macpherson 1989, 95–102.

——, 1989b. '"Rompe la tela de este dulce encuentro": San Juan's *Llama de amor viva* and the Courtly Context', in *Studies in Honor of Bruce W. Wardropper*, ed. Dian Fox, Harry Sieber, & Robert Ter Horst (Newark, Delaware: Juan de la Cuesta). pp. 193–203.

Morales, José L., 1971. *El Cántico espiritual de San Juan de la Cruz: su relación con el Cantar de los Cantares y otras fuentes escriturísticas y literarias* (Madrid: Espiritualidad).

O'Reilly, Terence, 1982. 'The Literary and Devotional Context of the *Pastorcico*', *FMLS*, 18: 363–70.

Parker, A. A., 1985. *The Philosophy of Love in Spanish Literature 1480–1680*, ed. Terence O'Reilly (Edinburgh: UP, 1985).

Riehle, Wolfgang, 1981. *The Middle English Mystics* (London: Routledge).

Rojas, Fernando de, 1976. *La Celestina: Tragicomedia de Calisto y Melibea*, ed. Dorothy S. Severin, with an introduction by Stephen Gilman, 4th ed. (Madrid: Alianza, 1976).

Rougemont, Denis de, 1940. *L'Amour et l'Occident* (Paris: Plon, 1939), translated by Montgomery Belgion as *Passion and Society* (London: Faber, 1940; revised edition 1956).

St Bonaventure, 1864–71. *Opera omnia*, 15 vols (Paris: Vives).

San Juan de la Cruz, 1980. *Obras completas*, ed. José Vicente Rodríguez & Federico Ruiz Salvador, 2nd ed. (Madrid: Espiritualidad).

———, 1981. *Cántico espiritual*, ed. Eulogio Pacho (Madrid: Fundación Universitaria Española).

San Pedro, Diego de, 1982. *Cárcel de amor*, ed. Keith Whinnom, 2nd ed. (Madrid: Castalia, 1982).

Severin, Dorothy Sherman, 1989. 'From the Lamentations of Diego de San Pedro to Pleberio's Lament', in Deyermond & Macpherson 1989, 178–84.

Smalley, Beryl, 1983. *The Study of the Bible in the Middle Ages*, 3rd ed. (Oxford: Blackwell).

Terry, Arthur, 1988. 'Lectures in Love's Philosophy: A. A. Parker on Human and Divine Love in Golden-Age Literature', *BHS*, 65: 169–74.

Thompson, Colin P., 1977. *The Poet and the Mystic: A Study of the Cántico Espiritual of San Juan de la Cruz* (Oxford: UP).

———, 1990. Review of *En torno a San Juan de la Cruz*, ed. José Servera Baño (Madrid: Júcar), *MLR* 85: 224–25.

Tillier, Jane Yvonne, 1985. 'Passion Poetry in the *Cancioneros*', *BHS*, 62: 65–78.

Voragine, Jacobus de, 1900. *The Golden Legend*, translated by William Caxton, 7 vols (London: Dent).

Wardropper, Bruce W., 1960. 'The Color Problem in Spanish Traditional Poetry', *MLN*, 75: 415–21.

Whinnom, Keith, 1968. *Spanish Literary Historiography: Three Forms of Distortion* (Exeter: Univ.).

———, 1981. *La poesía amatoria en la época de los Reyes Católicos* (Durham: Univ.).

Zimic, Stanislav, 1981. '*Don Duardos*: espiritualización de la aventura caballeresca', *BBMP*, 57: 47–103.

# XII

76

**ABSTRACT**  Este artículo tiene por tema la teoría que propuso Alexander Parker para explicar por qué la poesía mística española del siglo dieciséis se servía de los conceptos y de la retórica del amor cortés. En la primera parte del artículo se considera su idea de que el lenguaje de los cancioneros era esencialmente religioso; en la segunda se examina su creencia de que los poetas cancioneriles aspiraban a un amor purificado y perfecto. La última parte del artículo trata de un poema místico en el cual, según Parker, estas ideas se ejemplifican: la *Llama de amor viva* de San Juan de la Cruz.

**Keywords**  1  Spanish literature—sixteenth century
2  poetry—San Juan de la Cruz—*Llama de amor viva*
3  mysticism—courtly love

# XIII

## ST JOHN OF THE CROSS AND THE TRADITIONS
## OF MONASTIC EXEGESIS

For George Every

Modern scholarship has drawn to our attention the importance of Scripture in the writings of St John of the Cross.[1] In
his prose works it is by far the most cited source, and it
informs all his poems, especially those he composed during
his captivity in Toledo. Many readers nowadays find this
love of Scripture attractive, among them Roman Catholics
influenced by the renewal of biblical studies in their church,
but the same readers are often disconcerted by St John's
method of interpretation, especially by the primacy he accords
to the 'spiritual' or 'allegorical' meaning of the biblical text,
which often seems arbitrary or eccentric.[2]

The type of exegesis St John practised was inherited
from the Middle Ages. Established by the Fathers of the
Church, it was prolonged in the writings and liturgy of the
monastic tradition, and in the late medieval period it was
developed further in the Scholastic schools of the Universi-
ties.[3] St John was familiar with each stage of its evolution. As
his contemporaries inform us, he was well-acquainted with

the 'positive' theology of the Fathers.[4] During the 1560s he studied Scripture in the University of Salamanca, then at the forefront of biblical research.[5] And throughout his life as a friar his day was shaped by the practice, originally monastic, of reading Scripture in a liturgical and devotional context.[6] This monastic tradition is the subject of the pages that follow, in particular the influence it exercised on his view of Scripture, and on his poems and commentaries, through what was known as *lectio divina*: the art or craft of reading the sacred text.

## Lectio Divina

In the *avisos spirituales* of St John there are two references to *lectio*. The first occurs in the manuscript conserved in Andújar:

> Si deseas hallar la paz y consuelo de tu alma y servir a Dios de veras, no te contentes con eso que has dejado . . . mas deja todas esotras cosas que te quedan y apártate a una sola que lo trae todo consigo, que es la soledad santa, acompañada con oración y santa y divina lección, y allí persevera en olvido de todas las cosas. . .[7]

Here, reading and prayer are connected closely. The nature of the connection is made clear in another *aviso* included in the *Puntos de amor*:

> Buscad leyendo y hallaréis meditando;
> llamad orando y abriros han contemplando.[8]

### St John and the Traditions of Monastic Exegesis

This *aviso* is not, in fact, original to St John, but a translation of words attributed to the Carthusian, Guigo II, a monastic writer of the twelfth century who was one of the first to analyse the process by which reading Scripture could lead to union with God.[9] In *lectio* during the Middle Ages and in St John's own time, the biblical text was read slowly, thoughtfully and repeatedly, often out loud or *sotto voce*. In this way a memory of the text was built up, based not only on the sight of the words but on their pronunciation and sound. The reader's mind became a concordance, able to link passages spontaneously according to sound and meaning. The purpose of *lectio*, however, was not to acquire information but to savour the sacred words inwardly. The following advice to a medieval novice is quoted by Jean Leclercq:

> When he reads, let him strive to taste not to know
> ... then he will not have to go to the oratory in order
> to start praying, but in reading itself he will find a
> way to prayer and contemplation.[10]

The activity of savouring the text could itself be prayer: 'Haec autem degustatio adhaesio est, unio est'.[11]

It is clear from the evidence of contemporaries that St John read Scripture in this way. According to fray Juan Evangelista, who was his secretary for many years:

> Era muy amigo de leer en la Sagrada Escritura, y
> así nunca jamás le vide leer otro libro sino la Biblia
> (la cual sabía casi toda de memoria), y en un S.
> Agustín *contra haereses*, y en el *Flos sanctorum*;
> y cuando predicaba alguna vez, que fueron pocas,
> o hacía pláticas, que era de ordinario, nunca leía
> otro libro sino la Biblia.[12]

Through constant reading he came to memorise the text and could then recall it with ease. Another friar, Pablo de Santa María, remarked:

> Tengo por cierto que sabía toda la Biblia, según juzgaba de diferentes lugares de ella en pláticas que hacía en capítulo y refectorio, sin estudiar para ello, sino ir por donde el espíritu le guiaba.[13]

For St John, reading Scripture and talking about it were ways into prayer. Another witness recalled the affection and devotion with which he read and re-read chapter seventeen of the Fourth Gospel;[14] and the same intimate link between reading and recollection was noted by fray Agustín de los Reyes, who told a friend in 1585: 'Arrimado a estas paredes hallé este día al padre fray Juan de la Cruz . . . con una Biblia en la mano, ocupado, como solía, en contemplación'.[15]

### The Mystical Sense

St John's practice of *lectio* explains several features of his approach to Scripture, including the importance he accorded to its 'spiritual' sense. The mystical interpretation of the Bible was long-established in the Carmelite Order, as Henri de Lubac has shown. An anonymous Carmelite text of the thirteenth century affirms, for instance:

> Within these secret words, held captive beneath images, are hidden meanings that are subtle and mystical, like treasures in the ground. To discover these secrets, by separating the spirit from the letter, is to draw up life, the life of the Spirit. Happy

is the person who in the misery of exile devotes all his spirit and all his love to the delights of these mysterious meanings![16]

St John did not set out a general theory or method of exegesis,[17] but it is clear from several passages in which he discussed the matter in passing that he considered the mystical sense to be paramount. In the *Subida del Monte Carmelo* he explains that the spiritual sense of prophecy, including scriptural prophecy, is the essential one, for it is the sense intended by the Holy Spirit who inspires it: 'el principal intento de Dios en aquellas cosas es decir y dar el espíritu que está allí encerrado'.[18] God's ways are not ours, however, and this 'hidden' meaning cannot be fully grasped:

> [los dichos y revelaciones de Dios] . . . son abismo y profundidad de espíritu, y quererlos limitar a lo que de ellos entendemos y puede aprehender el sentido nuestro, no es más que querer palpar el aire y palpar alguna mota que encuentra la mano en él; y el aire se va y no queda nada.[19]

A deep awareness of God's transcendence leads him to draw a sharp contrast between the literal meaning and the spiritual. The former may be apprehended by reason and common sense but the latter exceeds it utterly: '. . . el espíritu que está allí encerrado . . . es dificultoso de entender, y . . . es muy más abundante que la letra y muy extraordinario y fuera de los límites de ella'.[20] The same point is made in the prologue to the *Cántico*: in certain books of Scripture the meaning intended by the Spirit is so 'abundant' that on the literal level the text is unintelligible, and this spiritual meaning cannot be uncovered by exegesis, however hard it strives: 'los santos doctores, aunque mucho dicen y más digan, nunca pueden acabar de declararlo por palabras, así como tampoco por palabras se pudo ello decir'. In fact exegesis normally leaves most of the full meaning of Scripture unexpressed: 'así lo que dello se declara ordinariamente es lo menos que contiene en sí'.[21]

The question naturally arises: if such is the character of the spiritual sense, can it be apprehended at all? The answer St John gives is: never completely, and only in the 'darkness' of faith. It is communicated when and as God chooses, and is received passively, not in the intellect but in the will. To grasp the hidden sense of a prophecy, however imperfectly, 'se ha de renunciar la letra en este caso del sentido y quedarse a oscuras en fe, que es el espíritu'.[22] And the director of someone who has been granted visions and locutions is advised:

> impóngale en que se sepa estar en libertad y tiniebla de fe, en que se recibe la libertad de espíritu y abundancia y, por consiguiente, la sabiduría y inteligencia propia de los dichos de Dios.[23]

For St John the spiritual sense of Scripture can be apprehended only by a person who is inspired by the Spirit, a person who is open to receiving in contemplation the knowledge that comes through love.

### The Old Testament

St John's experience of *lectio divina* also helps to explain the importance he attached to the Old Testament. In the prose works, almost two thirds of the Scriptural quotations are

### St John and the Traditions of Monastic Exegesis

drawn from it, and when he tries to describe mystical experience, such as the Dark Night or union with God, it is in Old Testament writers that he normally finds illustrations.[24] This has puzzled some modern readers who have expected him to refer more often to the Gospels or the Epistles of St Paul, and various explanations have been suggested, including the possibility that in this matter he was influenced by his Jewish roots. One French writer has affirmed: 'he knows he is a Christian, but he still feels profoundly pre-Christian'.[25]

In monastic exegesis, however, the Old Testament regularly received more attention than the New.[26] The reason lay partly in the fact that the monastic office (with which St John was familiar through the breviary) was composed largely of Old Testament readings, canticles and psalms. In such a context the meaning of the Old Testament was never just historical, the history of the Jewish people; it was always figurative too, the history of the Church, but at an earlier phase, caught up in the mystery of salvation.[27] The person practising *lectio*, moreover, was encouraged to read the psalms personally. John Cassian, for instance, wrote in his famous *Conference X*:

> Nourished by this food, which he continually eats, he penetrates so deeply into the thinking of the psalms that he sings them not as though they had been composed by the prophet but as if he himself had written them, as if this were his own private prayer uttered amid the deepest compunction of heart. Certainly he thinks of them as having been specially composed for him, and he recognises that what they express was made real not simply once upon a time in the person of the prophet, but that now, every day, they are being fulfilled in himself.

> Then indeed the Scriptures lie ever more clearly
> open to us. They are revealed, heart and sinew.
> Our experience not only brings us to know them
> but actually anticipates what they convey. The
> meaning of the words comes through to us not just
> by way of commentaries but by what we ourselves
> have gone through.[28]

When, therefore, St John saw his own experience recorded in
the Old Testament he was following in a long tradition.[29]

One of their experiences that medieval monastic writers
found recorded in the Old Testament was eschatological
desire: the longing for the full union with God that is possible
only after death.[30] St Bernard, following St Paul, expressed
it thus:

> now we see in a mirror dimly and not yet face to
> face. So it will be while we live among the nations;
> among the angels it will be otherwise. For then we
> shall enjoy the very same happiness as they; even
> we shall see him as he is, in the form of God, no
> longer in shadow.[31]

For them there was a parallel between their desire for Heaven
and the desire of the Old Testament prophets for the coming
of the Messiah. To quote Bernard again:

> Just as we say that our ancestors possessed only
> shadows and images, whereas the truth itself shines
> on us by the grace of Christ present in the flesh, so
> also no one will deny that in relation to the world
> to come, we still live in the shadow of the truth .[32]

### St John and the Traditions of Monastic Exegesis

Seen in this way, Old Testament expressions of longing for salvation referred not only to the coming of Christ but to life in Heaven: their meaning was anagogical.

Eschatological desire is a recurrent theme in the writings of St John. In the *Llama de amor viva*, for instance, he writes of the soul's desire: 'El cual, aunque acá más juntura tenga con Dios, nunca se hartará y quietará hasta que parezca su gloria'.[33] And in the *Cántico* he notes that when the soul attains union: 'vive . . . con alguna satisfacción, aunque no con hartura, pues que David con toda su perfección la esperaba en el cielo, diciendo: "Cuando pareciere tu gloria, me hartaré" (Ps. 16:15)'.[34] It is longing of this kind that constitutes the pain of the Dark Night, when the soul, drawn to God, finds that it cannot rest in anything except Him, yet cannot attain to full union either. To describe it, St John turns regularly to expressions of messianic desire in Job, David, Jeremiah.[35]

The Old Testament book to which he returns most often, the *Song of Songs*, was also the book most read and commented on in the medieval cloister.[36] For the medieval monks the *Song*'s image of lovers seeking each other but never finding rest was a vivid expression of the desire for heaven, ever growing but never fully satisfied. St Gregory, for instance, wrote:

> The Spouse hides himself when he is sought, that not being found he may be sought for with the more ardent affection, and she in seeking is withheld, that she cannot find him, in order that being rendered of larger capacity by the delay she undergoes, she may one day find a thousandfold what she sought.[37]

And St Bernard, in the same vein, affirmed:

> Is it strange that I should use the bride's voice to
> call him back when he goes away, if I am driven by
> a desire that, though not identical, in some way
> resembles hers? As long as I live I shall make my
> own the phrase with which she calls him back . . .
> and I shall repeat it as often as he goes away . . . I
> shall never cease to clamour with the ardent desire
> of my heart, begging him to return, to renew in me
> his saving joy, to give me himself.[38]

It is this tradition that St John takes up in the opening verse
of the *Cántico* which voices the girl's anguished cry: '¿Adónde
te escondiste,/Amado, y me dejaste con gemido?'. He writes:

> la ausencia de el Amado causa continuo gemir en
> el amante, porque, como fuera dél nada ama, en
> nada descansa ni recibe alivio. De donde en esto se
> conocerá el que de veras a Dios ama, si con
> ninguna cosa menos que El se contenta.[39]

### The Poems

In ways such as these *lectio divina* had a profound influence
on St John's approach to Scripture. It also left its mark on his
poems, especially those he composed in captivity. During
the months that he spent in prison his only reading matter,
apart from a *libro de devoción*, was the breviary.[40] In this
same period, according to early witnesses, he composed and
committed to memory the *romances*, the lyric 'Que bien sé yo

### St John and the Traditions of Monastic Exegesis

la fonte', and the first 31 stanzas of the *Cántico*.[41] Since *lectio* was at this time his only activity, it is not surprising that in these poems the influence of Scripture is particularly marked. In the monastic tradition, as Jean Leclercq has shown, one's memory was 'completely shaped by the Bible, entirely nourished on biblical words and on the images they evoked'. It was therefore natural to express oneself in a biblical vocabulary. This vocabulary, moreover, had a poetic character that made it a suitable means for religious expression:

> it was often more valuable for its power of evocation, than for its clarity or precision: it suggested more than it said. But for this very reason it was all the more suited to expressing spiritual experience.[42]

These words are true of St John's style also, particularly in the *Cántico*, where the influence of Scripture is apparent not only in the structure and syntax but in individual phrases, recurrent images and themes, and particular words. And this biblical material is edited with great freedom. It is altered, amplified and adapted to serve the poet's ends:

> Certainly his is a borrowed language, but he has made it his own, because he controls the images and redirects their tremendous power into the channels he has prepared for them.[43]

St John's method of reading the Bible also appears to have shaped his understanding of how his mystical poetry originated, and of how it should be interpreted. This may be inferred from the prologue to the *Cántico* in which there are some striking parallels between his remarks on the poem and

115

his views about Scripture. From the very beginning he makes it plain that the poem, which grew out of mystical experience, was inspired by the Holy Spirit. Its primary meaning is therefore to be found not in its literal but in its spiritual sense. This, however, cannot be apprehended by reason or expressed in words. The Spirit is a transcendent being whose words have an abundant significance that far exceeds their literal meaning, and to some extent ('en alguna manera') this feature also marks the utterances of those to whom He is united 'en inteligencia mística'. He goes on, in a well-known passage, to make an explicit connection between the style of his poem and that of certain biblical books:

> Las cuales semejanzas, no leídas con la sencillez del espíritu de amor e inteligencia que ellas llevan, antes parecen dislates que dichos puestos en razón, según es de ver en los divinos Cantares de Salomón y en otros libros de la Escritura divina, donde, no pudiendo el Espíritu Santo dar a entender la abundancia de su sentido por términos vulgares y usados, habla misterios en extrañas figuras y semejanzas.[11]

But if, on the literal level, the text is not intelligible, and if the mystical meaning cannot be grasped, how is the poem to be read and interpreted? St John insists that it must be read in the spirit in which it was composed, and to this end he offers a 'general' interpretation ('alguna luz general'), leaving the reader free to draw from the text whatever understanding the Spirit enables. Its meaning, like that of scriptural prophecy, is communicated in the darkness of faith. It is received in the will, not the intellect, and consists not of knowledge but of the wisdom that is attained through love:

> Aunque en alguna manera se declaran, no hay para qué atarse a la declaración, porque la sabiduría mística, la cual es por amor, de que las presentes *Canciones* tratan, no ha menester distintamente entenderse para hacer efecto de amor y afición en el alma, porque es a modo de la fe, en la cual amamos a Dios sin entenderle.[45]

Only a contemplative, he implies, can read the poem properly, a contemplative who is familiar with the conventions of *lectio divina*.

## The Commentaries

In the prose works, as in the poems, the presence of Scripture is pervasive, not only in the many biblical quotations they contain but also in St John's method of interpreting his lyrics, which is often said to resemble medieval commentaries on the Bible. In the Middle Ages two kinds of Scriptural exegesis coexisted, interrelated but distinct.[46] One was elaborated in the scholastic schools, the other in the cloister. Both took as their starting point a close reading of the Vulgate text, but in other respects they differed. The scholastic commentaries, which developed out of *quaestio* and *disputatio*, tended to be impersonal in tone. They were designed to instruct the reader's understanding by defining and resolving, with academic detachment, the problems of interpretation to which the text gave rise, and by elucidating the Christian doctrine it contained. The monastic commentaries, which grew out of *meditatio* and *contemplatio*, were distinct. They were more personal in tone and more literary in style, and they were directed, not to the Church in general, but to particular individuals and communities who shared, with the authors, a contemplative calling. Unlike scholastic commentaries, they did not aim necessarily to be exhaustive or complete: in the case of *The Song of Songs*, for instance, it was not unusual for them to deal with only a small number of verses.[47] Yet this did not matter, for their main purpose was not to instruct the intellect but to nourish the reader's inner life, and in doing so to draw him or her beyond knowledge towards wisdom.

In all these respects it is with the monastic tradition that St John's prose works have most in common. They were written at the request of people he knew, often as friends, and they were directed to contemplatives who shared his own calling. In the prologue to the *Subida del Monte Carmelo* he affirmed:

> Ni aun mi principal intento es hablar con todos, sino con algunas personas de nuestra sagrada Religión de los primitivos del Monte Carmelo, así frailes como monjas, por habérmelo ellos pedido, a quien Dios hace merced de meter en la senda deste Monte . . . [48]

As those who witnessed their composition recorded, they grew directly out of his own experience of prayer and *lectio*. According to fray Juan Evangelista, he did not consult many books when writing them, but drew instead on his own mystical knowledge. The only works in his cell, apart from a *Flos sanctorum*, were a bible and the breviary.[49] The process of writing was a contemplative act, rather than a scholarly or academic exercise: he wrote his commentary on the *Cántico* not seated or standing but on his knees.[50] Furthermore, the exegesis of the poems that the prose works contain is (as St John acknowledged) incomplete: the *Subida del Monte Carmelo* and the *Noche oscura* expound only part of the lyric on which they are based, and the prologues to the *Cántico espiritual* and the *Llama de amor viva* make clear that as commentaries they are inadequate, merely partial. The reader, however, is asked not to be discouraged by this, for their main purpose is to impart not knowledge but wisdom. Ana de Jesús was an unlettered nun, but St John was able to reassure her that ignorance of scholastic theology was no impediment to reading his text in the way he desired:

> aunque a V.R. le falte el ejercicio de teología escolástica con que se entienden las verdades divinas, no le falta el de la mística, que se sabe por amor en que, no solamente se saben, mas juntamente se gustan.[51]

----------------

In their different ways, the poems and the prose works both grew out of *lectio divina*, and both were intended, in turn, to serve as *lectio* for others. They assume, in fact, a context of contemplative prayer. This raises the question: is it possible, outside a contemplative context, to read them properly? St John, surely, would have answered: no. Such an answer does not render other approaches invalid, but it does, perhaps, confirm a certain truth about the nature of religious language which was recognised and noted by Wittgenstein:

> In religion every level of devoutness must have its appropriate form of expression which has no sense at a lower level. [A] doctrine, which means

something at a higher level, is null and void for
someone who is still at the lower level; he *can* only
understand it *wrongly* . . . [52]

This no doubt is why the finest interpreters of St John's
thought, such as Elisabeth of the Trinity, have been
contemplatives themselves, able to draw understanding from
experience as well as scholarship, from what they have tasted
as well as from what they have learned.

St John and the Traditions of Monastic Exegesis

# NOTES

1.  The classic study is Jean Vilnet, *Bible et mystique chez saint Jean de la Croix* (Paris, 1949).

2.  Colin P. Thompson, *The Poet and the Mystic. A Study of the Cántico Espiritual of San Juan de la Cruz* (Oxford, 1977), p. 16: 'it is this movement away from the obvious meaning into subjective and frequently eccentric interpretations that most disconcerts the modern reader'.

3.  Henri de Lubac, S.J., *Exégèse médiévale. Les quatre sens de l'Ecriture*, 4 vols (Paris, 1959-64).

4.  Fray Juan Evangelista testified that, 'era hombre que sabía muy bien teología escolástica y, con ventaja, (teología) positiva' (quoted in Crisógono de Jesús, *Vida de San Juan de la Cruz*, ed. Matías del Niño Jesús, 11th edn (Madrid, 1982), p. 299). See Manuel Diego Sánchez, 'La herencia patrística de San Juan de la Cruz', in *Experiencia y pensamiento en San Juan de la Cruz*, ed. Federico Ruiz (Madrid, 1990), pp. 83-111.

5.  On Spanish exegesis of the period, see Melquíades Andrés and others, *Historia de la teología española*, vol. I (Madrid, 1983), pp. 634-647.

6   .See Jesús Castellano Cervera, 'La experiencia del misterio litúrgico en San Juan de la Cruz', in *Experiencia y pensamiento en San Juan de la Cruz*, pp. 113-154.

7.  *Dichos de luz y amor*, 78: 'If you desire to find the peace and consolation of your soul and to really serve God, do not rest content with what you have renounced . . . but leave all those other things that you have yet to relinquish, and draw apart to one thing that brings all with it, namely holy solitude, accompanied by prayer and by reading that is holy and divine, and there persevere in forgetfulness of everything . . .'. All references are to *Vida y obras de San Juan de la Cruz*, ed. Crisógono de Jesús, Matías del Niño Jesús and Lucinio Ruano, 7th edn (Madrid, 1973).

8. *Dichos de luz y amor*, 157: 'Seek in reading and you will find in meditation; knock in prayer and it will be opened to you in contemplation'.

9. *PL* 40, 998: 'Quaerite legendo, et invenietis meditando; pulsate orando et aperietur vobis contemplando' (quoted in San Juan de la Cruz, *Obras completas*, ed José Vicente Rodríguez and Federico Ruiz Salvador, 2nd edn (Madrid, 1980), p. 128, n. 19). On Guigo II see Simon Tugwell, O.P., *Ways of Imperfection. An Exploration of Christian Spirituality* (London, 1984), pp. 93-102.

10. Jean Leclercq, O.S.B., *Initiation aux auteurs monastiques du moyen âge: l' amour des lettres et le désir de Dieu*, 2nd edn (Paris, 1963), p. 73.

11. Guiges du Pont, *De Contemplatione*, ed. Dom P. Dupont, O.S.B., *Analecta Cartusiana* 72 (1985), p. 232.

12. Quoted in Thompson, p. 3: 'He was very fond of reading Holy Scripture, and so it was that I never saw him read any book other than the Bible (almost all of which he knew by heart), and a volume of St Augustine *contra haereses*, and the *Flos sanctorum*; and whenever he preached, which was seldom, or gave homilies, as he normally did, the Bible was the only book he read'.

13. Quoted in Crisógono de Jesús, p. 301, n. 46: 'I am sure he knew the whole Bible, in view of how he commented on various passages from it during homilies he delivered in chapter and in the refectory, without preparing for this by study, but following where he was led by the Spirit'.

14. Federico Ruiz Salvador, O.C.D., *Introducción a San Juan de la Cruz. El escritor, los escritos, el sistema* (Madrid, 1968), p. 82.

15. Quoted in Ruiz Salvador, p. 83: 'Today I found Fr Juan de la Cruz leaning against these walls . . . with a bible in his hand, absorbed, as usual, in contemplation'.

St John and the Traditions of Monastic Exegesis

16. Quoted in de Lubac, vol. 4, pp. 498-9.

17. Ruiz Salvador, p. 85: 'No posee un sistema o método propio de exégesis. Hay asomas o esbozos de teoría, pero queda restringida al tema que por el momento le ocupa'.

18. *Subida* 2. 19, 5: 'the principal purpose of God in those things is to utter and impart the spirit enclosed there'.

19. *Subida* 2. 19, 10: 'The utterances and revelations of God . . . are a spiritual abyss or depth, and trying to limit them to those aspects that we understand and that our sense can apprehend is merely trying to seize hold of the air, and grasping some speck in it that our hand encounters; and the air slips away and nothing remains'.

20. *Subida* 2. 19, 5: '. . . the spirit that is enclosed there . . . is difficult to understand, and . . . it is much more abundant than the letter and most extraordinary and beyond its limits'.

21. *Cántico B*. Prólogo, 2: 'the holy doctors, although they say a good deal, and however much more they might say, can never expound it completely in words, just as words were not able to express it, thus the part of it that is expounded is normally the least that it contains'.

22. *Subida* 2. 19, 5: 'one must, in this case, renounce the literal meaning and remain in darkness in faith, which is the spirit'.

23. *Subida* 2. 19, 11: 'insist that he learn to dwell in freedom and darkness of faith, where one receives the freedom of spirit and abundance, and thus the wisdom and understanding that accords with the utterances of God'.

24. Ruiz Salvador, p. 81.

25. Jean Baruzi, quoted in de Lubac, vol. 4, p. 502.

26. Leclercq, pp. 79-80.

27. Leclercq, p. 80: 'l'histoire que retrace l'Ancien Testament n'est pas celle d'Israël, c'est déjà celle de l'Eglise dont Israël est un commencement'.

28. John Cassian, *Conferences*, translated by Colm Luibheid and introduced by Owen Chadwick (New York, 1985), p. 137.

29. See de Lubac, vol. 4, p. 501.

30. Leclercq. p. 82.

31. *Sermones super Cantica canticorum*, 31:8. The text has been edited by Jean Leclercq and others in *Sancti Bernardi Opera Omnia* (Rome, 1957-1977); the most recent Engish version is Bernard of Clairvaux, *On the Song of Songs*, translated by Kilian Walsh (Kalamazoo, 1976 onwards).

32. *Sermones super Cantica canticorum*, 31:8.

33. *Llama B*. I, 27: 'which, however united with God it may be in this life, will never find fulfilment and rest until his glory appears'.

34. *Cántico B*. I, 14: 'she lives . . . with some contentment, but not fulfilled, for David, with all his perfection, hoped for this in heaven, saying: "when your glory appears, I shall be filled" (*Ps.* 16, 15).' On the theme of eschatological desire in St John's thought see José Damián Gaitán, 'San Juan de la Cruz: un canto en tierra extraña. Exégesis y actualidad de un romance', *Revista de Espiritualidad* 149 (1978), 601-21.

35. Ruiz Salvador, p. 86.

36. Leclercq, p. 83.

## St John and the Traditions of Monastic Exegesis

37. *Moralia* 5:6 (*PL* 75, 783), quoted in Leclercq, p. 85; translated into English as St Gregory the Great, *Morals on the Book of Job*, vol. I (London, 1844), p. 246.

38. *Sermones super Cantica canticorum*, 74:7.

39. *Cántico B*. I, 14: 'the absence of the Beloved causes in the lover a continuous lament, for since she loves nothing apart from him, she can rest and find relief in nothing. The sign, therefore, that someone loves God truly, is their inability to find contentment in anything less than him'.

40. San Juan de la Cruz, *Cántico espiritual*, ed. Eulogio Pacho (Madrid, 1981), p. 18.

41. Eulogio Pacho, *Iniciación a San Juan de la Cruz. Pautas para la lectura y estudio de sus obras* (Burgos, 1982), p. 37.

42. Leclercq, p. 75.

43. Thompson, p. 69.

44. *Cántico B*. Prólogo, 1: 'These images, if not read with the simplicity of the spirit of love and understanding that they carry, appear to be nonsense rather than rational statements, as may be seen in the divine songs of Solomon and in other books of Sacred Scripture, where the Holy Spirit, being unable to convey his abundant meaning in common and popular terms, utters mysteries in strange figures and images'.

45. *Cántico B*., Prólogo, 2: 'Although they are, in some fashion, explained, there is no need to keep to the explanation offered, because mystical wisdom, which comes through love, and which these *Songs* treat, does not have to be understood clearly in order to arouse love and affection in the soul, for it operates like faith, in which we love God without understanding him'.

46. Leclercq. pp. 9-14, 70-72, 83-84.

47. Leclercq, p. 84.

48. *Subida*. Prólogo, 9: 'it is not even my main intention to speak to everyone, but to some people who belong to our sacred Order of Mount Carmel, both friars and nuns, since they have asked me to do so, - people whom God has favoured by putting them on the path up this Mountain'.

49. Crisógono de Jesús, p. 299.

50. Crisógono de Jesús, p. 295, n. 16.

51. *Cántico B*. Prólogo, 3: 'Even if Your Reverence lacks the practice of scholastic theology by which divine truths are understood, you do not lack the practice of mystical theology, which one knows through love, in which they are not only known but also tasted'.

52. Ludwig Wittgenstein, *Culture and Value*, edited by G. H. von Wright in collaboration with Heikki Nyman, translated by Peter Winch (Oxford, 1980), p.32.

# XIV

## THE LITERARY AND DEVOTIONAL CONTEXT OF THE *PASTORCICO*

"A poem is most beautiful and most meaningful to us when it is read in terms of the tradition which gave it birth" (Rosemund Tuve).[1]

In recent years a number of scholars in English and French studies have shown that to understand and appreciate fully the religious lyric of the Counter Reformation, one must be familiar with its scriptural, liturgical and devotional context. Yet despite the pioneer articles of the late Edward Wilson[2] there is no general study of the influence of devotional literature on Golden Age poetry; and there is still truth in the remark made in 1946 by María Rosa Lida: "La huella de la Biblia en la lengua y en la literatura española es campo no explorado".[3] This is surprising when one considers that the works of spirituality and exegesis which had most influence in late sixteenth-century England and Catholic Europe were written by Spaniards.[4]

One Spanish lyric which appears to be informed by traditions that have not been explored is the *Pastorcico*, a short poem by St John of the Cross:

> Un pastorcico solo está penado,
> ajeno de placer y de contento,
> y en su pastora puesto el pensamiento,
> y el pecho del amor muy lastimado.
>   No llora por haberle amor llagado,
> que no le pena verse así afligido,
> aunque en el corazón está herido;
> mas llora por pensar que está olvidado.
>   Que sólo de pensar que está olvidado
> de su bella pastora, con gran pena,
> se deja maltratar en tierra ajena,
> el pecho del amor muy lastimado.
>   Y dice el pastorcico: ¡Ay desdichado
> de aquel que de mi amor ha hecho ausencia,
> y no quiere gozar la mi presencia,
> y el pecho por su amor muy lastimado!
>   Y a cabo de un gran rato se ha encumbrado
> sobre un árbol, do abrió sus brazos bellos,
> y muerto se ha quedado, asido de ellos,
> el pecho del amor muy lastimado.[5]

In 1946 Dámaso Alonso drew attention to the need for a study of its devotional context, but no such study has appeared.[6] One reason may be the discovery by José Manuel Blecua in 1949 of a secular love song from which St John's poem seems to have derived:

> Un pastorcillo solo está penado,
> ajeno de placer y de contento,
> y en su pastora firme el pensamiento,
> y el pecho del amor muy lastimado.

> No llora por pensar que está olvidado,
> que ningún miedo tiene del olvido,
> mas porque el corazón tiene rendido,
> y el pecho del amor muy lastimado.
>  Mas dice el pastorcico:˙ ¡Desdichado!
> ¿qué haré cuando venga el mal de ausencia,
> pues tengo el corazón en la presencia
> y el pecho del amor muy lastimado?
>  Imagínase ya estar apartado
> de su bella pastora en tierra ajena,
> y quédase tendido en el arena,
> y el pecho del amor muy lastimado.[7]

After the publication of these lines Dámaso Alonso wrote: "San Juan de la Cruz ha tomado un poema eglógico profano y lo ha reproducido con ligeras variantes",[8] and some critics have concluded that apart from the final verse the substance of St John's poem was already present in the source. However, as Margaret Wilson has pointed out, "this is to ignore the refining and refashioning which has clearly taken place".[9] St John made no important alteration in the first verse, which sets the mood of melancholy in both poems, but in the remaining verses he made several small changes which affect the theme. First he altered the cause of the shepherd's sorrow. In the source the shepherd is distressed because he is in love and cannot bear to leave his beloved, and when he speaks it is to lament his misfortune. In St John's poem the shepherd is less self-centred. He is sorrowful because his love has been rejected, and attention is drawn to this fact by the absence of the refrain in the second verse and by the echo of its last line at the beginning of the third. However, unlike a conventional lover, St John's shepherd is not preoccupied with his misery but with the needs of his shepherdess, and when he speaks it is her misfortune that he laments, not his own. Second, St John elaborated the mysterious effects of the melancholy portrayed. The last verse of the source appears to inform two verses of St John: in verse three the exile that the original shepherd feared has actually occurred, and in verse five the sand in which he stretched has become a tree. The first shepherd is led by melancholy into resignation and passivity, a loosening of his hold on life; St John's shepherd is led further, into pain and death.

For these amendments there were precedents in secular love poetry. The theme of grief caused by unrequited love had received classic statement in the poems of Garcilaso, and the notion that a lover's melancholy could cause his death was commonplace in the courtly love tradition. Reasons for them may be found, too, in the allegory. St John's poem focuses on the sadness of Jesus when rejected by the sinful soul, and the theme of His grief, the *tristitia Christi*, was long established in exegesis and popular devotion. It derived from Patristic commentaries on the words of Jesus in Gethsemane, "My soul is sorrowful unto death" (Mtt.26:38). The reasons for His sadness were much debated. According to St Jerome it was not caused primarily by fear of dying but by compassion for all who would be responsible for His passing.[10] This view was followed by St Thomas in the *Summa Theologica*, and it was popularised in the *Legenda aurea*.[11] In the sixteenth century it was made controversial by an exchange of letters between Erasmus, who disagreed with Jerome, and John Colet, who defended him. Their discussion, which Erasmus wrote up as a treatise, was published with the first edition of the *Enchiridion* in 1503, and it was often reprinted.[12]

St John's poem, however, does more than focus on Christ's sadness: it implies that it exceeded his physical pain and caused his death. In verse three the shepherd's grief is so profound that he submits to violence with seeming indifference; and the fact that in real life his position in the tree at the end would be impossible to sustain indicates that the cause of his demise is not external but spiritual. This remarkable emphasis on inner anguish, and the absence of any allusion to the instruments of the Passion, has prompted Dámaso Alonso and others to draw parallels with the spirituality of Erasmus, who recoiled from the graphic portrayal of Christ's physical agony which was common in the late fifteenth century, preferring instead forms of mental prayer which centred on the hidden significance of His death.[13] Erasmus himself, however, did not write many meditations on the Passion, and St John's poem has more in common with the spirituality of two men whom Bataillon considered heirs of Erasmus in Spain, Juan de Ávila and Diego de Estella. In their meditations on the "beneficio de Cristo" both draw attention repeatedly to the interior anguish of Jesus. In his *Meditaciones del amor de Dios*, published in 1576, Estella writes:

> Juntas todas las tristezas que en el mundo han tenido todos los hombres, no llegan a la tristeza que tuvo Cristo, nuestro Señor, en su pasión. Veía la ingratitud de los hombres, conocía los pocos que de su pasión se habían de aprovechar.[14]

Both affirm that this anguish was greater than his physical pain and actually caused his death. In the second edition of the *Audi filia* in 1574, the reader is urged to consider Christ's love:

> del cual amor, como de fuente, nació lo mucho que exteriormente padeció; y . . . fue mucho más lo que padeció en lo interior.[15]

And both use the image of the heart of Jesus wounded by love, an image implied in line seven of St John's lyric. According to Estella the sadness of Jesus "afligía más su Corazón que los clavos y azotes",[16] and Ávila writes:

> miralde su sacratísimo corazón, tan lleno de amor para con todos, que excedía tanto a lo que de fuera padecía, aunque era inefable, cuanto excede el cielo a la tierra.[17]

St John's poem brings together two traditions, one of them secular, the other divine, in which unrequited love is a cause of sadness and death. Long before it was written, however, these traditions had met and intertwined. It was common in *cancionero* poetry to apply to the lover's distress texts drawn from the liturgy of Holy Week, including lines associated specifically with Jesus the Man of Sorrows.[18] As Patrick Gallagher has shown, this custom was popularised in Spain during the early sixteenth century by the verse of Garci Sánchez de Badajoz, and it left its mark on the first Eclogue of Garcilaso.[19] In the *Pastorcico* a theme from secular love poetry which already had sacred origins and associations is, once again, "vuelto a lo divino".

## II

These reflections inevitably raise the question of St John's debt to Sebastián de Córdoba. Dámaso Alonso has repeatedly defended the view that the last verse owes its central image to Córdoba's divinisation of Garcilaso's Second Eclogue in which Christ is glimpsed as a shepherd, wounded and in a tree.[20] On close examination, however, the differences between the two texts are more striking than the similarities. Córdoba's shepherd is a passive victim in a static scene bereft of the utterance and the drama in St John. He is covered in blood and bears a crown of thorns: no mention is made of interior distress.[21] Alonso concedes some of these differences but argues that in the poetic tradition immediately before St John it is only Córdoba who brings together and divinises the pastoral motifs of the shepherd and the tree. Yet although this may be so it does not follow that Córdoba was St John's source for, as Arthur Terry has pointed out,[22] the two images are brought together in Scripture, in the First Epistle of Peter:

> Christ also suffered for us . . . Who his own self bore our sins in his body upon the tree . . . For you were as sheep going astray: but you are now converted to the shepherd and bishop of your souls (I Pet.2:21,24,25).

The last verse, moreover, contains several images which do not occur in Córdoba but which may be found in popular iconography and in Scripture, notably the Song of Songs. One is the act of climbing by which the shepherd enters the tree. It was conventional to apply to Christ crucified the words of the bridegroom in Chapter 7 of the Song: "I will go up into the palm tree, and will take hold of the fruit thereof" (Cant.7:8). The image of Christ ascending his cross was interpreted by the Fathers to mean that He willingly chose to die for love of man.[23] It is used in this sense by Luis de la Palma in his popular *Historia de la Sagrada Pasión*:

> Subía el Señor vuelto el rostro hacia la cruz, mirándola de cerca con tanto amor y voluntad, con cuanto la había deseado tantos años.[24]

Secondly, there is the image of the shepherd opening his arms, an action which, in the poem, transforms the tree into a cross. The posture of Jesus crucified was traditionally interpreted as a gesture of longing and supplication, partly because of its resemblance to the classical Christian stance for prayer. It was associated in particular with the exegesis of two texts: the plea of the Bride in the Song, "Draw me: we will run after thee" (Cant.1:3), and the words of Jesus, interpreted as the Bridegroom's answer, "I, if I be lifted up from the earth, will draw all things to myself" (John 12:32).[25] In the *Audi, filia* Juan de Ávila affirms:

> tendió sus brazos para ser crucificado, en señal que tenía su corazón abierto con amor,[26]

and Diego de Estella writes:

> extendiste tus brazos en la cruz deseando abrazar y recibir entre ellos a todos los que huyen a ti.[27]

The image of the outstretched arms reinforces the theme that Christ died freely, and of love. It also combines with that of the tree to suggest subtly the redemptive effect of His passing: for the allegorical meaning of the poem depends not only on the description of the cross as a tree, which occurs in Scripture, but on the tradition which identified the tree in Eden by which man fell with the tree on Calvary by which he was redeemed. This tradition, which runs through the liturgy of Holy Week, supplied a dominant motif of medieval iconography.[28] One of the key texts invoked to expound it occurs in the Song:

> Under the apple tree I raised thee up: there thy mother was corrupted: there she was defloured that bore thee (Cant.8:5).

As Dámaso Alonso has acknowledged, "sin . . . la interpretación patrística de los 'dos árboles' . . . no existiría el poema".[29]

Lastly, there is the image of silence. In St John's poem the shepherd's words are followed by a long pause which does not occur in the source, after which he ascends the tree and dies without a sound. The reason for this image may lie in devotional explanations of the silence of Jesus. Luis de la Palma ascribes His refusal to answer His accusers to humility and patience,[30] and Juan de Ávila praises the interior silence of Christ which had a redemptive purpose:

> !Oh, bendito sea tu callar, Señor, que de dentro y de fuera en el día de tu pasión callaste: de fuera, no maldiciendo ni respondiendo; y en lo de dentro, no contradiciendo, mas aceptando con mucha paciencia los golpes y voces, y penas de tu pasión, pues tanto hablaste en las orejas de Dios, que antes que hablemos seamos oídos![31]

Pertinent too, perhaps, is the notion that His silence was a sign of His sadness which informs two verses of George Herbert's *The Sacrifice*, a poem that offers other parallels with St John's lyric:

> O all ye who passe by, behold and see;
> Man stole the fruit, but I must climbe the tree;
> The tree of life to all, but onely me:
>     Was ever grief like mine?
>
> Lo, here I hang, charg'd with a world of sinne,
> The greater world o' th' two; for that came in
> By words, but this by sorrow I must win:
>     Was ever grief like mine?[32]

### III

Dámaso Alonso has implied that without the last verse the meaning of the *Pastorcico* would be secular,[33] and it is certainly true that because the description of the shepherd's death lacks verisimilitude the reader is impelled to interpret it allegorically. There are, however, several lines earlier in the poem that do not make literal sense. In verse three, for instance, it is implied that the shepherd has left the shepherdess, although there is no literal reason for his being in a foreign land, nor for the violence he suffers there; but in verse four he laments that she has left *him*. Moreover, in lines thirteen and fourteen he refers to her in masculine terms as "desdichado" and "aquel". In English translations it is common to apply these lines to Satan. Roy Campbell has:

> "Alas! Alas! for him," the Shepherd cries,
> "Who tries from me my dearest love to part . . . "[34]

and Lynda Nicholson gives:

> "Ah woe to the one," the young shepherd said,
> "Who has stolen my dearest away . . . "[35]

Both agree that the next two lines,

> y no quiere gozar la mi presencia,
> y el pecho por su amor muy lastimado!

must refer to the shepherdess; and so, unlike St John, they are obliged to change the subject at the beginning of line fifteen. In other Golden Age texts the normal meaning of "hacer ausencia de" is not "to take away" but "to go away". This is its sense in the third act of *El condenado por desconfiado* when Enrico says to the voice that had told him to say in jail:

> ¿No dijiste que a mi vida
> la importaba de la cárcel
> no hacer ausencia?[36]

St John's shepherd is grieving because his beloved has deserted him; and the change in gender can be explained only in allegorical terms. Some critics have described the last verse as "unexpected",[37] but in fact the ending of the poem is carefully prepared from verse three onward.[38]

As in most of St John's poems the two levels of meaning cannot be detached. A recent writer considers that in this respect the lyric is flawed. According to Margaret Wilson the allegory is "not technically perfect" because the poem "only really makes sense if the underlying meaning is invoked" and "allegory should succeed at both levels".[39] However, as L. J. Woodward has pointed out, one cannot read the *Cántico espiritual* as a poem of human love without being faced in almost every verse with nonsense; and St John warns that unless his verses are read in a certain way "antes parecen dislates que dichos puestos en razón".[40] In the *Pastorcico* the occasional dislocation of the literal sense makes the poem more, not less, compelling. It obliges the reader to seek a deeper, hidden significance, and he finds it in mysterious images which communicate with him long before the poem has been analysed. These images belong to a common and widespread heritage of symbols quite familiar to St John and his contemporaries.[41] As Bataillon noted in another context, "se mueve a sus anchas en el simbolismo que le suministra la tradición".[42]

369

## NOTES

[1] Rosemund Tuve, *A Reading of George Herbert* (London, 1952), p.22.

[2] E. M. Wilson, "Spanish and English religious poetry of the seventeenth century", *JEH* IX (1958), 38-53; "A key to Calderón's *Psalle et Sile*", in *Hispanic Studies in honour of I. González Llubera* (Oxford, 1959), pp.1-12; E. Muller-Bochat, "Técnicas literarias y métodos de meditación en la poesía sagrada del siglo de oro", in *Actas del Tercer Congreso Internacional de Hispanistas* (Mexico City, 1970), pp.611-617.

[3] María Rosa Lida, "La poesía de San Juan de la Cruz", *RFH* V (1943), 388.

[4] On the influence of Spanish spirituality in England and France, see L. L. Martz, *The Poetry of Meditation* (Yale, 1954), T. C. Cave, *Devotional Poetry in France c. 1570-1613* (Cambridge, 1969); on Spanish exegesis, see *The Cambridge History of the Bible. The West from the Reformation to the Present Day*, edited by S. L. Greenslade (Cambridge, 1963), pp.213-215.

[5] The poem is included in *An Anthology of Spanish Poetry 1500-1700: Part 1* edited by Arthur Terry (Oxford, 1965), p.145.

[6] D. Alonso, *La poesía de San Juan de la Cruz*, second edition (Madrid, 1946); see his comments in the third edition (Madrid, 1958), pp.193-194.

[7] José M. Blecua, "Los antecedentes del poema del *Pastorcico* de San Juan de la Cruz", *RFE* XXXIII (1949), 378-380; reprinted in José M. Blecua, *Sobre poesía de la Edad de Oro* (Madrid, 1970), pp.96-99.

[8] D. Alonso, *Poesía española*, fourth edition (Madrid, 1962), p.262.

[9] Margaret Wilson, *San Juan de la Cruz: Poems* (London, 1975), p.31; see too Joaquín Gimeno Casalduero, "El pastorcico de San Juan y el pastorcillo de las *redondillas*", *HR* XXVII (1979), 77-85.

[10] PL 26, col.197.

[11] *Summa Theologica*. 3 q.46 a.6; The *Legenda Aurea* dwells at length on the sorrow of Jesus; and it gives as one of its causes the fact that "He was despised and forsaken of His friends"; *The Golden Legend* translated by William Caxton, vol.I (London, 1900), pp.66-73, especially p.67.

[12] The *Disputatiuncula de tedio, pavore, tristitia Iesu* was first published in the *Lucubratiunculae* (Antwerp, 1503), which also included the *Enchiridion*. It was reprinted in *Opera Omnia* (Leyden, 1703-1706, vol.V, cols.1265-1294. The letters of Erasmus that form the substance of the treatise may be seen in *The Correspondence of Erasmus: 1484 to 1500*, translated by R. A. B. Mynors and D. F. S. Thomson (Toronto, 1974), pp.202-219. The *De Tristitia Christi* of Thomas More was a later contribution to this debate: see Dermot Fenlon, *JTS* XXX (1979), p.370.

[13] D. Alonso, *La poesía de San Juan*, third edition, p.193; Lida, art.cit, p.385; on Erasmus and devotion to the Passion, see M. Bataillon, *Erasmo y España* (Mexico City, 1966), p.589, and T. O'Reilly, "Saint Ignatius Loyola and Spanish Erasmianism", *AHSI* XLIII (1974), pp.301-321.

[14] Diego de Estella, *Meditaciones del amor de Dios*, edited by A. García Ruiz (Madrid, 1965), p.182.

[15] *Obras completas del Santo Maestro Juan de Ávila*, edited by Luis Sala Balust and Francisco Martín Hernández, vol.I (Madrid, 1970), p.759.

[16] Estella, pp.182-183.

[17] Ávila, p.744; on the image of the wound of love in secular love poetry and in devotional literature see Wolfgang Riehle, *The Middle English Mystics* (London, 1981), pp.44-45, and Louis Gougaud, *Devotional and Ascetic Practices in the Middle Ages* (London, 1927), pp.75-130.

[18] "O all ye that pass by the way attend and see if there be any sorrow like to my sorrow" (Lam.1:12).

[19] P. Gallagher, "Garcilaso's First Eclogue and the Lamentations of Love", *FMLS* IX (1973), pp.192-199. The two traditions were combined also in exegesis: see the commentary on Mtt.26:38 by Juan Maldonado S.J., *Commentarii in quatuor evangelistas* (Mainz, 1602), vol.I, col.592.

[20] D. Alonso, *La poesía de San Juan*, pp.43-48 and 193-196; *Poesía española*, pp.245-247 and 263.

[21] These points are made tellingly by Lida, art.cit., pp.383-386. St John's lyric has much more in common with a poem by Hernando de Acuña (1518-1580), "Apenas el aurora había mostrado", in which a melancholy shepherd "a un árbol arrimado" complains that his beloved, by deserting him, has brought him close to death. It has been reprinted recently in *Antología de albas, alboradas y poemas afines*, edited by Dionisia Empaytaz (Madrid, 1976), p.31.

[22] Terry, p.168; the images occur together in Góngora's poem "Oveja perdida, ven" (1609): in this case Scripture is clearly a more likely inspiration than either Córdoba or St John! See D. Alonso, *Góngora y el "Polifemo"*, fifth edition (Madrid, 1967) vol.II, pp.110-111.

[23] F. P. Pickering, *Literature and Art in the Middle Ages* (London, 1970), pp.255 and 276.

[24] *Obras del Padre Luis de la Palma*, edited by Francisco X. Rodríguez Molero (Madrid, 1967), p.243.

[25] See Gougaud, pp.3-7, who quotes St Maximus of Turin, "Man has only to raise up his hands to make his body into the likeness of the cross; that is why we are taught to stretch out our hands in

prayer, for by such a position we show forth the Passion of the Lord"; also Pickering, pp.254-255, 263, 276, and Riehle, pp.39-40.

[26] Ávila, p.758.

[27] Estella, p.176. In the influential *Meditationes vitae Christi*, long attributed to St Bonaventure, Jesus is said to have ascended the Cross by a short ladder and to have turned, on reaching the top, to stretch out His hands in a gesture of love: "Cum ergo in superiori parte istius parvae scalae pervenit ad crucem, renes vertit, *et illa regalia aperit brachia, et extendens manus pulcherrimas*, in excelsum eas porrigit suis crucifixoribus." The parallel with St John's words: "abrió sus brazos bellos" is remarkable (the italics are mine). *Bonaventurae Opera Omnia* vol.XII (Paris, 1868), p.606. On the influence of the *Meditationes* in the early Golden Age, see K. Whinnom, "The supposed sources of inspiration of Spanish fifteenth century narrative religious verse", *Symposium* XVII (1963), 268-291.

[28] See Eleanor S. Greenhill, "The Child in the Tree, a study of the cosmological tree in Christian tradition", *Traditio* X (1954), pp.327-371; Gerhart B. Ladner, "Medieval and Modern understanding of symbolism: a comparison", *Speculum* LIV (1979), 223-256, especially 235-238 and the works cited.

[29] D. Alonso, *La poesía de San Juan*, p.193.

[30] Luis de la Palma, pp.161, 189-190.

[31] Ávila, p.779.

[32] George Herbert, *The English Poems*, edited by C. A. Patrides (London, 1974), p.54. The purpose of the silence of Jesus is pointed out in the *Legenda Aurea*: "... Eve sinned by speaking, and Jesus would make satisfaction by being still and not speaking": *Golden Legend*, p.73.

[33] "El poema no descubriría su nueva intención a lo divino, a no ser por una estrofa que el Santo le añade", *Poesía española*, p.262.

[34] *St John of the Cross: Poems: with a translation by Roy Campbell* (London, 1960), p.59.

[35] Gerald Brenan, *St John of the Cross: His Life and Poetry* (Cambridge, 1973), p.169; different translations, closer to the original, are offered in Willis Barnstone, *The Poems of St John of the Cross* (New York, 1972), p.71, and in *The Collected Works of St John of the Cross* translated by Kieran Kavanaugh O.C.D. and Otilo Rodríguez O.C.D. (Washington, 1973), p.722-723.

[36] *El condenado por desconfiado: a Play Attributed to Tirso de Molina*, edited by Daniel Rogers (Oxford, 1974), p.130.

[37] M. Wilson, p.32.

[38] Lida, art.cit., p.388.

[39] M. Wilson, pp.32-33.

[40] L. J. Woodward in *BHS* XXXIX (1962), p.103; Crisógono de Jesus, Matías del Nino, Lucinio Ruano, *Vida y obras de San Juan de la Cruz*, 7th edition (Madrid, 1973), p.703. I am grateful to Professor Woodward for the comment that in the last line of verse 4 the words "por su amor" balance, rhythmically, the "de mi amor" of two lines earlier, and the contrast is echoed by the play on "ausencia" and "presencia". He notes that "San Juan often builds up his strophes in this way to force the mind to seek resolution."

[41] Several of them occur in an anonymous fifteenth-century English poem mentioned by Dámaso Alonso, op.cit., pp.193-194. This poem, best known by its refrain "Quia amore langueo", may be seen in the *New Oxford Book of English Verse 1250-1950*, edited by Helen Gardner (Oxford, 1972), pp.9-12; see too, Rosemary Woolf, *The English Religious Lyric in the Middle Ages* (Oxford, 1968), pp.187-191; Douglas Gray, *Themes and Images in the Medieval Religious Lyric* (London, 1972), pp.143-145; J. I. Wimsatt, "The Canticle of Canticles, two Latin poems and 'In a valey of this restles mynde'", *Modern Philology* LXXV (1978), pp.327-345.

[42] M. Bataillon, "La tortolica de *Fonte-frida* y del *Cántico espiritual*" *NRFE* VII (1953), p.305: quoted in C. Thompson, *The Poet and the Mystic* (Oxford, 1977), p.79.

# The *Cántico Espiritual* of Saint John of the Cross and the Mystical Interpretation of the *Song of Songs*

For Elisabeth Stopp

The last twenty five years have seen the publication of several studies which have as their theme the influence exercised by the *Song of Songs* on the *Cántico espiritual* of St John of the Cross.[1] These have confirmed that the *Song* is the most important source of the poem, in which its presence may be discerned in the imagery and the diction, as well as in the syntax and the structure.[2] All of them, however, have limited their attention to what St John would have called the "literal" sense of the scriptural text. None has considered in detail the possible influence on the poem of the mystical interpretation of the *Song* which was developed by the Fathers of the Church and prolonged throughout the Middle Ages into the period of St John himself.[3] During the 1580s, when the *Cántico* was being completed, several Latin commentaries on the *Song* were published in Spain, but with one exception they have not been studied in connection with St John's text.[4]

For such reticence there are several reasons, two of which are especially worthy of note. First, in his prose commentaries on the *Cántico* St John often quotes passages from the *Song* and interprets them in a spiritual sense, but he does not normally support his exegesis by citing patristic or later authorities; and second, when scholars have compared his readings of the *Song* with those advanced by the most famous commentators (notably Origen, St Gregory, St Bernard, or St John's great contemporary, Luis de León) the differences have usually appeared to them more striking than the similarities.[5] This evidence has led, in turn, to a twofold conclusion: in seeing the *Song* as a mystical poem St John was faithful to the main lines of the exegetical tradition, but when commenting on specific images within it he normally derived his interpretation not from previous authorities but from his own interior experience and knowledge of souls. Such a conclusion, however, is not easy to sustain. The more familiar one becomes with the exegetical tradition, the deeper seems its influence on the *Cántico*, not only indirectly, on the prose commentaries, but directly too, on the process of poetic composition itself.[6]

During the Middle Ages the *Song of Songs* was the scriptural book that received most exegesis in monastic circles, and the number of surviving commentaries is sizeable.[7] The modern reader who peruses them, however, is likely to be struck not simply by their number but by the many features they have in common. In the remote beginnings of the exegetical tradition each verse of the *Song* acquired a series of connotations and associations on which subsequent exegetes drew. These connotations recur constantly in the commentaries, and to such an extent that one can speak of a literary convention in which the same elements are repeated and reproduced unceasingly. Often a commentary stands out from others not because its interpretation of the *Song* is unique but because of the theological acumen or literary elegance with which conventional elements are articulated.[8] Although, therefore, it is difficult, perhaps impossible, for us to ascertain the specific commentaries that St John knew well, it is possible to enquire how familiar he was with the mystical associations of the scriptural text, which would have been accessible to him not only in works of exegesis but, less directly, in works of devotion and theology, as well as in the liturgy and the Office.

### The Prose Commentaries

A useful starting point for such an enquiry may be found in St John's interpretation of four images of the *Cántico espiritual* which also appear in the *Song of Songs*. The first occurs in stanza 24 of *Cántico A*:[9]

> No quieras despreciarme,
> que, si color moreno en mí hallaste,
> ya bien puedes mirarme
> después que me miraste,
> que gracia y hermosura en mí dejaste.

> *Do not despise me,*
> *for, if you found dark colouring on me,*
> *well may you look upon me,*
> *for on me you left grace and beauty.*

These lines derive in part from words uttered by the bride in the opening chapter of the *Song*: "Nigra sum, sed formosa, filiae Ierusalem" [Sg 1,4] ["*I am black but beautiful, daughters of Jerusalem*"]. In his commentary St John explains that the dark complexion of the girl in his poem represents her defects and imperfections which the grace of divine love transmutes into holiness:

> Como si dijera... Que si, antes queme miraras, hallaste en mí fealdad
> de culpas e imperfecciones y bajeza de condición natural... *Después*
> *que me miraste*, quitando de mí ese color moreno y desgraciado con

que no estaba de ver, *ya bien puedes mirarme* más veces;  porque no sólo me quitaste el color moreno mirándome la primera vez, pero también me hiciste más digna de ver... [CA 24, 2-4]

*It is as if she were to say... For if, before you looked upon me, you found within me the ugliness of faults and imperfections and the wretchedness of my natural condition... After you looked upon me, and removed from me that dark and unfortunate complexion which made me unsightly, well may you look upon me again and again; for not only did you remove from me the dark complexion, when you looked upon me for the first time, but you also made me more worthy of being seen...*

St John goes on to quote and discuss the relevant verse of the *Song*:

Esto da a entender la esposa a las hijas de Jerusalén en los divinos Cantares (1, 4), diciendo: *Nigra sum sed formosa, filiae Ierusalem, ideo dilexit me rex et introduxit me in cubiculum suum...* Lo qual es tanto como si dijera: Hijas de Jerusalén, no os maravilléis porque el Rey celestial me haya hecho tan grandes mercedes... porque, aunque soy morena de mío, por lo qual no las merecía, ya soy hecha hermosa de él, por haberme él mirado... [CA 24, 5]

*This is conveyed by the Bride to the daughters of Jerusalem in the divine Songs, with the words Dark am I but beautiful, daughters of Jerusalem, so the king has loved me and brought me into his chamber... Which is as if she were to say: daughters of Jerusalem, do not marvel that the heavenly King should have done me such great favours... for although for my part I am dark, and therefore did not deserve them, I have now been made beautiful through him, because he has looked upon me..*

In the exegetical tradition one encounters the same contrast between sin and grace, imperfection and holiness.  St Ambrose (c.339-397) wrote:  "*Fusca sum et decora... fusca per culpam, decora per gratiam... fusca sum quia peccavi, decora quia jam me diligit Christus...*" [P.L. 15, 1863]. [*Swarthy am I and comely... swarthy because of fault, comely because of free gift... I am swarthy because I sinned, comely because Christ now shows me his love*".][10] Two centuries later St Gregory (c.540-604) observed:[11]

Considerat quid fuit, quid facta est:  et confitetur praeteritas culpas, ne superba sit, confitetur praesentem uitam, ne ingrata;  et dicit: *Nigra sum, sed formosa*. Nigra per meritum, formosa per gratiam; nigra per uitam praeteritam, formosa per conversationem sequentem.

*She ponders on what she was, on what she has become;  she both acknowledges past failings, lest she become proud, and present good living, lest she be ungrateful; and she says: Dark of skin am I, yet comely. Dark by her own deserving, comely by gift receiving; dark from her past life, comely from the changed life that has come later.*

And in the fifteenth century Denis the Carthusian (1402-1471) affirmed:[12]

Ecclesia nigram se nominat... quoniam multi imperfecti, fragiles et infirmi ac peccatores in ea sunt... Verumtamen ipsa se formosam fatetur, quoniam semper multi virtuosi et sancti in ea consistunt, et omnes qui ei vere incorporantur, caritate virtutibusque infusis ac donis Spiritus Sancti ornantur.

*The Church calls herself dark... because there are many imperfect, frail and sickly people as well as sinners in her... still, she herself describes herself as beautiful, since there are always many virtuous and holy people who take their place in her, and all those truly incorporated in her are embellished with love and the infused virtues and the gifts of the Holy Spirit.*

None of these texts may be described as a "source" of St John's commentary, but in each of them may be found certain exegetical themes which St John took and developed in his own way.[13]

The second image is the bed on which the lovers in the *Cántico* are united. It is mentioned by the bride in stanza 15:

> Nuestro lecho florido
> de cuevas de leones enlazado,
> en púrpura tendido,
> de paz edificado,
> de mil escudos de oro coronado.

> *Our flowering bed,*
> *entwined with lions' dens,*
> *decked out in purple,*
> *built of peace,*
> *crowned with a thousand shields of gold.*

The first line is a literal translation of words spoken by the *sponsa* at the end of the opening chapter of the *Song*: "Lectulus noster floridus" (Sg 1, 15). In his commentary St John indicates that this bed is the second person of the Trinity, the Word made flesh:

Este lecho florido es el pecho y amor del Amado, en que el alma, hecha esposa, está ya unida [CA 15, 2]... el *lecho* no es otra cosa que su mismo Esposo el Verbo, Hijo de Dios... en el cual ella, por medio de la dicha unión de amor, se recuesta.

[CB 24, 1].

*This flowering bed is the breast and the love of the Beloved, on which the soul, who has become the bride, is now united... the* bed *is nothing less than her very Spouse the Word, Son of God... on which, by means of this union of love, she reclines.*

A similar interpretation occurs in the famous commentary on the *Song* composed in the third century by Origen (c.185-c.254): the body Christ assumed is a bed that he shares with the bride, and in this bed the Church has been united with him and enabled to participate in the life of the Word of God.[14] The same notion appears in the twelfth-century commentary of Alan of Lille (d.1203): "Lectulus Christi dicitur caro quam assumpsit... Et eleganter dixit *lectulus noster floridus*, quia caro Christi, quae prius in vita floruit, per mortem effloruit, et per resurrectionem refloruit." [P.L. 210, 63]

*["The bed of Christ means the flesh he assumed... Tastefully does the text say our bed is all flowers, because Christ's flesh, which first flourished during his life, bloomed at his death and bloomed yet again at his resurrection."]*

And it recurs in the commentary of his older contemporary, Honorius of Autun (early 12th century):

Lectulus est homo Dominicus, in quo Deo sponsus cum sponsa sua humana natura requievit. *Deus, quippe, erat in Christo, mundum reconcilians sibi* (2 Co 5, 19), ideo autem *lectulus noster* dicitur, quia Ecclesia per carnem Christi est Deo conjuncta [P.L. 172, 380-381]

*The bed is the Lord-Man, in which God the bridegroom rested with his bride, our nature. Yes, God was in Christ, reconciling the world to himself [2 Co 5, 19], and so it is called our bed because through the flesh of Christ the Church is joined to God.*

The third image is that of the Beloved feeding among the flowers which St John uses in the last line of stanza 26: "y pacerá el Amado entre las flores" *["and the Beloved will feed among the flowers"]*. These words derive from two passages in the *Song* in which the Beloved is said to feed among the lilies: "Dilectus meus mihi, et ego illi, qui pascitur inter lilia" [Sg 2, 16; 6, 2] *["My beloved to me, and I to him who feeds among the lilies".]*. On citing these passages in his commentary St John explains that the garden in which the Beloved feeds is the soul, and that the lilies represent her virtues: "es a saber, que se deleita en mi alma, que es el huerto, entre los lirios de mis virtudes y perfecciones y gracias" *["which is to say, he delights in my soul, which is the garden, among the lilies of my virtues and perfections and graces"]*. He also draws attention to the fact that the Beloved feeds among the flowers, not on them. His food is the soul herself: "Y es de notar, que no dice que pacerá las flores, sino entre las flores... lo que pace es la misma alma transformándola en sí" [CA 26, 9] *["And it is noteworthy that she does not say he will feed on the flowers, but among the flowers... what he feeds on is the soul herself, transforming her into himself."]*

All the elements in this interpretation may be found in the earlier exegetical tradition. The image of the lilies that represent the virtues of the soul occurs often in the commentaries, for instance in the one formally attributed to Cassiodorus (c.485 - c.580): "hoc est, delectatur et jucundatur inter candidas et odoriferas virtutes sanctorum" [P.L. 70, 1067] ["*that is, he is delighted and made cheerful amid the bright and fragrant virtues of the saints*"]. And Anselm of Laon (d.1117) observes, in turn: "delectatur et reficitur... in operibus illorum qui sunt lilia, id est candidati in virtutibus" [P.L. 162, 1201] ["*he is delighted and refreshed... by the deeds of those who are lilies, that is, those bright with virtues*"]. The notion that the Lord feeds within the soul was expressed in the eighth century by St Bede (c.673-735): "In utraque etenim vita dilectus inter lilia pascitur, quia Dominus electorum suorum, et foris pura operatione, et dulci interius aeternorum contemplatione delectatur, atque in membris suis reficitur" [P.L. 91, 1116] ["*For in both kinds of living the Beloved feasts among the lilies, because the Lord is delighted both by the external, well-intentioned doing and the internal contemplating of what is eternal by his very own chosen ones, and finds refreshment in his members.*"]   Three centuries later it reappears in the sermons of St Bernard (1090-1153) who insists, like St John, on the importance of the phrase *inter lilia*: "tu forte vigilantius advertisti, non pabulum hoc loco designari, sed locum;  nec enim dictum 'liliis' eum pasci, sed *inter lilia*" ["*possibly you have been so perceptive as to notice that this text refers not to provision but to position;  for it is not stated that he fed 'on lilies' but among lilies*"]. And he continues: "Mandor cum arguor, glutior cum instituor, decoquor cum immutor, digeror cum transformor, unior cum conformor" ["*I am chewed when rebuked, swallowed when taught, boiled when changed, digested when transformed, made one when conformed*"].[15]  In the fifteenth century these various exegetical elements are brought together in the commentary of Denis the Carthusian:  "*Qui pascitur inter lilia*, id est, in cordibus continentium ac pure viventium et in splendore virtutum delectatur, quiescit, et quasi nutriri se protestatur." (p.337) ["*He who feeds among the lilies, that is, delights, finds rest, in the hearts of the chaste and upright-living and in the brightness of [their] virtues, and declares that he is, as it were, fed.*"]

The fourth and final image is the mysterious figure of Aminadab who appears in the closing lines of St John's poem:

> Que nadie lo miraba,
> Aminadab tampoco parecía
> y el cerco sosegaba
> y la caballería
> a vista de las aguas descendía.

> *For nobody was looking...*
> *Nor did Aminadab appear;*
> *and the siege was subsiding,*
> *and the cavalry*
> *in sight of the waters was descending.*

In the commentary Aminadab is identified with Satan who strives to prevent the bride from entering into her peace:

El cual Aminadab en la Escritura divina significa el demonio adversario del alma esposa, el cual la combatía siempre y turbaba con su innumerable munición de tentaciones y asechanzas, porque no se entrase en esta fortaleza y escondrijo del recogimiento interior con el Amado. En el cual puesto está el alma tan favorecida y fuerte en virtudes y victoriosa, que el demonio no osa parecer delante de ella. [CA 39, 3]

*This Aminadab in divine Scripture signifies the devil, the adversary of the soul and bride, who was always fighting against her and disturbing her with his countless armaments of temptations and snares in order to prevent her entering into this fortress and hiding-place of interior recollection with the Beloved. In this place the soul is so favoured and strong in virtues and victorious that the devil does not dare to appear before her.*

The source of the image is the *Song*, chapter six, where the bride at one point exclaims: "Nescivi: anima mea conturbavit me, propter quadrigas Aminadab" (Sg 6, 11) ["*I knew not: my soul troubled me on account of the chariots of Aminadab"*]. Elsewhere in his writings St John quotes this text, and repeats the identification of Aminadab with the devil.[16]

A number of modern critics have found St John's interpretation puzzling, partly, it seems, because in the *Song* Aminadab is mentioned only in passing, and does not have a significant role, and partly because many celebrated exegetes (including St Gregory, St Bede, Denis the Carthusian and Luis de León) do not interpret Aminadab in the same way. Elisabeth Howe, for instance, describes St John's reading as "novel", and explains: "Fray Luis de León... discerns no correspondence between Aminadab and Satan... nor do most Biblical commentators. Cassiodorus, in fact, considers him a prefiguration of Christ, not Satan".[17] Other critics go further and argue that St John's interpretation is "arbitrary", "disconcerting" and "cavalier".[18] On closer inspection, however, the exegetical tradition turns out to be complex, and to consist of various strands, some of which provide antecedents and parallels for the reading St John advances. In the Eastern Church, the early commentary of Theodoret (c.393 - c.466) interprets Aminadab as the prince of this world who oppresses the Church and enslaves her,[19] a view echoed in the West in the commentary of Apponius (early 5th century) where Aminadab is identified with the evil spirits who have refused to serve God.[20] In the course of the Middle Ages negative interpretations of the image recur. Nicholas of Lyra (c.1270-1340) identifies Aminadab with the Assyrians and Babylonians who took Israel into captivity.[21] Two centuries later, the Carthusian Henry Herp (d.1477) sees him as the soul's unrestrained will that makes her ignorant and blind,[22] while for his contemporary, Jaime Pérez de Valencia (d.1490), he symbolises the earthly powers that persecuted the early Church.[23] In St John's own day similar readings may be found in two of the Spanish commentaries on the *Song* that appeared in the 1580s. The Cistercian, Cipriano de la Huerga (d.1560) finds in Aminadab an allusion to the oppressors of the Church in every age,[24] while for Cosme Damián de Hortolá (1493-1568) he is the Antichrist.[25]

Although the confines of this article do not permit a detailed analysis of further examples, it is clear that one could find an exegetical background to St John's interpretation of other images of the *Song* that occur in the *Cántico*, among them the wounded stag who is Christ (CA1 and 12); the foxes in the vineyard (CA 25); the chaste and solitary turtle-dove (CA 34); the paradisial apple-tree (CA 28); the strand of the bride's hair that makes the Beloved captive (CA 22); her eye that wounds him (CA 22); and the caverns of stone to which the lovers hope to climb (CA 36). In each of these cases, St John "moves at his ease amid the symbolism that tradition supplies".[26] This symbolism is more than the literal sense of the *Song*: it includes the mystical connotations that the scriptural text had acquired in patristic and medieval exegesis.

## The Poem

The influence of the exegetical tradition on the prose commentaries of St John raises the question of how the poem was composed. It seems likely that through the practice of *lectio divina* he came to know the *Song of Songs* by heart, and was able to call it to mind with ease during his incarceration in Toledo (between December 1577 and August 1578) when the first 31 stanzas of the *Cántico* took shape.[27] Is it possible that in his prison cell he had in mind not only the text of the *Song* but its traditional associations? There are at least two stanzas which imply that it may be so.

The first is inspired by a passage in chapter four of the *Song* where the bridegroom summons the winds to enter his garden: "Surge, aquilo; et veni, auster; perfla hortum meum, et fluant aromata illius" (Sg 4, 16) [*Arise, north wind, and come, south wind; blow through my garden and let its aromatical spices flow"*]. In the *Cántico*, stanza 26, the winds are addressed not by the bridegroom but by the bride, who summons only one of them, begging the other to cease:

> Detente, cierzo muerto;
> ven austro, que recuerdas los amores,
> aspira por mi huerto,
> y corran sus olores,
> y pacerá el Amado entre las flores.

> *Cease, you dead north wind;*
> *come, you south wind, reawakening love;*
> *blow through my garden,*
> *and let its scents run free,*
> *and the Beloved will feed among the flowers.*

St John's poem alters first the speaker and then the command.[28] A possible reason for this latter change becomes clear in the commentary where he affirms that the north wind represents spiritual aridity:

El *cierzo* es un viento frío seco, y marchita las flores; y, porque la sequedad espiritual hace ese mismo efecto en el alma donde mora, la llama *cierzo*... Y, deseando la esposa conservarse en la suavidad de su amor, dice a la sequedad que se detenga... (CA 26, 2)

*The north wind is a cold and dry wind, and it withers the flowers; and because spiritual aridity has that same effect on the soul in which it dwells, she calls it north wind... And the bride, wishing to maintain herself in the sweetness of her love, tells aridity to cease...*

The south wind, on the other hand, represents for him the presence of the Holy Spirit, for whom the soul longs: "El *austro* es otro viento... es aire apacible... tiene los efectos contrarios a cierzo. Y así, por este aire      entiende aquí el alma al Espíritu Santo..." [CA 26, 3]  [*"The south wind is another wind... it is a gentle breeze... its effects are contrary to those of the north wind. And so, by this breeze, the soul here understands the Holy Spirit..."*]. This interpretation of the two winds may be found in earlier exegesis of the *Song*, along with precedents for the alteration in the command. St Ambrose, for instance, notes: "Plerique haec ita accipiunt, quasi projiciatur aquilo, et invitetur auster. Quod si ita accipiunt, exturbatur ab Ecclesia perfidiae glacialis asperitas... et invitatur australis verna temperies." [P.L. 15, 1916] [*"Many take these words to mean that the north wind is waved off and the south wind is welcomed. Understood like this, the icy severity of unbelief is thrust out of the Church... and the springtime mildness of the south wind is welcomed."*] St Gregory, in his commentary on *Job*, applies the text to the individual soul:[29]

Per Austrum vero, qui nimirum ventus calidus est, non immerito Spiritus sanctus designatur, quo quisque, dum tangitur, ab iniquitatis suae torpore liberatur... Aquilo enim jubetur ut surgat, ut nimirum is qui mortalium corda restringit adversarius spiritus fugiat. [P.L. 76, 436-437]

*Rightly is the Holy Spirit indicated by the south wind, which, of course, is a warm wind thanks to which, once it is experienced, one is freed from the oppression resulting from one's wickedness... For the north wind is urged to rise that the spirit adversary that hinders the hearts of mortals may unhesitatingly depart.*

In the twelfth century the same exegesis is advanced by Richard of St Victor (d.1173): "Aquilonem surgere jube, id est recedere, et austrum flare, id est adversitatem cessare, et Spiritus sui consolationem advenire" [P.L. 196, 494] [*"Order the north wind to rise, that is, withdraw, and the south wind to blow, that is, adversity to cease, and the comfort of his Spirit to come close"*]. And according to Honorius of Autun: "Rex ergo adveniens, dicit: O aquilo hostis maligne, de latebris tuis surge, et de horto meo discede: tu autem, auster, cultor horti, veni, perfla hortum meum" [P.L. 172, 429]. [*"Consequently, the King at his coming says, 'North wind, wicked foe, rise from your hiding-place, and depart from my garden; but you, south wind, true gardener of the garden, come and blow through my garden"*].

The second passage occurs in chapter six of the *Song*, where the bridegroom begs the bride to avert her eyes: "Averte oculos tuos a me, quia ipsi me avolare fecerunt" [Sg 6, 4] *["Turn your eyes away from me, for they have made me fly away"]*. In the *Cántico* the same words are assigned to the bride: "¡Apártalos, Amado/que voy de vuelo!" [CA 12] *["Turn them away, Beloved, for I go flying!"]*. In his commentary St John explains that the bride makes this request because the soul, longing to be united with God, cannot endure his presence without danger to her life:

> ...tal es la miseria del natural en esta vida que aquello que al alma le es más vida y ella con tanto deseo desea, que es la comunicación y conocimiento de su Amado, cuando se le vienen a dar, no lo puede recibir sin que casi le cueste la vida, de suerte que los ojos que con tanta solicitud y ansias y por tantas vías buscaba, venga a decir cuando los reciben: ¡apártalos, Amado! [CA 12, 2]

> *... such is the wretchedness of (our) nature in this life that that which is most truly life to the soul, and desired by her with such longing, namely the knowledge and communication of her Beloved, cannot be received by her, when given, without almost costing her her life, so that when she receives (the gaze of) the eyes that she sought with such solicitude and fervour and in so many ways, she says: "Turn them away, Beloved!"*

The reason for the bride's plea as explained by St John has much in common with the motive of the bridegroom in the *Song* as described in medieval exegesis. St Ambrose, for instance, states: "*Averte*, inquit, *oculos tuos a me*: eo quod plenitudinem divinitatis ejus et splendorem veri luminis sustinere non possit" [P.L. 15, 1942]. *["Turn, he says, your eyes from me: because she cannot bear the fullness of his divinity and the brightness of the true light"].* The same notion is developed in the commentary of Bede:

> averte oculos tuae mentis a contemplatione divinae majestatis et essentiae, quia *ipsi me avolare fecerunt*, id est, ipsi tui sensus spirituales, quibus me perfecte cognoscere desiderasti... non in hac vita me ad perfectum comprehendere sufficiunt. [P.L. 91, 1177]

> *turn away your mind's eyes from contemplating the majesty and being of God because they have made me fly away, that is, your spiritual senses themselves, through which you were desirous of knowing me perfectly... are not capable in this life of fully grasping me.*

And the tradition recurs in Honorius of Autun: "Quasi dicat... Et ne quaeras me ex toto in hac vita videre, quod non poteris prae tua fragilitate" [P.L. 172, 447-448]. *["As if he were saying... 'And do not seek to see me fully in this life, since you will not be able to because of your frailty'."]*

These two stanzas that St John composed in captivity appear to derive not simply from the literal sense of the *Song*, which they modify, but from its mystical sense, originally established by the Fathers, which they conserve. In this respect they illustrate a truth which the other examples examined here confirm: when composing his poem, and writing the commentaries, St John proceeded like the householder praised by Christ who managed to draw from his storeroom things old as well as new. To comprehend and appreciate his work the modern reader must therefore become familiar with the traditions that shaped it, and it is no exaggeration to say that of these the most important yet least explored is the mystical sense of the *Song of Songs*.

## References

1. This article is an extended version of a paper forthcoming in the proceedings of *Encuentros sobre San Juan de la Cruz*, a conference organised in Granada in December 1991 to mark the fourth centenary of the death of St John of the Cross.

2. Colin P. Thompson, *The Poet and the Mystic: A Study of the "Cántico espiritual"* of *San Juan de la Cruz*, (Oxford, 1977), 60-69.

3. See the article, "Cantique des Cantiques: histoire de l'interprétation spirituelle" in *Dictionnaire de Spiritualité* 2, 93-109.

4. The exception is the commentary of Luis de León (Salamanca, 1580). Other commentaries of the decade include those of Blessed Alonso de Orozco (Burgos, 1581), Cipriano de la Huerga (Alcalá, 1582) and Cosme Damián de Hortolá (Barcelona, 1583). The unfinished commentary of St Thomas of Villanueva was included in the edition of his *Conciones sacrae* published in Alcaá in 1581. See *Repertorio de historia de las ciencias eclesásticas de España*, 7 vols. (Salamanca, 1967-79), vol. 3, 539, vol. 5, 239; *Catalogue of Books printed in Spain... before 1601 now in the British Library*, second edition, edited by Dennis E. Rhodes (London, 1989).

5. José L. Morales, *El "Cántico espiritual" de San Juan de la Cruz: su relación con el Cantar de los cantares y otras fuentes escriturísticas y morales* (Madrid, 1971), 52-57, 89, 190; Colin P. Thompson, *The Strife of Tongues. Fray Luis de León and the Golden Age of Spain* (Cambridge, 1988), 117; Manuel Diego Sánchez, "La herencia patrística de Juan de la Cruz" in *Experiencia y pensamiento en San Juan de la Cruz*, edited by Federico Ruiz (Madrid, 1990), 95 nn. 26 and 28.

6. On St John and medieval exegesis in general see Henri de Lubac, S.J., *Exégèse mediévale. Les quatre sens de l'Ecriture*, 4 vols. (Paris, 1959-64), vol. 4, 500-5.

7. Jean Leclercq, O.S.B., *The Love of Learning and the Desire for God. A Study of Monastic Culture*, translated by Catharine Misrahi (London, 1978), 106.

8. On the notion of a literary convention see Terence O'Reilly, "Courtly Love and Mysticism in Spanish Literature of the Golden Age", *Journal of Hispanic Research* 1 (1992-3), 55-56.

9. All references to St John's works are to *San Juan de la Cruz. Obras completas*, edited by José Vincente Rodríguez and Federico Ruiz Salvador, second edition (Madrid, 1980). The abbreviations *CA* and *CB* refer to the two redactions of St John's text: *Cántico A* and *Cántico B*. Translations of the poem generally follow Thompson, *The Poet and the Mystic*, 173-177. Translations of passages from the commentary are my own.

10. I am grateful to Fr Hugh McCaffrey of Mount Melleray Abbey who kindly supplied me with translations into English of the Latin passages quoted here. These I have reproduced, with occasional modifications, apart from translations

of the *Song*, which usually follow the Douay version.

11. *Expositiones in Canticum canticorum* 36: 6-10, in *Grégoire le Grand: Commentaire sur le Cantique des Cantiques* (Sources Chrétiennes, 314), edited by Rodrigue Bélanger (Paris, 1984).

12. *Enarratio in Canticum canticorum Salomonis*, in *D. Dionysii Cartusiani. In Sacram Scripturam Commentaria*, vol. 7 (Montreuil-sur-mer, 1898), 302.

13. As Manuel Diego Sánchez has observed (see n.5 above) the influence on St John of patristic thought cannot be measured simply by his direct allusions to the Fathers for it was mediated to him through a tradition that was the shared inheritance of all mystical writers (85). The point is made too by Thompson, 1-20.

14. R.P. Lawson, *Origen: the Song of Songs. Commentary and Homilies* (London, 1957), 174.

15. *Sermones in Canticum* 70, i; 71, 5. I have followed the edition in *Obras completas de San Bernardo*, vol. 5 (Madrid, 1987).

16. *Noche oscura*, book 2, chapter 23, 5.

17. Elizabeth Teresa Howe, *Mystical Imagery: Santa Teresa de Jesús and San Juan de la Cruz* (New York, 1988), 228.

18. Morales, 233; John Venard, O.C.D., *The Spiritual Canticle of St John of the Cross* (Sydney, 1980), 277.

19. See María Inés de Jesús, "*Aminadab tampoco parecía*. Aportación a un pequeño enigma sanjuanista", *San Juan de la Cruz* 7 (1991), 141-143.

20. *In Canticum Canticorum expositionem*, edited by B. de Vregille and L. Neyrand (Corpus Christianorum, Series Latina, xix) (Turnholt, 1986), 232-233.

21. Richard Frederick Little, *A Commentary on the Song of Songs from Ancient and Medieval Sources* (London, 1869), 295.

22. Littledale, 296-297.

23. *Expositio in Cantica Canticorum Salomonis* (Valencia, 1486). I have used the edition uf Lyons, 1517 [fol. xlii (r)].

24. *Commentaria in librum beati Job et in Cantica Canticorum Salomonis Regi* (Alcalá, 1582), 263.

25. *In Canticum canticorum Salomonis explanatio* (Barcelona, 1583), 415-421.

26. "Se mueve a sus anchas en el simbolismo que le suministra la tradición": Marcel Bataillon, *Varia lección de clásicos españoles* (Madrid, 1964), 163.

27. Terence O'Reilly, "St John of the Cross and the traditions of monastic exegesis", in *Leeds Papers on Saint John of the Cross*, edited by Margaret A. Rees (Leeds, 1991), 105-120.

28. See the observations in Thompson, 68.

29. A similar passage eleshwere in the writings of St Gregory was noted by Crisógono de Jesús Sacramentado, O.C.D.: see Morales, 190.

# INDEX

Acuña, Hernando de: XII 63

Alba, dukes of: V 6,9

Alcalá de Henares: I 443-45,454; II 301-3,321; III 116-20,126; IV 376,378; V 13,14

Alcaraz: see Ruiz de Alcaraz

Alexandria, Patriarchate of: I 453

*Alumbrados:* I 440; II 302; IV 369,371,373-76, 378-80; V 12,15,16,18

Álvarez Gato, Juan: XII 58

*Amadís de Gaula:* VI 105

Ambrose, St.: XV 7,13-14

Ana de Jesús: XIII 119

Andújar: XIII 106

Antwerp: I 443

Apponius: XV 11

Aquaviva, Claudio: I 460

Aquinas, Thomas, St.: III 126; VI 107; XI 110; XII 60; XIV 365

Araoz, Antonio de: V 2-3

Arcediano del Alcor: see Fernández de Madrid, Alonso

Ardèvol, Jeroni: III 117

Assisi, Francis of, St.: I 456; V 15; XI 110

Augustine, St.: II 313,319; IV 373; V 20,21; XI 111-12

Autun, Honorius of: XV 9,13-14

Ávila, John of, St.: I 440; XII 56-57; XIV 365-67

Ávila, Teresa of, St.: XII 53,56,65-67

Azpeitia: I 449

Babylon: I 449

Balma, Hugh of: VII 288,292,323-24

Barcelona: I 445; II 302-4; III 115,117-19; VI 101-2; VIII 301

Basil, St.: V 17

Battista Ribera, G.: V 2

Beda, Noel: III 127

Bede, St.: IX 422; XV 10-11,14

Beltrán, Felipe: V 5

Bernard St.: VII 292,315; XII 60,69; XIII 112,114; XV 5,10

Bethlehem: I 446

Bobadilla, Nicolás Alonso de: I 445

Boethius: XI 107

Bollandists: I 440

Bonanat, Ioachim: VIII 302

Bonaventure, St.: III 126; VII 288,318; XI 107,110 Borgia, Francis, St.: I 455,460

Brazil: I 448

Bustamante, Bartolomé: I 460

Calvin, John: I 443; II 314

Camaldoli: VI 107

Canisius, Peter, St.: I 447,455

Cano, Melchor: III 126; IV *passim*; V *passim*

Carafa, Giampietro: see Paul IV, Pope

Cardoner: VIII 303

Carranza de Miranda, Bartolomé: IV 370,373-75

Carrillo, Gonzalo: XII 61

Cartagena: XII 56,58

Cassian, John: VII 292; XIII 111

Cassiodorus: XV 9,11

Castillo, Hernando del: XII 56

Castro, Juan: I 445,457

*Celestina:* XII 66

Cervini, Marcello: see Marcellus II, Pope

Chanones, Jean: I 456; VIII 302,323

Charles V, Emperor: I 455

Ciruelo, Pedro: III 125

Cisneros, García Jiménez de: VII *passim*; VIII *passim*
-*Exercitatorio de la vida espiritual:* II 308,311; VII *passim*; VIII *passim*; XI 110

Clement VIII, Pope: I 462

Clement XIV, Pope: V 5

Clichtove, Josse van: III 120

Coimbra: V 5

Colet, John: XIV 365

Collège de Furet, Paris: I 443

Collège de Montaigu, Paris: I 443; III 120

Collège de Sainte Barbe, Paris: I 443;

III 120
Cologne: I 447
Constantinople: I 448
Contarini, Gasparo: I 446,458,461-62;
    VI 107
Cop, Nicholas: I 443
Córdoba, Sebastián de: XIV 366
Cruz, Isabel de la: IV 378
Cyprus: I 448

David: V 20; XIII 113
Denis the Carthusian: XI 109; XV 8,
    10-11
*Devotio moderna:* II 311; III 125; VII 287,
    VIII 302
*Dejados:* see *dexados*
*Dexados:* I 443; II 301,304; IV
    369,371,373-74,376-80; V
    12,15,16,18
Díez de Games, Gutierre: XII 71
Dionysius, the Pseudo-Areopagite:
    XI 107
Dominic, St.: I 456; V 15
*Don Quixote:* XII 59

Eguía, Diego de: I 445
Eguía, Esteban de: I 445
Eguía, Miguel de: I 445; II 302,321;
    III 120
Eiximenis, Francesc: VII 288
*El condenado por desconfiado:* XIV 368
Elduayen, Amador de: I 445
Elisabeth of the Trinity: XIII 120
Elisha: X 109-110
Encina, Juan del: XII 66-67
Erasmus: I 445,452,458,461-62, II 301-
    4,306-307,310-19,321; III *passim;*
    VI 101-6,108-10; X *passim;* XIV
    365
    -*De praeparatione ad mortem:* II
    315-16
    -*Enchiridion militis christiani:* II
    301-7,311-18,320-21; III 115-
    20,123; VI 101-3; X 95-98; XIV
    365
    -*Inquisitio de fide:* II 306,308,318
    -*Paraphrasis in Evangelium Lucae:*
    X 91
    -*Paraphrasis in Evangelium*

*Matthaei:* III 119
    -*Supputationes errorum in censuris*
    -*Beddae:* III 119
    -*The Praise of Folly:* X 91,98
Estella, Diego de: XIV 365,367
Ethiopia: I 448,453
*Exposcit debitum:* I 446,451-52

Farnese, Alessandro: IV 372; V 13,15
Favre, Pierre, Blessed: I 445,449,457; V
    5,12,14
Fernández de Madrid, Alonso: II 307,313-
    14,318-21
Ficino, Marsilio: II 313
Fonseca, Alonso de: II 314; III 120
Fresnada, Bernardo de: V 2

García de Santa María, Gonzalo: IX 423
Garcilaso de la Vega: XII 63,71; XIV
    364,366
Gerson, Jean: VII 288
Gethsemane: XII 60-61; XIV 364
Ghinucci, Girolamo: I 451,458,461
Girón, Francisco: VIII 302
Giustiniani, Paolo: VI 107
Gonçalves da Cámara, Luis: I
    440,447,455,462; II 303,311; III
    116-19; VI 103,105; VIII 301
Gonzaga, Giulia: II 308,314-15
Gouveia, Andrés de: I 443
Gouveia, Diego de: I 443; III 125
Granada, Luis de: IV 373
Gregory the Great, St.: VII 315; X 96;
    XIII 113; XV 5,7,11,13
Guastalda, Countess of: V 5,15,18
Guidiccioni, Bartolomeo: I 458
Guigo II: XIII 107

Herbert, George: XIV 367
Herp, Henry: XV 11
Hoces, Diego: I 444
Hortolá, Cosmé Damián de: XV 11
Huerga, Cipriano de la: XV 11

*Imitation of Christ:* I 442; II
    303,308,311,313,321; VIII 303;
    XII 56-59
Ingolstadt: I 447
Iriarte, Tomás de: V 10

Japan: I 448
Jeremiah: XIII 113
Jerome, St.: VII 315; IX 422-23; XII 60; XIV 364-65
Jerusalem: I 444-46,448-50,454,463; III 122; VI 101
Job: XIII 113
John, St.: V 12; VII 295
John of the Cross, St.: IX 423; XI 111; XII 53,55,63-64,66-72; XIII *passim*; XIV *passim*; XV *passim*
Juan Evangelista: XIII 107,118
Julius III, Pope: I 455

Kempf, Nicholas: VII 288
Kempis, Thomas à: II 311; VII 288

*La Gran Conquista de Ultramar:* IX 422
Laínez, Diego: I 440,445,455; IV 370 n.9; V 2,5,12,14,21; VI 104-5
Laon, Anselm of: XV 10
Laredo, Bernardino de: XII 65
*Lazarillo de Tormes:* X *passim*
Le Jay, Claude: I 455
León, Luis de: XI *passim*; XV 5,11
Lerma, Juan de: VIII 302
Lille, Alan of: XV 9
Lombard, Peter: III 126; VII 293; XI 110
López, Iñigo: V 3
Loyola: I 444-45,456; III 125; VI 103-5,110
Loyola, Ignatius of, St.: I *passim*; II *passim*, III *passim*, IV *passim*; V *passim*; VI *passim*; VII *passim*; VIII *passim*, IX *passim*, XII 56
-*Autobiography:* I 440,444
-*Constitutions:* I 449,460,461
-*Rules for Thinking with the Church:* I 449,452-53,455,461; II 305; III 119-24,126; VI 108
-*Spiritual Exercises:* I 444-45,449-50,456,461;II302,304,308-17,320-21; III 115,119,123,125,127; IV 369-70,372-80; V 8,20,21; VI 102-3,108-10; VII *passim*; VIII *passim*; IX *passim*
Ludolph of Saxony: see Ludolph the Carthusian
Ludolph the Carthusian:

-*Vita Christi:* I 444; II 308,311; III 125; VI 104,110; VII 288; VIII 303-4; IX 423-24; X 91-92,94-97; XII 61-62,65
Luke, St.: IX 422; X 92
Luther, Martin: I 439,441-43,447-48; II 313-14; III 115,121,125-127; IV 377, V 19,20; VI 101,108
Lyra, Nicholas of: XV 11

Macías: XII 60
Madama: see Margaret of Austria
Madrid, Alonso de: XII 65
Maffei, Gian Pietro: I 439-40,442
Mainardi, Agostino: I 444
Málaga: I 444
Maldonado, Juan: II 314
Manresa: I 445,453,456; II 302; VI 103-6,109-10; VIII 301,303-4; IX 421
Manrique, Jorge: XII 57-8,61
Marcellus II, Pope: I 455,461-62
Margaret of Austria: IV 372 n.13; V 13,15
Matthew, St.: IX 421,423; X 92
*Meditationes vitae Christi:* VII 288; XII 60-61; XIV 370 n.27
Miona, Manuel: III 120; IV 377 n.21,378
Mombaer, John: II 311; VII 288,300; VIII 323
Montesino, Ambrosio: IX 423; XII 65
Montmartre: I 446,449-50,457; III 122
Montserrat: I 445-46; III 125; IV 104-6; VIII 301-3,323
More, Thomas, St.: III 122
Morone, Giovanni: I 461-62

Nadal, Jerónimo: I 441,444,446,450
Nebrija, Elio Antonio de: IX 422
Nieto, Laurentius: VIII 302
Nazareth: II 309

Origen: II 313,319; XV 5,9
Ortiz, Pedro: IV 376; V 14
Osuna, Francisco de: II 306-7; XII 65

Palestine: I 444,449; IX 421
Palma, Luis de la: XIV 366-67
Pamplona: I 442,444,449; VI 103
Paris: I 443-45,447,449,454,457; II 118-

20,125-26; VI 101
Paul, St.: II 305,311,316; III 123; IV 375,378; V 18,19,21; XIII 111-12
Paul III, Pope: I 446,450,455,458,461,463; IV 377
Paul IV, Pope: I 455,461-62,464; III 125-26; IV 370,379-80; V 1,4
Pelagius: V 20
Peralta, Pedro de: I 445
Pérez de Castro: XII 71
Pérez de Valencia, Jaime: XV 11
Peter, St.: I 449; V 15; XIV 366
Pius IV, Pope: V4
Pius V, St., Pope: I 462
Pico della Mirandola, Giovanni: II 313
Plato: II 305,319; XI 107
Plotinus: XI 107
Polanco, Juan Alfonso de: I 440-41,446,454-55,457; VI 104
Pole, Reginald: I 461-62
Prudentius: XII 65

Rabanus Maurus: IX 422
Ranke, Leopold von: I 442
Recogidos: II 301,304,306-7
Regensburg: I 462
Regimini militantis ecclesiae: I 446,451
Regla, Juan de: IV 374
Reyes, Agustín de los: XIII 108
Ribadeneira, Pedro de: I 439-42,448,451,453,456; II 302-4,311; III 115-19; V 2,3-4,7; VI 101-2; VIII 302
Ribera, Francisco de: XII 65
Rodrigues, Simao: I 445,460
Rodríguez, Alonso: I 442
Rome, city of: I 442,444,446-50,453-54,461,463; III 122,125; IV 371-72,379-80; V 1-3,7-9,12-13; VI 102
Rosas: V 2
Roser, Isabel: IV 377; V 15 n.23
Ruiz de Alcaraz, Pedro: IV 378
Ruiz de Virués, Alonso: II 314
Rull: XII 58
Ruysbroeck, Jan van: XII 60

Sá, Calisto de: I 445
Sadoleto, Jacopo: I 461
St. Victor, Richard of: VII 315-16; XI

108; XV 13
Salamanca: I 443,454; II 302; V 1,5,14 ; X 92; XIII 106
Salinas, Francisco: XI 109-13
Salmerón, Alfonso: I 445; IV 370 n.9; V 5,12,14
Sánchez de Badajoz, Garci: XII 60; XIV 366
San Esteban, Dominican House, Salamanca: I 454
San Pedro, Diego de: XII 59,62,67
Santa Fe, Michael de: VIII 302
Santa María, Pablo de: XIII 108
Santa Maria Maggiore, basilica of: I 446
Schopp, Gaspar: IV 370; V 4
Segovia: V 1
Seville: I 460
Sicily: I 448
Socrates: II 305
Sorbonne: III 125
Soria: XII 56-57,61
Sosa, Lope de: XII 57
Spirituali: I 440
Suso, Henry: VII 315

Tavara, Marqués de: IV 374
Theodoret: XV 11
Toledo: I 443; IV 369; V 4; X 93,97; XIII 105; XV 12
Tolomei, Lattanzio: I 461
Torres, Miguel de: I 460; IV 376,377 n.21; V 5,12,14
Tovar, Bernardino: III 120; IV 377 n.21
Trent, Council of: I 439-40,456,462; III 115; IV 370 n.9; V 5,14; VI 102; XI 110
Trieste: I 455

Valdés, Alfonso de: II 314,320
Valdés, Juan de: II 306-7,310,314; X 91
  -Alfabeto cristiano: II 308,314-15
  -Diálogo de doctrina cristiana: II 306-8,315,318-19,321
Vall de Cristo, Charterhouse of: I 457
Valla, Lorenzo: III 125
Valladolid: V 2
Vargas, Alfonso de: see Schopp, Gaspar
Vega, Juan de: I 448
Venice: I 444-47, III 125

Vergara, Juan de:  II 314
Vicente, Gil:  XII 64
Vienna:  I 455; V 5
Virués:  see Ruiz de Virués
*Vitae patrum*:  VI 108
Voragine, Jacopo di:
    -*Legenda aurea*:   I 444,456;  VI
    110; VIII 303; XII 60,62; XIV
    365

Vives, Juan Luis:  III 120

Wittgenstein, Ludwig:  XIII 119

Xavier, Francis, St.:  I 445

Zerbolt of Zutphen, Gerard: II 311; VII
    287,318,324; VIII 323

Vergara, Juan de: II 314
Vicente, Gil: XII 64
Vienna: I 455; V 5
Virués: see Ruiz de Virués
Vitae patrum: VI 108
Voragine, Jacopo di:
-Legenda aurea: I 444,456; VI
110; VIII 303; XII 60,62; XIV
365

Vives, Juan Luis: III 120

Wittgenstein, Ludwig: XIII 119

Xavier, Francis, St.: I 445

Zarbolt of Zutphen, Gerard: II 311, VII
287,318,324; VIII 323